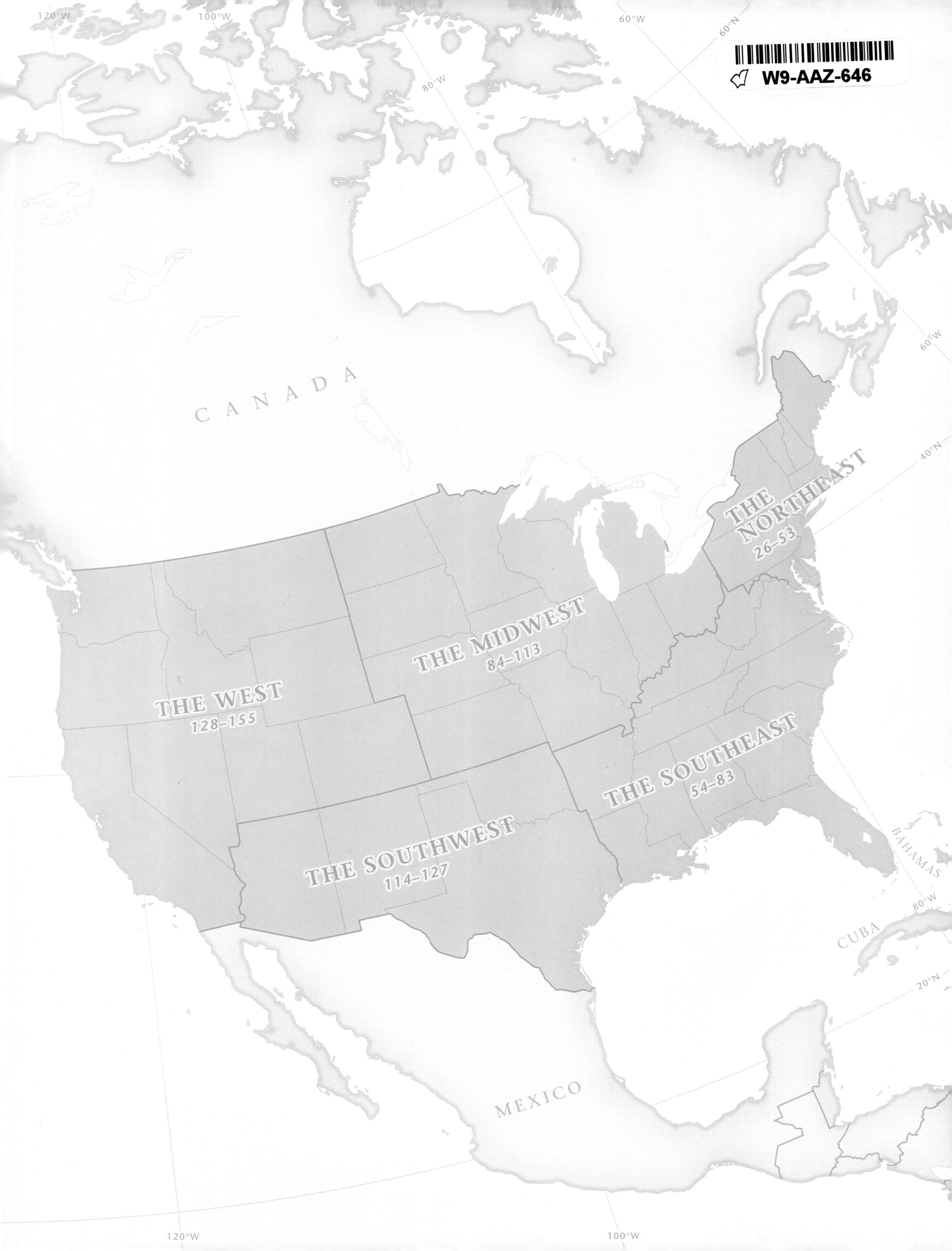

120°W
100°W
60°W
60°N
80°W
W9-AAZ-646
CANADA
60°W
40°N
THE NORTHEAST
26–53
THE MIDWEST
84–113
THE WEST
128–155
THE SOUTHEAST
54–83
THE SOUTHWEST
114–127
BAHAMAS
80°W
CUBA
20°N
MEXICO
120°W
100°W

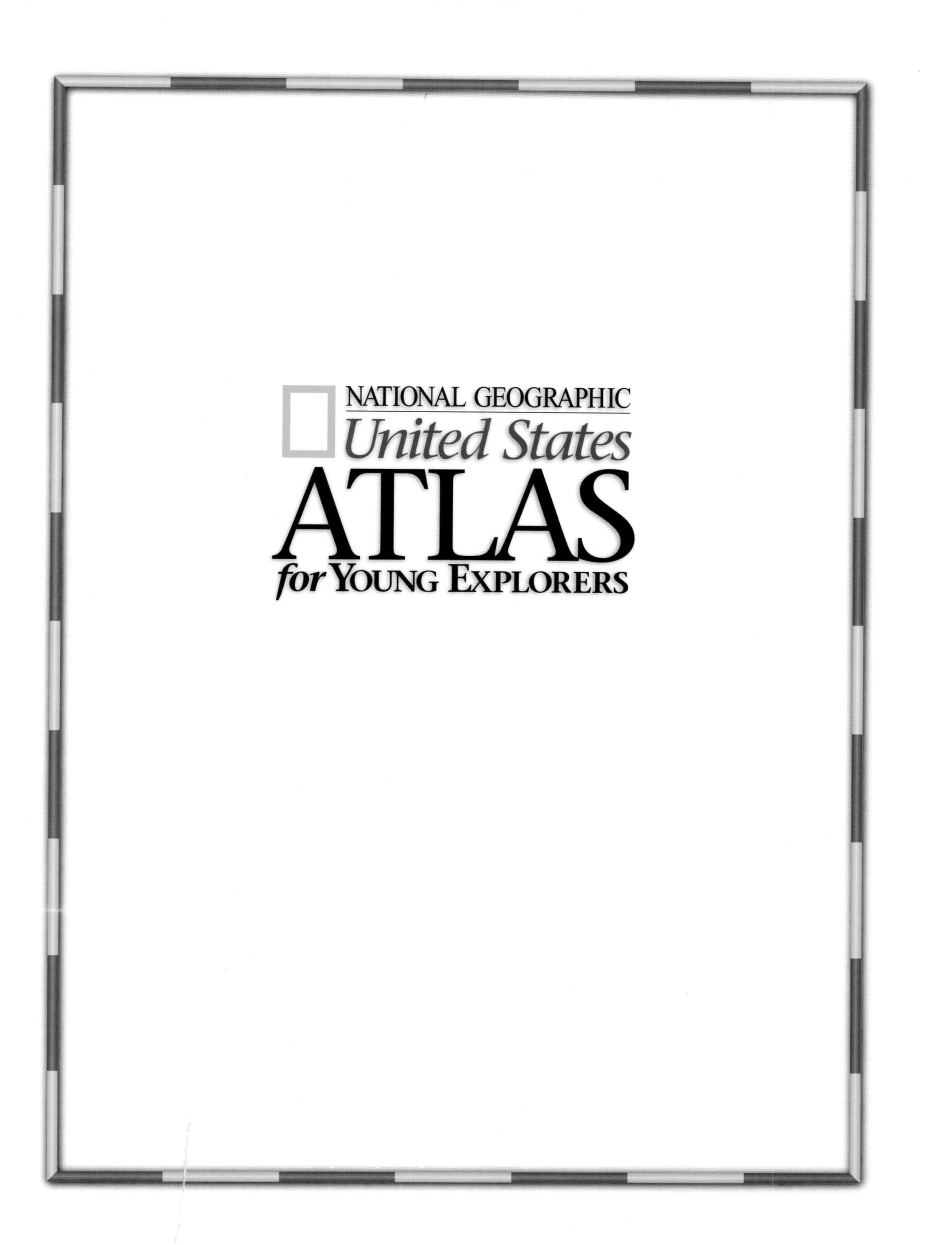

NATIONAL GEOGRAPHIC
United States
ATLAS
for YOUNG EXPLORERS

From the rugged West (near right) to the rounded mountains of the East (far right), the United States has a landscape as diverse as its people. The varied land and vegetation of the contiguous United States can be seen in the large photograph, which was made by combining satellite images.

NATIONAL GEOGRAPHIC United States ATLAS for YOUNG EXPLORERS

NATIONAL GEOGRAPHIC

WASHINGTON, D.C.

Photographs from Getty Images

Contents

Sailing, page 31

Cotton, page 59

A rainbow arches over Denali National Park, in Alaska.

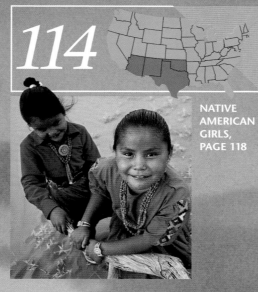

How To Use This Atlas

The maps in this atlas can tell you many things about the United States. Those that immediately follow this section give you information about the whole country, such as its physical features, federal lands, and population.

Then you'll see the states organized into five regions. Each regional section opens with a large photograph showing a landscape in the region and a smaller one that relates to human use of the land. Then a physical map of the region shows mountains, lakes, rivers, deserts, and so forth. After that, a photographic essay lets you "see" the area in words and pictures.

From there, you're ready to meet the states themselves. Each is represented by a political map (like the one of New York, detailed below), a description of the state, and a box with statistics and other useful facts. The back of this atlas has more statistics about the U.S., a glossary, and an index that will help you find any place-name in this atlas.

The Regions of the United State

In this atlas, the 50 states are grouped into five regions: the Northeast, Southeast, Midwes Southwest, and West. This breakdown is based on what i being taught in most U.S. schools. States within a regio have some things in commo Agriculture unites states in th Midwest, for example, where wheat and corn grow in seemingly endless fields. Colo make it easy to identify the st within each region.

Map Icons

The key below names the small pictures, or icons, that tell you where important economic activities take place in each state. It also identifies the symbols that show towns, boundaries, and natural features.

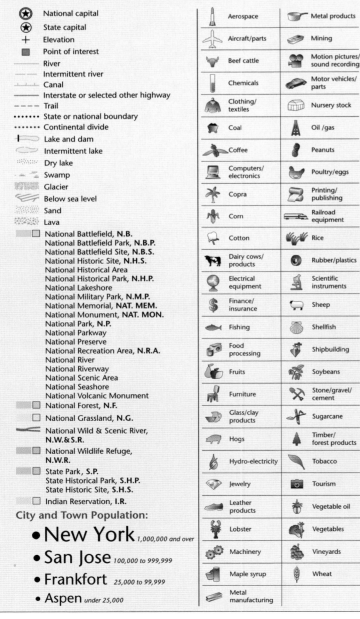

- National capital
- State capital
- Elevation
- Point of interest
- River
- Intermittent river
- Canal
- Interstate or selected other highway
- Trail
- State or national boundary
- Continental divide
- Lake and dam
- Intermittent lake
- Dry lake
- Swamp
- Glacier
- Below sea level
- Sand
- Lava
- National Battlefield, **N.B.**
  National Battlefield Park, **N.B.P.**
  National Battlefield Site, **N.B.S.**
  National Historic Site, **N.H.S.**
  National Historical Area
  National Historical Park, **N.H.P.**
  National Lakeshore
  National Military Park, **N.M.P.**
  National Memorial, **NAT. MEM.**
  National Monument, **NAT. MON.**
  National Park, **N.P.**
  National Parkway
  National Preserve
  National Recreation Area, **N.R.A.**
  National River
  National Riverway
  National Scenic Area
  National Seashore
  National Volcanic Monument
- National Forest, **N.F.**
- National Grassland, **N.G.**
- National Wild & Scenic River, **N.W.&S.R.**
- National Wildlife Refuge, **N.W.R.**
- State Park, **S.P.**
  State Historical Park, **S.H.P.**
  State Historic Site, **S.H.S.**
- Indian Reservation, **I.R.**

City and Town Population:

- **New York** *1,000,000 and over*
- **San Jose** *100,000 to 999,999*
- **Frankfort** *25,000 to 99,999*
- **Aspen** *under 25,000*

Aerospace	Metal products
Aircraft/parts	Mining
Beef cattle	Motion pictures/ sound recordings
Chemicals	Motor vehicles/ parts
Clothing/ textiles	Nursery stock
Coal	Oil /gas
Coffee	Peanuts
Computers/ electronics	Poultry/eggs
Copra	Printing/ publishing
Corn	Railroad equipment
Cotton	Rice
Dairy cows/ products	Rubber/plastics
Electrical equipment	Scientific instruments
Finance/ insurance	Sheep
Fishing	Shellfish
Food processing	Shipbuilding
Fruits	Soybeans
Furniture	Stone/gravel/ cement
Glass/clay products	Sugarcane
Hogs	Timber/ forest products
Hydro-electricity	Tobacco
Jewelry	Tourism
Leather products	Vegetable oil
Lobster	Vegetables
Machinery	Vineyards
Maple syrup	Wheat
Metal manufacturing	

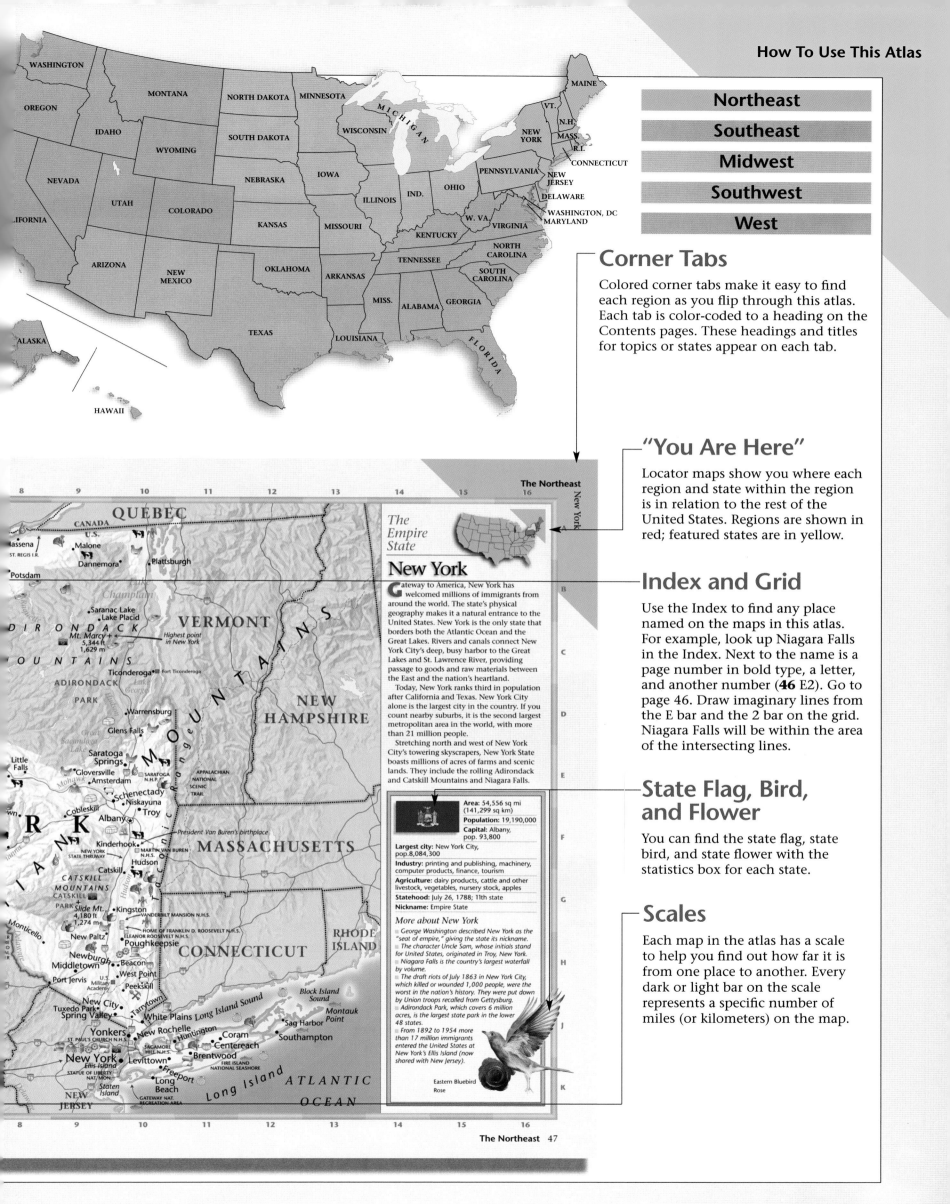

Northeast
Southeast
Midwest
Southwest
West

Corner Tabs

Colored corner tabs make it easy to find each region as you flip through this atlas. Each tab is color-coded to a heading on the Contents pages. These headings and titles for topics or states appear on each tab.

"You Are Here"

Locator maps show you where each region and state within the region is in relation to the rest of the United States. Regions are shown in red; featured states are in yellow.

Index and Grid

Use the Index to find any place named on the maps in this atlas. For example, look up Niagara Falls in the Index. Next to the name is a page number in bold type, a letter, and another number (**46** E2). Go to page 46. Draw imaginary lines from the E bar and the 2 bar on the grid. Niagara Falls will be within the area of the intersecting lines.

State Flag, Bird, and Flower

You can find the state flag, state bird, and state flower with the statistics box for each state.

Scales

Each map in the atlas has a scale to help you find out how far it is from one place to another. Every dark or light bar on the scale represents a specific number of miles (or kilometers) on the map.

The Northeast

New York

The Empire State

New York

Gateway to America, New York has welcomed millions of immigrants from around the world. The state's physical geography makes it a natural entrance to the United States. New York is the only state that borders both the Atlantic Ocean and the Great Lakes. Rivers and canals connect New York City's deep, busy harbor to the Great Lakes and St. Lawrence River, providing passage to goods and raw materials between the East and the nation's heartland.

Today, New York ranks third in population after California and Texas. New York City alone is the largest city in the country. If you count nearby suburbs, it is the second largest metropolitan area in the world, with more than 21 million people.

Stretching north and west of New York City's towering skyscrapers, New York State boasts millions of acres of farms and scenic lands. They include the rolling Adirondack and Catskill Mountains and Niagara Falls.

Area: 54,556 sq mi (141,299 sq km)
Population: 19,190,000
Capital: Albany, pop. 93,800
Largest city: New York City, pop.8,084,300
Industry: printing and publishing, machinery, computer products, finance, tourism
Agriculture: dairy products, cattle and other livestock, vegetables, nursery stock, apples
Statehood: July 26, 1788; 11th state
Nickname: Empire State

More about New York

- *George Washington described New York as the "seat of empire," giving the state its nickname.*
- *The character Uncle Sam, whose initials stand for United States, originated in Troy, New York.*
- *Niagara Falls is the country's largest waterfall by volume.*
- *The draft riots of July 1863 in New York City, which killed or wounded 1,000 people, were the worst in the nation's history. They were put down by Union troops recalled from Gettysburg.*
- *Adirondack Park, which covers 6 million acres, is the largest state park in the lower 48 states.*
- *From 1892 to 1954 more than 17 million immigrants entered the United States at New York's Ellis Island (now shared with New Jersey).*

Eastern Bluebird
Rose

The Northeast 47

The Physical United States

From sea to shining sea, the United States spans about 3,000 miles (4828 km) from its east to west coasts. Its total area is 3,794,000 square miles (9,827,000 sq km). On this physical map you will see natural features of the land, such as rivers, lakes, mountains, and deserts. Shading shows differences in elevation, or height of the land above sea level. Colors identify vegetation regions. The map shows state boundaries so that you can check out the landscape in each state. At the top of the page, a cross-section of the country from west to east shows the elevation of the land on a line between San Francisco and Washington, D.C.

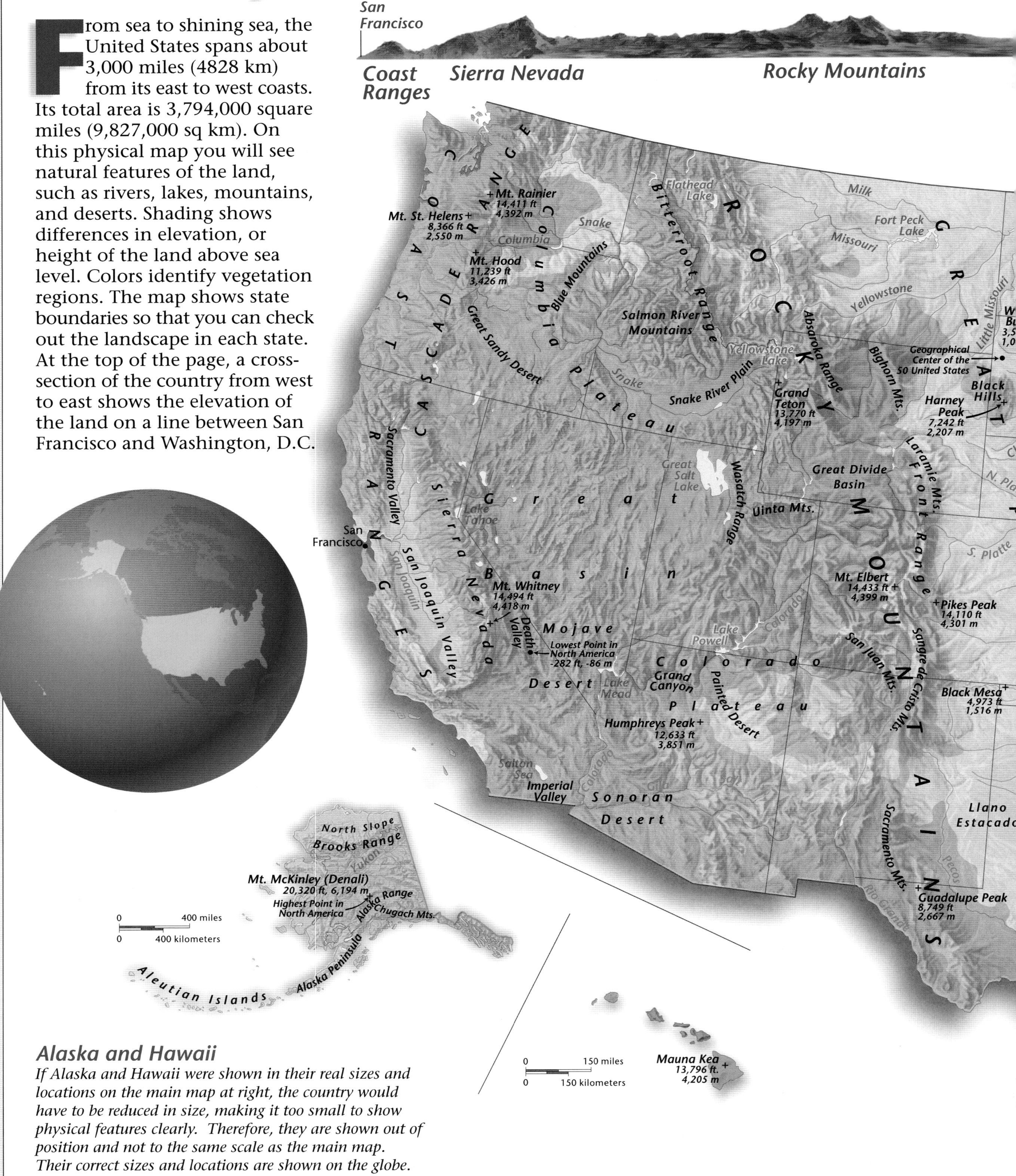

Alaska and Hawaii

If Alaska and Hawaii were shown in their real sizes and locations on the main map at right, the country would have to be reduced in size, making it too small to show physical features clearly. Therefore, they are shown out of position and not to the same scale as the main map. Their correct sizes and locations are shown on the globe.

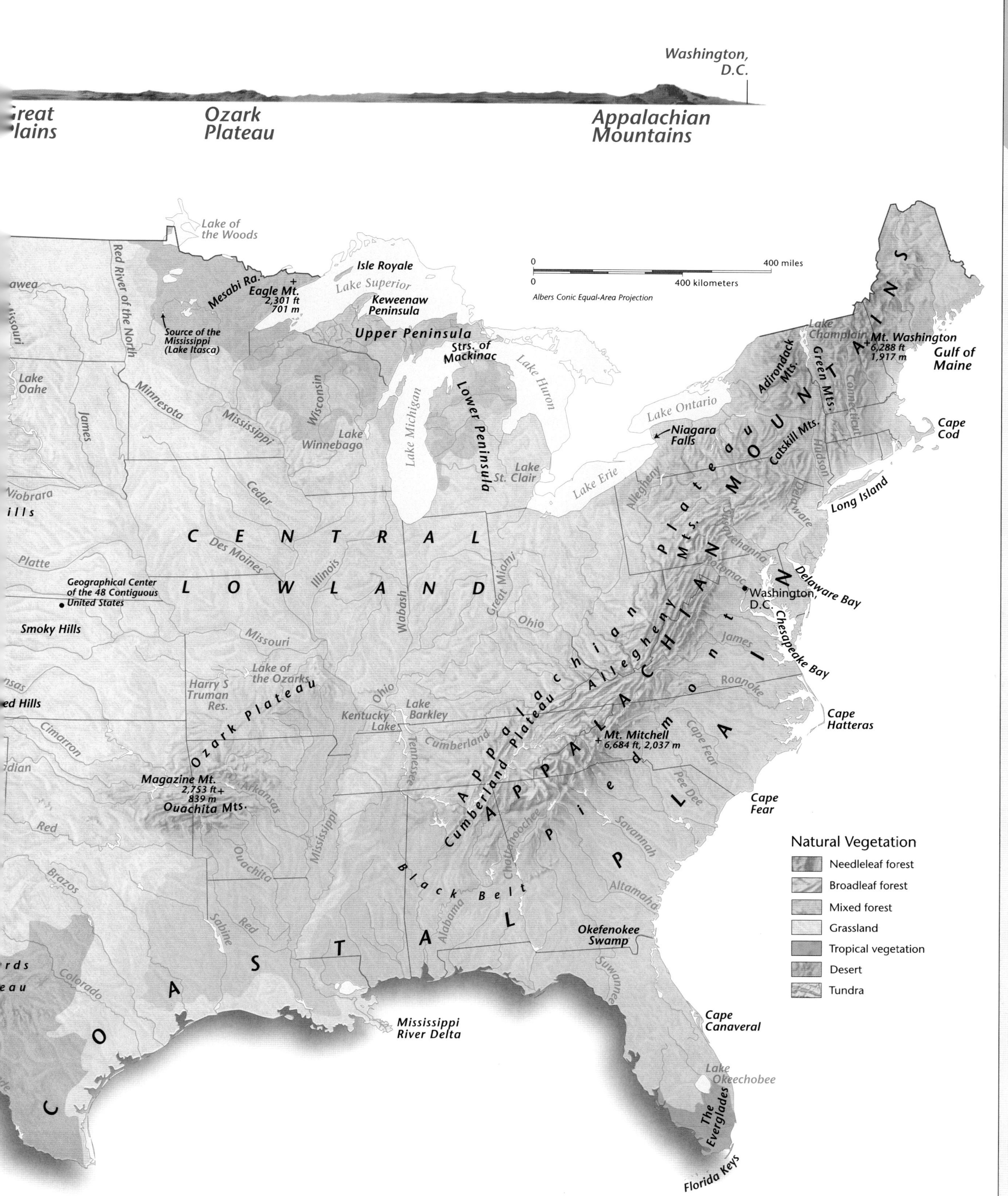
Washington, D.C.
Great Plains
Ozark Plateau
Appalachian Mountains
Lake of the Woods
Isle Royale
Lake Superior
Keweenaw Peninsula
Upper Peninsula
Mesabi Ra.
Eagle Mt. 2,301 ft 701 m
Source of the Mississippi (Lake Itasca)
Red River of the North
Strs. of Mackinac
Lake Huron
Lake Michigan
Lower Peninsula
Wisconsin
Lake Winnebago
Minnesota
Mississippi
Lake Oahe
James
Lake St. Clair
Lake Erie
Lake Ontario
Niagara Falls
0 400 miles
0 400 kilometers
Albers Conic Equal-Area Projection
Lake Champlain
Adirondack Mts.
Green Mts.
Mt. Washington 6,288 ft 1,917 m
Gulf of Maine
Connecticut
Catskill Mts.
Hudson
Cape Cod
Long Island
Delaware
Allegheny
Susquehanna
Potomac
Delaware Bay
Washington, D.C.
Chesapeake Bay
James
Roanoke
Cape Hatteras
Niobrara
Platte
Cedar
Des Moines
Illinois
CENTRAL LOWLAND
Geographical Center of the 48 Contiguous United States
Smoky Hills
Missouri
Wabash
Great Miami
Ohio
Lake of the Ozarks
Harry S Truman Res.
Ozark Plateau
Kentucky Lake
Lake Barkley
Cumberland
Tennessee
Cimarron
Appalachian Plateau
Allegheny Plateau
Cumberland Plateau
APPALACHIAN MOUNTAINS
Piedmont
Mt. Mitchell 6,684 ft, 2,037 m
Cape Fear
Pee Dee
Cape Fear
Magazine Mt. 2,753 ft 839 m
Ouachita Mts.
Arkansas
Red
Ouachita
Mississippi
Brazos
Savannah
Chattahoochee
Black Belt
Alabama
Altamaha
Sabine
Red
Okefenokee Swamp
Suwannee
COASTAL PLAIN
Colorado
Mississippi River Delta
Cape Canaveral
Lake Okeechobee
The Everglades
Florida Keys
Natural Vegetation
Needleleaf forest
Broadleaf forest
Mixed forest
Grassland
Tropical vegetation
Desert
Tundra

Natural Environment

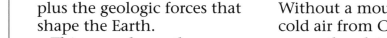

The natural world that surrounds you is called the natural environment. It includes weather and climate plus the geologic forces that shape the Earth.

This map shows the country's many climate regions. Climate is determined by location—in mountains, near oceans, or deep in the continental interior—as well as by prevailing winds and distance from the Equator.

Climate regions have predictable weather patterns, but day-to-day weather can change suddenly, sometimes disastrously. Cool air from the Rockies that meets warm air from the Gulf of Mexico can spawn tornadoes. These are particularly common from Texas to Nebraska in a belt known as Tornado Alley. Without a mountain barrier, cold air from Canada sweeps across the plains and the Great Lakes, causing ice and snow storms. Snowmelt and heavy rains can lead to severe spring flooding. Each summer, the dry, leeward slopes of western mountains are ravaged by wildfires sparked by lightning.

Geology is another source of natural disasters. Earthquakes and volcanoes mark the Pacific coast, where vast geologic plates interact with each other.

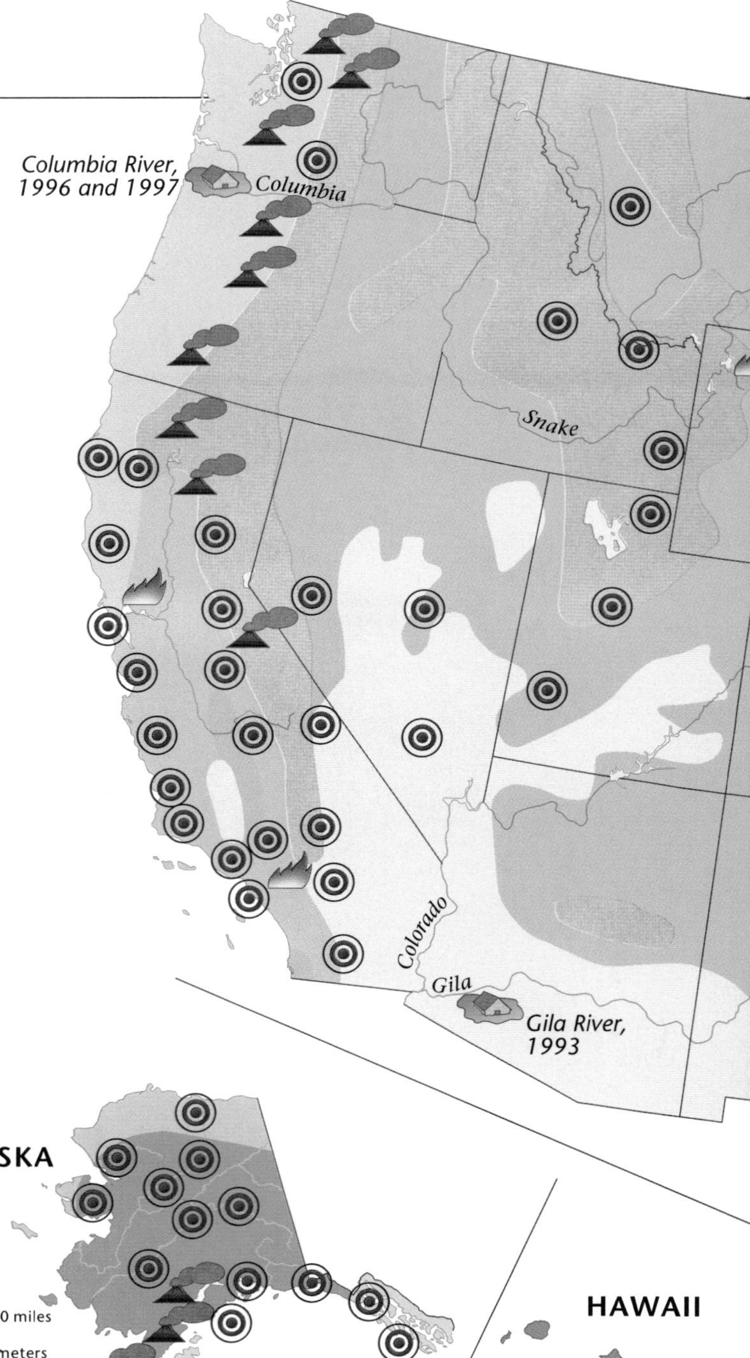

◄ ***Slim and** deadly, a tornado touches down in Texas. Some 800 to 1,000 twisters kill 70 to 80 people a year in the United States.*

◄ ***Blinding** snow forces a farmer to use a guide rope to get from his house to his barn and back. In blizzards people can get lost just a few feet from home.*

► ***Battling** floodwaters, people try to paddle a canoe through the streets of an Iowa town in the great Midwest flood of 1993.*

► ***Blazing** inferno, a forest fire engulfs trees in California. The U.S. spends at least $1 billion a year fighting wildfires.*

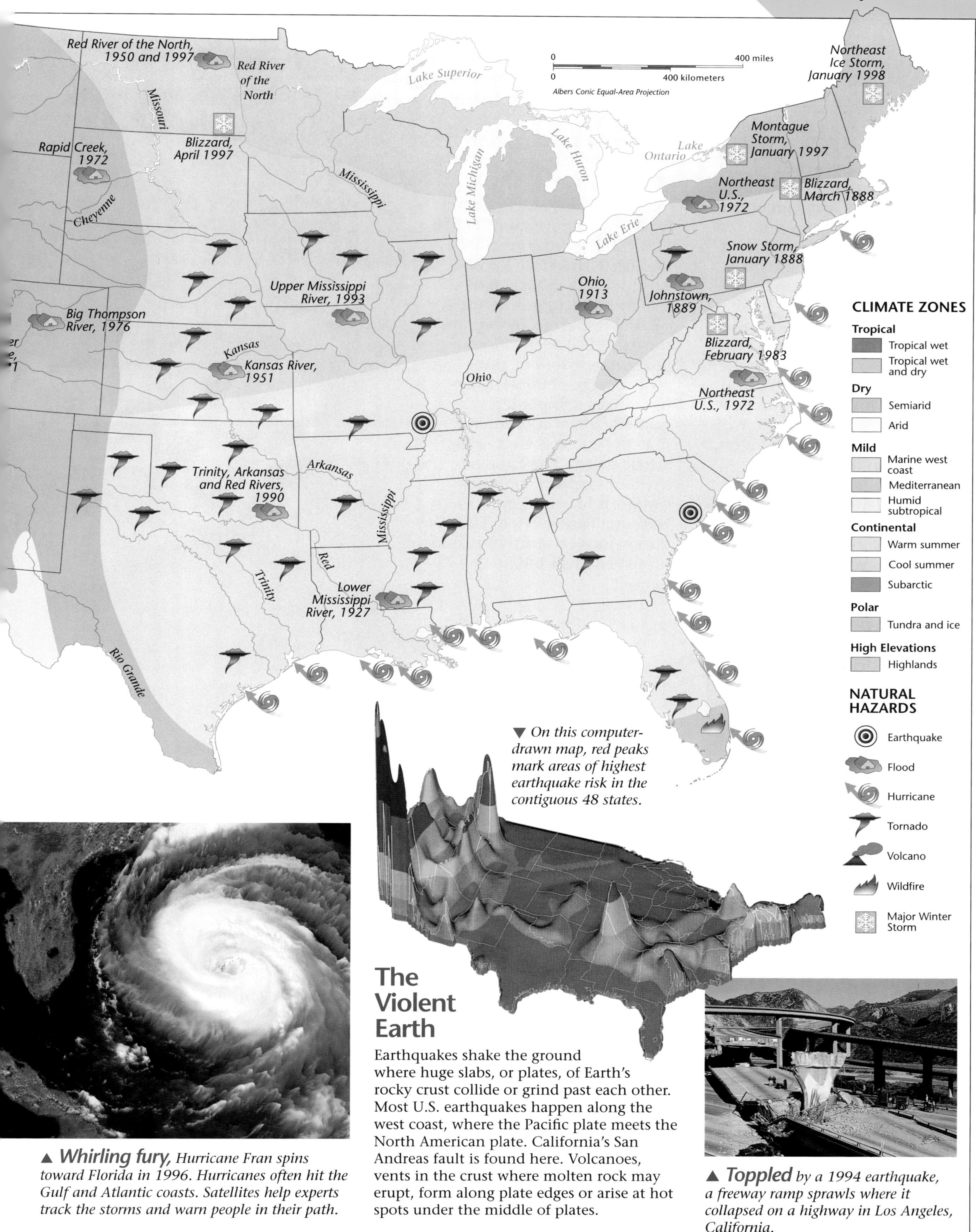

▼ *On this computer-drawn map, red peaks mark areas of highest earthquake risk in the contiguous 48 states.*

▲ ***Whirling fury,*** *Hurricane Fran spins toward Florida in 1996. Hurricanes often hit the Gulf and Atlantic coasts. Satellites help experts track the storms and warn people in their path.*

The Violent Earth

Earthquakes shake the ground where huge slabs, or plates, of Earth's rocky crust collide or grind past each other. Most U.S. earthquakes happen along the west coast, where the Pacific plate meets the North American plate. California's San Andreas fault is found here. Volcanoes, vents in the crust where molten rock may erupt, form along plate edges or arise at hot spots under the middle of plates.

▲ ***Toppled*** *by a 1994 earthquake, a freeway ramp sprawls where it collapsed on a highway in Los Angeles, California.*

Federal Lands

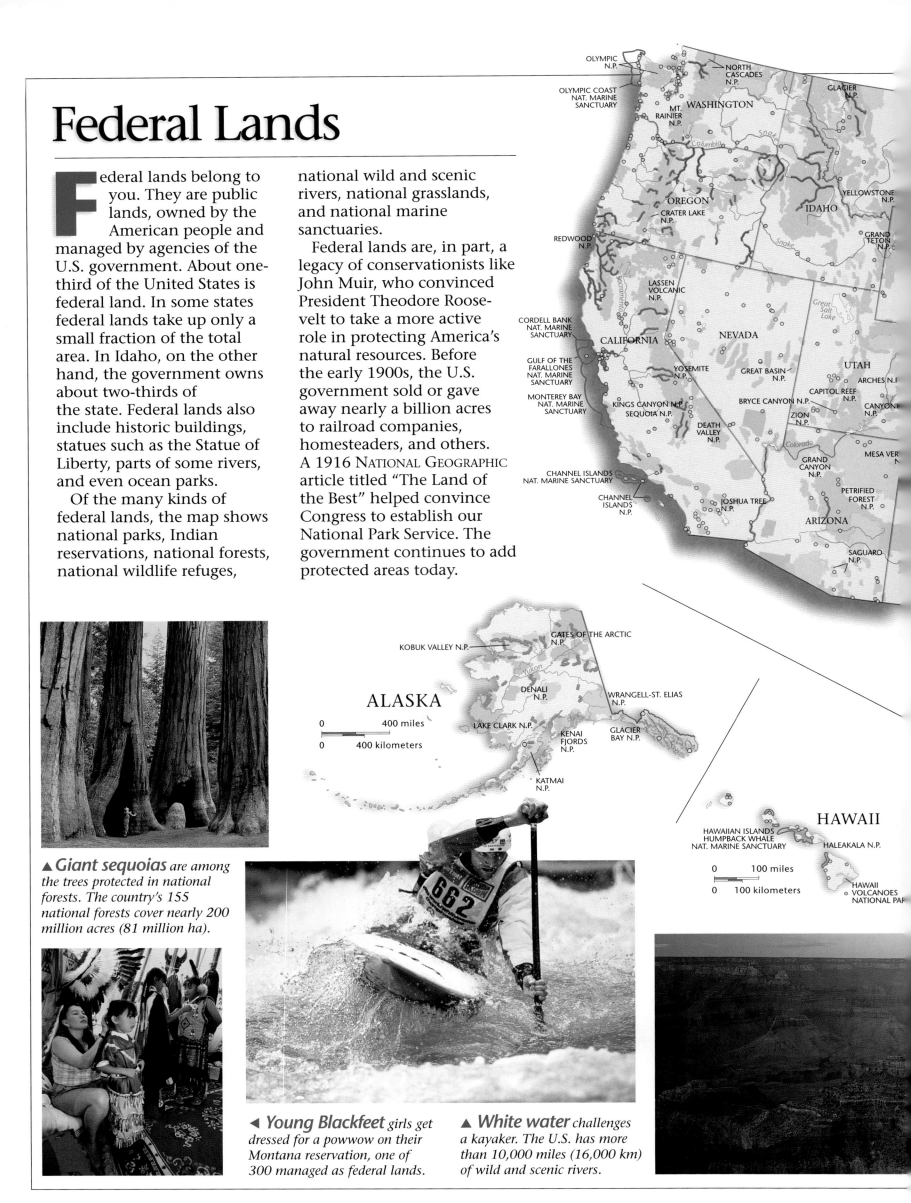

Federal lands belong to you. They are public lands, owned by the American people and managed by agencies of the U.S. government. About one-third of the United States is federal land. In some states federal lands take up only a small fraction of the total area. In Idaho, on the other hand, the government owns about two-thirds of the state. Federal lands also include historic buildings, statues such as the Statue of Liberty, parts of some rivers, and even ocean parks.

Of the many kinds of federal lands, the map shows national parks, Indian reservations, national forests, national wildlife refuges, national wild and scenic rivers, national grasslands, and national marine sanctuaries.

Federal lands are, in part, a legacy of conservationists like John Muir, who convinced President Theodore Roosevelt to take a more active role in protecting America's natural resources. Before the early 1900s, the U.S. government sold or gave away nearly a billion acres to railroad companies, homesteaders, and others. A 1916 NATIONAL GEOGRAPHIC article titled "The Land of the Best" helped convince Congress to establish our National Park Service. The government continues to add protected areas today.

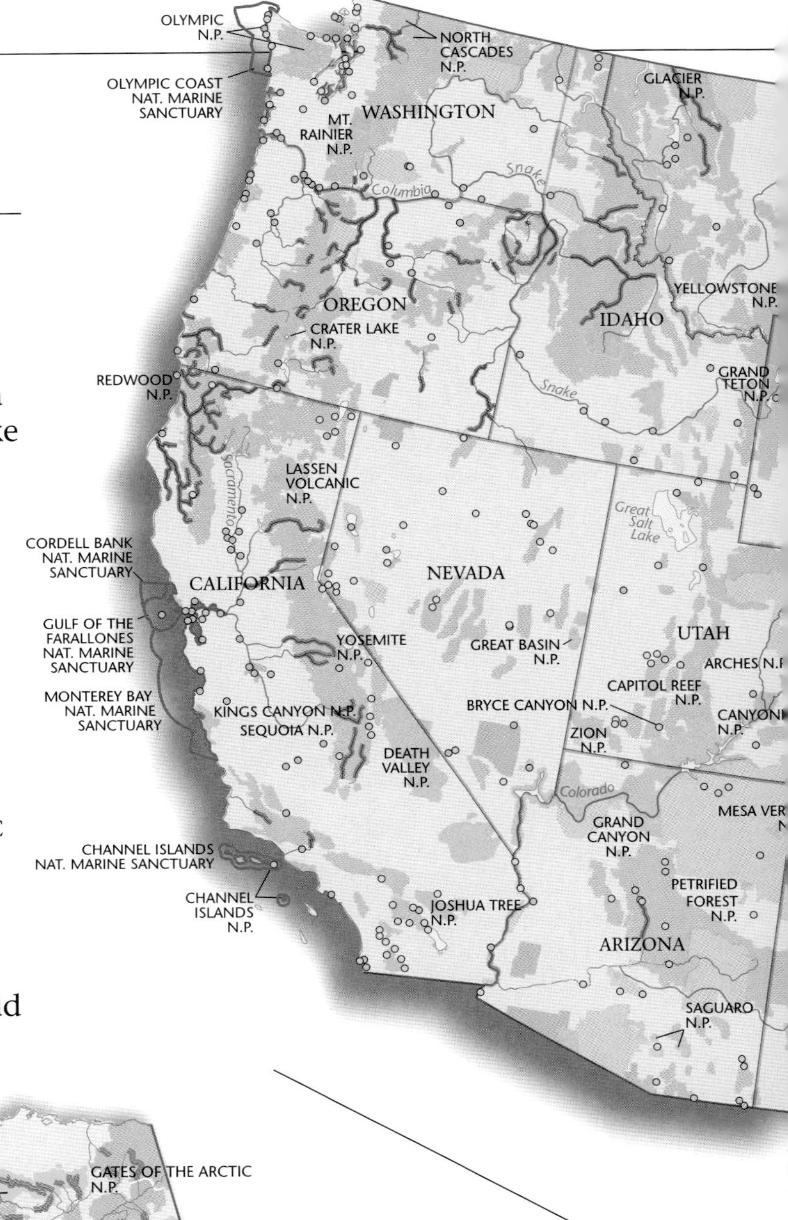

▲ ***Giant sequoias*** *are among the trees protected in national forests. The country's 155 national forests cover nearly 200 million acres (81 million ha).*

◄ ***Young Blackfeet*** *girls get dressed for a powwow on their Montana reservation, one of 300 managed as federal lands.*

▲ ***White water*** *challenges a kayaker. The U.S. has more than 10,000 miles (16,000 km) of wild and scenic rivers.*

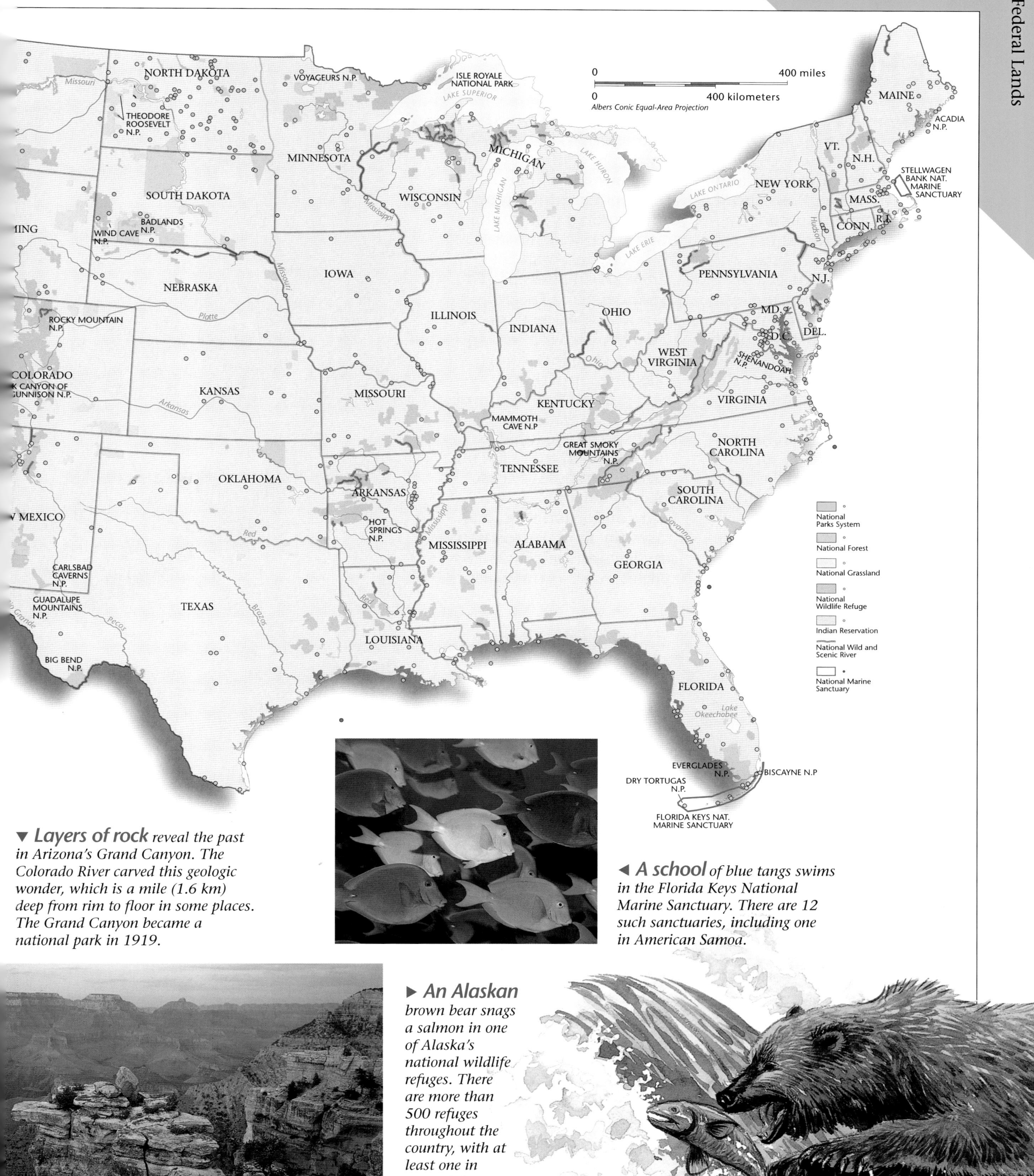

▼ ***Layers of rock*** *reveal the past in Arizona's Grand Canyon. The Colorado River carved this geologic wonder, which is a mile (1.6 km) deep from rim to floor in some places. The Grand Canyon became a national park in 1919.*

◀ ***A school*** *of blue tangs swims in the Florida Keys National Marine Sanctuary. There are 12 such sanctuaries, including one in American Samoa.*

▶ ***An Alaskan*** *brown bear snags a salmon in one of Alaska's national wildlife refuges. There are more than 500 refuges throughout the country, with at least one in every state.*

Endangered Species

From Alaska to Florida and from Hawaii to Maine, hundreds of species of animals and plants that once flourished now struggle to survive.

The greatest threat to wildlife is loss of habitat, or living space. The U.S. population is increasing by 3.3 million people a year. Today about 95 percent of our original forests are gone. Many wetlands, vital to fish, birds, and other animals, have been drained.

Animals have been hunted into near-extinction for food, fur, or blubber to make oil. Wolves and other predators have been killed to protect domestic herds. The bison, which once rumbled across the plains in vast herds, was nearly wiped out by hunters in the 19th century. In addition, people have harmed fish and the animals that eat them by unintentionally poisoning waters with toxic wastes, fertilizers, and pesticides.

In 1973 Congress passed the Endangered Species Act to protect species that were in danger of dying out. The law prohibits killing, collecting, or harming these species. Today, almost 400 animals and 600 plant species are listed as endangered in the U.S. The map shows some of these endangered animals and their connection to human use of the land. Fortunately, new laws are helping many species make a comeback.

◀ ***Wings spread*** wide, a bald eagle dives for a fish. Once extremely endangered, the birds are increasing in numbers.

▼ ***A Crocodile*** native to Florida gives her babies a lift. Hunted for its skin, which was used to make belts, purses, and other items, this species became endangered.

▼ ***Biologists*** examine a captive-bred red wolf that was introduced into the wild in North Carolina. These endangered wolves are now successfully breeding in their natural habitat.

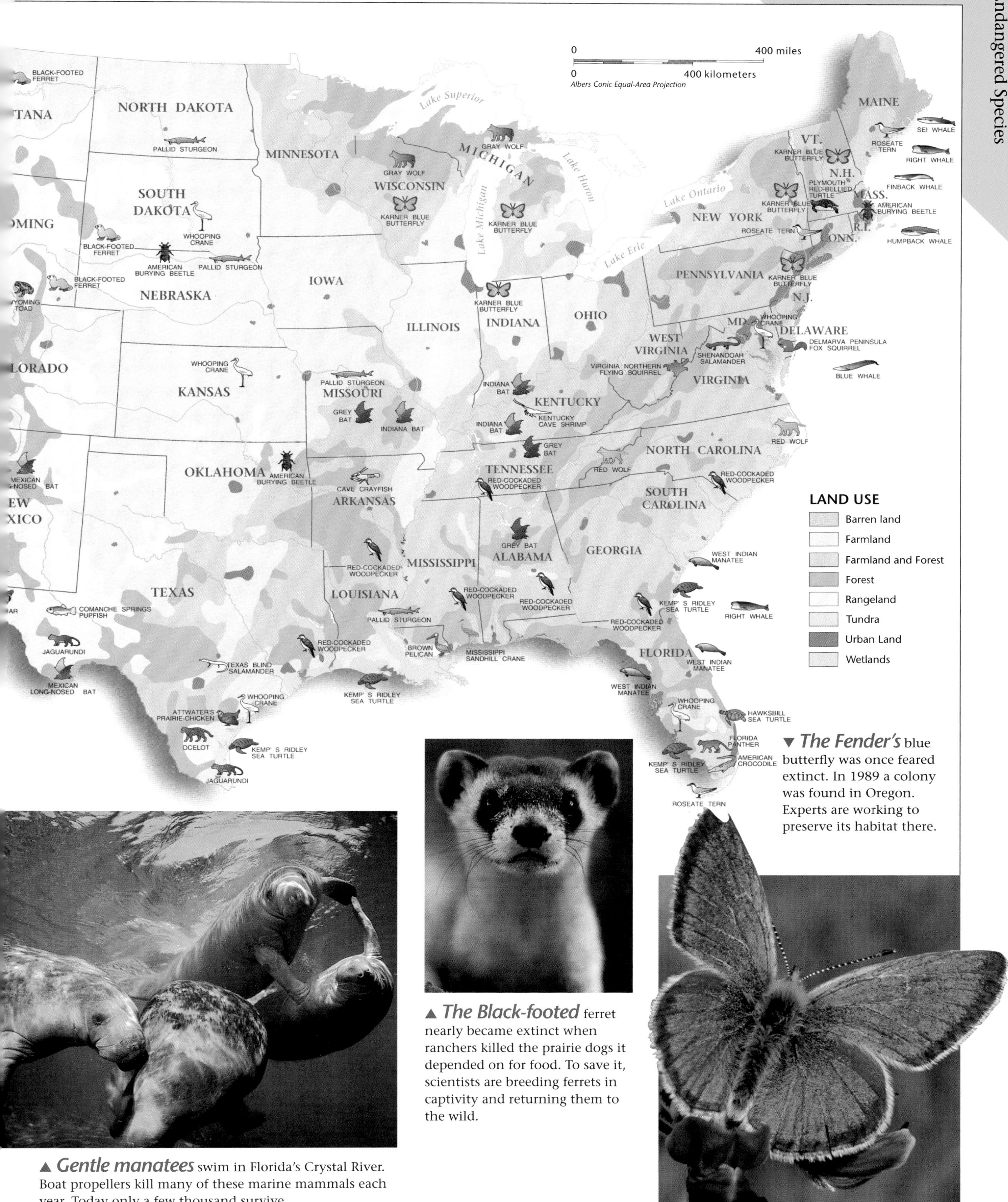

▼ *The Fender's* blue butterfly was once feared extinct. In 1989 a colony was found in Oregon. Experts are working to preserve its habitat there.

▲ *The Black-footed* ferret nearly became extinct when ranchers killed the prairie dogs it depended on for food. To save it, scientists are breeding ferrets in captivity and returning them to the wild.

▲ *Gentle manatees* swim in Florida's Crystal River. Boat propellers kill many of these marine mammals each year. Today only a few thousand survive.

The Political United States

Political maps reflect the way people organize themselves into towns, cities, states, and countries. This map shows state boundaries, state capitals, and large cities as well as some major natural features. Rivers and mountains often serve as boundaries. The 48 states that are connected—called the contiguous or conterminous United States—make up the large map. Alaska and Hawaii are shown as separate insets, each to its own scale. The globe below shows these two states in their real locations.

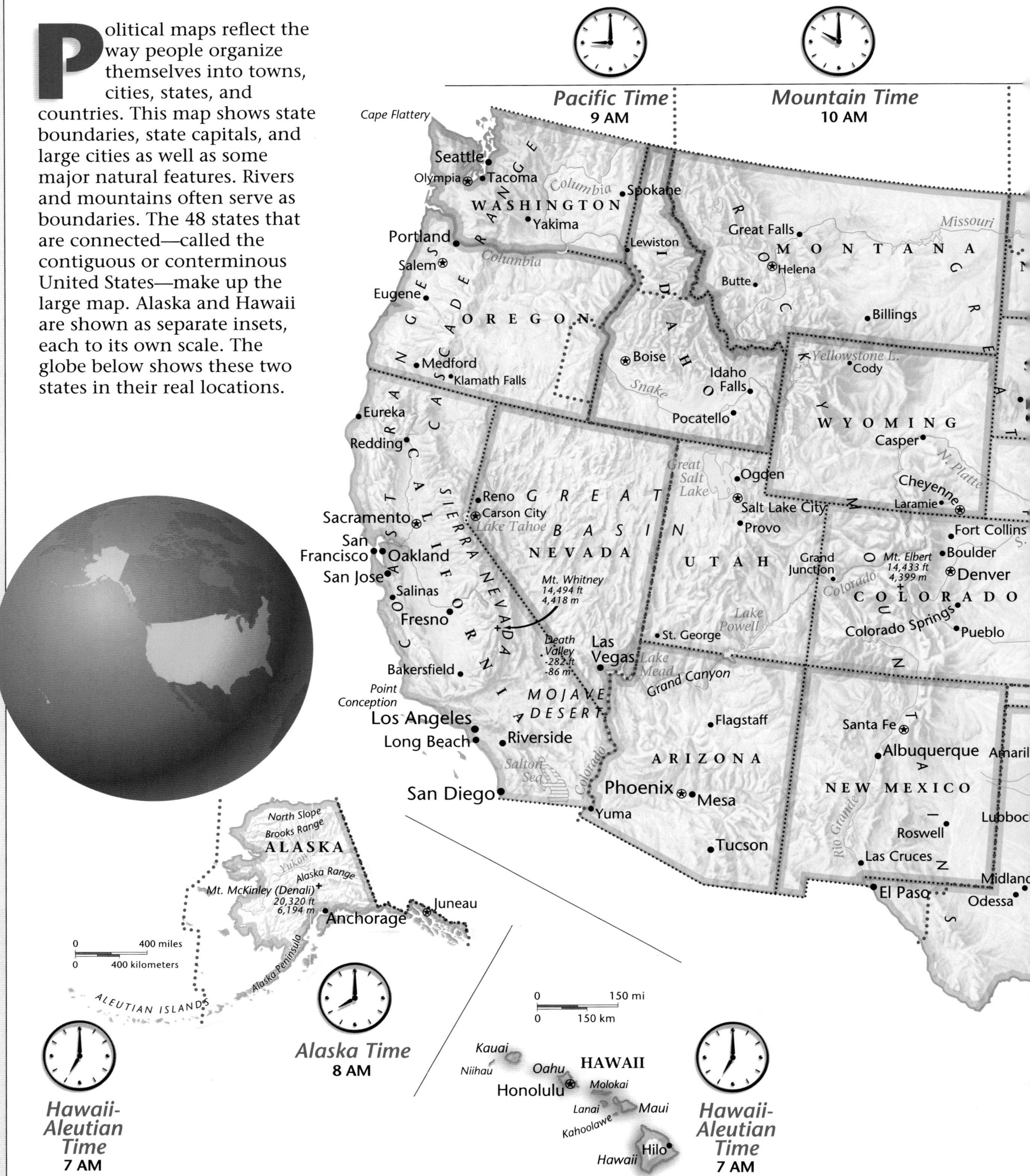

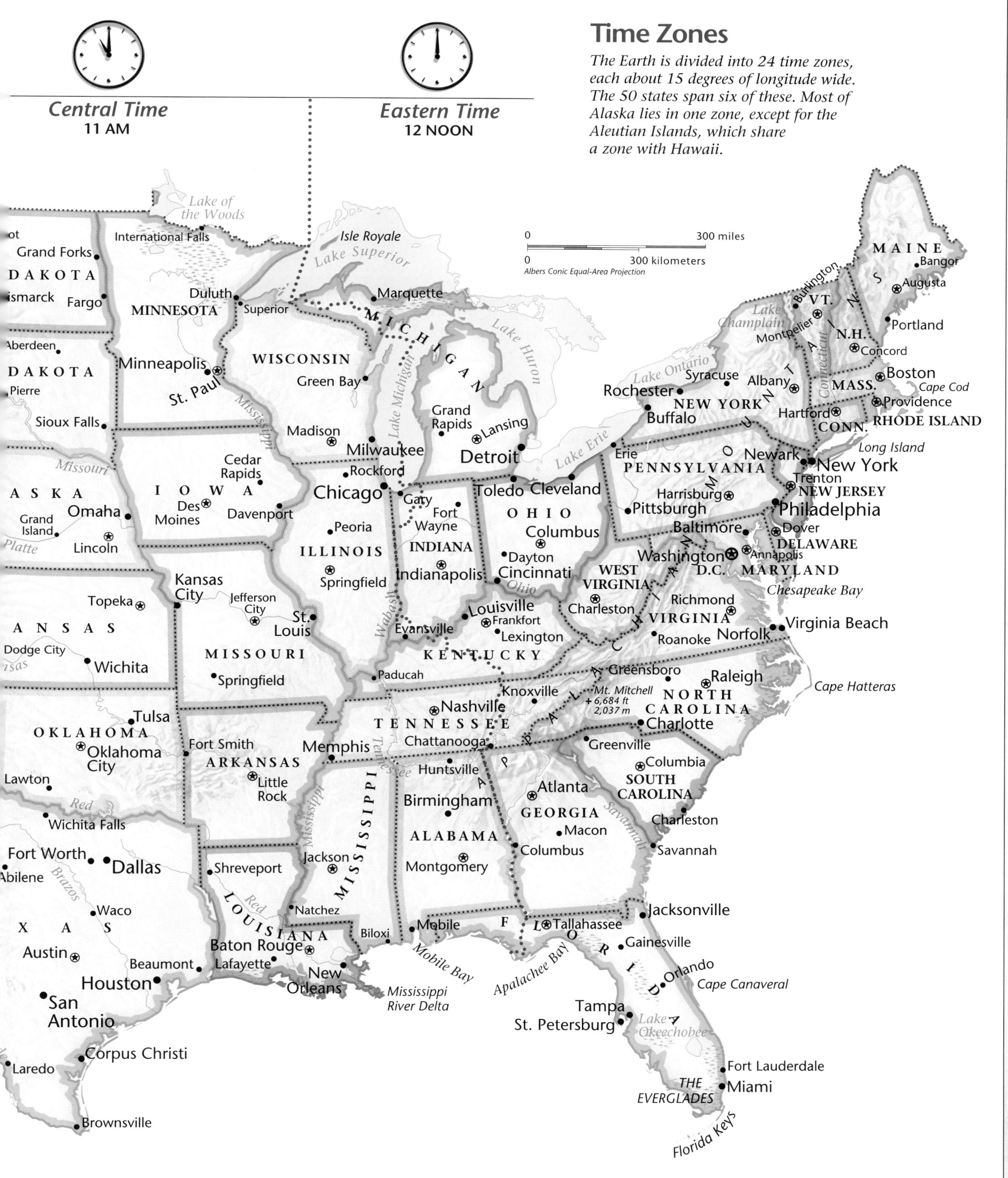
Time Zones
The Earth is divided into 24 time zones, each about 15 degrees of longitude wide. The 50 states span six of these. Most of Alaska lies in one zone, except for the Aleutian Islands, which share a zone with Hawaii.
Central Time
11 AM
Eastern Time
12 NOON
0
300 miles
0
300 kilometers
Albers Conic Equal-Area Projection
Lake of the Woods
International Falls
Isle Royale
Lake Superior
Grand Forks
DAKOTA
Fargo
Duluth
MINNESOTA
Superior
Marquette
MICHIGAN
Lake Huron
Aberdeen
DAKOTA
Pierre
Minneapolis
St. Paul
WISCONSIN
Green Bay
Mississippi
Sioux Falls
Madison
Lake Michigan
Grand Rapids
Lansing
Milwaukee
Detroit
Missouri
Cedar Rapids
IOWA
Des Moines
Davenport
Rockford
Chicago
Gary
Toledo
Cleveland
Lake Erie
Omaha
Grand Island
Lincoln
Platte
Peoria
Fort Wayne
OHIO
Columbus
ILLINOIS
INDIANA
Dayton
Springfield
Indianapolis
Cincinnati
Ohio
Kansas City
Jefferson City
Topeka
St. Louis
Wabash
Evansville
Louisville
Frankfort
Lexington
KENTUCKY
Dodge City
Wichita
MISSOURI
Springfield
Paducah
Tulsa
OKLAHOMA
Oklahoma City
Lawton
Fort Smith
ARKANSAS
Little Rock
Memphis
Nashville
TENNESSEE
Chattanooga
Knoxville
Tennessee
Huntsville
Red
Wichita Falls
Fort Worth
Dallas
Abilene
Brazos
Waco
TEXAS
Austin
Houston
San Antonio
Corpus Christi
Laredo
Brownsville
Shreveport
Red
LOUISIANA
Natchez
Jackson
MISSISSIPPI
Mississippi
Baton Rouge
Lafayette
Beaumont
New Orleans
Mississippi River Delta
Biloxi
Mobile
Mobile Bay
Birmingham
ALABAMA
Montgomery
Atlanta
GEORGIA
Macon
Columbus
FLORIDA
Tallahassee
Apalachee Bay
Gainesville
Jacksonville
Orlando
Cape Canaveral
Tampa
St. Petersburg
Lake Okeechobee
Fort Lauderdale
Miami
THE EVERGLADES
Florida Keys
Savannah
Savannah
Charleston
SOUTH CAROLINA
Columbia
Greenville
Charlotte
NORTH CAROLINA
Raleigh
Greensboro
Mt. Mitchell
+6,684 ft
2,037 m
Cape Hatteras
APPALACHIAN MOUNTAINS
Roanoke
Norfolk
Virginia Beach
VIRGINIA
Richmond
WEST VIRGINIA
Charleston
Washington D.C.
Annapolis
MARYLAND
Chesapeake Bay
Baltimore
Dover
DELAWARE
Philadelphia
NEW JERSEY
Trenton
Pittsburgh
Harrisburg
PENNSYLVANIA
Erie
Newark
New York
Long Island
Buffalo
Rochester
NEW YORK
Lake Ontario
Syracuse
Albany
Hartford
CONN.
RHODE ISLAND
Providence
Cape Cod
MASS.
Boston
Connecticut
Concord
N.H.
Portland
Lake Champlain
Montpelier
Burlington
VT.
MAINE
Bangor
Augusta

Territorial Growth

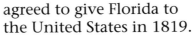

As Europeans began settling America in the 1600s, the 13 British colonies rose along the east coast. After the Revolutionary War ended in 1781, these colonies became the United States. The country grew quickly as Britain gave the new nation land stretching west to the Great Lakes and Mississippi River and south through Georgia.

The United States then expanded by buying land, fighting wars, or negotiating treaties. In 1803 the United States bought a huge parcel of land known as the Louisiana Purchase from France. This land doubled the country's size. The U.S. grew again when Spain agreed to give Florida to the United States in 1819.

Turning west, the United States fought with Mexico. By 1848 it had won most of the land from Texas to California. As settlers flooded the Oregon Country in the 1840s, Britain gave up most of this area to the U.S. As each new territory was settled, it eventually became a state (see big map). Settlers moving West pushed Native Americans off their lands. By 1900 the U.S. government had taken 95 percent of Indian lands.

In 1867 the U.S. bought Alaska from Russia, and in 1898 it annexed the Hawaiian Islands. In 1959 these lands became the 49th and 50th states.

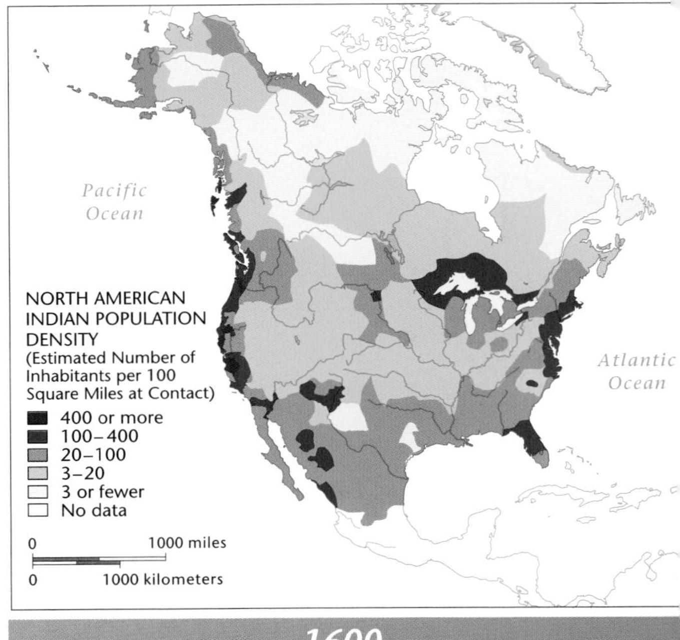

1600

In 1600, before European settlement, America was inhabited by Native Americans. This map shows where the largest numbers of these people lived.

The Westward Expansion

Beginning in the 1820s, thousands of pioneers packed their covered wagons and crossed the Great Plains to the far West. Both Americans and European immigrants wanted land. Some looked for gold or adventure. Others, such as the Mormons, sought religious freedom. The longest of the pioneer trails was the Oregon Trail, winding 2,000 miles (3,220 km) from Missouri to Oregon. It experienced some of its heaviest traffic after gold was discovered in California in 1848.

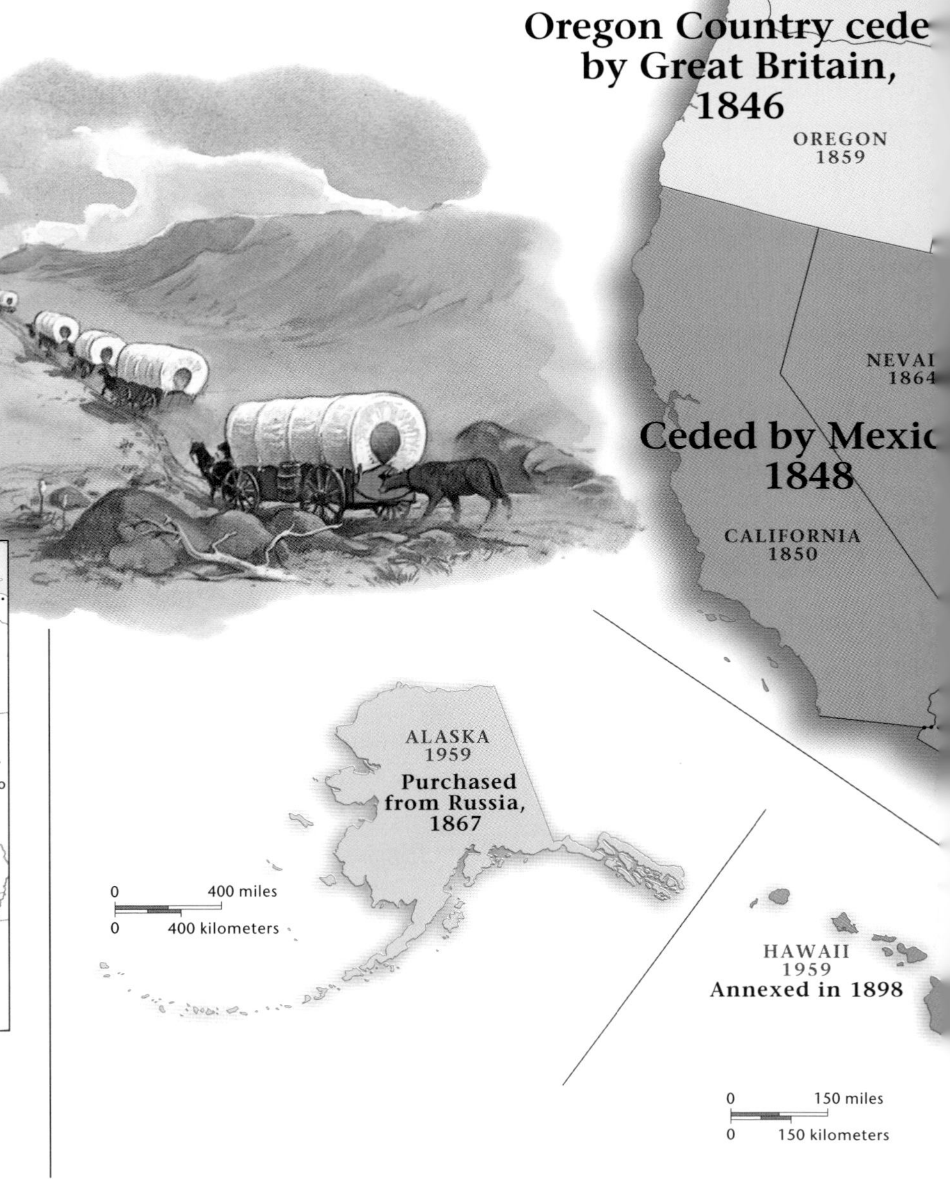

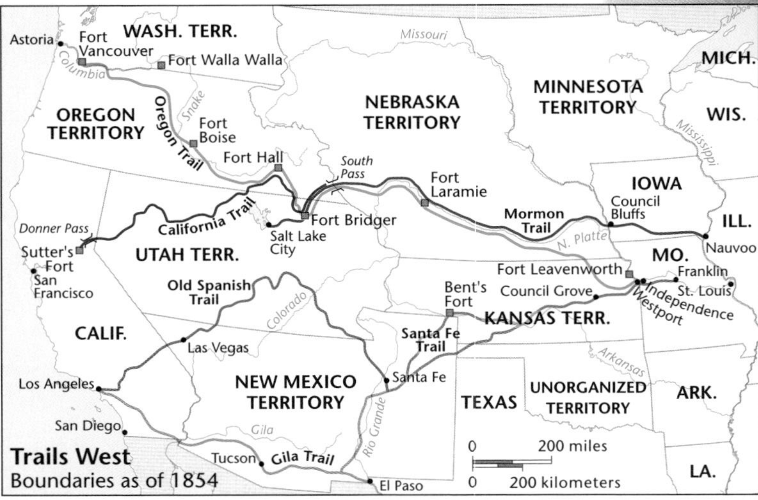

Trails West: Routes of the Pioneers

Pioneers followed many trails West in the 1800s. During the height of the westward movement in the 1840s and 1850s, thousands journeyed to Oregon, Utah, and California each year.

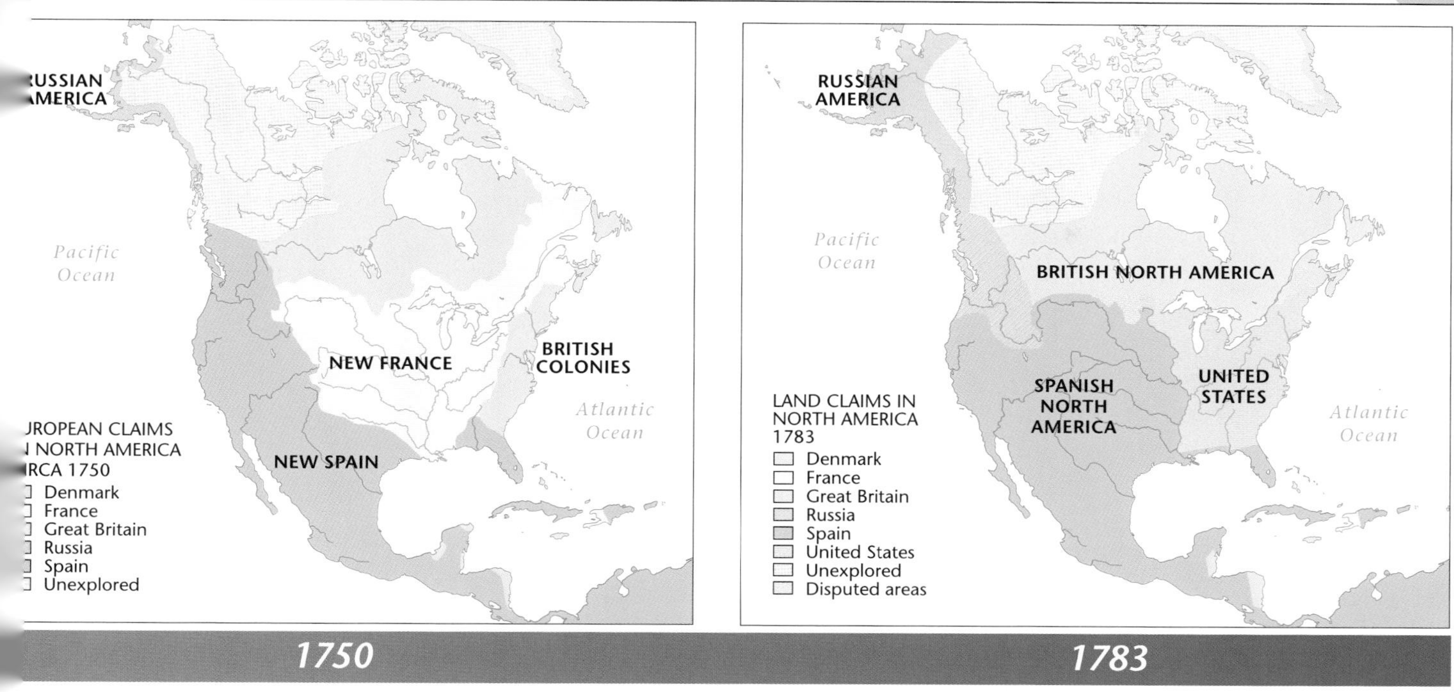

By 1750 Great Britain had 13 colonies in the East. France dominated the interior and Spain the West and Southwest. Russia had settlements in Alaska.

In the Treaty of 1783 Britain recognized the U.S. as a country, granting it land from Canada almost to the Gulf of Mexico and west to the Mississippi.

Building a Country

This map shows the country's major land acquisitions and the date each state was admitted to the Union. Current territories are shown on pages 156–159.

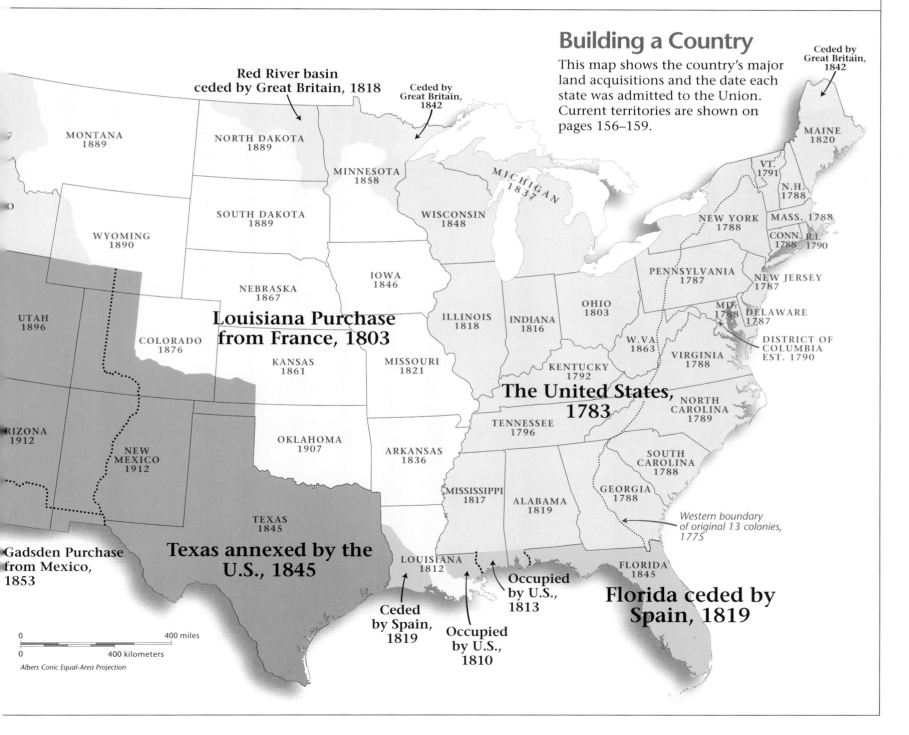

Ceded by Great Britain, 1842
Red River basin ceded by Great Britain, 1818
Ceded by Great Britain, 1842
MONTANA 1889
NORTH DAKOTA 1889
MINNESOTA 1858
MAINE 1820
MICHIGAN 1837
VT. 1791
N.H. 1788
SOUTH DAKOTA 1889
WISCONSIN 1848
NEW YORK 1788
MASS. 1788
WYOMING 1890
CONN. 1788
R.I. 1790
IOWA 1846
PENNSYLVANIA 1787
NEW JERSEY 1787
NEBRASKA 1867
UTAH 1896
Louisiana Purchase from France, 1803
ILLINOIS 1818
INDIANA 1816
OHIO 1803
MD. 1788
DELAWARE 1787
COLORADO 1876
W.VA. 1863
DISTRICT OF COLUMBIA EST. 1790
KANSAS 1861
MISSOURI 1821
VIRGINIA 1788
KENTUCKY 1792
The United States, 1783
NORTH CAROLINA 1789
ARIZONA 1912
TENNESSEE 1796
OKLAHOMA 1907
ARKANSAS 1836
SOUTH CAROLINA 1788
NEW MEXICO 1912
GEORGIA 1788
MISSISSIPPI 1817
ALABAMA 1819
TEXAS 1845
Western boundary of original 13 colonies, 1775
Gadsden Purchase from Mexico, 1853
Texas annexed by the U.S., 1845
LOUISIANA 1812
FLORIDA 1845
Occupied by U.S., 1813
Florida ceded by Spain, 1819
Ceded by Spain, 1819
Occupied by U.S., 1810
0 400 miles
0 400 kilometers
Albers Conic Equal-Area Projection

Population

Who are we? Where do we live? How many of us are there? These are basic aspects of population—aspects that are rapidly changing.

Five hundred years ago, the country's population was made up of Native Americans scattered across the land in hundreds of different tribal nations. After colonization began in the 1600s, the population included Europeans and a few Africans clustered in settlements, mainly along the eastern seaboard. By the 19th century, land and the promise of mineral wealth lured adventurous souls all the way to the west coast.

Big industrial areas grew up in the Northeast during the last 200 years, but by the middle of the 20th century these older cities began to decline as people looked for new opportunities. A lower cost of living, jobs, and warmer weather now attract many to the Sun Belt, a region of rapid growth in the South and West.

Metropolitan areas—cities and their suburbs—continue to attract people from less populated areas. Suburbs themselves are growing into "edge cities" where people both live and work. Immigration brings hundreds of thousands of new residents each year—mainly Hispanic and Asian—adding to our growing diversity.

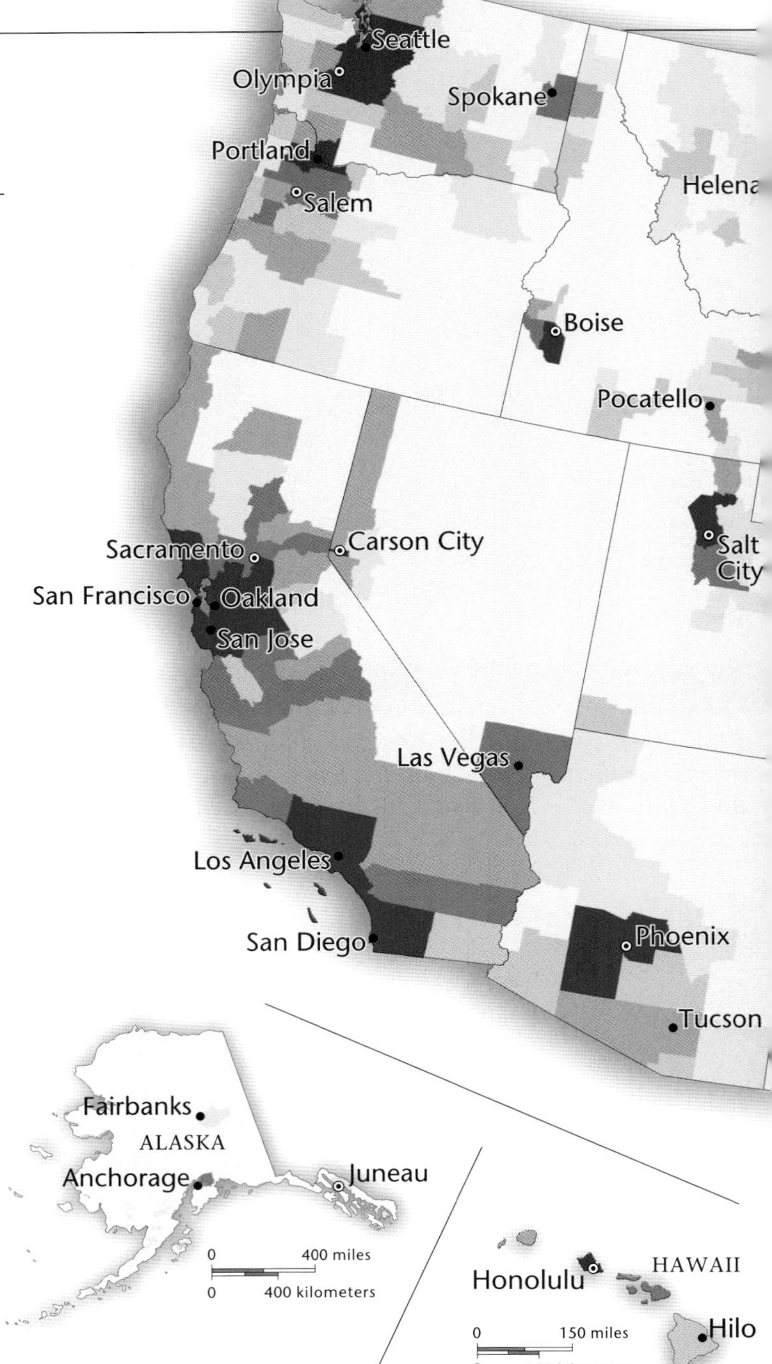

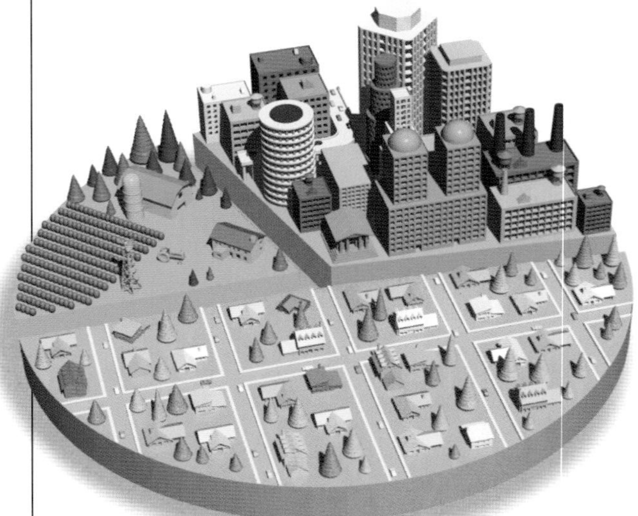

Where We Live

In 1900 about 40 percent of all Americans lived outside of urban areas on farms (green). Four out of five now live in metropolitan areas—in cities (blue) or their suburbs (orange), with the suburbs gaining the most people.

Source (left and below): U.S. Bureau of the Census

How Old Are We?

The median age—meaning the age at which half the population is older, half younger—in the U.S. was once quite young. In 1900 it was only 23 years. According to the 2000 census, it had reached 35. As people live longer and have smaller families, the median age is rising. By 2040, when the last "baby boomers" (shaded areas) born in the 1960s reach old age, almost one in four Americans will be over 65.

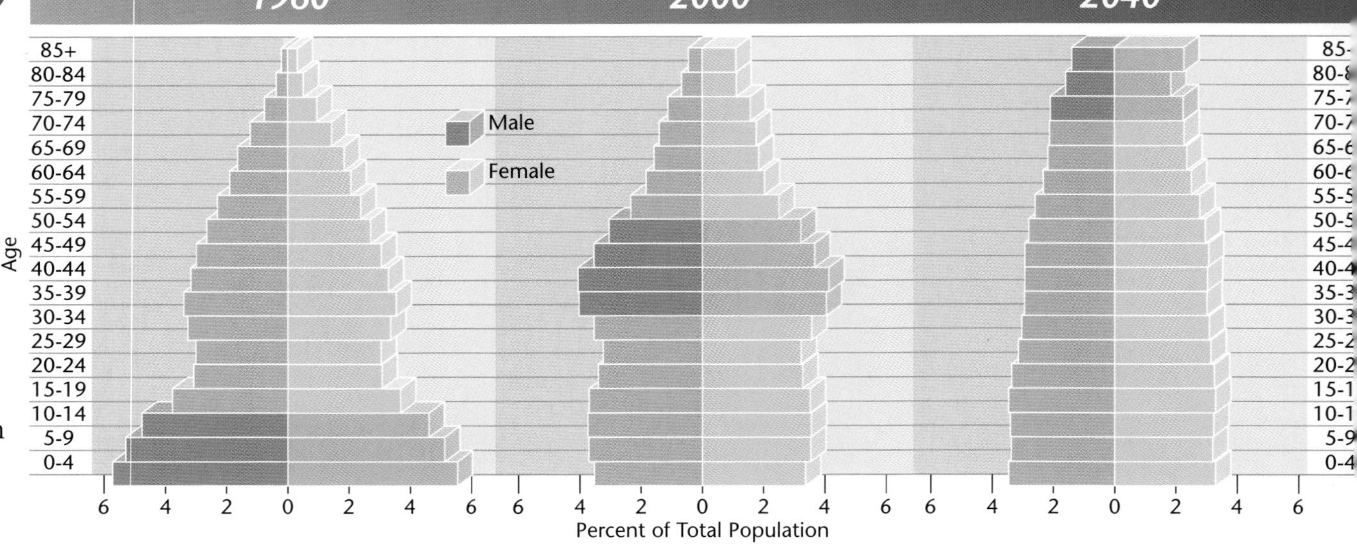

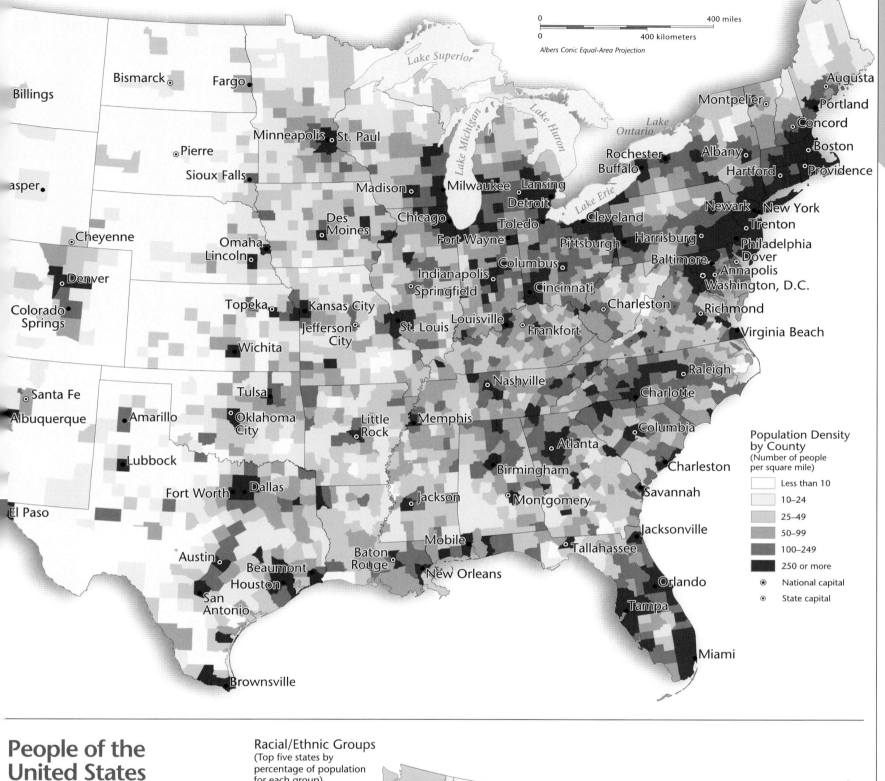

People of the United States

According to the U.S. Census Bureau, the people of the United States can be divided into five major groups: American Indian (including Eskimos and Aleuts), Asian/Pacific Islander, black, Hispanic, and white non-Hispanic. This map shows where the highest percentage of each group lives, based on state populations. Only the top five states for each group are shown. The percentages can be misleading. For instance, the percentage of Alaskans who are American Indian is double that of Oklahoma. But Oklahoma has three times as many American Indians as Alaska because Oklahoma's total population is larger.

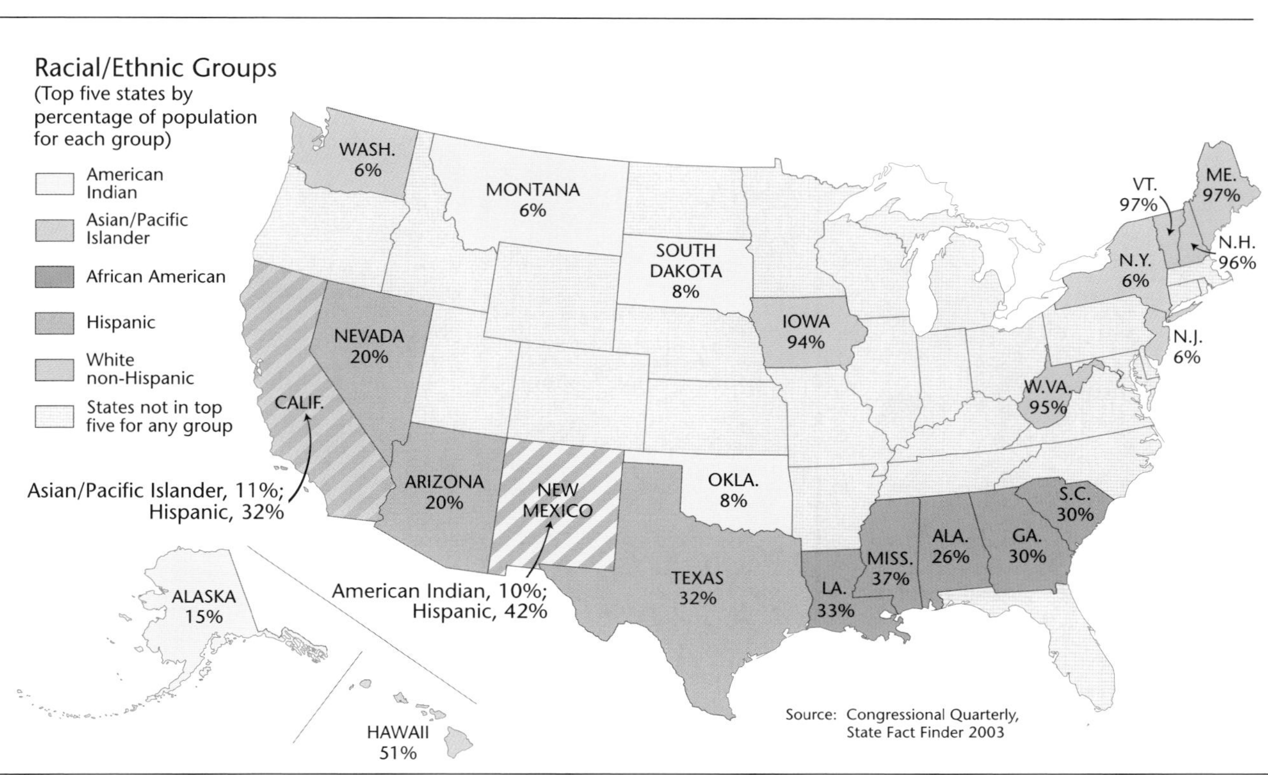

Transportation

Transportation in the United States has changed dramatically as the country has grown.

In colonial America, travel was slow and difficult. To go between colonies, most people sailed along the coast. Roads were little more than rutted dirt paths through the woods. In the early 1800s, people began moving West. Settlers used rivers as their highways. The steamboat, invented in 1807, helped speed travel along these waterways. When canals, like the Erie Canal, linked eastern cities to rivers, they opened the West even more.

At the same time, railroads began to expand. Steam-powered locomotives pulled trainloads of raw materials and goods to factories and markets. By 1870 railroad lines spanned the continent, and a cross-country trip that used to take months by wagon took just days.

The 20th century transformed travel with automobiles, trucks, buses, and aircraft. Today, a web of interstate highways crisscrosses the nation. Americans drive nearly three trillion miles a year. Some 11 million heavy duty trucks carry goods from fresh foods to gasoline. Barges and ships move cargo to busy seaports. Meanwhile, jet aircraft zip overhead, whisking people coast to coast in hours.

Planes, Trains, and Automobiles

The graph at right shows how American passenger travel between cities has changed since 1940. In the 1940s, during the war years, train travel jumped as gas rationing cut back on the use of cars. After the war, returning G.I.s wanted to get out on the road again. Interstate highways and improvements in automobile reliability and performance have increased intercity auto travel from nearly 300 billion miles in 1940 to 2,000 billion in 1995. The fastest-growing mode of travel has been by airplane. Between 1940 and 1995, while the U.S. population doubled, airplane travel miles jumped by 350 times.

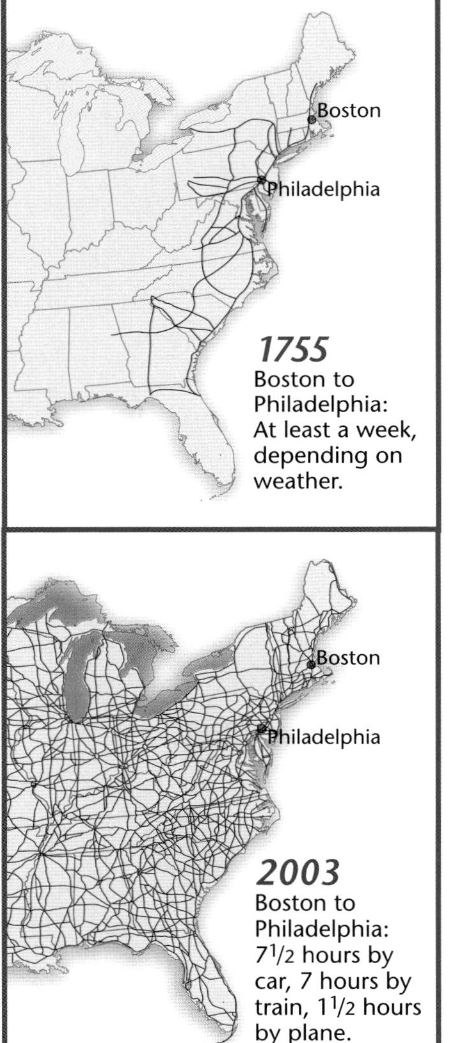

1755
Boston to Philadelphia: At least a week, depending on weather.

2003
Boston to Philadelphia: 7 1/2 hours by car, 7 hours by train, 1 1/2 hours by plane.

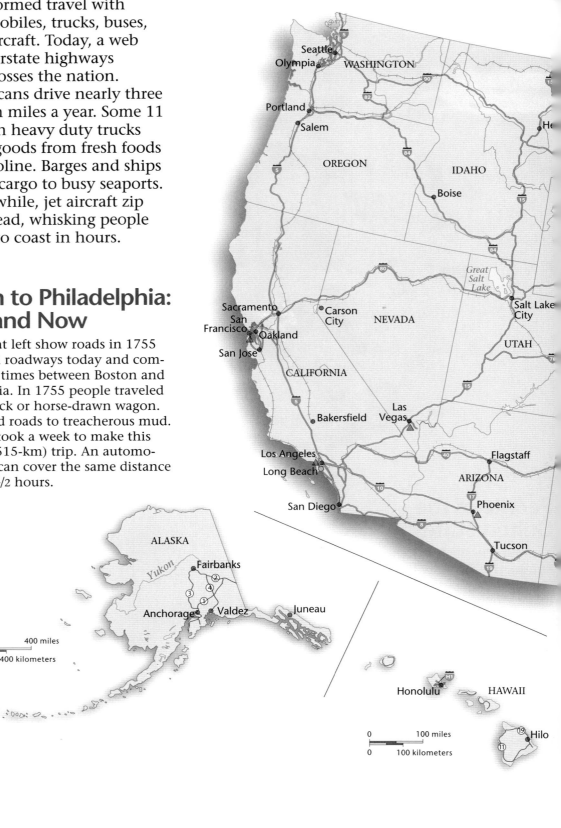

Boston to Philadelphia: Then and Now

The maps at left show roads in 1755 and federal roadways today and compare travel times between Boston and Philadelphia. In 1755 people traveled by horseback or horse-drawn wagon. Rain turned roads to treacherous mud. In 1755 it took a week to make this 320-mile (515-km) trip. An automobile today can cover the same distance in about 7 1/2 hours.

Transportation

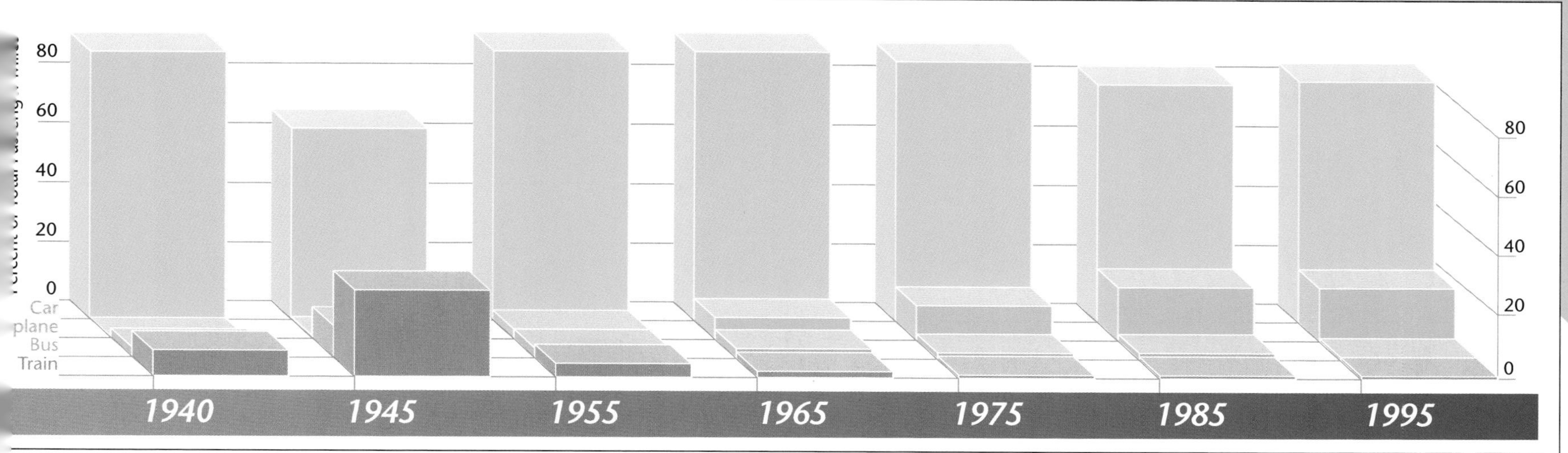

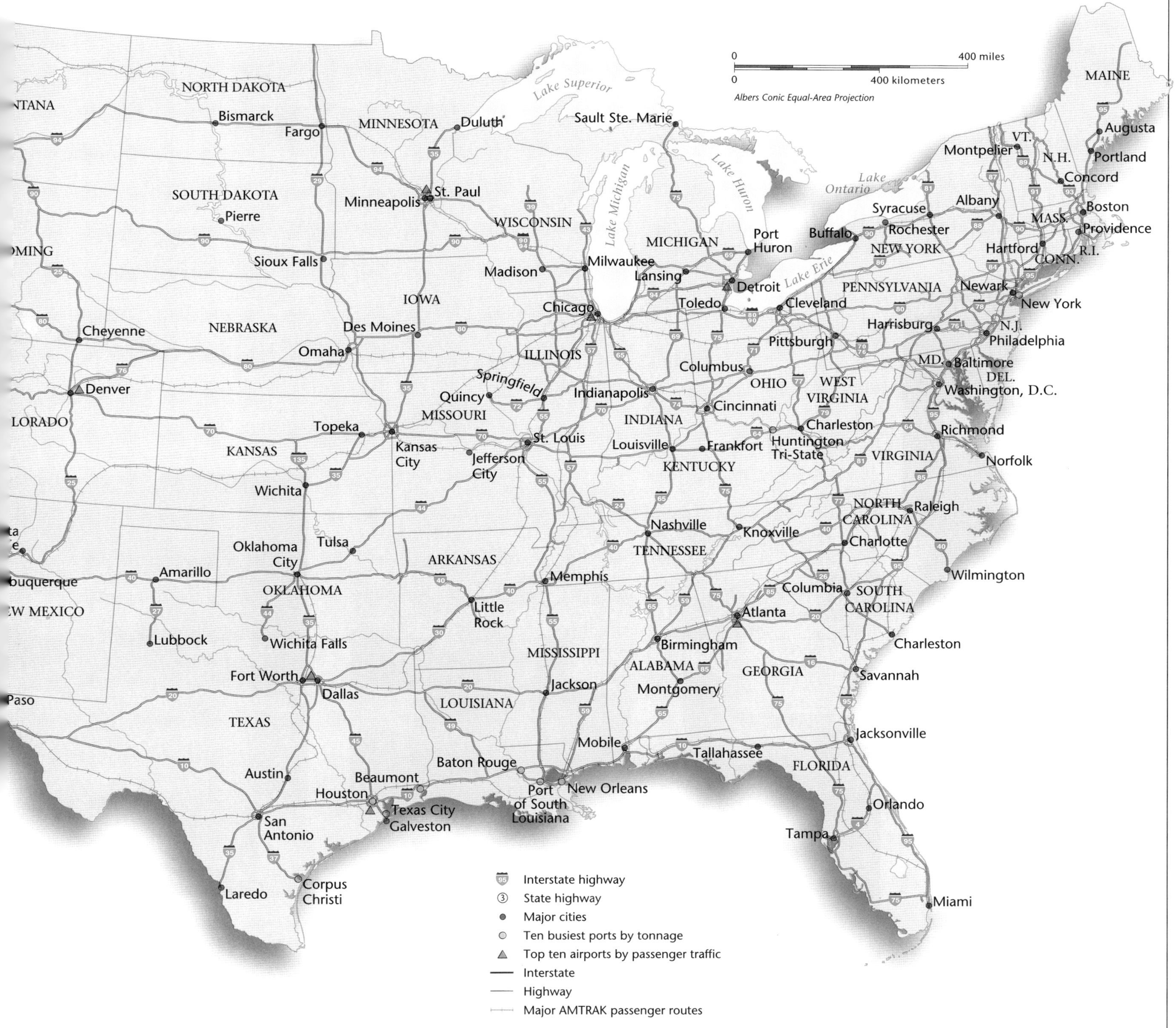

0 400 miles
0 400 kilometers
Albers Conic Equal-Area Projection

- Interstate highway
- State highway
- Major cities
- Ten busiest ports by tonnage
- Top ten airports by passenger traffic
- Interstate
- Highway
- Major AMTRAK passenger routes

Our Nation's Capital

The District of Columbia

Not a state, but not merely a city, the District of Columbia is the capital of the United States. Planned in the late 18th century as the seat of the federal government, it is better known as Washington, D.C., in honor of the nation's first President.

Today, nearly a quarter of a million people report to work at government offices in the District. Hundreds of thousands more do work related to government. The U.S. Congress meets here, in the domed Capitol building at the head of the Mall, a grassy promenade surrounded by monuments and the museums of the Smithsonian Institution. More than a collection of monuments, though, the District is also home to more than 560,000 people. Many of them are descendants of African Americans who settled here after the Civil War.

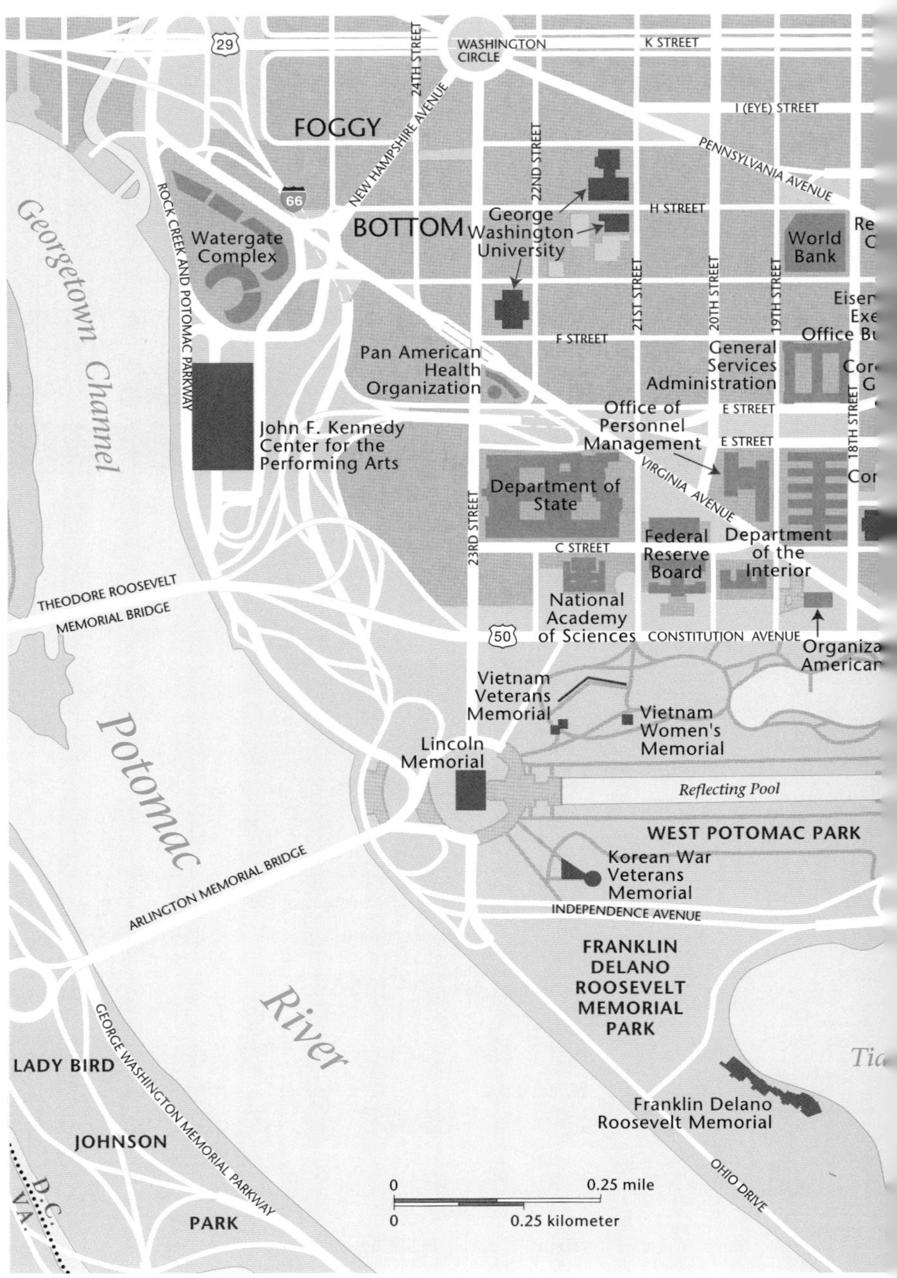

▲ *A visitor touches a name on the granite wall of the Vietnam Veterans Memorial. The wall commemorates those who died in the Vietnam War.*

▼ *Crisp dollar bills from the Bureau of Engraving and Printing represent the millions of dollars in currency that roll off presses there each day.*

▼ *The Washington Monument, framed by the Capitol and the temple-like Lincoln Memorial, soars 555 feet (169 m) above the Mall.*

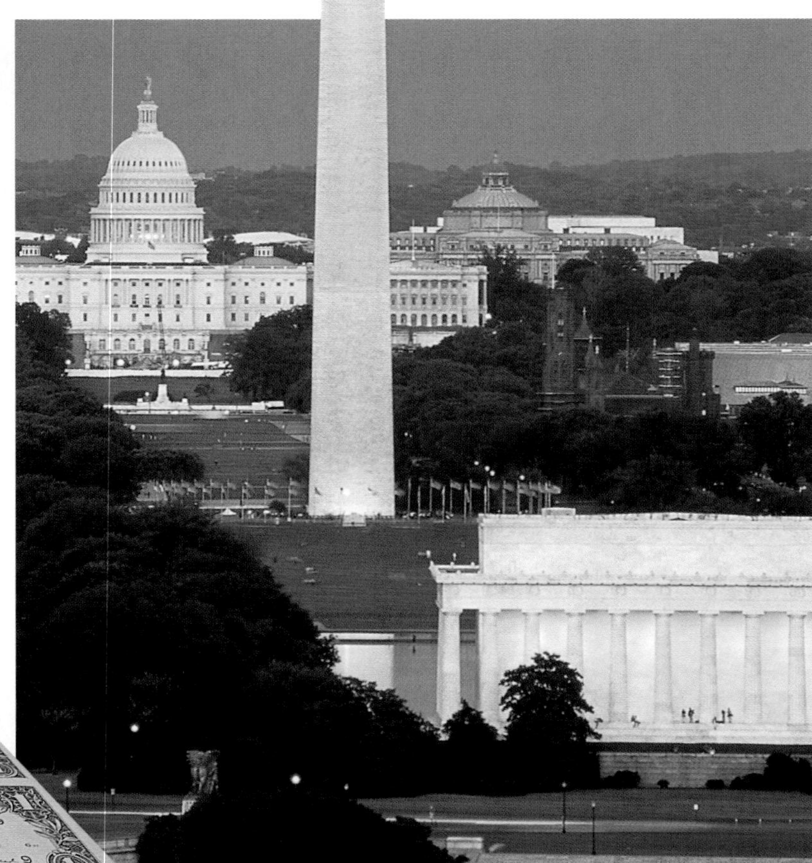

▲ *Earth Day draws a gathering of thousands to the Mall. The two-mile-long (3.2 km) Mall has long served as the site of public celebration—and public protest.*

The District of Columbia

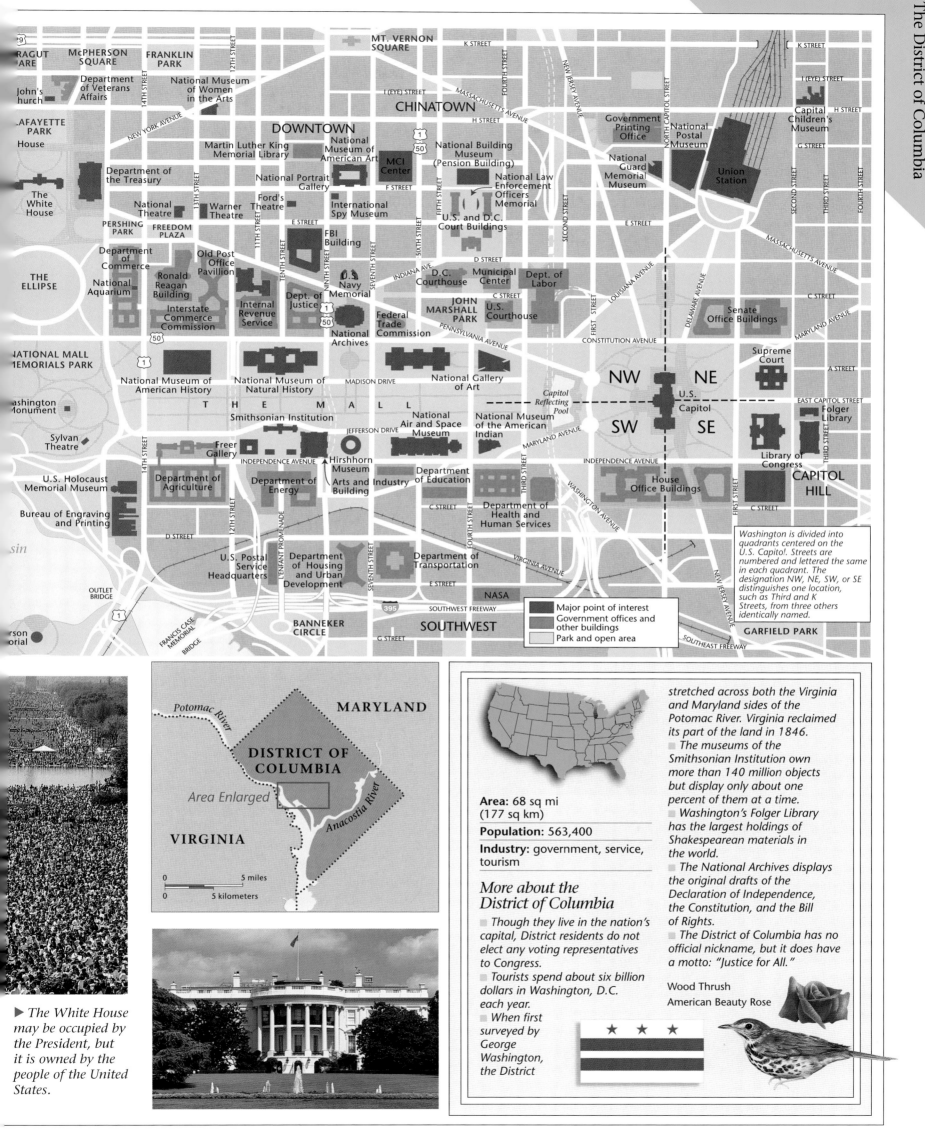

K STREET
MT. VERNON SQUARE
McPHERSON SQUARE
FRANKLIN PARK
12TH STREET
14TH STREET
Department of Veterans Affairs
National Museum of Women in the Arts
I (EYE) STREET
CHINATOWN
MASSACHUSETTS AVENUE
FOURTH STREET
NEW JERSEY AVENUE
NORTH CAPITOL STREET
Government Printing Office
National Postal Museum
Union Station
Capital Children's Museum
H STREET
G STREET
LAFAYETTE PARK
NEW YORK AVENUE
DOWNTOWN
Martin Luther King Memorial Library
National Museum of American Art
MCI Center
National Building Museum (Pension Building)
National Guard Memorial Museum
The White House
Department of the Treasury
National Portrait Gallery
F STREET
National Law Enforcement Officers Memorial
13TH STREET
National Theatre
Warner Theatre
Ford's Theatre
International Spy Museum
FIFTH STREET
U.S. and D.C. Court Buildings
SECOND STREET
E STREET
PERSHING PARK
FREEDOM PLAZA
11TH STREET
FBI Building
SIXTH STREET
SECOND STREET
THIRD STREET
FOURTH STREET
THE ELLIPSE
Department of Commerce
National Aquarium
Old Post Office Pavilion
Ronald Reagan Building
Interstate Commerce Commission
TENTH STREET
NINTH STREET
SEVENTH STREET
D STREET
Internal Revenue Service
Dept. of Justice
U.S. Navy Memorial
INDIANA AVE.
D.C. Courthouse
Municipal Center
Dept. of Labor
LOUISIANA AVENUE
DELAWARE AVENUE
C STREET
JOHN MARSHALL PARK
U.S. Courthouse
FIRST STREET
Senate Office Buildings
MARYLAND AVENUE
National Archives
Federal Trade Commission
PENNSYLVANIA AVENUE
CONSTITUTION AVENUE
NATIONAL MALL MEMORIALS PARK
National Museum of American History
National Museum of Natural History
MADISON DRIVE
National Gallery of Art
Supreme Court
A STREET
NW
NE
Washington Monument
THE MALL
Capitol Reflecting Pool
U.S. Capitol
EAST CAPITOL STREET
Folger Library
Smithsonian Institution
National Air and Space Museum
National Museum of the American Indian
SW
SE
JEFFERSON DRIVE
Sylvan Theatre
Freer Gallery
INDEPENDENCE AVENUE
Hirshhorn Museum
Arts and Industry Building
Department of Education
THIRD STREET
Library of Congress
CAPITOL HILL
U.S. Holocaust Memorial Museum
Department of Agriculture
Department of Energy
WASHINGTON AVENUE
House Office Buildings
Bureau of Engraving and Printing
D STREET
L'ENFANT PROMENADE
C STREET
Department of Health and Human Services
U.S. Postal Service Headquarters
Department of Housing and Urban Development
Department of Transportation
VIRGINIA AVENUE
NEW JERSEY AVENUE
OUTLET BRIDGE
E STREET
NASA
SOUTHWEST FREEWAY
FRANCIS CASE MEMORIAL BRIDGE
BANNEKER CIRCLE
G STREET
SOUTHWEST
GARFIELD PARK
SOUTHEAST FREEWAY

Major point of interest
Government offices and other buildings
Park and open area

Washington is divided into quadrants centered on the U.S. Capitol. Streets are numbered and lettered the same in each quadrant. The designation NW, NE, SW, or SE distinguishes one location, such as Third and K Streets, from three others identically named.

▶ *The White House may be occupied by the President, but it is owned by the people of the United States.*

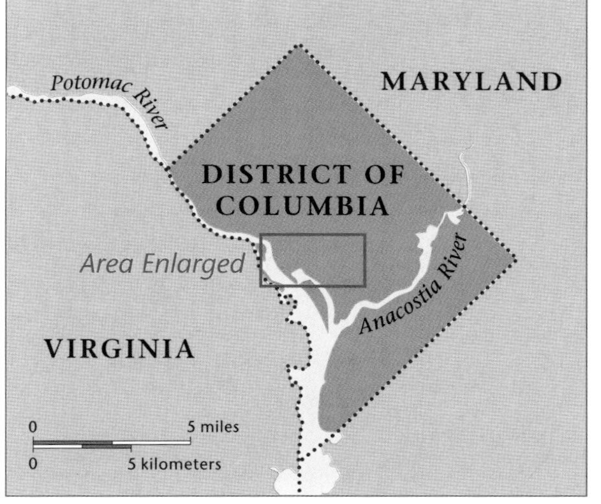

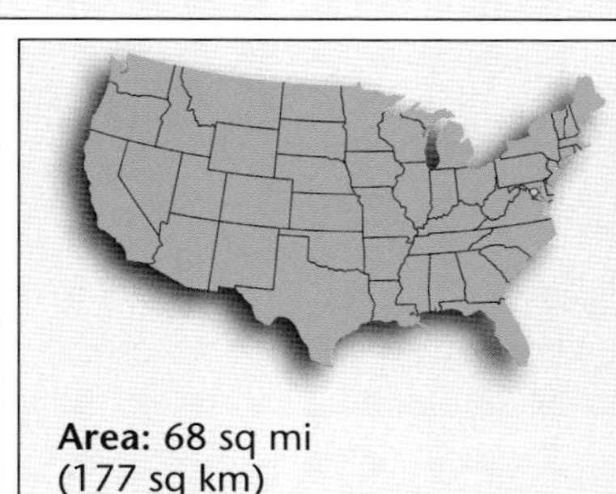

Area: 68 sq mi (177 sq km)

Population: 563,400

Industry: government, service, tourism

More about the District of Columbia

- *Though they live in the nation's capital, District residents do not elect any voting representatives to Congress.*
- *Tourists spend about six billion dollars in Washington, D.C. each year.*
- *When first surveyed by George Washington, the District stretched across both the Virginia and Maryland sides of the Potomac River. Virginia reclaimed its part of the land in 1846.*
- *The museums of the Smithsonian Institution own more than 140 million objects but display only about one percent of them at a time.*
- *Washington's Folger Library has the largest holdings of Shakespearean materials in the world.*
- *The National Archives displays the original drafts of the Declaration of Independence, the Constitution, and the Bill of Rights.*
- *The District of Columbia has no official nickname, but it does have a motto: "Justice for All."*

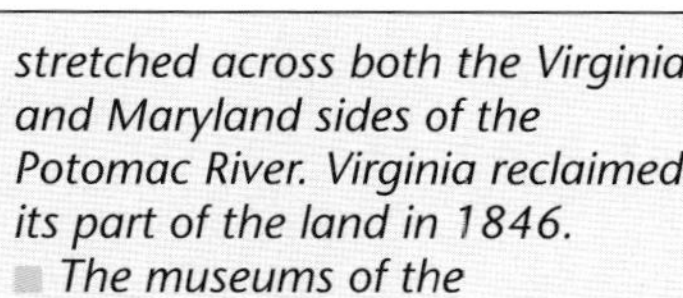

Wood Thrush

American Beauty Rose

The North

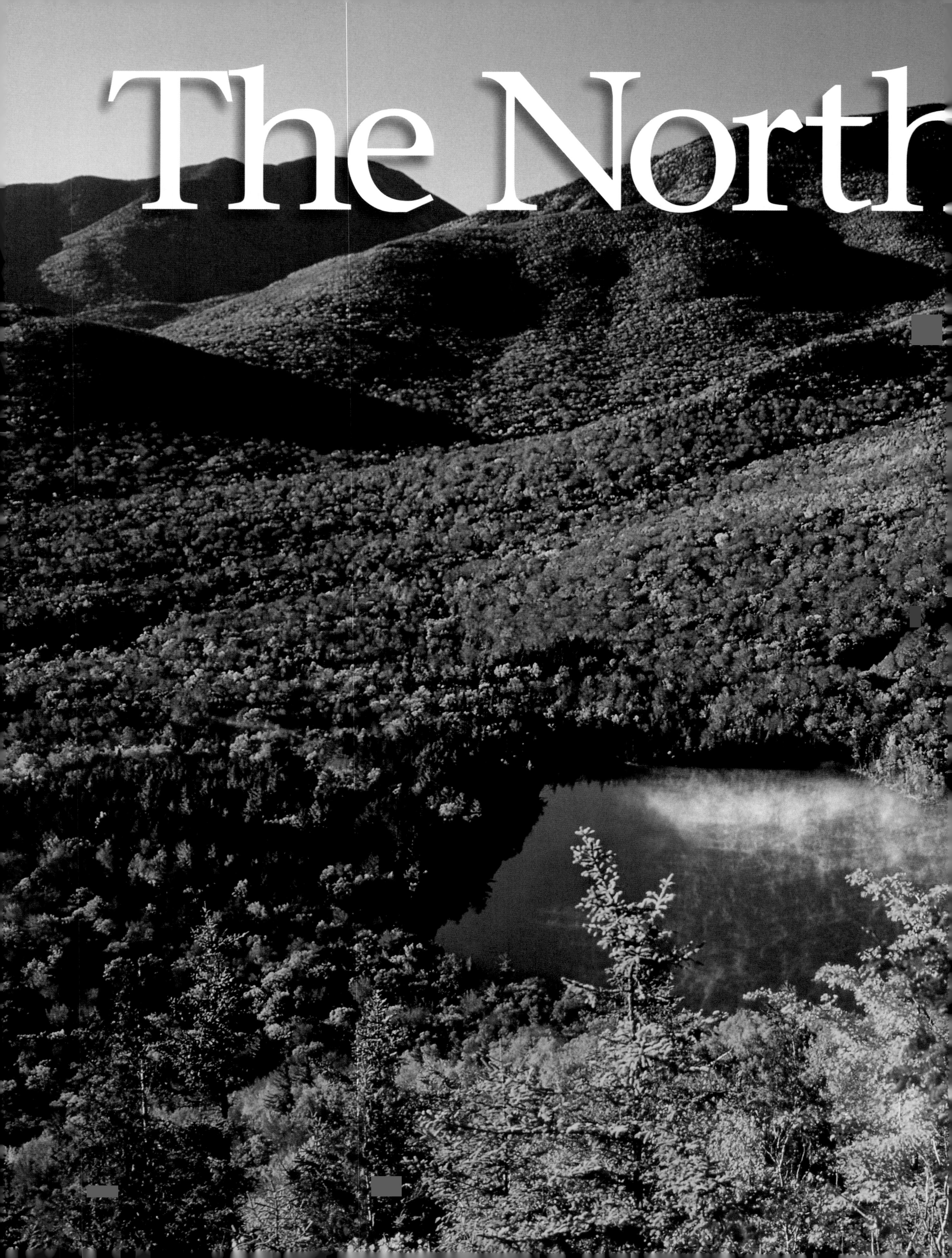

east

The Northeast

Connecticut
Delaware
Maine
Maryland
Massachusetts
New Hampshire
New Jersey
New York
Pennsylvania
Rhode Island
Vermont

Jostling crowds (above) pack Fifth Avenue in the heart of New York, the largest city in the United States. Not far from its densely populated cities, the Northeast also holds quiet beauty, such as New York's Adirondack Mountains (left), clothed in brilliant fall colors. The view from the Adirondacks takes in three states and one Canadian province.

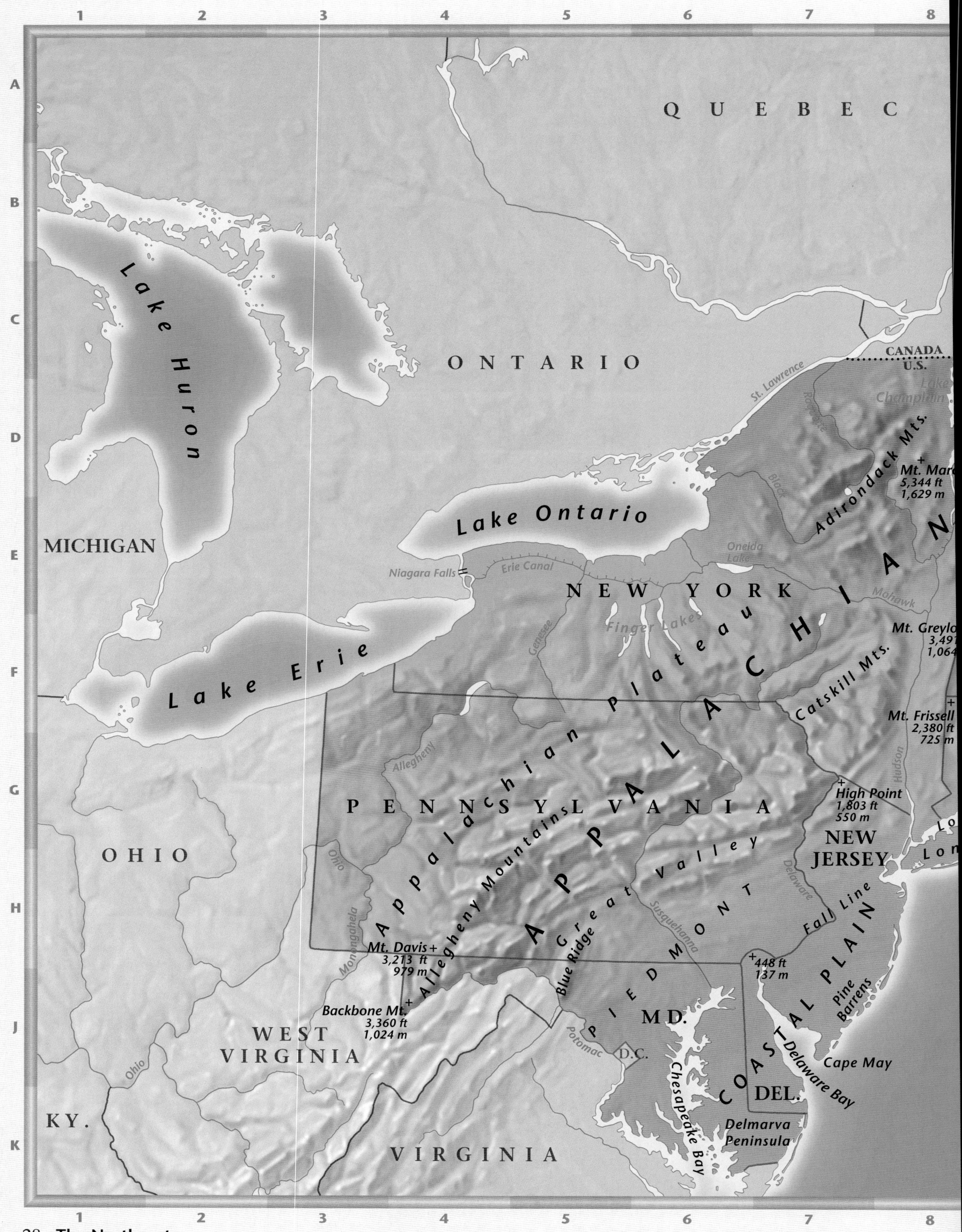
QUEBEC
ONTARIO
Lake Huron
Lake Ontario
Lake Erie
MICHIGAN
CANADA
U.S.
St. Lawrence
Lake Champlain
Adirondack Mts.
Mt. Marcy
5,344 ft
1,629 m
Oneida Lake
Niagara Falls
Erie Canal
NEW YORK
Mohawk
Finger Lakes
Genesee
Appalachian Plateau
APPALACHIAN
Mt. Greylock
Catskill Mts.
Mt. Frissell
2,380 ft
725 m
Hudson
Allegheny
PENNSYLVANIA
High Point
1,803 ft
550 m
NEW JERSEY
OHIO
Ohio
Appalachian Mountains
Allegheny Mountains
Great Valley
Delaware
Susquehanna
PIEDMONT
Fall Line
Monongahela
Mt. Davis
3,213 ft
979 m
Blue Ridge
448 ft
137 m
COASTAL PLAIN
Pine Barrens
Backbone Mt.
3,360 ft
1,024 m
MD.
WEST VIRGINIA
Potomac
D.C.
Delaware Bay
Cape May
Chesapeake Bay
DEL.
Delmarva Peninsula
KY.
VIRGINIA

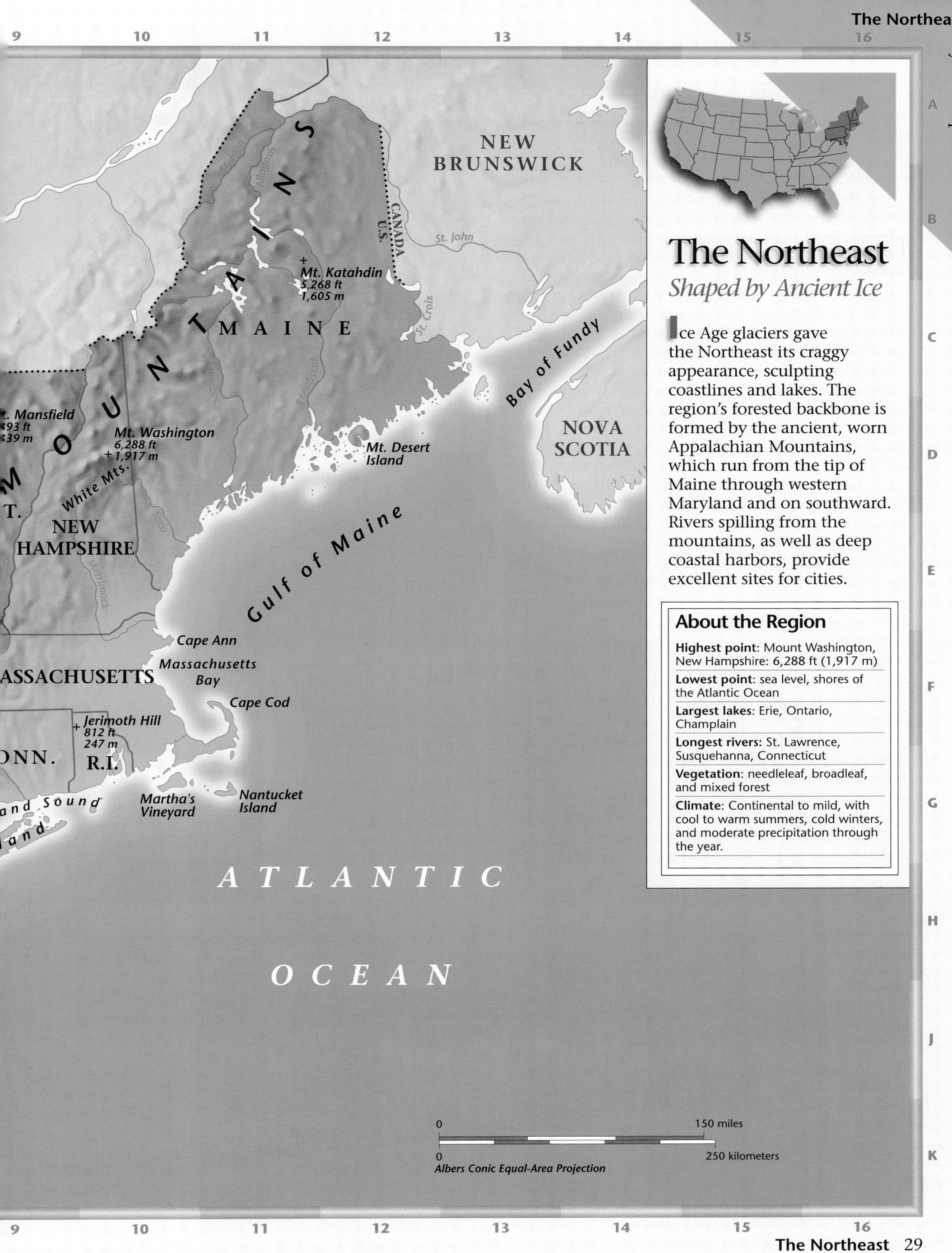

The Northeast

Shaped by Ancient Ice

Ice Age glaciers gave the Northeast its craggy appearance, sculpting coastlines and lakes. The region's forested backbone is formed by the ancient, worn Appalachian Mountains, which run from the tip of Maine through western Maryland and on southward. Rivers spilling from the mountains, as well as deep coastal harbors, provide excellent sites for cities.

About the Region

Highest point: Mount Washington, New Hampshire: 6,288 ft (1,917 m)

Lowest point: sea level, shores of the Atlantic Ocean

Largest lakes: Erie, Ontario, Champlain

Longest rivers: St. Lawrence, Susquehanna, Connecticut

Vegetation: needleleaf, broadleaf, and mixed forest

Climate: Continental to mild, with cool to warm summers, cold winters, and moderate precipitation through the year.

The Northeast

Birthplace of a Nation

Stretching down the Atlantic coast from Maine to Maryland, the Northeast has some of the nation's oldest settlements and most densely populated areas. About a fifth of the country's people live here, many in a string of giant cities—running from Boston through New York to Washington, D.C.—that blend into one huge urban area called a megalopolis.

Excellent harbors first made most of these big cities international trade centers. Then the rise of factories and manufacturing helped them grow into booming metropolises connected by roads, rivers, and railroads.

The Northeast is the birthplace of much of the nation's early history. European settlers came here in 1620, seeking freedom and a new life. Here, the Revolutionary War began, and leaders of the 13 original colonies forged a new nation. Hemmed by mountains and seashores, the Northeast is a place of great variety and beauty. Even near the largest cities, pockets of wilderness remain, including some of the country's most scenic lands.

▲ **LIBERTY STANDS** *strong before a smoke-filled New York skyline the day after terrorist attacks destroyed the World Trade Center's Twin Towers.*

▲ **A COVERED** *bridge in Arlington, Vermont, crosses the Batten Kill River. Vermont has more than a hundred of these structures.*

▶ **WORKERS INSPECT** *chocolate kisses at a Hershey, Pennsylvania, factory. Food processing is a major element of the Northeast's economy.*

▶ **RACING** *downhill, a skier enjoys a fast run on Olympic slopes near Lake Placid, New York.*

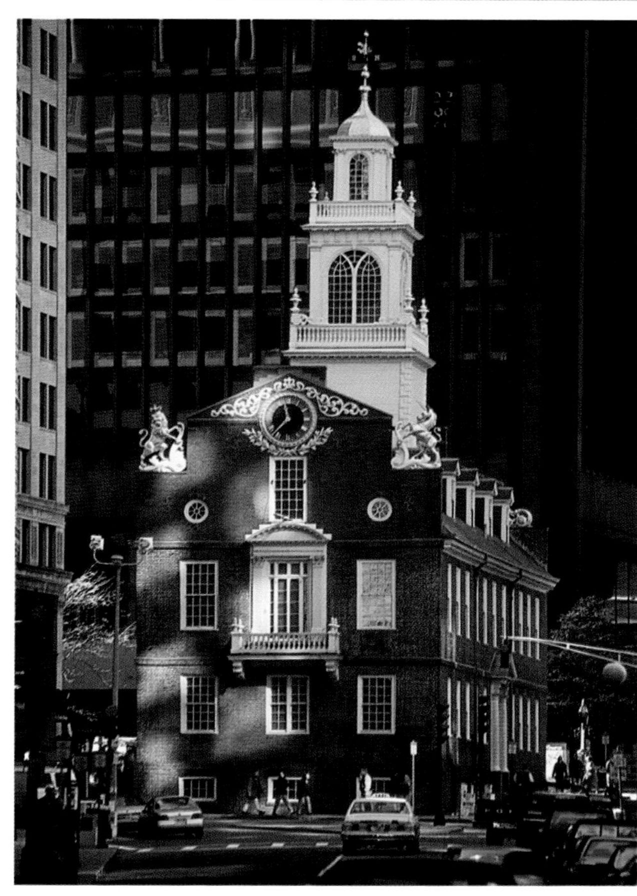

▶ **THE OLD STATE** *House, built in 1713, is a historic landmark in Boston, Massachusetts. It was the center of events, such as the Boston "Massacre," that led up to the American Revolution.*

▲ **JUICY RED** *cranberries grow in peaty bogs. Massachusetts is the top grower of the berries, which are harvested in September and October.*

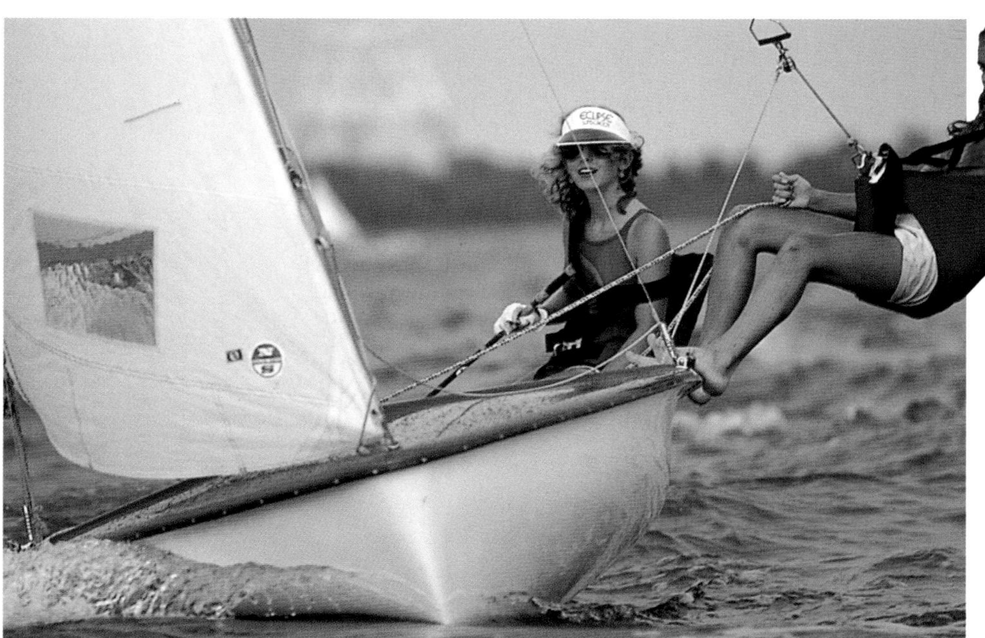

▶ **RIDING THE WIND,** *two young boaters enjoy a summer sail on a breezy river. During warm months, sailing, motorboating, fishing, and swimming are popular pastimes along the Northeast's many waterways.*

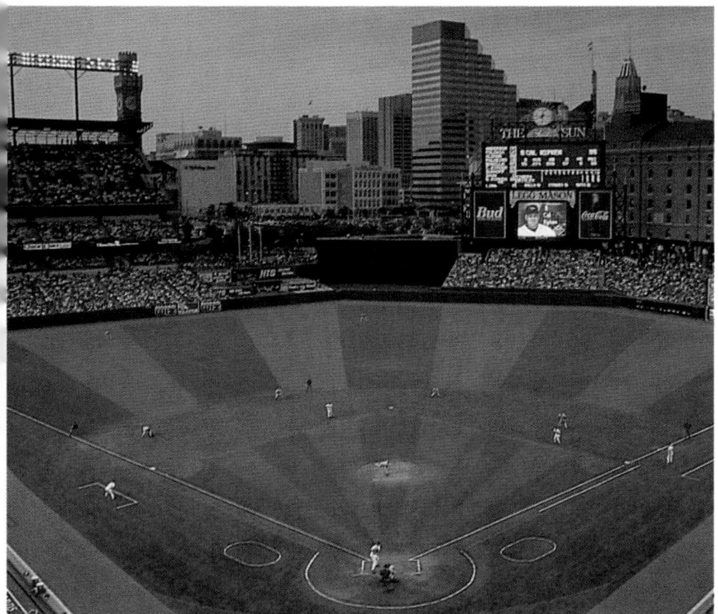

▲ **BASEBALL FANS CROWD** *Camden Yards Stadium in Baltimore, Maryland. The Northeast is home to many of the country's oldest ball clubs as well as the Baseball Hall of Fame in Cooperstown, New York.*

▼ **BLUE CRABS** *from the Chesapeake Bay make for tasty eating. The bay, bordered by Maryland and Virginia, is one of the country's richest sources of seafood. Chesapeake Bay waterman haul in millions of pounds of crabs, oysters, and clams a year.*

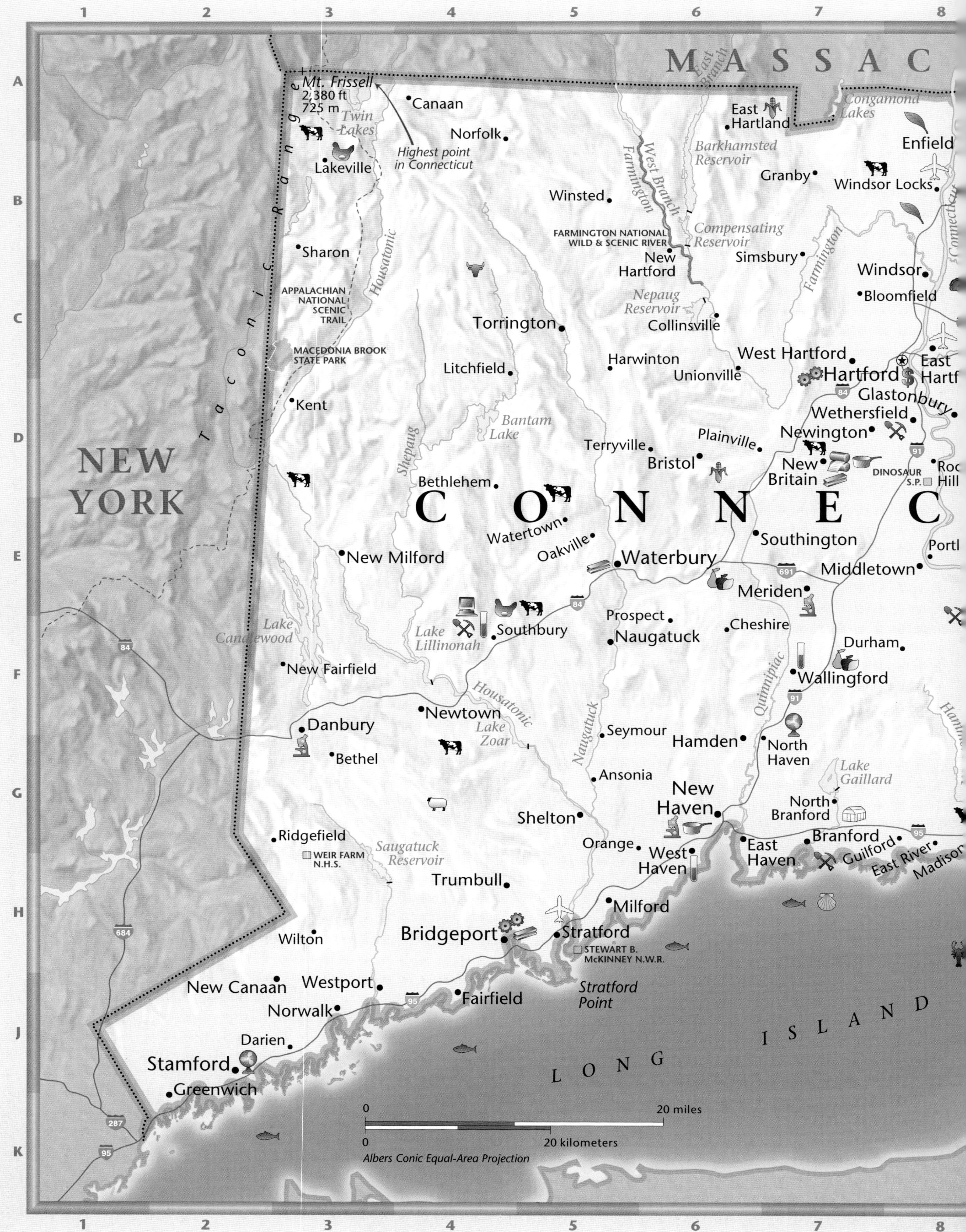

MASSACHUSETTS
NEW YORK
CONNECTICUT
LONG ISLAND
Mt. Frissell
2,380 ft
725 m
Highest point in Connecticut
Twin Lakes
Canaan
Norfolk
Lakeville
Taconic Range
East Branch
Congamond Lakes
East Hartland
Barkhamsted Reservoir
Enfield
Granby
Windsor Locks
Winsted
Farmington
West Branch
FARMINGTON NATIONAL WILD & SCENIC RIVER
Compensating Reservoir
Sharon
Housatonic
New Hartford
Simsbury
Windsor
Bloomfield
APPALACHIAN NATIONAL SCENIC TRAIL
Nepaug Reservoir
Collinsville
Torrington
MACEDONIA BROOK STATE PARK
Litchfield
Harwinton
Unionville
West Hartford
Hartford
East Hartford
Glastonbury
Wethersfield
Kent
Bantam Lake
Shepaug
Terryville
Plainville
Newington
Bristol
New Britain
DINOSAUR S.P.
Rocky Hill
Bethlehem
Watertown
Oakville
Southington
Waterbury
New Milford
Middletown
Meriden
Lake Candlewood
Prospect
Cheshire
Lake Lillinonah
Southbury
Naugatuck
Durham
New Fairfield
Wallingford
Quinnipiac
Housatonic
Newtown
Lake Zoar
Danbury
Seymour
Hamden
North Haven
Bethel
Ansonia
Lake Gaillard
New Haven
North Branford
Shelton
Ridgefield
Orange
West Haven
East Haven
Branford
Guilford
East River
Madison
WEIR FARM N.H.S.
Saugatuck Reservoir
Trumbull
Milford
Wilton
Bridgeport
Stratford
STEWART B. McKINNEY N.W.R.
New Canaan
Westport
Fairfield
Stratford Point
Norwalk
Darien
Stamford
Greenwich
0
20 miles
0
20 kilometers
Albers Conic Equal-Area Projection

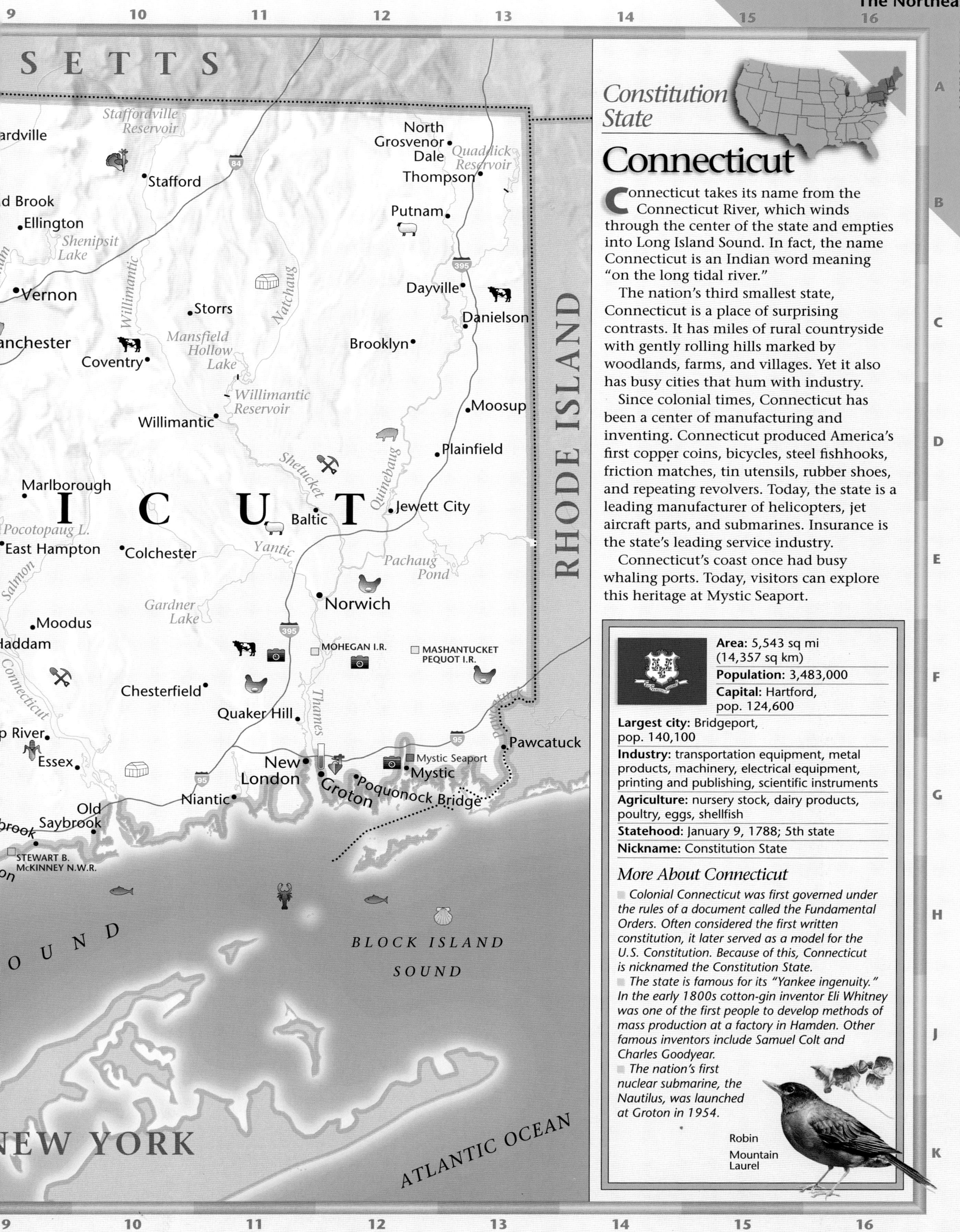

Constitution State

Connecticut

Connecticut takes its name from the Connecticut River, which winds through the center of the state and empties into Long Island Sound. In fact, the name Connecticut is an Indian word meaning "on the long tidal river."

The nation's third smallest state, Connecticut is a place of surprising contrasts. It has miles of rural countryside with gently rolling hills marked by woodlands, farms, and villages. Yet it also has busy cities that hum with industry.

Since colonial times, Connecticut has been a center of manufacturing and inventing. Connecticut produced America's first copper coins, bicycles, steel fishhooks, friction matches, tin utensils, rubber shoes, and repeating revolvers. Today, the state is a leading manufacturer of helicopters, jet aircraft parts, and submarines. Insurance is the state's leading service industry.

Connecticut's coast once had busy whaling ports. Today, visitors can explore this heritage at Mystic Seaport.

Area: 5,543 sq mi (14,357 sq km)

Population: 3,483,000

Capital: Hartford, pop. 124,600

Largest city: Bridgeport, pop. 140,100

Industry: transportation equipment, metal products, machinery, electrical equipment, printing and publishing, scientific instruments

Agriculture: nursery stock, dairy products, poultry, eggs, shellfish

Statehood: January 9, 1788; 5th state

Nickname: Constitution State

More About Connecticut

Colonial Connecticut was first governed under the rules of a document called the Fundamental Orders. Often considered the first written constitution, it later served as a model for the U.S. Constitution. Because of this, Connecticut is nicknamed the Constitution State.

The state is famous for its "Yankee ingenuity." In the early 1800s cotton-gin inventor Eli Whitney was one of the first people to develop methods of mass production at a factory in Hamden. Other famous inventors include Samuel Colt and Charles Goodyear.

The nation's first nuclear submarine, the Nautilus, was launched at Groton in 1954.

Robin

Mountain Laurel

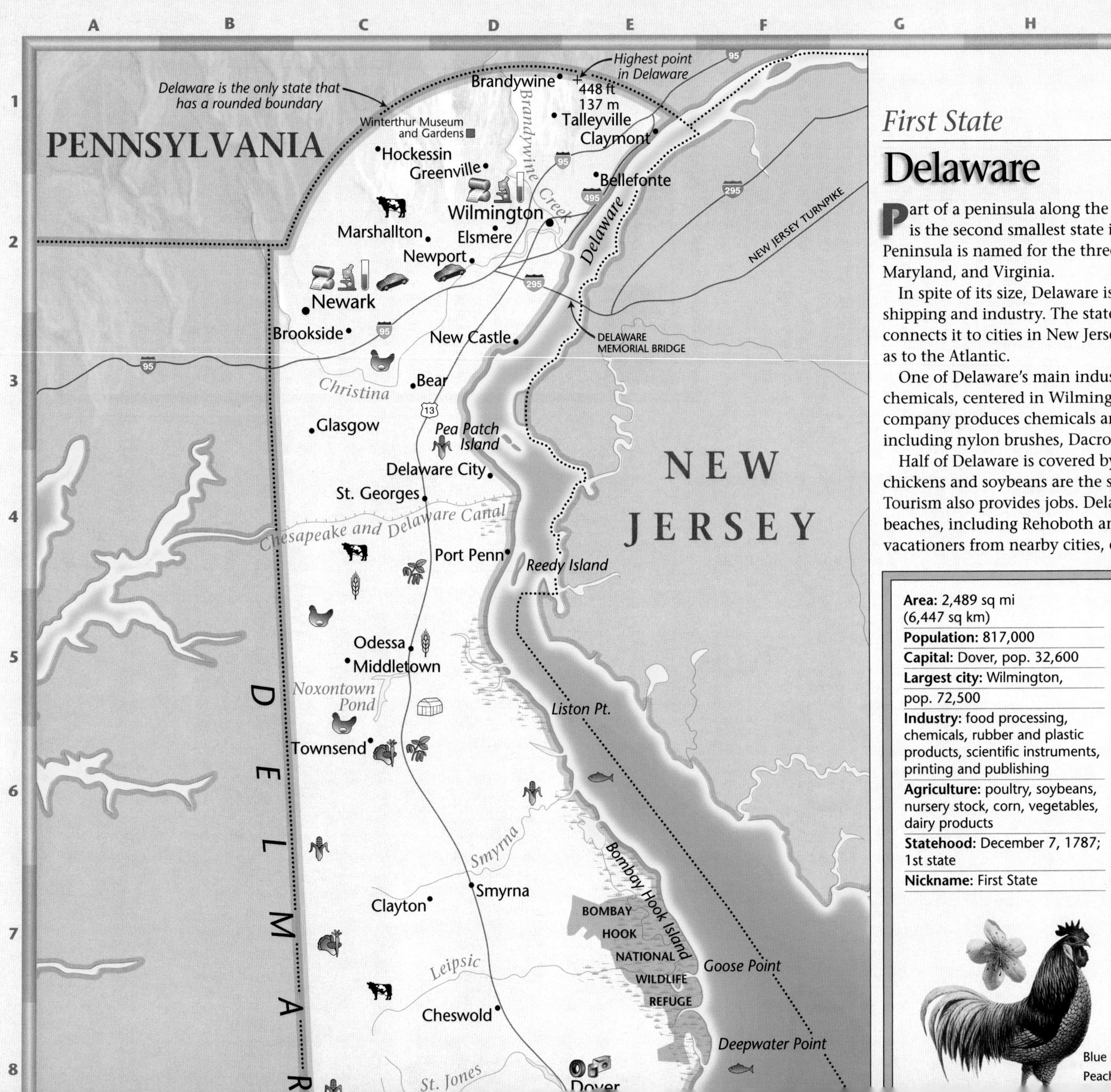

First State

Delaware

Part of a peninsula along the Atlantic Ocean, Delaware is the second smallest state in the nation. The Delmarva Peninsula is named for the three states that share it: Delaware, Maryland, and Virginia.

In spite of its size, Delaware is an important center of shipping and industry. The state's largest river, the Delaware, connects it to cities in New Jersey and Pennsylvania as well as to the Atlantic.

One of Delaware's main industries is the manufacture of chemicals, centered in Wilmington. There, the giant Du Pont company produces chemicals and products made from them, including nylon brushes, Dacron fabric, and Teflon pans.

Half of Delaware is covered by farmland, and broiler chickens and soybeans are the state's main farm products. Tourism also provides jobs. Delaware's beautiful ocean beaches, including Rehoboth and Bethany Beaches, draw vacationers from nearby cities, especially Washington, D.C.

Area: 2,489 sq mi (6,447 sq km)

Population: 817,000

Capital: Dover, pop. 32,600

Largest city: Wilmington, pop. 72,500

Industry: food processing, chemicals, rubber and plastic products, scientific instruments, printing and publishing

Agriculture: poultry, soybeans, nursery stock, corn, vegetables, dairy products

Statehood: December 7, 1787; 1st state

Nickname: First State

More About Delaware

- *Delaware got its name when a ship from Virginia colony sailed into what is now Delaware Bay in 1610. The captain named the bay De La Warr for Lord De La Warr, governor of Virginia. The name later became Delaware.*
- *Delaware is called the First State because it was the first state to ratify the U.S. Constitution on Dec. 7, 1787.*
- *The first log cabins in North America were built by Swedes and Finns who settled in Delaware.*
- *In 1817 Thomas Gilpin created the nation's first modern papermaking machine. Paper manufacturing is still a big business in the state.*

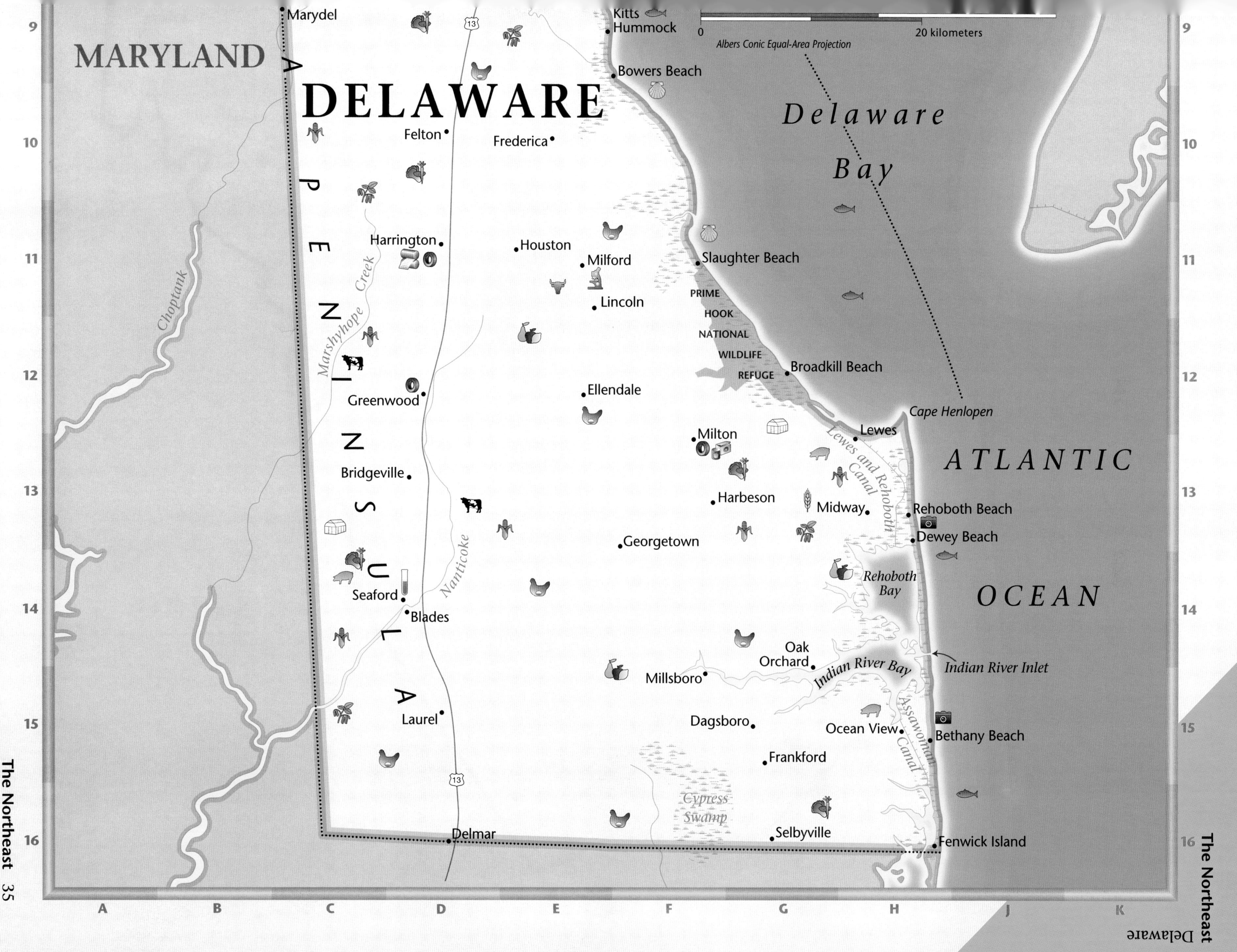
MARYLAND
DELAWARE
DELMARVA PENINSULA
Delaware Bay
ATLANTIC OCEAN
0
20 kilometers
Albers Conic Equal-Area Projection
Marydel
Kitts Hummock
Bowers Beach
Felton
Frederica
Harrington
Houston
Milford
Slaughter Beach
Lincoln
PRIME HOOK NATIONAL WILDLIFE REFUGE
Broadkill Beach
Greenwood
Ellendale
Cape Henlopen
Lewes
Milton
Lewes and Rehoboth Canal
Bridgeville
Harbeson
Midway
Rehoboth Beach
Dewey Beach
Georgetown
Rehoboth Bay
Seaford
Blades
Nanticoke
Marshyhope Creek
Choptank
Oak Orchard
Indian River Bay
Indian River Inlet
Millsboro
Laurel
Dagsboro
Ocean View
Assawoman Canal
Bethany Beach
Frankford
Cypress Swamp
Selbyville
Delmar
Fenwick Island
13
A B C D E F G H J K
9 10 11 12 13 14 15 16

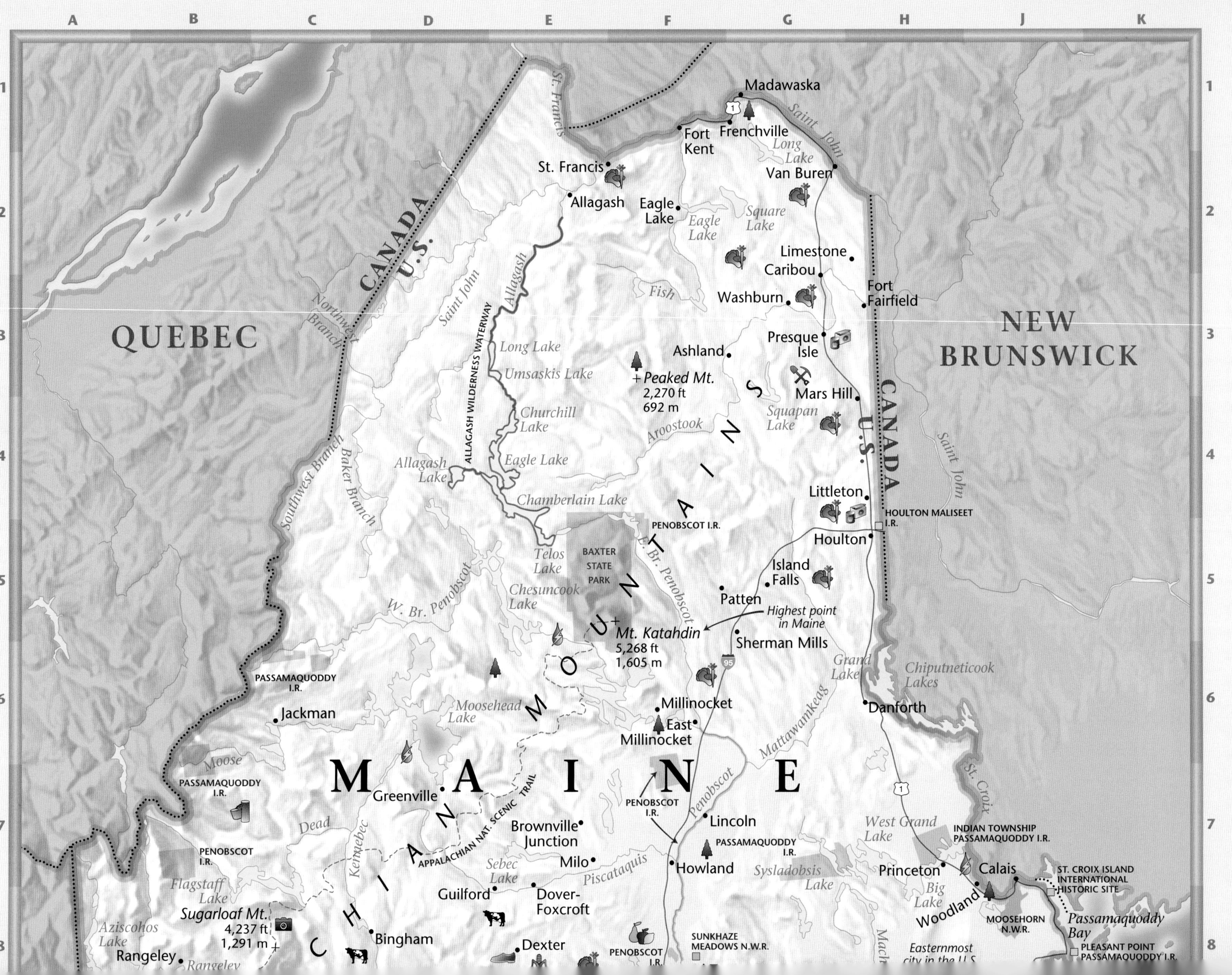
QUEBEC
NEW BRUNSWICK
MAINE
CANADA
U.S.
MOUNTAINS
Madawaska
Frenchville
Fort Kent
St. Francis
Allagash
Eagle Lake
Van Buren
Limestone
Caribou
Washburn
Fort Fairfield
Presque Isle
Ashland
Peaked Mt. 2,270 ft 692 m
Mars Hill
Littleton
HOULTON MALISEET I.R.
Houlton
Island Falls
Patten
Highest point in Maine
Mt. Katahdin 5,268 ft 1,605 m
Sherman Mills
BAXTER STATE PARK
PENOBSCOT I.R.
PASSAMAQUODDY I.R.
Jackman
Millinocket
East Millinocket
Danforth
Greenville
Brownville Junction
Milo
Guilford
Dover-Foxcroft
Dexter
Bingham
Rangeley
Sugarloaf Mt. 4,237 ft 1,291 m
Lincoln
Howland
Princeton
Calais
Woodland
INDIAN TOWNSHIP PASSAMAQUODDY I.R.
ST. CROIX ISLAND INTERNATIONAL HISTORIC SITE
MOOSEHORN N.W.R.
SUNKHAZE MEADOWS N.W.R.
PLEASANT POINT PASSAMAQUODDY I.R.
Passamaquoddy Bay
Easternmost city in the U.S.
ALLAGASH WILDERNESS WATERWAY
APPALACHIAN NAT. SCENIC TRAIL
St. Francis
Saint John
Allagash
Northwest Branch
Southwest Branch
Baker Branch
Fish
Aroostook
E. Br. Penobscot
W. Br. Penobscot
Penobscot
Mattawamkeag
Piscataquis
Kennebec
Dead
Moose
St. Croix
Long Lake
Square Lake
Eagle Lake
Umsaskis Lake
Churchill Lake
Allagash Lake
Chamberlain Lake
Telos Lake
Chesuncook Lake
Squapan Lake
Moosehead Lake
Grand Lake
Chiputneticook Lakes
West Grand Lake
Sysladobsis Lake
Big Lake
Sebec Lake
Flagstaff Lake
Aziscohos Lake

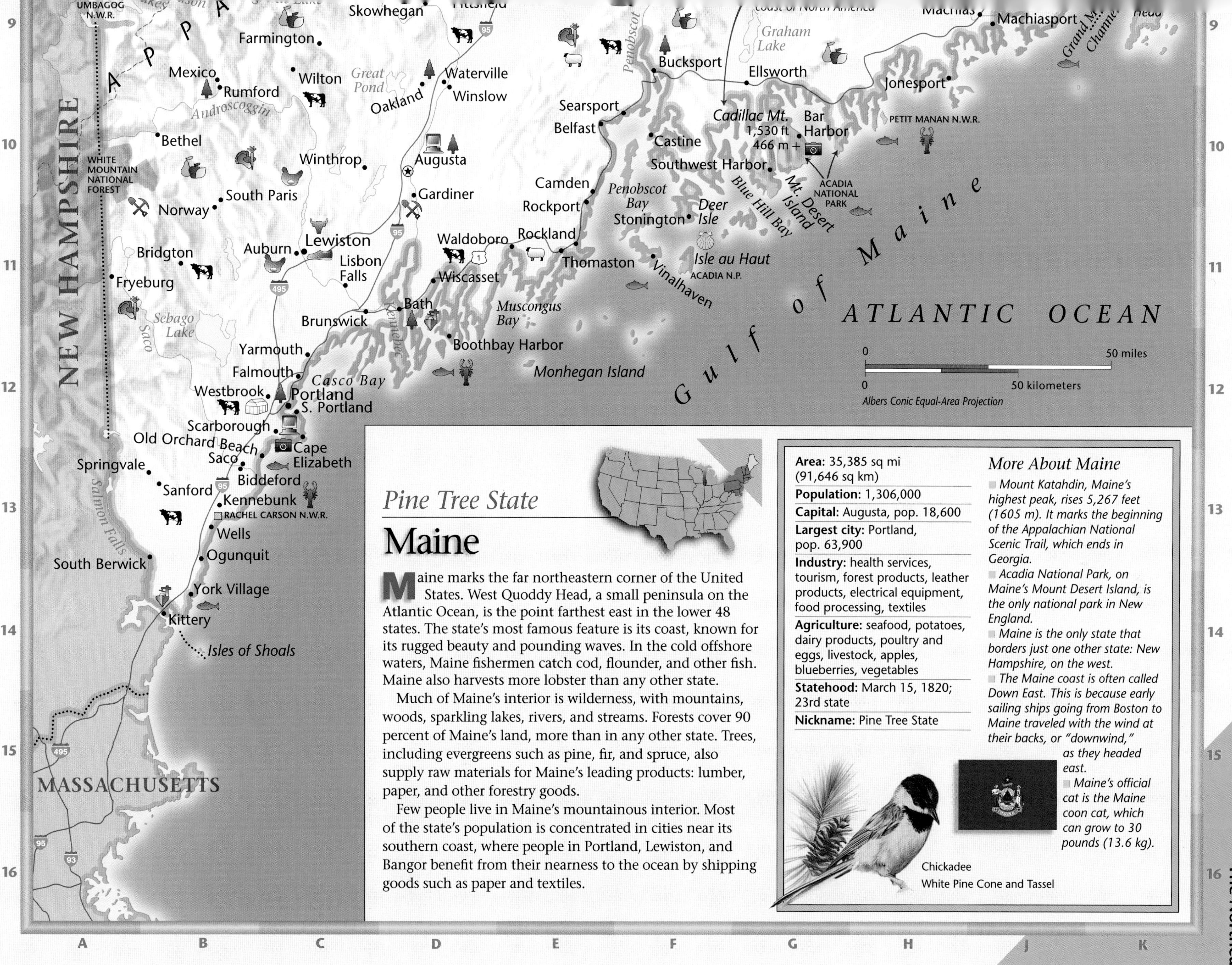

Pine Tree State

Maine

Maine marks the far northeastern corner of the United States. West Quoddy Head, a small peninsula on the Atlantic Ocean, is the point farthest east in the lower 48 states. The state's most famous feature is its coast, known for its rugged beauty and pounding waves. In the cold offshore waters, Maine fishermen catch cod, flounder, and other fish. Maine also harvests more lobster than any other state.

Much of Maine's interior is wilderness, with mountains, woods, sparkling lakes, rivers, and streams. Forests cover 90 percent of Maine's land, more than in any other state. Trees, including evergreens such as pine, fir, and spruce, also supply raw materials for Maine's leading products: lumber, paper, and other forestry goods.

Few people live in Maine's mountainous interior. Most of the state's population is concentrated in cities near its southern coast, where people in Portland, Lewiston, and Bangor benefit from their nearness to the ocean by shipping goods such as paper and textiles.

Area: 35,385 sq mi (91,646 sq km)

Population: 1,306,000

Capital: Augusta, pop. 18,600

Largest city: Portland, pop. 63,900

Industry: health services, tourism, forest products, leather products, electrical equipment, food processing, textiles

Agriculture: seafood, potatoes, dairy products, poultry and eggs, livestock, apples, blueberries, vegetables

Statehood: March 15, 1820; 23rd state

Nickname: Pine Tree State

More About Maine

- *Mount Katahdin, Maine's highest peak, rises 5,267 feet (1605 m). It marks the beginning of the Appalachian National Scenic Trail, which ends in Georgia.*
- *Acadia National Park, on Maine's Mount Desert Island, is the only national park in New England.*
- *Maine is the only state that borders just one other state: New Hampshire, on the west.*
- *The Maine coast is often called Down East. This is because early sailing ships going from Boston to Maine traveled with the wind at their backs, or "downwind," as they headed east.*
- *Maine's official cat is the Maine coon cat, which can grow to 30 pounds (13.6 kg).*

Chickadee
White Pine Cone and Tassel

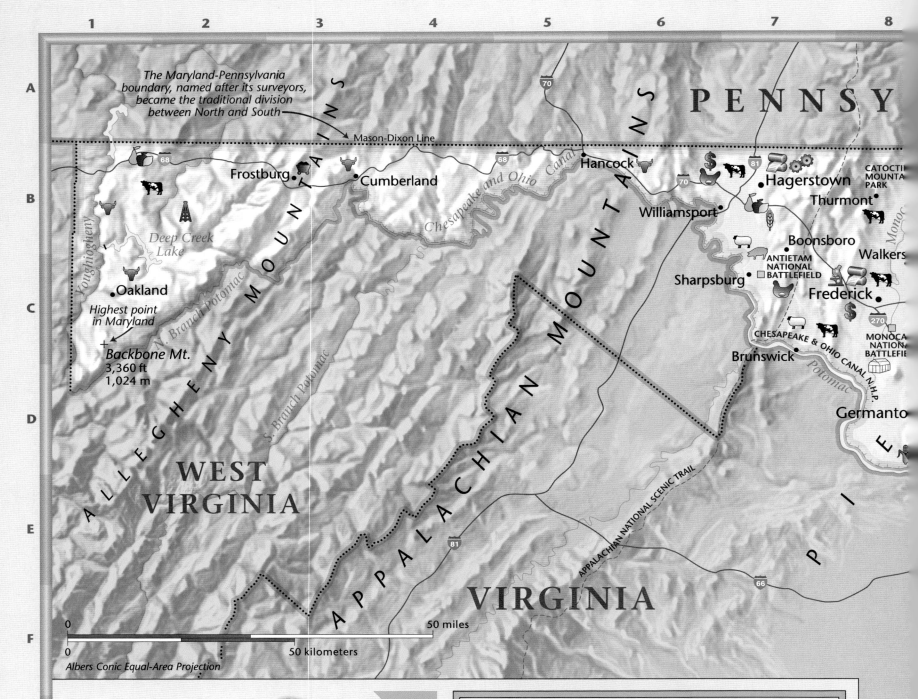

The Maryland-Pennsylvania boundary, named after its surveyors, became the traditional division between North and South

Mason-Dixon Line

PENNSY

WEST VIRGINIA

VIRGINIA

ALLEGHENY MOUNTAINS

APPALACHIAN MOUNTAINS

Frostburg, Cumberland, Oakland, Hancock, Williamsport, Hagerstown, Thurmont, Boonsboro, Sharpsburg, Frederick, Brunswick, Germanto

Deep Creek Lake

Youghiogheny

N. Branch Potomac

S. Branch Potomac

Chesapeake and Ohio Canal

Highest point in Maryland

Backbone Mt.
3,360 ft
1,024 m

ANTIETAM NATIONAL BATTLEFIELD

CHESAPEAKE & OHIO CANAL N.H.P.

APPALACHIAN NATIONAL SCENIC TRAIL

0 — 50 miles

0 — 50 kilometers

Albers Conic Equal-Area Projection

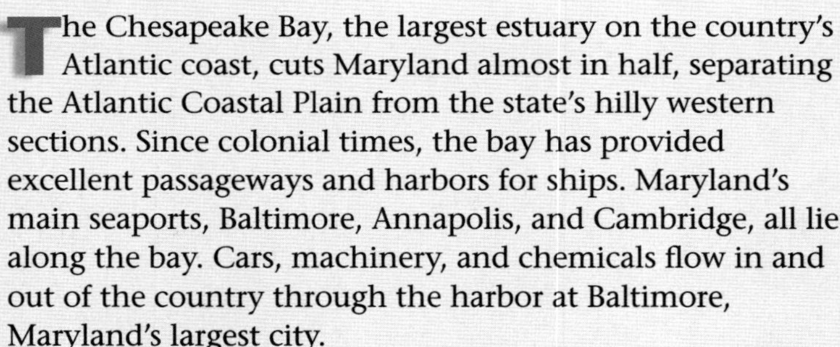

Old Line State

Maryland

The Chesapeake Bay, the largest estuary on the country's Atlantic coast, cuts Maryland almost in half, separating the Atlantic Coastal Plain from the state's hilly western sections. Since colonial times, the bay has provided excellent passageways and harbors for ships. Maryland's main seaports, Baltimore, Annapolis, and Cambridge, all lie along the bay. Cars, machinery, and chemicals flow in and out of the country through the harbor at Baltimore, Maryland's largest city.

The Chesapeake's waters, teeming with oysters, crabs, clams, and fish, have long provided a living for watermen. "Chesapeake" comes from an Indian word that means "great shellfish bay." Maryland ranks among the top states for harvests of oysters and blue crabs.

Health care and computer services employ many Marylanders. Some farm, growing crops or raising chickens. Others work in the state's factories. Many commute to jobs in Washington, D.C., especially with the federal government.

Area: 12,407 sq mi (32,133 sq km)

Population: 5,509,000

Capital: Annapolis, pop. 36,200

Largest city: Baltimore, pop. 638,600

Industry: real estate, federal government, health services, business services, engineering services, electrical and gas services, communications, banking, insurance

Agriculture: poultry and eggs, dairy products, nursery stock, soybeans, corn, seafood, cattle, vegetables

Statehood: April 28, 1788; 7th state

Nickname: Old Line State

More About Maryland

- *Maryland earned its nickname from the praise its "troops of the line" won from George Washington during the Revolutionary War.*
- *Francis Scott Key wrote "The Star Spangled Banner" after watching the British attack Baltimore's Fort McHenry during the War of 1812.*
- *Baltimore lawyer Thurgood Marshall became the country's first African-American Supreme Court Justice in 1964.*
- *Maryland was named for the wife of England's King Charles I. In 1632 he granted the land of Maryland to Lord Baltimore, who founded the Maryland colony.*

Northern (Baltimore) Oriole
Black-eyed Susan

MARYLAND
NEW JERSEY
DELAWARE
VIRGINIA
ANIA
D.C.
DELMARVA PENINSULA
ATLANTIC OCEAN
Baltimore
Annapolis
Towson
Catonsville
Ellicott City
Columbia
Glen Burnie
Dundalk
Essex
Parkville
Cockeysville
Reisterstown
Manchester
Bel Air
Havre de Grace
Aberdeen
Edgewood
Perry Hall
Elkton
Chestertown
Severna Park
Bowie
Silver Spring
Bethesda
Rockville
Hyattsville
Suitland
Deale
Chesapeake Beach
Waldorf
St. Charles
La Plata
Indian Head
Prince Frederick
Golden Beach
Solomons
Lexington Park
St. Marys City
Grasonville
St. Michaels
Easton
Denton
Federalsburg
Hurlock
Cambridge
Bucktown
Salisbury
Fruitland
Ocean Pines
Berlin
Ocean City
Snow Hill
Pocomoke City
Crisfield
U.S. center of population in 1800
HAMPTON N.H.S.
FT. McHENRY NAT. MON. & HISTORIC SHRINE
PATUXENT NATIONAL WILDLIFE REFUGE
GREENBELT PARK
WILLIAM PRESTON LANE JR. MEMORIAL BRIDGE (CHESAPEAKE BAY BRIDGE)
EASTERN NECK N.W.R.
OXON COVE PARK & OXON HILL FARM
FT. FOOTE PARK
FT. WASHINGTON PARK
PISCATAWAY PARK
BLACKWATER NATIONAL WILDLIFE REFUGE
ASSATEAGUE ISLAND NATIONAL SEASHORE
Susquehanna
Chesapeake and Delaware Canal
Sassafras
Chester
Severn
Patuxent
Choptank
Nanticoke
Pocomoke
Potomac
Chesapeake Bay
Kent Island
Eastern Bay
Fishing Bay
Bloodsworth Island
Tangier Sound
Point Lookout
Smith Island
Pocomoke Sound
Chincoteague Bay
Assateague Island
95
295
83
795
695
70
495
97
50

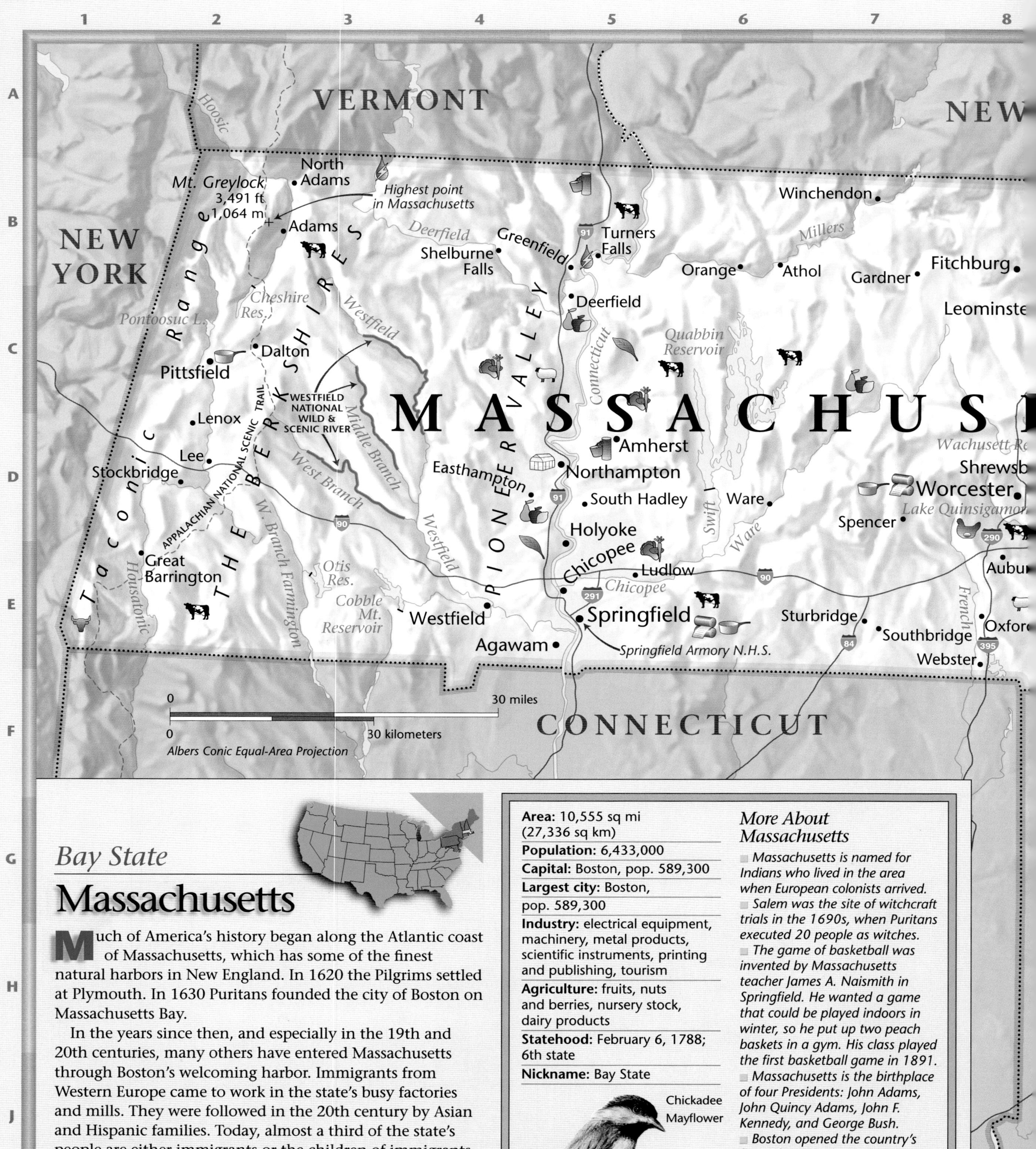

Bay State

Massachusetts

Much of America's history began along the Atlantic coast of Massachusetts, which has some of the finest natural harbors in New England. In 1620 the Pilgrims settled at Plymouth. In 1630 Puritans founded the city of Boston on Massachusetts Bay.

In the years since then, and especially in the 19th and 20th centuries, many others have entered Massachusetts through Boston's welcoming harbor. Immigrants from Western Europe came to work in the state's busy factories and mills. They were followed in the 20th century by Asian and Hispanic families. Today, almost a third of the state's people are either immigrants or the children of immigrants.

Boston is still a busy seaport. A center of business, culture, and learning, it is one of the largest cities on the East Coast. More than 50 universities and colleges draw students to the Boston area. In turn, the universities supply expert workers to companies in Massachusetts that specialize in computers, electronics, and medical research.

Area: 10,555 sq mi (27,336 sq km)

Population: 6,433,000

Capital: Boston, pop. 589,300

Largest city: Boston, pop. 589,300

Industry: electrical equipment, machinery, metal products, scientific instruments, printing and publishing, tourism

Agriculture: fruits, nuts and berries, nursery stock, dairy products

Statehood: February 6, 1788; 6th state

Nickname: Bay State

Chickadee

Mayflower

More About Massachusetts

- *Massachusetts is named for Indians who lived in the area when European colonists arrived.*
- *Salem was the site of witchcraft trials in the 1690s, when Puritans executed 20 people as witches.*
- *The game of basketball was invented by Massachusetts teacher James A. Naismith in Springfield. He wanted a game that could be played indoors in winter, so he put up two peach baskets in a gym. His class played the first basketball game in 1891.*
- *Massachusetts is the birthplace of four Presidents: John Adams, John Quincy Adams, John F. Kennedy, and George Bush.*
- *Boston opened the country's first subway in 1897.*

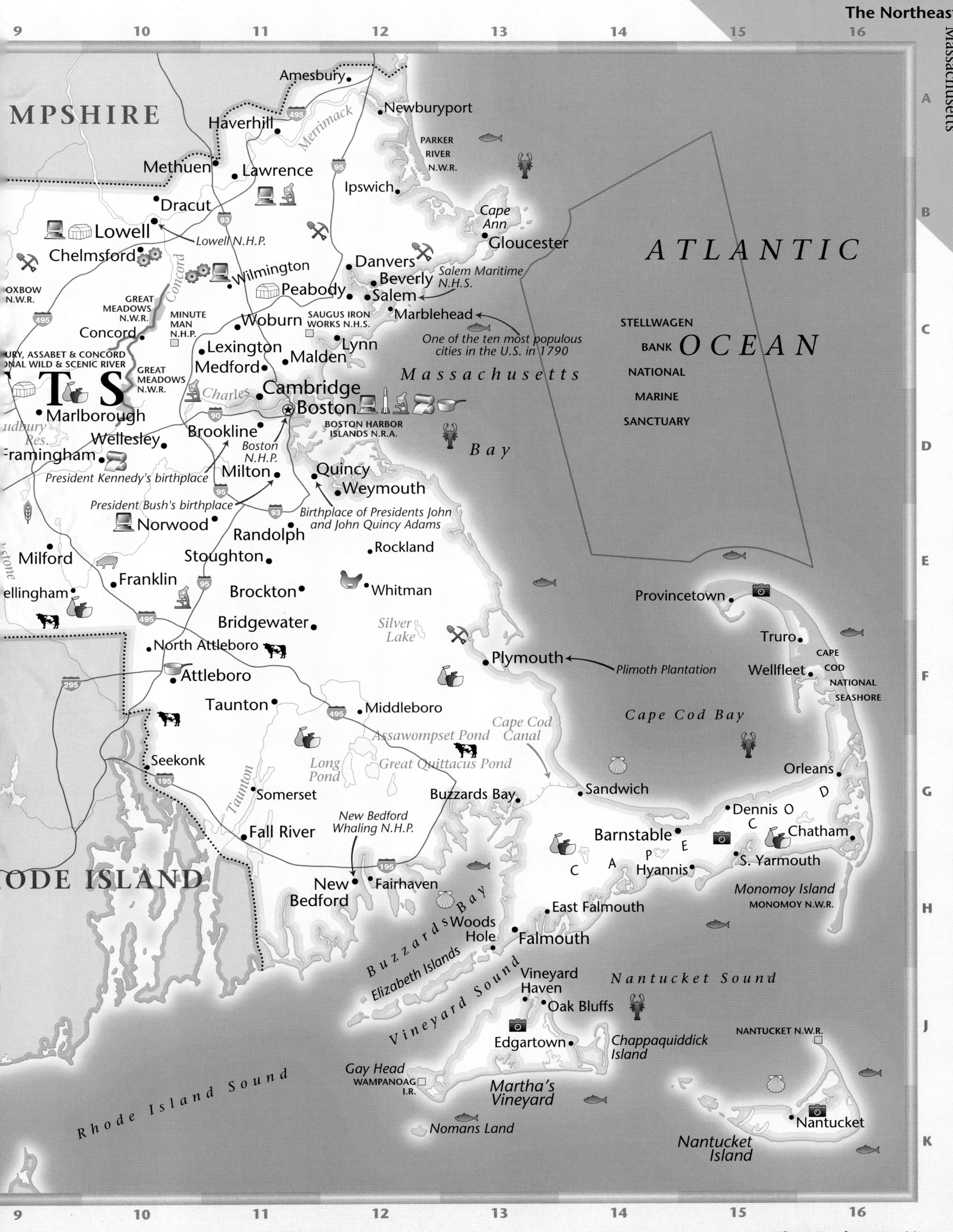
MPSHIRE
ATLANTIC OCEAN
STELLWAGEN BANK NATIONAL MARINE SANCTUARY
Massachusetts Bay
Cape Cod Bay
Nantucket Sound
Vineyard Sound
Buzzards Bay
Rhode Island Sound
ODE ISLAND
Amesbury
Newburyport
Haverhill
Merrimack
Methuen
Lawrence
Ipswich
PARKER RIVER N.W.R.
Dracut
Lowell
Lowell N.H.P.
Chelmsford
Cape Ann
Gloucester
Danvers
Beverly
Salem
Salem Maritime N.H.S.
Wilmington
Peabody
Concord
OXBOW N.W.R.
GREAT MEADOWS N.W.R.
MINUTE MAN N.H.P.
Woburn
SAUGUS IRON WORKS N.H.S.
Marblehead
Lynn
One of the ten most populous cities in the U.S. in 1790
Lexington
Malden
Medford
Cambridge
Charles
Boston
Marlborough
Brookline
BOSTON HARBOR ISLANDS N.R.A.
Wellesley
Framingham
Boston N.H.P.
Milton
Quincy
Weymouth
President Kennedy's birthplace
President Bush's birthplace
Birthplace of Presidents John and John Quincy Adams
Norwood
Randolph
Rockland
Milford
Stoughton
Franklin
Whitman
Brockton
Bridgewater
Silver Lake
North Attleboro
Plymouth
Plimoth Plantation
Attleboro
Taunton
Middleboro
Assawompset Pond
Cape Cod Canal
Great Quittacus Pond
Long Pond
Seekonk
Somerset
Buzzards Bay
Sandwich
New Bedford Whaling N.H.P.
Fall River
New Bedford
Fairhaven
Provincetown
Truro
CAPE COD NATIONAL SEASHORE
Wellfleet
Orleans
Dennis
Barnstable
Chatham
Hyannis
S. Yarmouth
CAPE COD
Monomoy Island
MONOMOY N.W.R.
East Falmouth
Woods Hole
Falmouth
Elizabeth Islands
Vineyard Haven
Oak Bluffs
Edgartown
Chappaquiddick Island
NANTUCKET N.W.R.
Gay Head
WAMPANOAG I.R.
Martha's Vineyard
Nomans Land
Nantucket
Nantucket Island
9 10 11 12 13 14 15 16
A B C D E F G H J K

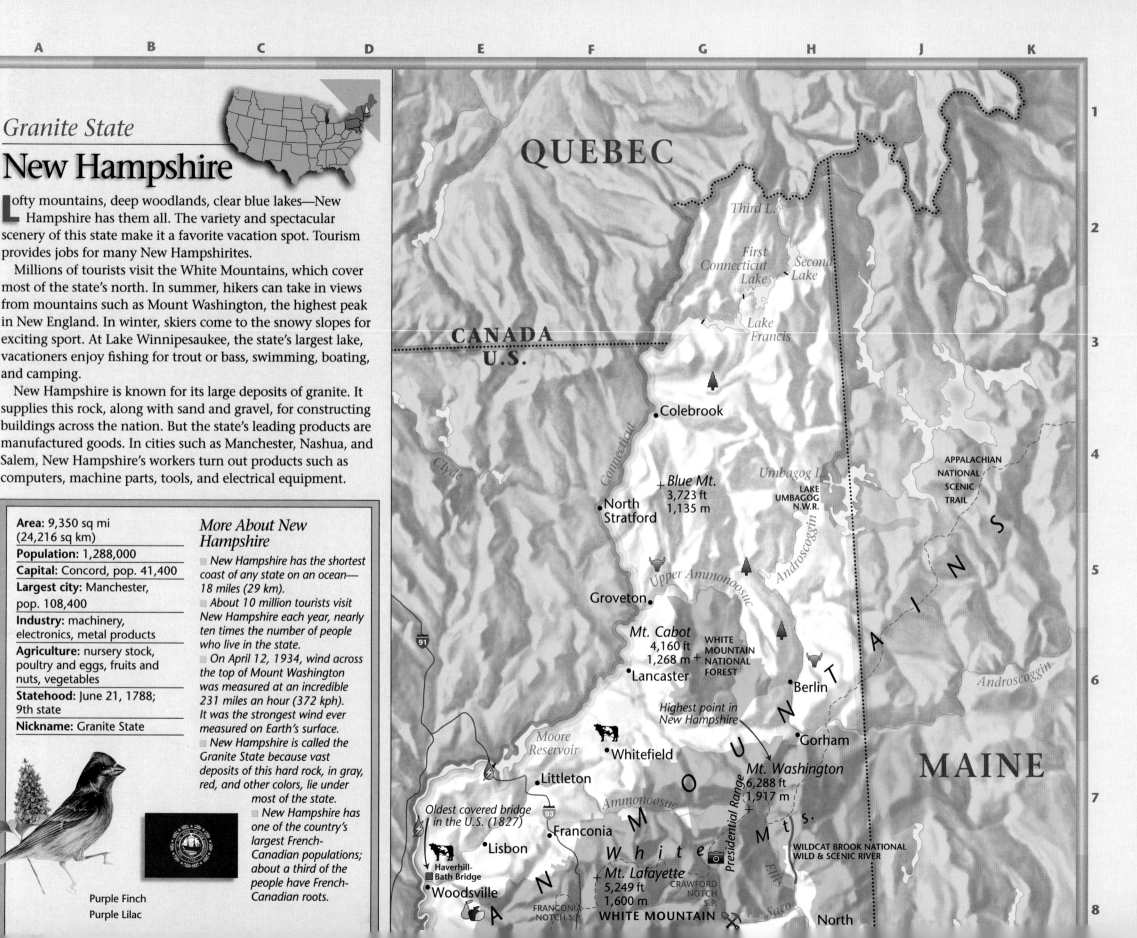

Granite State

New Hampshire

Lofty mountains, deep woodlands, clear blue lakes—New Hampshire has them all. The variety and spectacular scenery of this state make it a favorite vacation spot. Tourism provides jobs for many New Hampshirites.

Millions of tourists visit the White Mountains, which cover most of the state's north. In summer, hikers can take in views from mountains such as Mount Washington, the highest peak in New England. In winter, skiers come to the snowy slopes for exciting sport. At Lake Winnipesaukee, the state's largest lake, vacationers enjoy fishing for trout or bass, swimming, boating, and camping.

New Hampshire is known for its large deposits of granite. It supplies this rock, along with sand and gravel, for constructing buildings across the nation. But the state's leading products are manufactured goods. In cities such as Manchester, Nashua, and Salem, New Hampshire's workers turn out products such as computers, machine parts, tools, and electrical equipment.

Area: 9,350 sq mi (24,216 sq km)

Population: 1,288,000

Capital: Concord, pop. 41,400

Largest city: Manchester, pop. 108,400

Industry: machinery, electronics, metal products

Agriculture: nursery stock, poultry and eggs, fruits and nuts, vegetables

Statehood: June 21, 1788; 9th state

Nickname: Granite State

More About New Hampshire

- *New Hampshire has the shortest coast of any state on an ocean—18 miles (29 km).*
- *About 10 million tourists visit New Hampshire each year, nearly ten times the number of people who live in the state.*
- *On April 12, 1934, wind across the top of Mount Washington was measured at an incredible 231 miles an hour (372 kph). It was the strongest wind ever measured on Earth's surface.*
- *New Hampshire is called the Granite State because vast deposits of this hard rock, in gray, red, and other colors, lie under most of the state.*
- *New Hampshire has one of the country's largest French-Canadian populations; about a third of the people have French-Canadian roots.*

Purple Finch
Purple Lilac

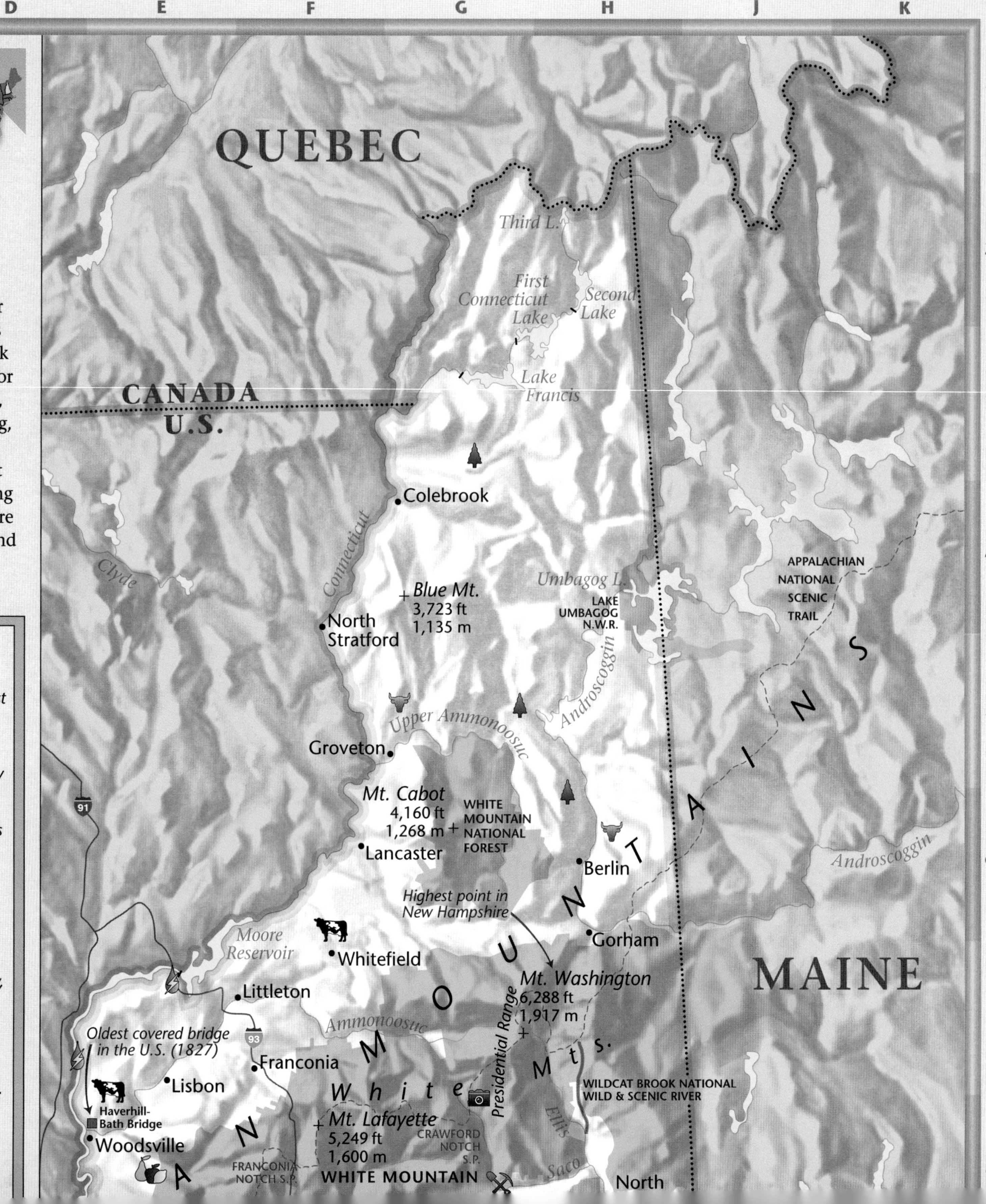

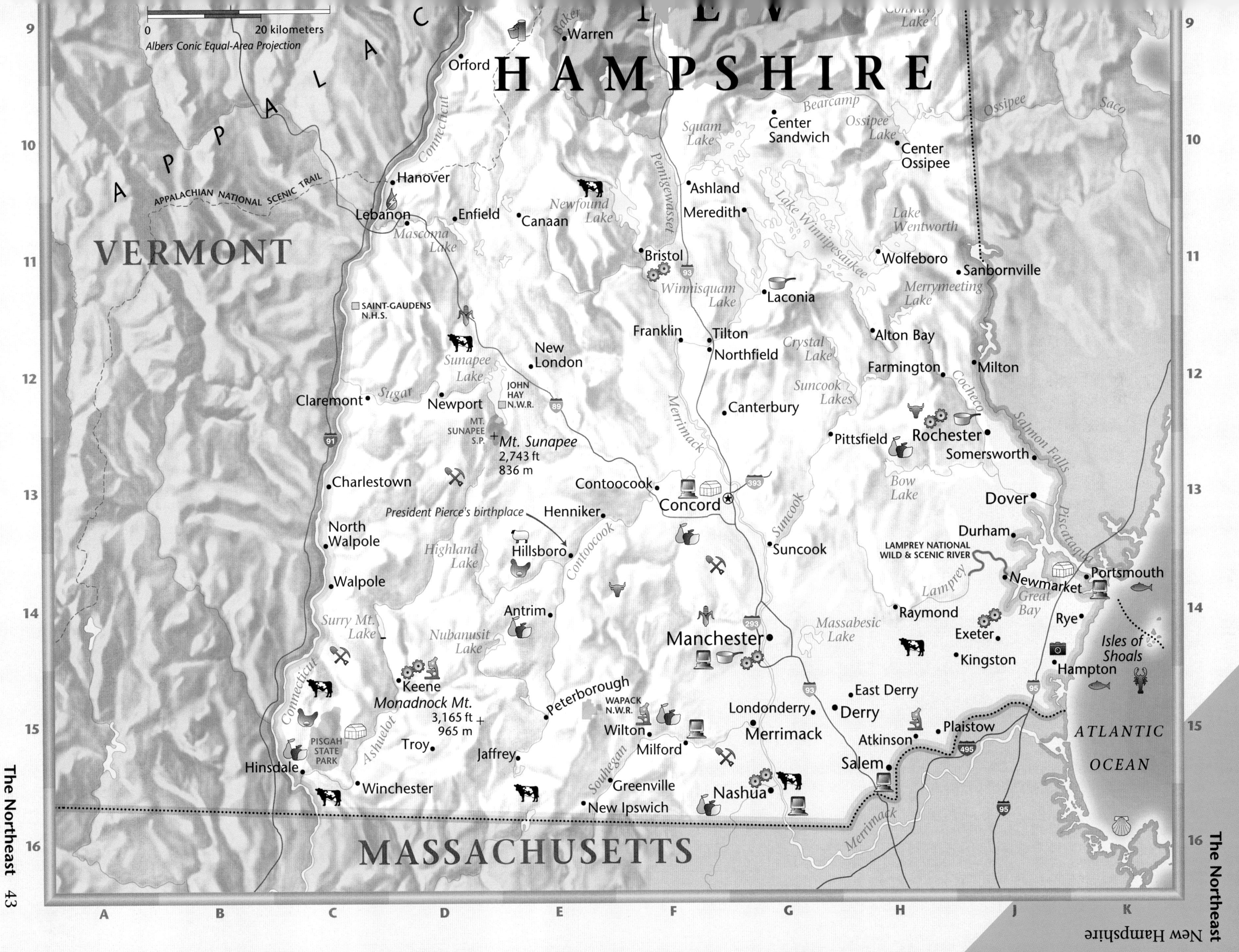
NEW HAMPSHIRE
VERMONT
MASSACHUSETTS
ATLANTIC OCEAN
APPALACHIA
APPALACHIAN NATIONAL SCENIC TRAIL
0 20 kilometers
Albers Conic Equal-Area Projection
Concord
Manchester
Nashua
Portsmouth
Dover
Rochester
Somersworth
Durham
Newmarket
Exeter
Kingston
Hampton
Rye
Raymond
Plaistow
Atkinson
Salem
Derry
East Derry
Londonderry
Merrimack
Milford
Wilton
Greenville
New Ipswich
Peterborough
Jaffrey
Antrim
Hillsboro
Henniker
Contoocook
Keene
Troy
Winchester
Hinsdale
Walpole
North Walpole
Charlestown
Claremont
Newport
New London
Lebanon
Hanover
Enfield
Canaan
Orford
Warren
Bristol
Franklin
Tilton
Northfield
Canterbury
Laconia
Ashland
Meredith
Center Sandwich
Center Ossipee
Wolfeboro
Sanbornville
Alton Bay
Farmington
Milton
Pittsfield
Suncook
Mt. Sunapee 2,743 ft 836 m
Monadnock Mt. 3,165 ft 965 m
President Pierce's birthplace
SAINT-GAUDENS N.H.S.
JOHN HAY N.W.R.
MT. SUNAPEE S.P.
WAPACK N.W.R.
PISGAH STATE PARK
LAMPREY NATIONAL WILD & SCENIC RIVER
Isles of Shoals
Lake Winnipesaukee
Squam Lake
Newfound Lake
Winnisquam Lake
Sunapee Lake
Mascoma Lake
Highland Lake
Nubanusit Lake
Surry Mt. Lake
Crystal Lake
Suncook Lakes
Massabesic Lake
Bow Lake
Merrymeeting Lake
Lake Wentworth
Ossipee Lake
Great Bay
Connecticut
Merrimack
Pemigewasset
Contoocook
Souhegan
Ashuelot
Sugar
Piscataqua
Salmon Falls
Cocheco
Lamprey
Suncook
Bearcamp
Ossipee
Saco
Baker
A B C D E F G H J K
9 10 11 12 13 14 15 16

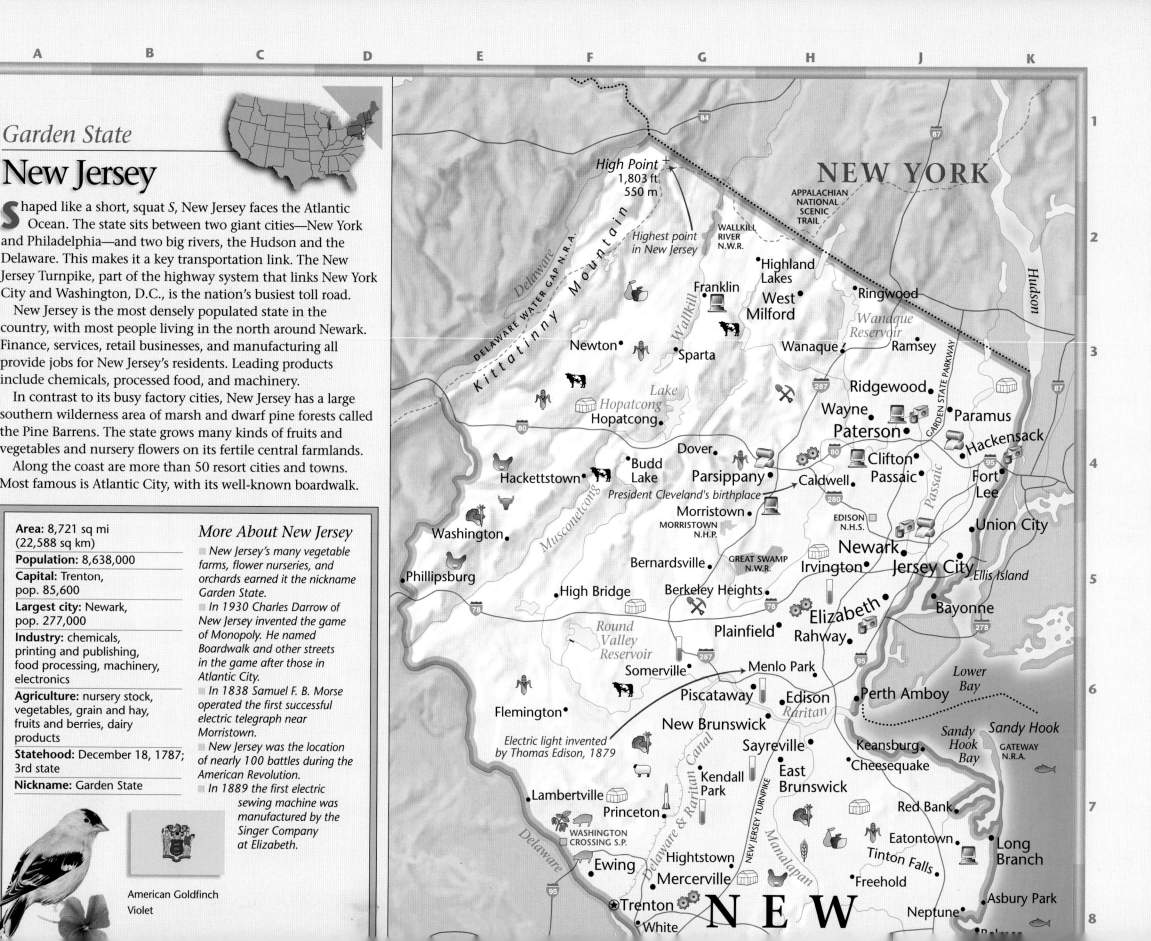

Garden State

New Jersey

Shaped like a short, squat *S*, New Jersey faces the Atlantic Ocean. The state sits between two giant cities—New York and Philadelphia—and two big rivers, the Hudson and the Delaware. This makes it a key transportation link. The New Jersey Turnpike, part of the highway system that links New York City and Washington, D.C., is the nation's busiest toll road.

New Jersey is the most densely populated state in the country, with most people living in the north around Newark. Finance, services, retail businesses, and manufacturing all provide jobs for New Jersey's residents. Leading products include chemicals, processed food, and machinery.

In contrast to its busy factory cities, New Jersey has a large southern wilderness area of marsh and dwarf pine forests called the Pine Barrens. The state grows many kinds of fruits and vegetables and nursery flowers on its fertile central farmlands.

Along the coast are more than 50 resort cities and towns. Most famous is Atlantic City, with its well-known boardwalk.

Area: 8,721 sq mi (22,588 sq km)

Population: 8,638,000

Capital: Trenton, pop. 85,600

Largest city: Newark, pop. 277,000

Industry: chemicals, printing and publishing, food processing, machinery, electronics

Agriculture: nursery stock, vegetables, grain and hay, fruits and berries, dairy products

Statehood: December 18, 1787; 3rd state

Nickname: Garden State

More About New Jersey

- *New Jersey's many vegetable farms, flower nurseries, and orchards earned it the nickname Garden State.*
- *In 1930 Charles Darrow of New Jersey invented the game of Monopoly. He named Boardwalk and other streets in the game after those in Atlantic City.*
- *In 1838 Samuel F. B. Morse operated the first successful electric telegraph near Morristown.*
- *New Jersey was the location of nearly 100 battles during the American Revolution.*
- *In 1889 the first electric sewing machine was manufactured by the Singer Company at Elizabeth.*

American Goldfinch

Violet

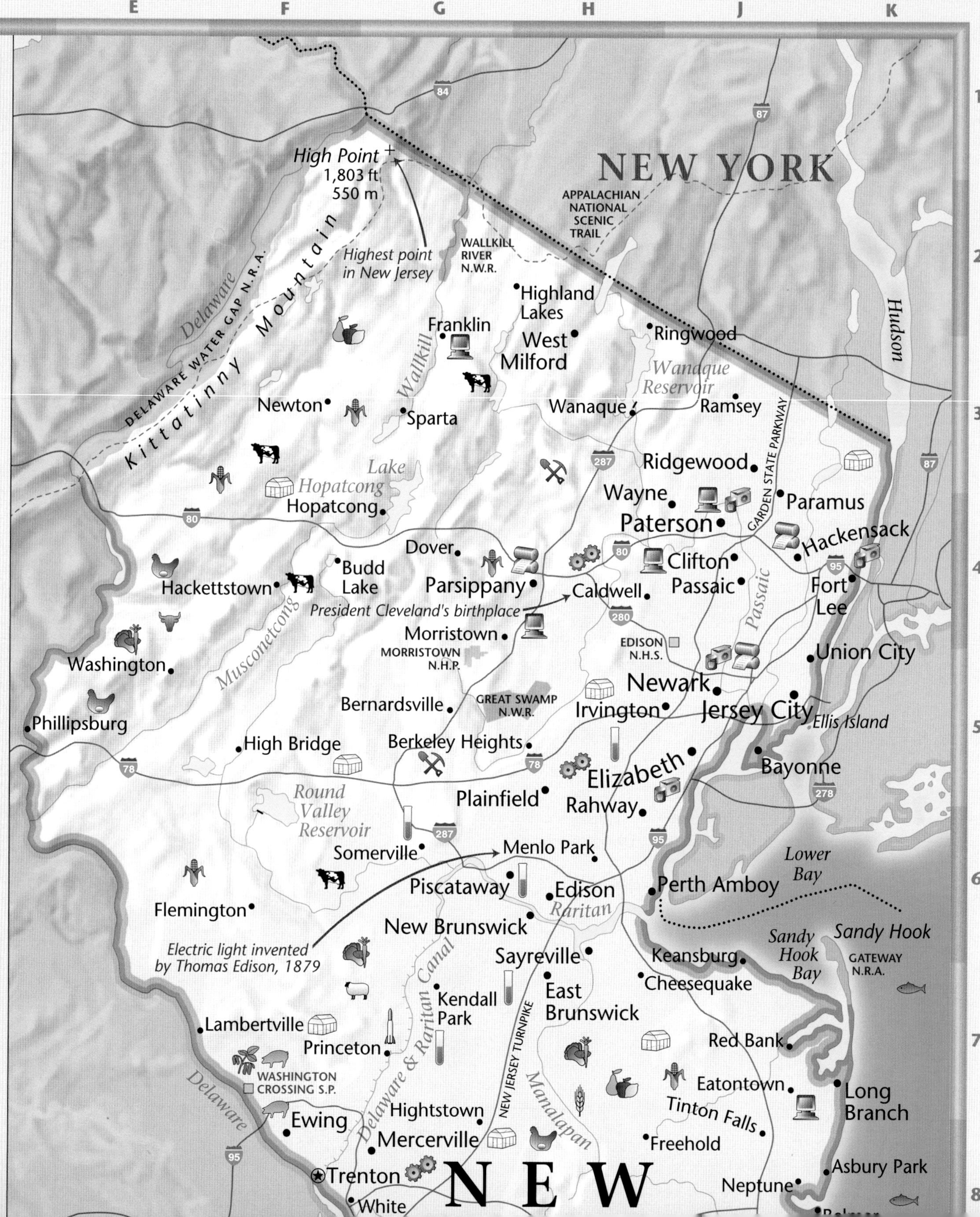

New Jersey

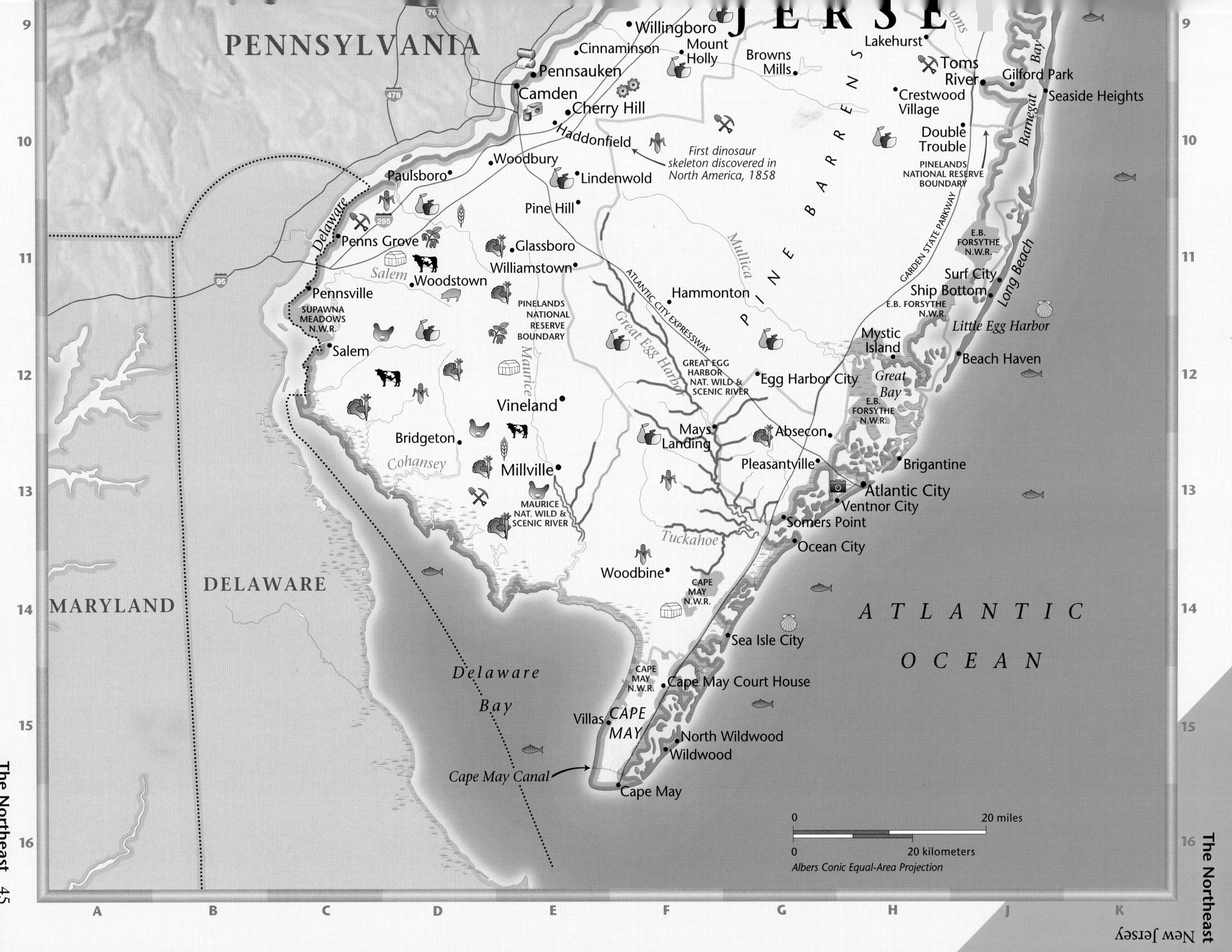
PENNSYLVANIA
JERSE
PINE BARRENS
DELAWARE
MARYLAND
ATLANTIC OCEAN
Delaware Bay
Delaware
Barnegat Bay
Long Beach
Little Egg Harbor
Great Bay
Mullica
Great Egg Harbor
Tuckahoe
Maurice
Cohansey
Salem
CAPE MAY
Cape May Canal
Willingboro
Cinnaminson
Mount Holly
Browns Mills
Lakehurst
Toms River
Gilford Park
Seaside Heights
Crestwood Village
Double Trouble
Pennsauken
Camden
Cherry Hill
Haddonfield
First dinosaur skeleton discovered in North America, 1858
Woodbury
Paulsboro
Lindenwold
Pine Hill
PINELANDS NATIONAL RESERVE BOUNDARY
GARDEN STATE PARKWAY
E.B. FORSYTHE N.W.R.
Penns Grove
Glassboro
Williamstown
Woodstown
Pennsville
SUPAWNA MEADOWS N.W.R.
Salem
ATLANTIC CITY EXPRESSWAY
Hammonton
Surf City
Ship Bottom
Mystic Island
Beach Haven
GREAT EGG HARBOR NAT. WILD & SCENIC RIVER
Egg Harbor City
Vineland
Bridgeton
Mays Landing
Absecon
Pleasantville
Brigantine
Millville
MAURICE NAT. WILD & SCENIC RIVER
Atlantic City
Ventnor City
Somers Point
Ocean City
Woodbine
CAPE MAY N.W.R.
Sea Isle City
Cape May Court House
Villas
North Wildwood
Wildwood
Cape May
0 20 miles
0 20 kilometers
Albers Conic Equal-Area Projection
A B C D E F G H J K
9 10 11 12 13 14 15 16

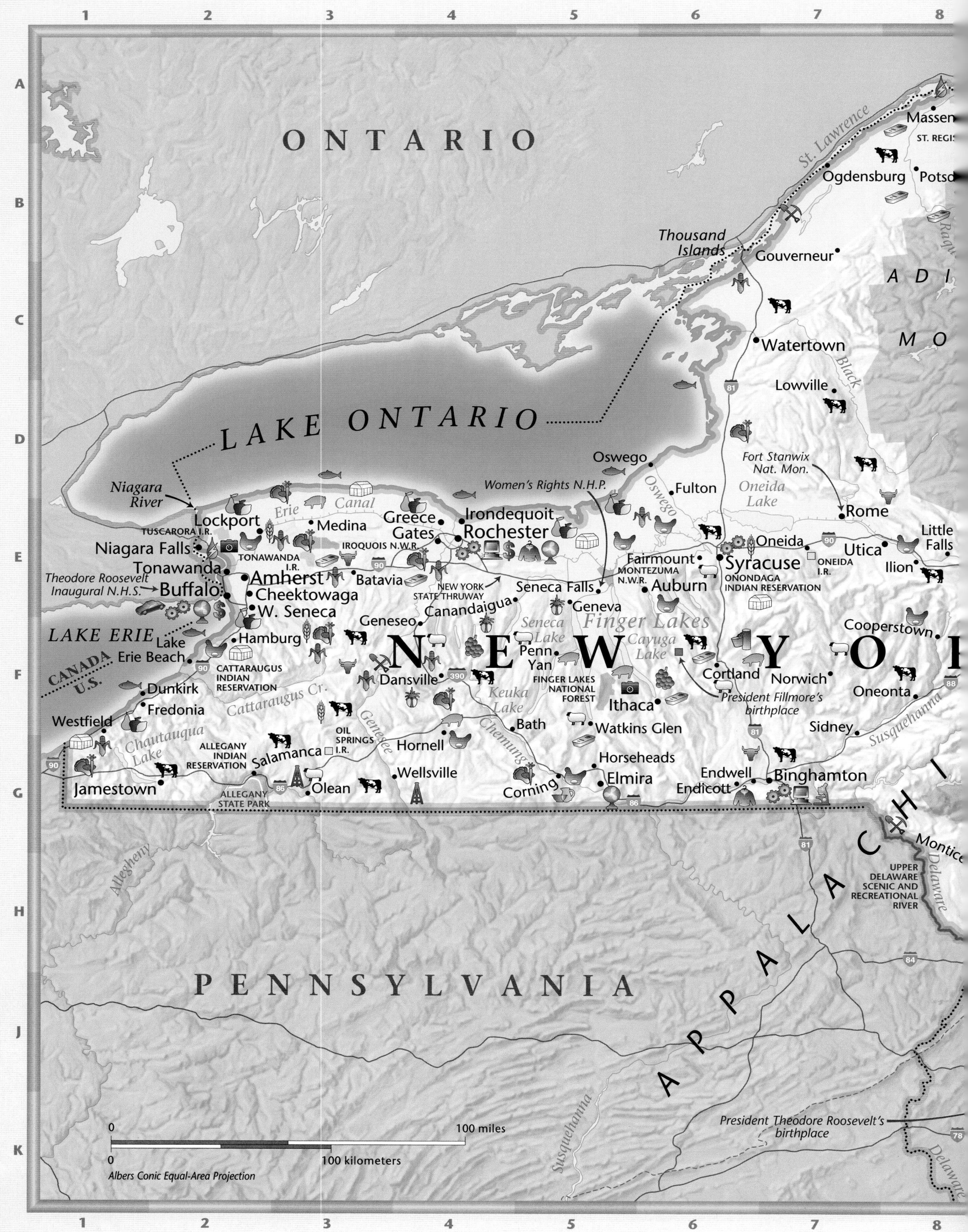
ONTARIO
LAKE ONTARIO
LAKE ERIE
CANADA
U.S.
NEW YORK
PENNSYLVANIA
APPALACHIAN
Finger Lakes
Niagara River
Thousand Islands
St. Lawrence
Lockport
Medina
Greece
Gates
Irondequoit
Rochester
Niagara Falls
Tonawanda
Buffalo
Amherst
Cheektowaga
W. Seneca
Batavia
Geneseo
Canandaigua
Seneca Falls
Geneva
Auburn
Syracuse
Oswego
Fulton
Oneida
Rome
Utica
Little Falls
Ilion
Watertown
Lowville
Ogdensburg
Gouverneur
Hamburg
Lake Erie Beach
Dunkirk
Fredonia
Westfield
Jamestown
Salamanca
Olean
Wellsville
Hornell
Dansville
Bath
Penn Yan
Ithaca
Watkins Glen
Horseheads
Elmira
Corning
Cortland
Norwich
Oneonta
Cooperstown
Sidney
Endwell
Endicott
Binghamton
TUSCARORA I.R.
TONAWANDA I.R.
IROQUOIS N.W.R.
Theodore Roosevelt Inaugural N.H.S.
NEW YORK STATE THRUWAY
Women's Rights N.H.P.
Fairmount
MONTEZUMA N.W.R.
ONONDAGA INDIAN RESERVATION
ONEIDA I.R.
Fort Stanwix Nat. Mon.
Oneida Lake
Erie Canal
Seneca Lake
Cayuga Lake
Keuka Lake
FINGER LAKES NATIONAL FOREST
President Fillmore's birthplace
CATTARAUGUS INDIAN RESERVATION
Cattaraugus Cr.
Chautauqua Lake
ALLEGANY INDIAN RESERVATION
OIL SPRINGS I.R.
ALLEGANY STATE PARK
Genesee
Chemung
Oswego
Black
Susquehanna
Allegheny
Delaware
UPPER DELAWARE SCENIC AND RECREATIONAL RIVER
President Theodore Roosevelt's birthplace
0
100 miles
0
100 kilometers
Albers Conic Equal-Area Projection

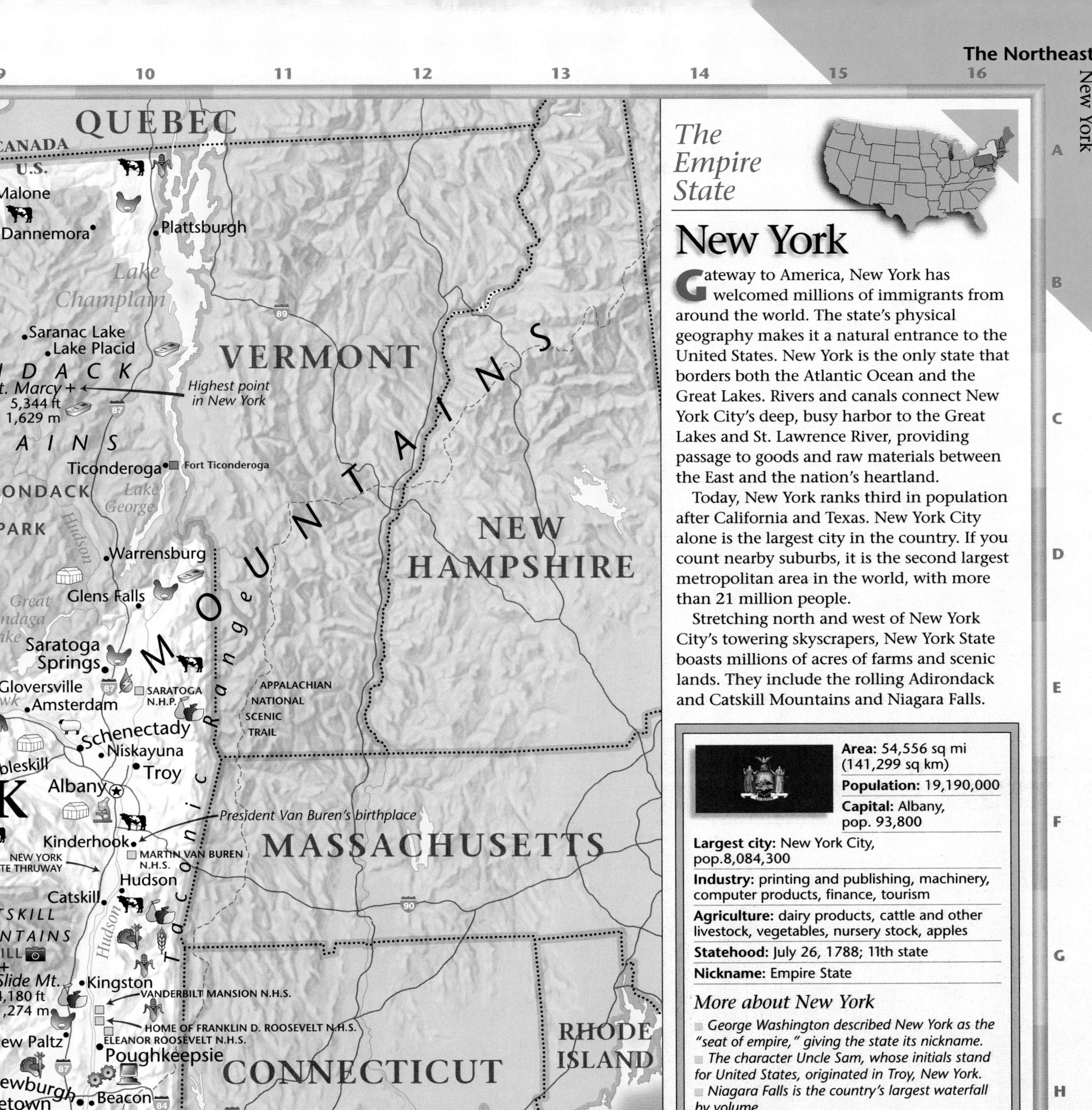

The Empire State

New York

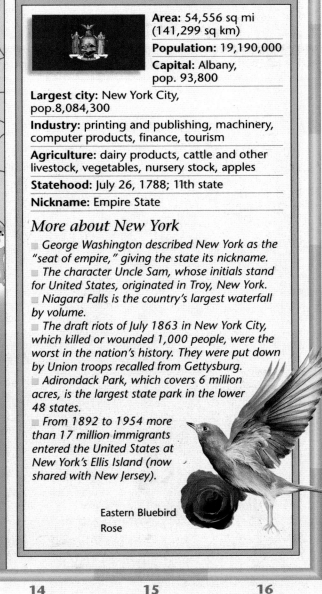

Gateway to America, New York has welcomed millions of immigrants from around the world. The state's physical geography makes it a natural entrance to the United States. New York is the only state that borders both the Atlantic Ocean and the Great Lakes. Rivers and canals connect New York City's deep, busy harbor to the Great Lakes and St. Lawrence River, providing passage to goods and raw materials between the East and the nation's heartland.

Today, New York ranks third in population after California and Texas. New York City alone is the largest city in the country. If you count nearby suburbs, it is the second largest metropolitan area in the world, with more than 21 million people.

Stretching north and west of New York City's towering skyscrapers, New York State boasts millions of acres of farms and scenic lands. They include the rolling Adirondack and Catskill Mountains and Niagara Falls.

Area: 54,556 sq mi (141,299 sq km)

Population: 19,190,000

Capital: Albany, pop. 93,800

Largest city: New York City, pop.8,084,300

Industry: printing and publishing, machinery, computer products, finance, tourism

Agriculture: dairy products, cattle and other livestock, vegetables, nursery stock, apples

Statehood: July 26, 1788; 11th state

Nickname: Empire State

More about New York

- *George Washington described New York as the "seat of empire," giving the state its nickname.*
- *The character Uncle Sam, whose initials stand for United States, originated in Troy, New York.*
- *Niagara Falls is the country's largest waterfall by volume.*
- *The draft riots of July 1863 in New York City, which killed or wounded 1,000 people, were the worst in the nation's history. They were put down by Union troops recalled from Gettysburg.*
- *Adirondack Park, which covers 6 million acres, is the largest state park in the lower 48 states.*
- *From 1892 to 1954 more than 17 million immigrants entered the United States at New York's Ellis Island (now shared with New Jersey).*

Eastern Bluebird

Rose

Lake Erie
NEW
OHIO
PENNSYLVANIA
WEST VIRGINIA
MARYLAND
VIRGINIA
Erie
Millcreek
Corry
Allegheny Reservoir
Warren
Bradford
Allegheny
Coudersport
Mansfield
Wellsboro
ERIE N.W.R.
Meadville
Titusville
ALLEGHENY NATIONAL WILD & SCENIC RIVER
ALLEGHENY NATIONAL FOREST
Pymatuning Reservoir
Pine Creek
Pine Creek Gorge
Emporium
Greenville
Oil City
Ridgway
St. Marys
Clarion
CLARION NATIONAL WILD & SCENIC RIVER
W. Branch Susquehanna
Sharon
Beaver
Grove City
Du Bois
Williamsport
Jersey Shore
Lock Haven
New Castle
Punxsutawney
Clearfield
Butler
Kittanning
ALLEGHENY MOUNTAINS
APPALACHIAN MOUNTAINS
Beaver Falls
State College
Indiana
Tyrone
Ohio
Aliquippa
McCandless
Lewistown
Juniata
Pittsburgh
Plum
Penn Hills
Conemaugh
ALLEGHENY PORTAGE RAILROAD N.H.S.
Altoona
Huntingdon
Hollidaysburg
McKeesport
Jeannette
JOHNSTOWN FLOOD NAT. MEM.
Raystown Lake
Tuscarora Mountain
Greensburg
Johnstown
Washington
Monessen
Windber
President Buchanan's birthplace
Mechanicsburg
Carlisle
PENNSYLVANIA TURNPIKE
Youghiogheny
Connellsville
Somerset
Bedford
Shippensburg
Waynesburg
Monongahela
Uniontown
Casselman
Highest point in Pennsylvania
Chambersburg
FRIENDSHIP HILL N.H.S.
FT. NECESSITY NATIONAL BATTLEFIELD
Mt. Davis 3,213 ft (979) m
Mercersburg
Gettysburg
EISENHOWER N.H.S.
Waynesboro
GETTYSBURG N.M.P.
Cheat
0
100 miles
0
100 kilometers
Albers Conic Equal-Area Projection

The Pennsylvania-Maryland boundary, named after its surveyors, became the traditional division between North and South

Independence N.H.P. includes Independence Hall, Liberty Bell, Christ Church, Franklin Court; Betsy Ross House; Edgar Allan Poe N.H.S., Deshler-Morris House, Gloria Dei Church N.H.S.

Busiest freshwater port in the U.S.

Keystone State

Pennsylvania

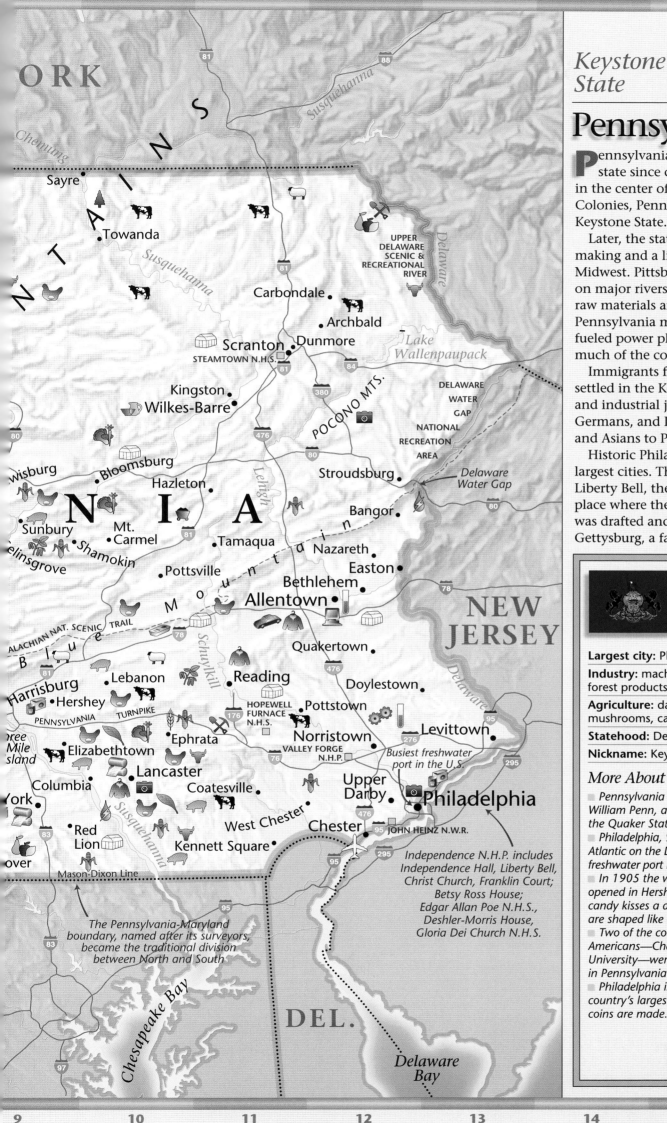

Pennsylvania's location has made it a key state since colonial times. Situated right in the center of the 13 original American Colonies, Pennsylvania won the nickname Keystone State.

Later, the state became a hub of steelmaking and a link between the East and the Midwest. Pittsburgh and Philadelphia, both on major rivers, became shipping centers for raw materials and manufactured goods. Pennsylvania mines yielded the coal that fueled power plants and steel factories across much of the country.

Immigrants from all over the world have settled in the Keystone State. Rich farmland and industrial jobs have attracted British, Germans, and Italians as well as Hispanics and Asians to Pennsylvania.

Historic Philadelphia is one of the East's largest cities. There, visitors can see the Liberty Bell, the house of Betsy Ross, and the place where the Declaration of Independence was drafted and signed. To the west is Gettysburg, a famous Civil War site.

Area: 46,055 sq mi (119,283 sq km)

Population: 12,365,000

Capital: Harrisburg, pop. 48,500

Largest city: Philadelphia, pop. 1,492,200

Industry: machinery, printing and publishing, forest products, metal products

Agriculture: dairy products, poultry and eggs, mushrooms, cattle, hogs, grains

Statehood: December 12, 1787; 2nd state

Nickname: Keystone State

More About Pennsylvania

- *Pennsylvania was founded by and named for William Penn, a Quaker. It is sometimes called the Quaker State.*
- *Philadelphia, 90 miles (145 km) from the Atlantic on the Delaware River, is the largest freshwater port in the world.*
- *In 1905 the world's largest chocolate factory opened in Hershey. Today, it produces 33 million candy kisses a day. Even the city's street lamps are shaped like Hershey kisses.*
- *Two of the country's first colleges for African-Americans—Cheyney University and Lincoln University—were founded in Pennsylvania in the 1800s.*
- *Philadelphia is home to the country's largest mint, where coins are made.*

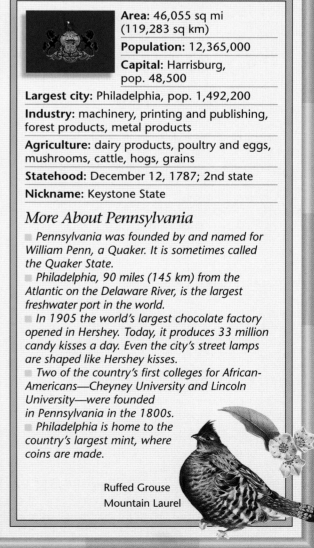

Ruffed Grouse
Mountain Laurel

MASSACHUSETTS
RHODE ISLAND
CONN.
Wallum Lake
Slatersville
Woonsocket
Union Village
Pawtucket Reservoir
Cumberland Hill
Manville
Harrisville
Glendale
Pascoag Lake
Pascoag
Blackstone
Ashton
Chepachet
Woonasquatucket Reservoir
Valley Falls
Lonsdale
Saylesville
Central Falls
Harmony
Esmond
Woonasquatucket
Pawtucket
Ponaganset Reservoir
Jerimoth Hill
812 ft
247 m
Highest point in Rhode Island
Greenville
North Providence
Seekonk
North Scituate
Johnston
Providence
East Providence
Roger Williams National Memorial
Ponaganset
Foster Center
Scituate Reservoir
Cranston
Pawtuxet
Providence
Palmer
Barrington
Warren
Hope
Harris
West Warwick
Anthony
Coventry Center
Rice City
Moosup
Warwick
Bay
Flat River Reservoir
Tiogue Lake
East Greenwich
Bristol
Mount Hope Bay
Stafford Pond
Tiverton
Island Park
Prudence Island
Portsmouth
Wood
Austin
Exeter
Wickford
Narragansett
Nonquit Pond
Rhode Island
Sakonnet
Adamsville
Rhode Island Red Monument
Hamilton
Conanicut Island
Queen
Allenton
95
195
295
395
495

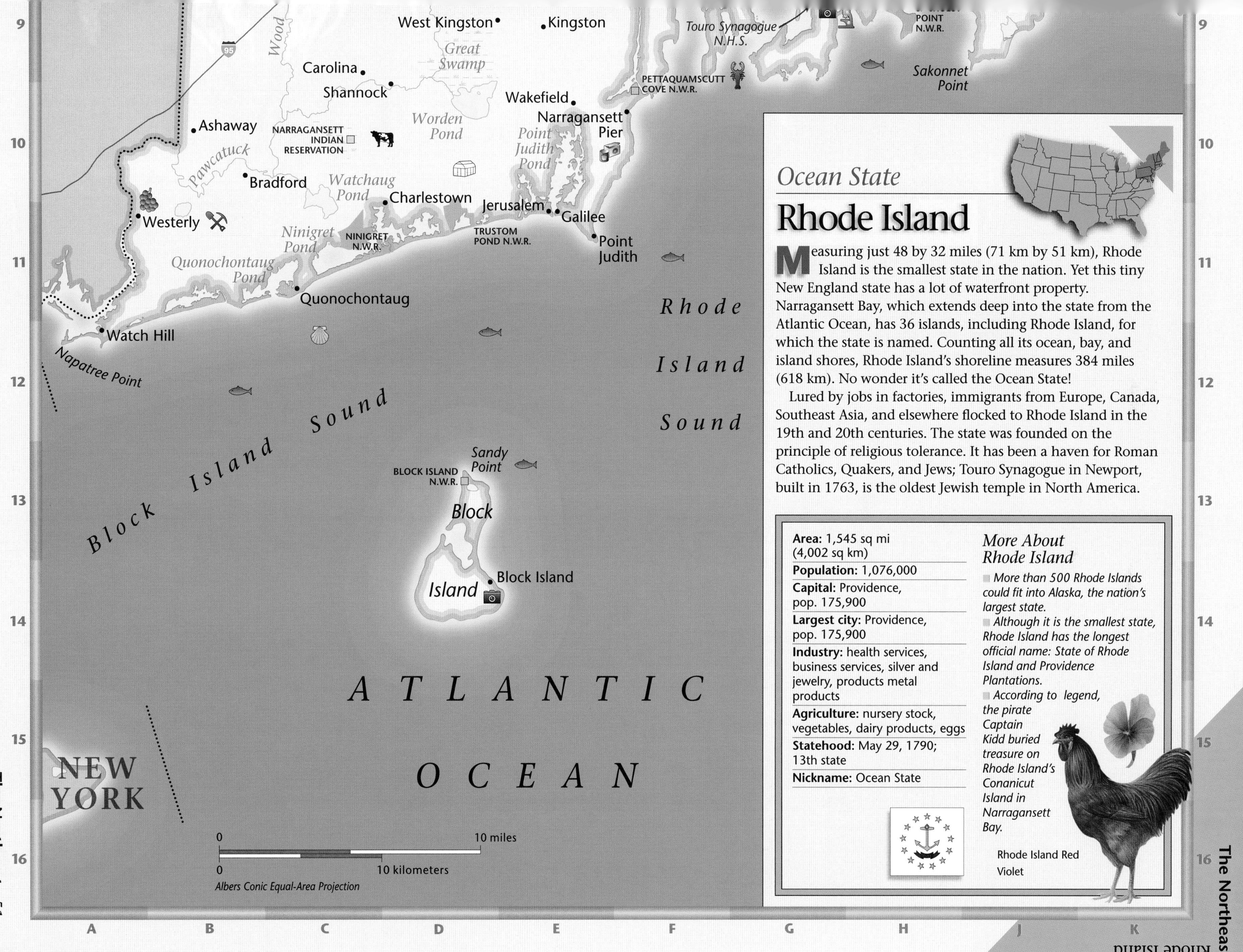

Ocean State

Rhode Island

Measuring just 48 by 32 miles (71 km by 51 km), Rhode Island is the smallest state in the nation. Yet this tiny New England state has a lot of waterfront property. Narragansett Bay, which extends deep into the state from the Atlantic Ocean, has 36 islands, including Rhode Island, for which the state is named. Counting all its ocean, bay, and island shores, Rhode Island's shoreline measures 384 miles (618 km). No wonder it's called the Ocean State!

Lured by jobs in factories, immigrants from Europe, Canada, Southeast Asia, and elsewhere flocked to Rhode Island in the 19th and 20th centuries. The state was founded on the principle of religious tolerance. It has been a haven for Roman Catholics, Quakers, and Jews; Touro Synagogue in Newport, built in 1763, is the oldest Jewish temple in North America.

Area: 1,545 sq mi (4,002 sq km)

Population: 1,076,000

Capital: Providence, pop. 175,900

Largest city: Providence, pop. 175,900

Industry: health services, business services, silver and jewelry, products metal products

Agriculture: nursery stock, vegetables, dairy products, eggs

Statehood: May 29, 1790; 13th state

Nickname: Ocean State

More About Rhode Island

- *More than 500 Rhode Islands could fit into Alaska, the nation's largest state.*
- *Although it is the smallest state, Rhode Island has the longest official name: State of Rhode Island and Providence Plantations.*
- *According to legend, the pirate Captain Kidd buried treasure on Rhode Island's Conanicut Island in Narragansett Bay.*

Rhode Island Red

Violet

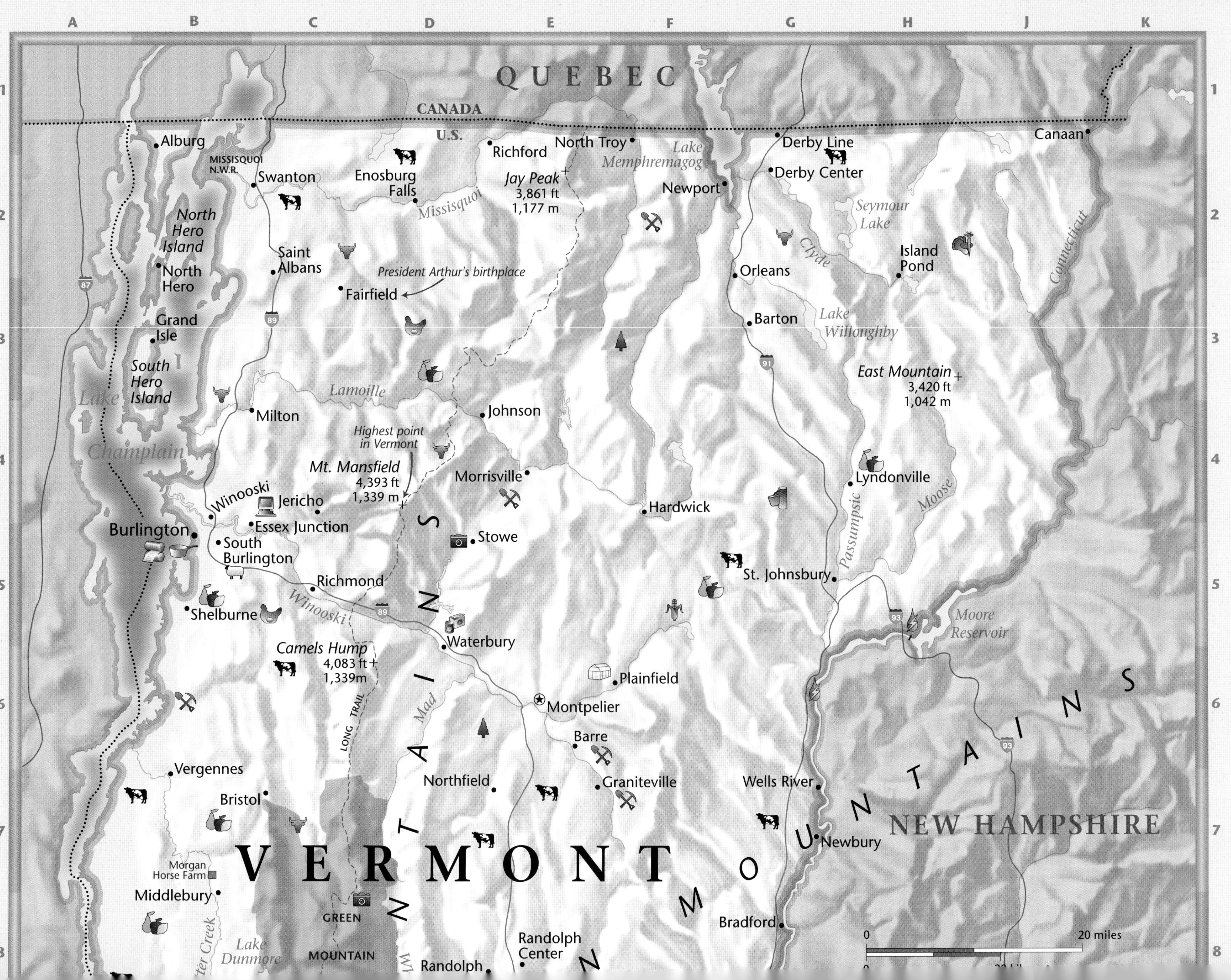

QUEBEC
CANADA
U.S.
NEW HAMPSHIRE
VERMONT
GREEN MOUNTAINS
GREEN
MOUNTAIN
LONG TRAIL
Alburg
MISSISQUOI N.W.R.
Swanton
Enosburg Falls
Missisquoi
Richford
North Troy
Jay Peak 3,861 ft 1,177 m
Lake Memphremagog
Newport
Derby Line
Derby Center
Canaan
Seymour Lake
Clyde
Island Pond
Connecticut
North Hero Island
North Hero
Saint Albans
President Arthur's birthplace
Fairfield
Orleans
Barton
Lake Willoughby
Grand Isle
South Hero Island
Lake Champlain
East Mountain 3,420 ft 1,042 m
Lamoille
Milton
Johnson
Highest point in Vermont
Mt. Mansfield 4,393 ft 1,339 m
Morrisville
Lyndonville
Moose
Winooski
Jericho
Essex Junction
Hardwick
Passumpsic
Burlington
South Burlington
Stowe
Richmond
St. Johnsbury
Shelburne
Winooski
Waterbury
Moore Reservoir
Camels Hump 4,083 ft 1,339m
Plainfield
Montpelier
Mad
Barre
Vergennes
Northfield
Graniteville
Wells River
Bristol
Newbury
Morgan Horse Farm
Middlebury
Bradford
Lake Dunmore
Randolph Center
Randolph
0
20 miles

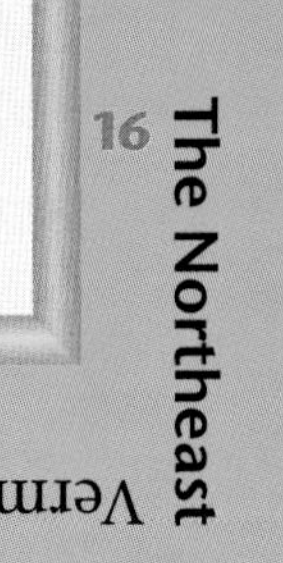

Green Mountain State

Vermont

Vermont gets its name from the tree-covered Green Mountains that run down the state's middle. "Vermont" comes from the French words "vert mont," meaning "green mountain." Forests cover three-fourths of the state, and trees such as maples, poplars, and birches blaze with fiery color in the fall, clothing the mountains in red, yellow, and orange.

Vermont is the only New England state with no seacoast, yet much of it is bordered by water. The Connecticut River forms the state's eastern boundary. Lake Champlain, New England's largest lake, lies along much of the western edge.

In winter, Vermont's mountains get a whopping 100 inches (254 cm) or more of snow. Ski resorts, such as Stowe and Killington, draw skiers and provide jobs for many Vermonters.

Farmers who boil down the sweet sap of sugar maple trees for syrup produce more maple syrup than those in any other state. Vermont is also rich in milk, apples, marble, granite, and manufactured goods ranging from electronic equipment to books.

Area: 9,614 sq mi (24,901 sq km)

Population: 619,000

Capital: Montpelier, pop. 8,000

Largest city: Burlington, pop. 39,500

Industry: health services, tourism, finance, real estate, computer components, electrical parts, printing and publishing, machine tools

Agriculture: dairy products, maple products, apples

Statehood: March 4, 1791; 14th state

Nickname: Green Mountain State

Hermit Thrush

Red Clover

More About Vermont

- *Vermont was an independent country from 1777 to 1791. It had its own money and its own postal service.*
- *Vermont has 85.3 percent of its electricity generated by nuclear energy. That's more than any other state.*
- *In 1777 Vermont was the first state to forbid slavery as part of the articles of its state constitution.*
- *Some of the nation's most important buildings, including the United States Capitol and the U.S. Supreme Court Building, in Washington, D.C., contain marble and granite from Vermont quarries.*
- *Vermont has 114 covered bridges, which were built to protect wooden roads from snow and ice.*

The South

east

The Southeast

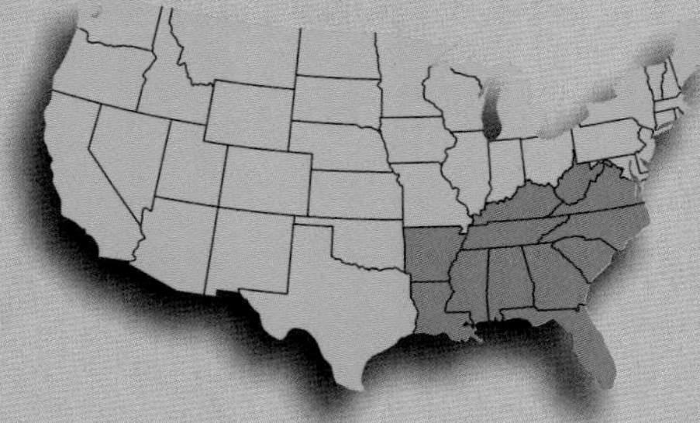

Alabama
Arkansas
Florida
Georgia
Kentucky
Louisiana
Mississippi
North Carolina
South Carolina
Tennessee
Virginia
West Virginia

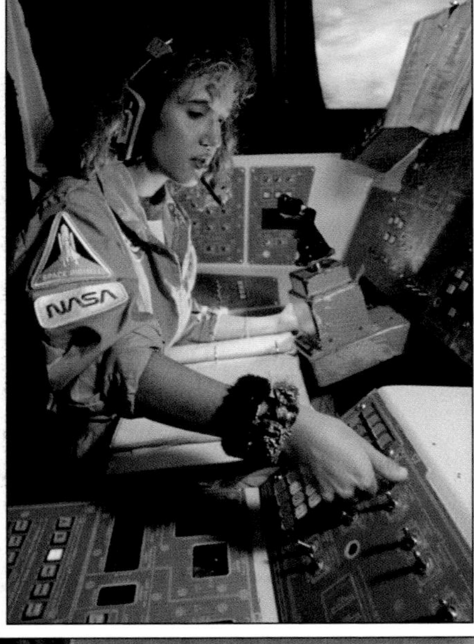

Ghostly, moss-draped bald cypress trees, silent reminders of the Old South's genteel lifestyle, rise from the quiet waters of Louisiana's Atchafalaya Bay (left). Looking to the future, a young girl (above) operates the controls of a space shuttle in a simulated mission at the U.S. Space Camp, in Huntsville, Alabama.

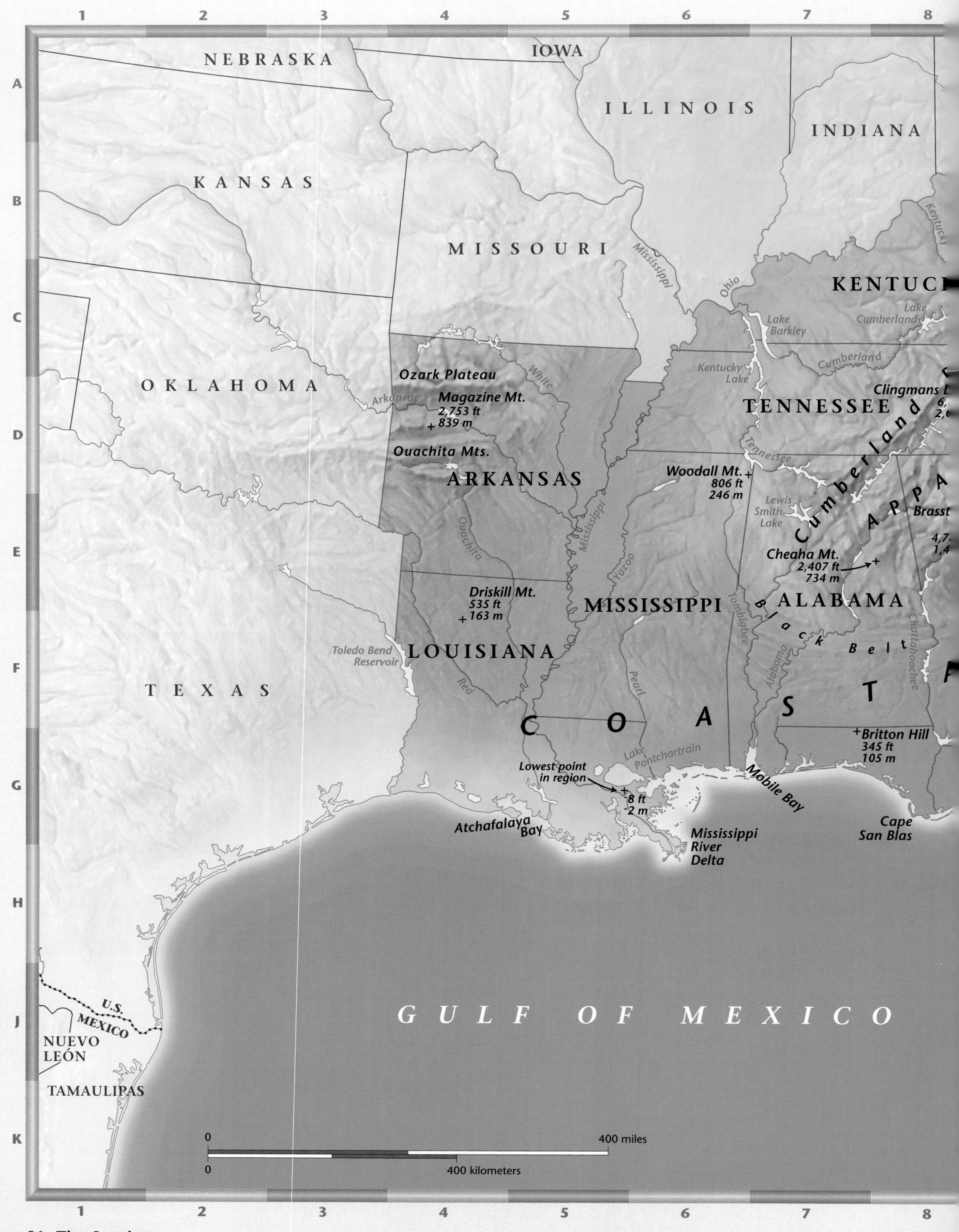
NEBRASKA
IOWA
ILLINOIS
INDIANA
KANSAS
MISSOURI
Mississippi
Ohio
KENTUC
Kentucky
Lake Cumberland
Lake Barkley
Cumberland
Kentucky Lake
OKLAHOMA
Ozark Plateau
White
Arkansas
Magazine Mt.
2,753 ft
839 m
TENNESSEE
Clingmans
Ouachita Mts.
ARKANSAS
Tennessee
Woodall Mt.
806 ft
246 m
Lewis Smith Lake
Cumberland
APPA
Brasst
Ouachita
Mississippi
Yazoo
Cheaha Mt.
2,407 ft
734 m
Driskill Mt.
535 ft
163 m
MISSISSIPPI
Tombigbee
ALABAMA
Black Belt
Toledo Bend Reservoir
LOUISIANA
Red
Pearl
Alabama
Chattahoochee
TEXAS
COAST
Britton Hill
345 ft
105 m
Lake Pontchartrain
Lowest point in region
-8 ft
-2 m
Mobile Bay
Atchafalaya Bay
Mississippi River Delta
Cape San Blas
U.S.
MEXICO
NUEVO LEÓN
TAMAULIPAS
GULF OF MEXICO
0
400 miles
0
400 kilometers

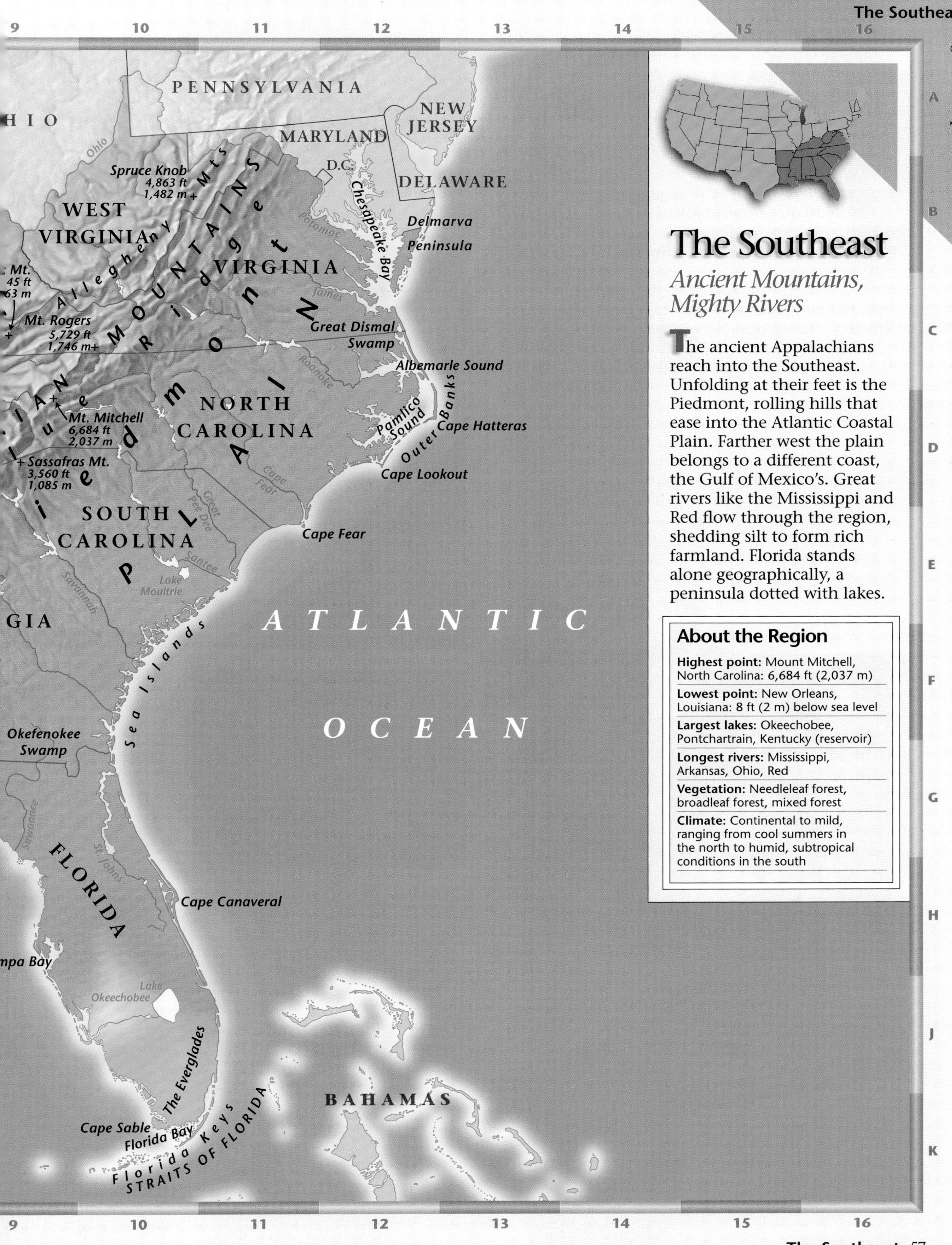

The Southeast

Ancient Mountains, Mighty Rivers

The ancient Appalachians reach into the Southeast. Unfolding at their feet is the Piedmont, rolling hills that ease into the Atlantic Coastal Plain. Farther west the plain belongs to a different coast, the Gulf of Mexico's. Great rivers like the Mississippi and Red flow through the region, shedding silt to form rich farmland. Florida stands alone geographically, a peninsula dotted with lakes.

About the Region

Highest point: Mount Mitchell, North Carolina: 6,684 ft (2,037 m)

Lowest point: New Orleans, Louisiana: 8 ft (2 m) below sea level

Largest lakes: Okeechobee, Pontchartrain, Kentucky (reservoir)

Longest rivers: Mississippi, Arkansas, Ohio, Red

Vegetation: Needleleaf forest, broadleaf forest, mixed forest

Climate: Continental to mild, ranging from cool summers in the north to humid, subtropical conditions in the south

The Southeast

Tradition Meets Technology

The Southeast is a blend of old and new: old mountains and artificial lakes, single-crop farming and multi-crop fields, time-honored crafts and high-tech industry.

In the eastern part of the region, early settlers moved into Appalachian valleys, building independent communities. Their descendants preserve this mountain heritage in music and art. Cities grew up on the coast and along the fall line. Here, rivers drop from the highlands to the flat Atlantic Coastal Plain. Energy produced from the falling water powered early factories.

Cotton once ruled the fertile lands of the Deep South. In the early 1900s, after the destructive boll weevil ruined this crop, farmers began to plant a wider variety of plants and started fish farms on flooded fields. Rich with shellfish and petroleum, the Gulf of Mexico in the far south provides a living for many. In Florida, land once covered by water is now covered with orchards that are the source of the state's famous orange juice.

▲ **TRADITIONAL MUSIC-MAKING** *fills leisure hours in communities of the Appalachian Mountains. Tunes played there often reflect the settlers' Scottish and Irish roots.*

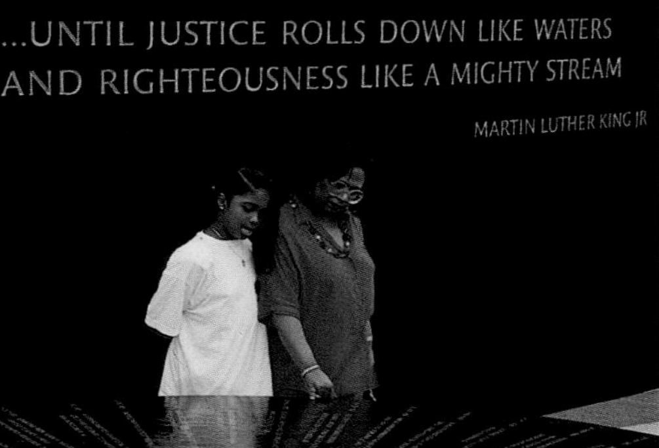

...UNTIL JUSTICE ROLLS DOWN LIKE WATERS
AND RIGHTEOUSNESS LIKE A MIGHTY STREAM
MARTIN LUTHER KING JR

◀ **POWERFUL WORDS** *on the Civil Rights Memorial in Montgomery, Alabama, echo a speech by Dr. Martin Luther King, Jr., civil rights crusader.*

▼ **FUN IN THE SUN** *takes many forms on Florida's Marco Island and in other resorts that line the Gulf of Mexico.*

▶ **RED AND READY,** *steamed crawfish form the basis of many Cajun dishes. Louisiana's diverse culture is reflected in its colorful, spicy cooking.*

◀ **THOROUGHBRED HORSES** *thunder from the starting gate at Churchill Downs, home of the famous Kentucky Derby, in Louisville. Horse breeding and racing is a valuable industry in many southeastern states.*

▲ **PURPLE HAZE** *covers the slopes of the Great Smoky Mountains, which straddle the border between North Carolina and Tennessee.*

◀ **SHOULDER-HIGH** *in white fluff, Alabama farmers inspect a field of cotton, still an important crop in the Southeast.*

▼ **MODERN AND BUSTLING** *Atlanta, Georgia, rose from the ashes of a city that burned to the ground during the Civil War. Atlanta today serves as a vital U.S. center of transportation, banking, and manufacturing.*

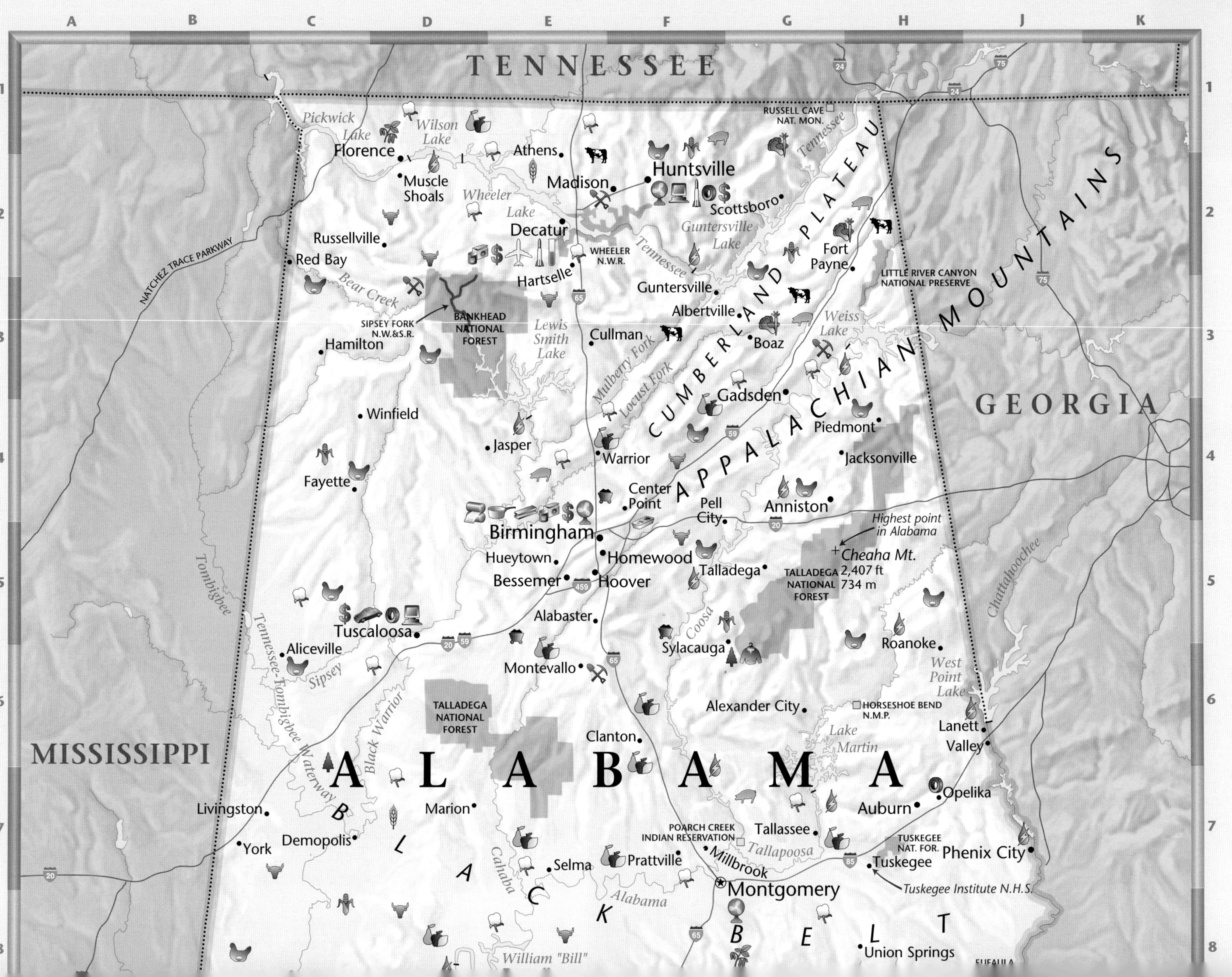

TENNESSEE
GEORGIA
MISSISSIPPI
ALABAMA
CUMBERLAND PLATEAU
APPALACHIAN MOUNTAINS
BLACK BELT
Huntsville
Madison
Athens
Decatur
Hartselle
Florence
Muscle Shoals
Russellville
Red Bay
Hamilton
Winfield
Fayette
Jasper
Cullman
Guntersville
Albertville
Boaz
Scottsboro
Fort Payne
Gadsden
Piedmont
Jacksonville
Anniston
Talladega
Sylacauga
Pell City
Center Point
Warrior
Birmingham
Homewood
Hoover
Hueytown
Bessemer
Alabaster
Montevallo
Clanton
Tuscaloosa
Aliceville
Marion
Selma
Demopolis
Livingston
York
Prattville
Millbrook
Montgomery
Tallassee
Alexander City
Roanoke
Lanett
Valley
Opelika
Auburn
Phenix City
Tuskegee
Union Springs
Highest point in Alabama
Cheaha Mt. 2,407 ft 734 m
RUSSELL CAVE NAT. MON.
LITTLE RIVER CANYON NATIONAL PRESERVE
WHEELER N.W.R.
BANKHEAD NATIONAL FOREST
SIPSEY FORK N.W.&S.R.
TALLADEGA NATIONAL FOREST
HORSESHOE BEND N.M.P.
TUSKEGEE NAT. FOR.
Tuskegee Institute N.H.S.
POARCH CREEK INDIAN RESERVATION
NATCHEZ TRACE PARKWAY
Tennessee
Pickwick Lake
Wilson Lake
Wheeler Lake
Guntersville Lake
Lewis Smith Lake
Weiss Lake
West Point Lake
Lake Martin
Bear Creek
Mulberry Fork
Locust Fork
Coosa
Tallapoosa
Alabama
Cahaba
Black Warrior
Sipsey
Tennessee-Tombigbee Waterway
Tombigbee
Chattahoochee
William "Bill"

Heart of Dixie

Alabama

Just like a karate expert, the state of Alabama has a black belt. Alabama's belt is a broad strip of dark, fertile soil in the state's center where farmers grow cotton, peanuts, soybeans, and corn. Two-thirds of the state is forested, providing wood for paper and other wood products that form one of the state's most profitable industries.

Alabama was one of the first southern states to industrialize. Iron ore, coal, and limestone mined from the ridges of the Appalachian Mountains made Birmingham a steelmaking center. High-tech business has a home in Huntsville, the headquarters of the state's space industry. Here, Saturn rockets and many other advances in spaceflight were developed.

Alabama products travel through the state on its many navigable rivers. The Tennessee-Tombigbee Waterway, which connects the Tennessee and Tombigbee river systems, has increased the importance of Mobile. Goods from all over the East can reach this port city. Deep shipping lanes allow oceangoing ships to dock in Mobile's waters, giving the city international connections.

Area: 52,419 sq mi (135,765 sq km)

Population: 4,501,000

Capital: Montgomery, pop. 201,400

Largest city: Birmingham, pop. 239,400

Industry: retail and wholesale trade, services, government, finance, insurance, real estate, transportation, construction, electrical equipment

Agriculture: poultry, forest products, cattle, nursery stock, cotton, eggs, peanuts, soybeans

Statehood: December 14, 1819; 22nd state

Nickname: Heart of Dixie

More about Alabama

- *The town of Enterprise erected a monument to the boll weevil, a cotton-destroying insect, because the weevil's attack on cotton early in the 20th century forced farmers to grow new kinds of crops.*
- *George Washington Carver, an agricultural scientist, discovered 300 uses for the peanut and 100 uses for the sweet potato while working at the Tuskegee Institute.*
- *The building of the Tenn-Tom waterway moved more earth than the excavation of the Panama Canal.*
- *Montgomery resident Rosa Parks sparked a boycott of the bus system when she was forcibly removed from a bus after refusing to give her seat to a white person. The boycott became a major event in the civil rights movement.*
- *Mobile shares the tradition of Mardi Gras, a pre-Lenten festival, with New Orleans.*

Northern Flicker

Camellia

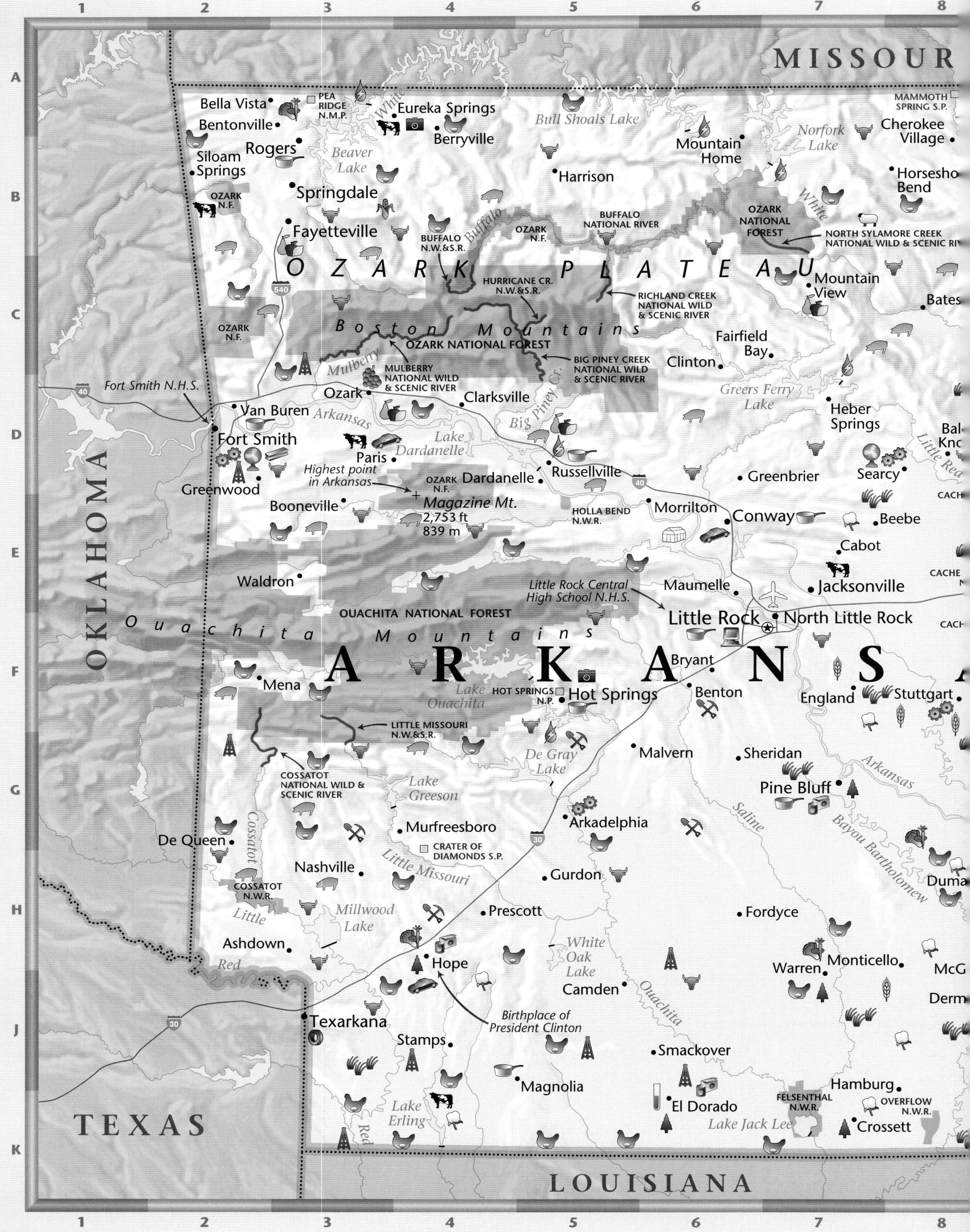
MISSOURI
OKLAHOMA
TEXAS
LOUISIANA
ARKANSAS
OZARK PLATEAU
Boston Mountains
Ouachita Mountains
OUACHITA NATIONAL FOREST
OZARK NATIONAL FOREST
OZARK N.F.
Bella Vista
Bentonville
Rogers
Siloam Springs
Springdale
Fayetteville
PEA RIDGE N.M.P.
Eureka Springs
Berryville
Beaver Lake
Bull Shoals Lake
Harrison
Mountain Home
Norfork Lake
MAMMOTH SPRING S.P.
Cherokee Village
Horseshoe Bend
BUFFALO NATIONAL RIVER
BUFFALO N.W.&S.R.
HURRICANE CR. N.W.&S.R.
RICHLAND CREEK NATIONAL WILD & SCENIC RIVER
OZARK NATIONAL FOREST
NORTH SYLAMORE CREEK NATIONAL WILD & SCENIC RIVER
Mountain View
Batesville
Fairfield Bay
Clinton
Greers Ferry Lake
Heber Springs
MULBERRY NATIONAL WILD & SCENIC RIVER
BIG PINEY CREEK NATIONAL WILD & SCENIC RIVER
Fort Smith N.H.S.
Van Buren
Fort Smith
Ozark
Clarksville
Lake Dardanelle
Paris
Highest point in Arkansas
Magazine Mt. 2,753 ft 839 m
Dardanelle
Russellville
Greenwood
Booneville
HOLLA BEND N.W.R.
Morrilton
Conway
Greenbrier
Searcy
Beebe
Cabot
Jacksonville
Waldron
Maumelle
Little Rock Central High School N.H.S.
Little Rock
North Little Rock
Bryant
Benton
Mena
Lake Ouachita
HOT SPRINGS N.P.
Hot Springs
LITTLE MISSOURI N.W.&S.R.
COSSATOT NATIONAL WILD & SCENIC RIVER
De Gray Lake
Malvern
Sheridan
England
Stuttgart
Pine Bluff
Lake Greeson
Murfreesboro
CRATER OF DIAMONDS S.P.
Arkadelphia
De Queen
Nashville
Gurdon
COSSATOT N.W.R.
Millwood Lake
Prescott
Fordyce
Ashdown
Hope
White Oak Lake
Camden
Warren
Monticello
Birthplace of President Clinton
Texarkana
Stamps
Smackover
Magnolia
El Dorado
FELSENTHAL N.W.R.
Hamburg
OVERFLOW N.W.R.
Crossett
Lake Erling
Lake Jack Lee
Arkansas
Ouachita
Saline
Bayou Bartholomew
Little Missouri
Red
Little
Cossatot
Mulberry
Big Piney Cr.
Buffalo
White
Little Red
40
540
30
1 2 3 4 5 6 7 8
A B C D E F G H J K

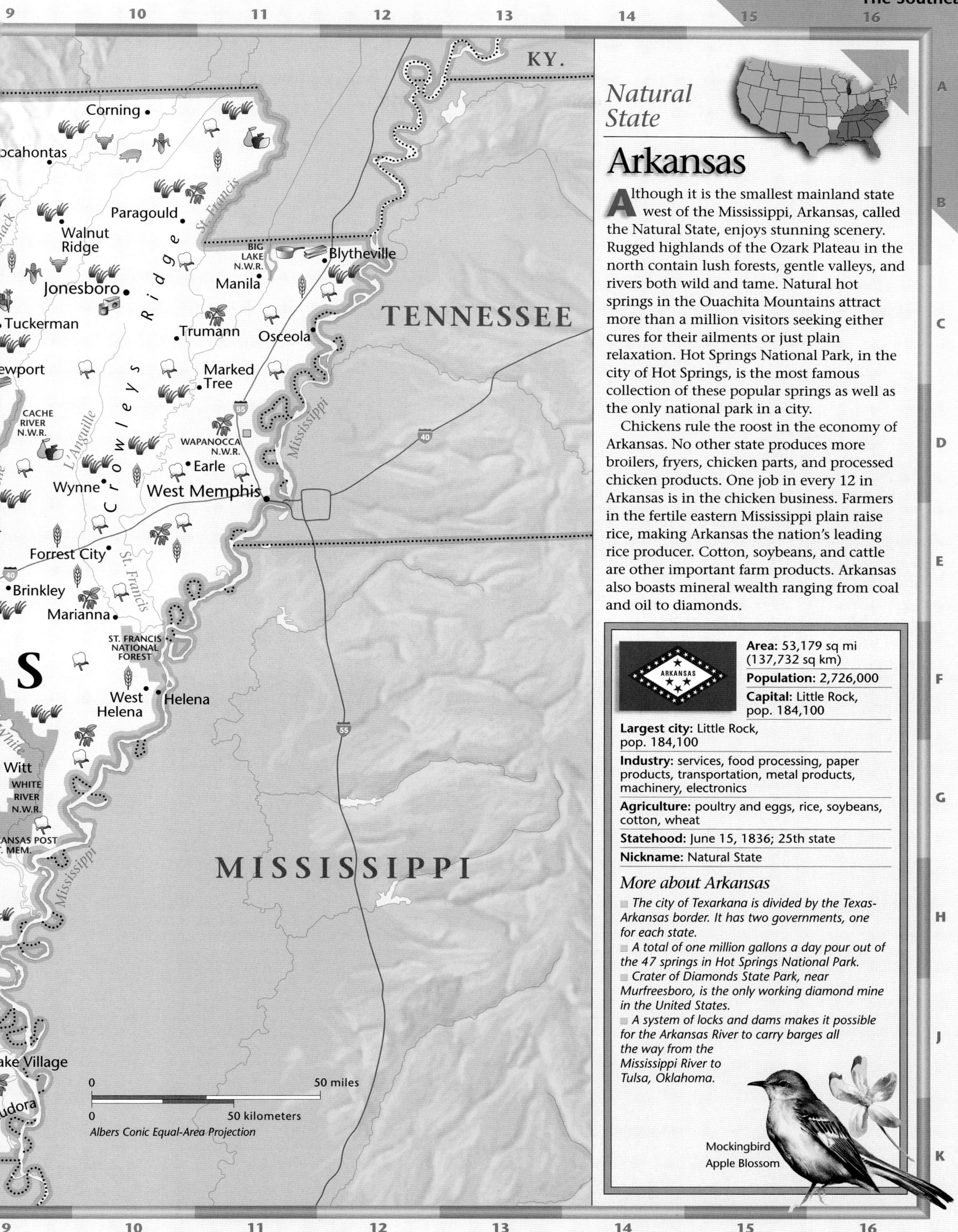

Natural State

Arkansas

Although it is the smallest mainland state west of the Mississippi, Arkansas, called the Natural State, enjoys stunning scenery. Rugged highlands of the Ozark Plateau in the north contain lush forests, gentle valleys, and rivers both wild and tame. Natural hot springs in the Ouachita Mountains attract more than a million visitors seeking either cures for their ailments or just plain relaxation. Hot Springs National Park, in the city of Hot Springs, is the most famous collection of these popular springs as well as the only national park in a city.

Chickens rule the roost in the economy of Arkansas. No other state produces more broilers, fryers, chicken parts, and processed chicken products. One job in every 12 in Arkansas is in the chicken business. Farmers in the fertile eastern Mississippi plain raise rice, making Arkansas the nation's leading rice producer. Cotton, soybeans, and cattle are other important farm products. Arkansas also boasts mineral wealth ranging from coal and oil to diamonds.

ARKANSAS

Area: 53,179 sq mi (137,732 sq km)

Population: 2,726,000

Capital: Little Rock, pop. 184,100

Largest city: Little Rock, pop. 184,100

Industry: services, food processing, paper products, transportation, metal products, machinery, electronics

Agriculture: poultry and eggs, rice, soybeans, cotton, wheat

Statehood: June 15, 1836; 25th state

Nickname: Natural State

More about Arkansas

- *The city of Texarkana is divided by the Texas-Arkansas border. It has two governments, one for each state.*
- *A total of one million gallons a day pour out of the 47 springs in Hot Springs National Park.*
- *Crater of Diamonds State Park, near Murfreesboro, is the only working diamond mine in the United States.*
- *A system of locks and dams makes it possible for the Arkansas River to carry barges all the way from the Mississippi River to Tulsa, Oklahoma.*

ALABAMA
MISSISSIPPI
LOUISIANA
GEO
POARCH CREEK I.R.
Highest point in Florida
Britton Hill
345 ft
105 m
Crestview
Marianna
Lake Seminole
Perdido
Choctawhatchee
Apalachicola
Ochlockonee
Niceville
Pensacola
Fort Walton Beach
Fort Pickens
GULF ISLANDS NATIONAL SEASHORE
Panama City
Tallahassee
APALACHICOLA NATIONAL FOREST
ST. MARKS N.W.R.
Perry
Intracoastal Waterway
FLO
ST. VINCENT N.W.R.
GULF OF MEXICO
0
100 miles
0
100 kilometers
Albers Conic Equal-Area Projection

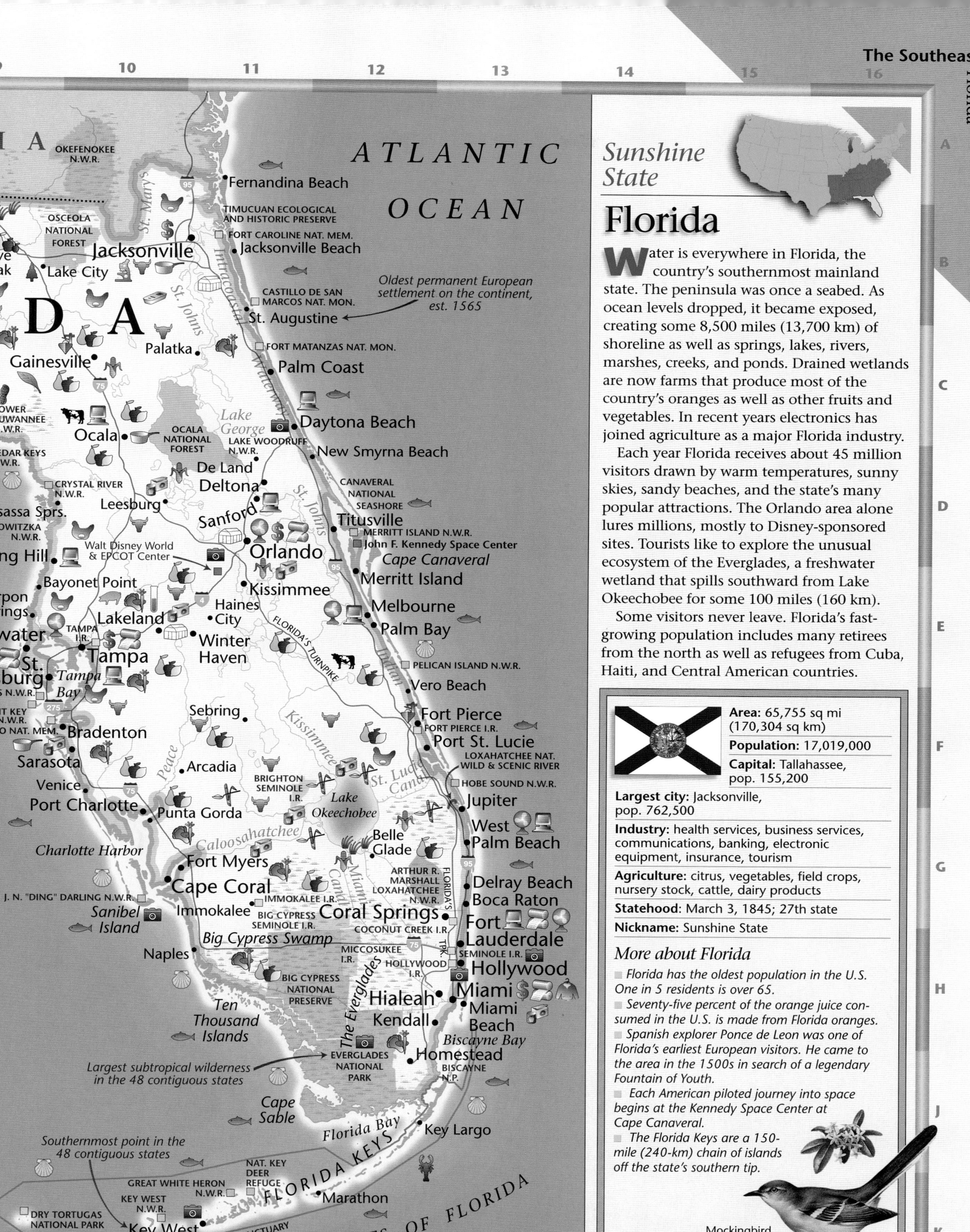

Sunshine State

Florida

Water is everywhere in Florida, the country's southernmost mainland state. The peninsula was once a seabed. As ocean levels dropped, it became exposed, creating some 8,500 miles (13,700 km) of shoreline as well as springs, lakes, rivers, marshes, creeks, and ponds. Drained wetlands are now farms that produce most of the country's oranges as well as other fruits and vegetables. In recent years electronics has joined agriculture as a major Florida industry.

Each year Florida receives about 45 million visitors drawn by warm temperatures, sunny skies, sandy beaches, and the state's many popular attractions. The Orlando area alone lures millions, mostly to Disney-sponsored sites. Tourists like to explore the unusual ecosystem of the Everglades, a freshwater wetland that spills southward from Lake Okeechobee for some 100 miles (160 km).

Some visitors never leave. Florida's fast-growing population includes many retirees from the north as well as refugees from Cuba, Haiti, and Central American countries.

Area: 65,755 sq mi (170,304 sq km)

Population: 17,019,000

Capital: Tallahassee, pop. 155,200

Largest city: Jacksonville, pop. 762,500

Industry: health services, business services, communications, banking, electronic equipment, insurance, tourism

Agriculture: citrus, vegetables, field crops, nursery stock, cattle, dairy products

Statehood: March 3, 1845; 27th state

Nickname: Sunshine State

More about Florida

- *Florida has the oldest population in the U.S. One in 5 residents is over 65.*
- *Seventy-five percent of the orange juice consumed in the U.S. is made from Florida oranges.*
- *Spanish explorer Ponce de Leon was one of Florida's earliest European visitors. He came to the area in the 1500s in search of a legendary Fountain of Youth.*
- *Each American piloted journey into space begins at the Kennedy Space Center at Cape Canaveral.*
- *The Florida Keys are a 150-mile (240-km) chain of islands off the state's southern tip.*

Mockingbird
Orange Blossom

TENNESSEE
NORTH CAROLINA
SOUTH CAROLINA
GEORGIA
ALABAMA
APPALACHIAN MOUNTAINS
BLUE RIDGE
APPALACHIAN NATIONAL SCENIC TRAIL
Brasstown Bald
4,784 ft
1,458 m
Highest point in Georgia
Rabun Gap
CHATTOOGA NATIONAL WILD & SCENIC RIVER
CHICKAMAUGA AND CHATTANOOGA N.M.P.
CHATTAHOOCHEE NATIONAL FOREST
CHATTAHOOCHEE NATIONAL FOREST
NEW ECHOTA S.H.S.
Springer Mt.
3,782 ft
1,153 m
KENNESAW MOUNTAIN N.B.P.
CHATTAHOOCHEE RIVER N.R.A.
Martin Luther King, Jr. N.H.S.
Stone Mountain
OCONEE N.F.
OCONEE NATIONAL FOREST
PIEDMONT N.W.R.
PIEDMONT N.W.R.
OCMULGEE NATIONAL MONUMENT
ANDERSONVILLE N.H.S.
JIMMY CARTER N.H.S.
President Carter's birthplace
SAVANNAH N.W.R.
FORT PULASKI NATIONAL MONUMENT
LaFayette
Dalton
Calhoun
Rome
Dahlonega
Toccoa
Gainesville
Hartwell
Elberton
Roswell
Marietta
Smyrna
Sandy Springs
Atlanta
East Point
Athens
Monroe
Washington
Carrollton
Covington
Peachtree City
Newnan
Griffin
Eatonton
Milledgeville
Thomson
Evans
Augusta
La Grange
Thomaston
Sandersville
Waynesboro
Millen
Macon
Warner Robins
Perry
Dublin
Swainsboro
Statesboro
Columbus
Vidalia
Eastman
Savannah
Coosawattee
Oostanaula
Etowah
Coosa
Chattahoochee
Chattooga
Tugaloo
Savannah
Broad
Flint
Ogeechee
Ohoop
Canooche
Ocon
Lake Sidney Lanier
Allatoona Lake
Hartwell L.
Richard B. Russell Lake
J. Strom Thurmond Reservoir
Lake Oconee
Lake Sinclair
West Point Lake
Lake Harding
Lake Oliver

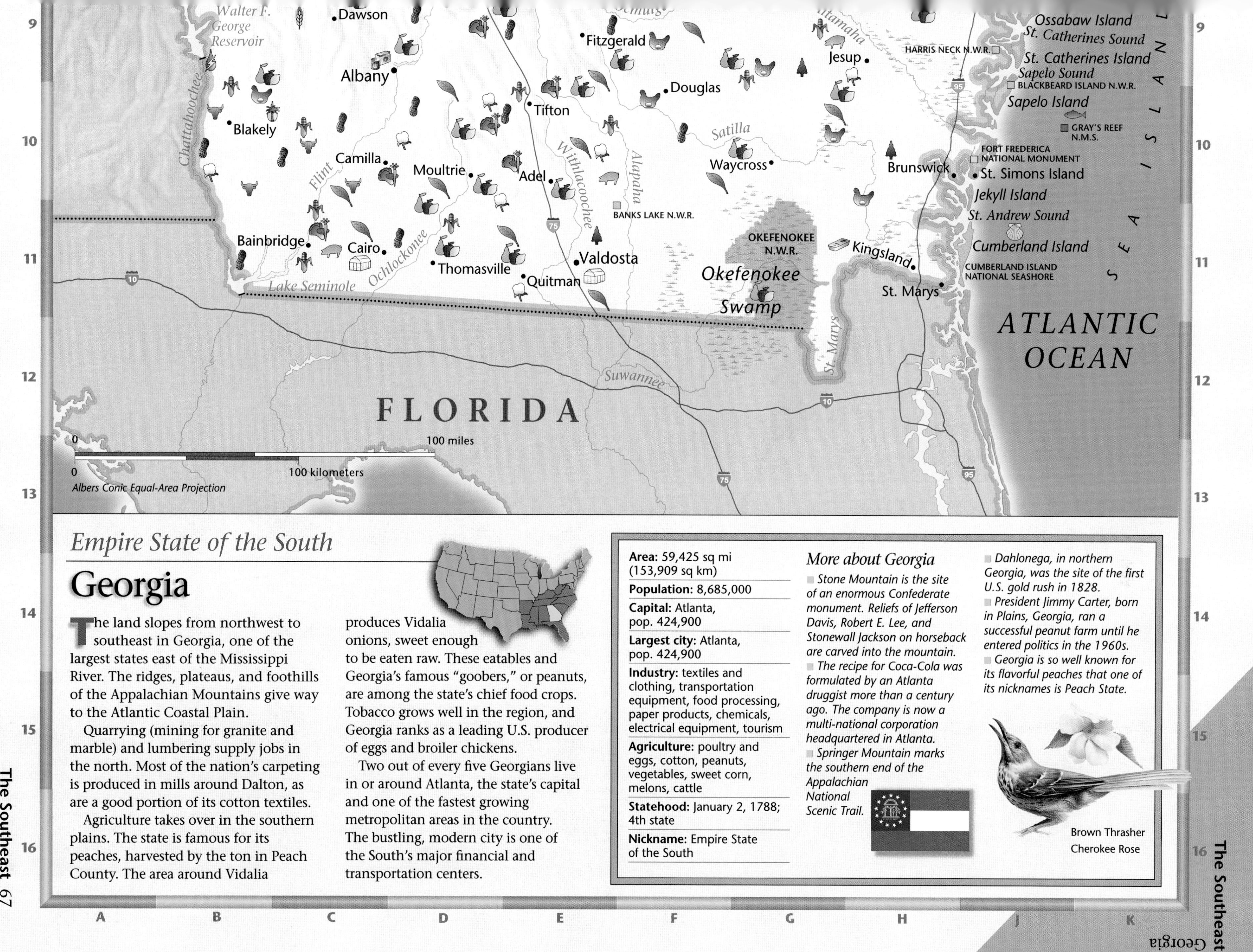

Empire State of the South

Georgia

The land slopes from northwest to southeast in Georgia, one of the largest states east of the Mississippi River. The ridges, plateaus, and foothills of the Appalachian Mountains give way to the Atlantic Coastal Plain.

Quarrying (mining for granite and marble) and lumbering supply jobs in the north. Most of the nation's carpeting is produced in mills around Dalton, as are a good portion of its cotton textiles.

Agriculture takes over in the southern plains. The state is famous for its peaches, harvested by the ton in Peach County. The area around Vidalia produces Vidalia onions, sweet enough to be eaten raw. These eatables and Georgia's famous "goobers," or peanuts, are among the state's chief food crops. Tobacco grows well in the region, and Georgia ranks as a leading U.S. producer of eggs and broiler chickens.

Two out of every five Georgians live in or around Atlanta, the state's capital and one of the fastest growing metropolitan areas in the country. The bustling, modern city is one of the South's major financial and transportation centers.

Area: 59,425 sq mi (153,909 sq km)

Population: 8,685,000

Capital: Atlanta, pop. 424,900

Largest city: Atlanta, pop. 424,900

Industry: textiles and clothing, transportation equipment, food processing, paper products, chemicals, electrical equipment, tourism

Agriculture: poultry and eggs, cotton, peanuts, vegetables, sweet corn, melons, cattle

Statehood: January 2, 1788; 4th state

Nickname: Empire State of the South

More about Georgia

- *Stone Mountain is the site of an enormous Confederate monument. Reliefs of Jefferson Davis, Robert E. Lee, and Stonewall Jackson on horseback are carved into the mountain.*
- *The recipe for Coca-Cola was formulated by an Atlanta druggist more than a century ago. The company is now a multi-national corporation headquartered in Atlanta.*
- *Springer Mountain marks the southern end of the Appalachian National Scenic Trail.*
- *Dahlonega, in northern Georgia, was the site of the first U.S. gold rush in 1828.*
- *President Jimmy Carter, born in Plains, Georgia, ran a successful peanut farm until he entered politics in the 1960s.*
- *Georgia is so well known for its flavorful peaches that one of its nicknames is Peach State.*

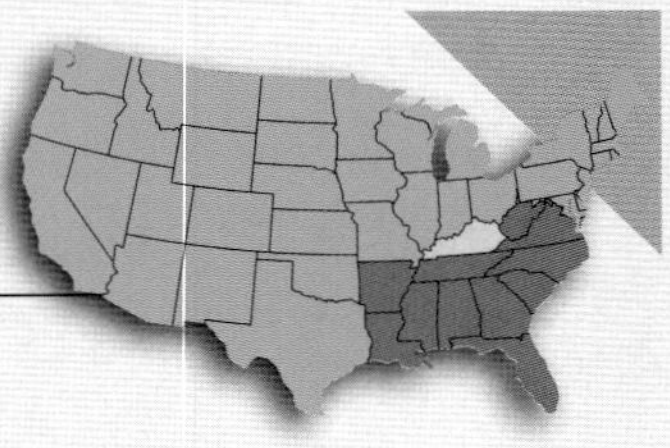

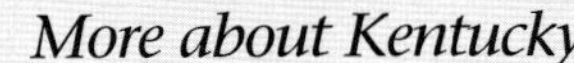

Bluegrass State

Kentucky

Like other professional athletes, Kentucky thoroughbred horses often bring in more than $1 million apiece. The valuable animals grow up on the rolling pastures of the Bluegrass region where underground limestone makes the grass rich in bone-strengthening lime and calcium. Each year the city of Louisville shows off the speed of these horses when it hosts the famous Kentucky Derby horse race. Kentucky's fertile soil also helps farmers raise cattle and grow light-bodied burley tobacco, corn, and soybeans.

In the east lie the Appalachian Mountains and the Cumberland Plateau, with their heavily forested ridges and peaks, fast rivers, and narrow valleys. Scotch-Irish people settled these lands, followed by southern and eastern European immigrants who mined the soft bituminous coal found in this region and the western part of the state.

Rivers lace the interior of the state, too, and one—the Ohio—forms its northern boundary. Altogether, Kentucky has more than a thousand miles of rivers.

Area: 40,409 sq mi (104,659 sq km)

Population: 4,118,000

Capital: Frankfort, pop. 27,700

Largest city: Louisville (metro), pop. 693,600

Industry: manufacturing, services, government, finance, insurance, real estate, retail trade, transportation, wholesale trade, construction, mining

Agriculture: tobacco, horses, cattle, corn, dairy products

Statehood: June 1, 1792; 15th state

Nickname: Bluegrass State

Cardinal
Goldenrod

More about Kentucky

- *Kentucky bluegrass is green not blue. It gets its name from the tiny bluish flowers that bloom briefly each May.*
- *U.S. President Abraham Lincoln and Confederate President Jefferson Davis were both born in Kentucky less than 100 miles (160 km) apart.*
- *Fort Knox contains more than $6 billion in gold bullion, deposited there by the U.S. government and representing nearly all the gold belonging to the country.*
- *In 1775 Daniel Boone led pioneers from Tennessee into Kentucky via the Cumberland Gap. They named their town Boonesborough.*

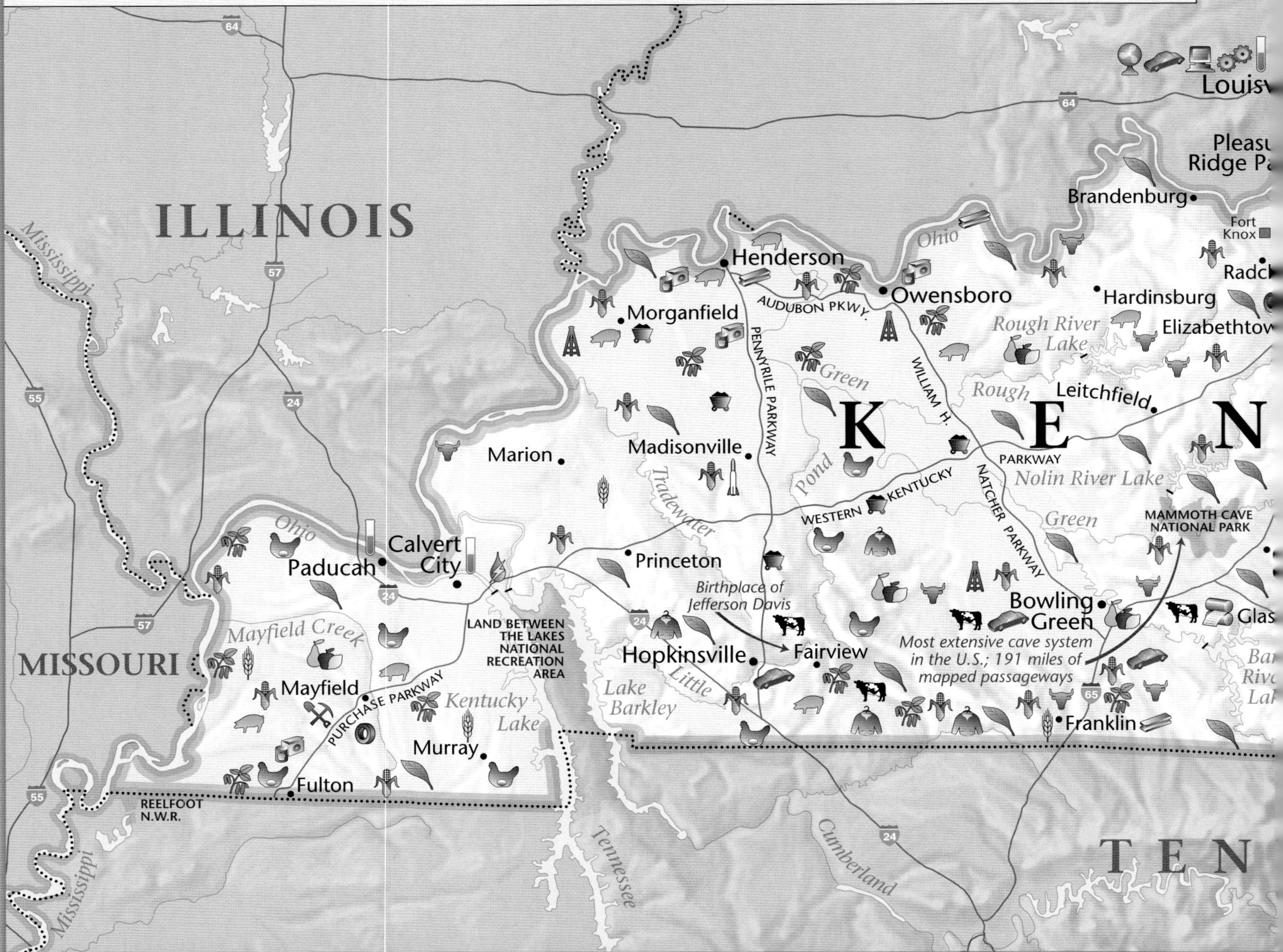

ILLINOIS
MISSOURI
KEN
TEN
Louisv
Pleasu Ridge Pa
Brandenburg
Fort Knox
Radc
Hardinsburg
Elizabethtow
Henderson
Owensboro
Morganfield
AUDUBON PKWY.
PENNYRILE PARKWAY
WILLIAM H. NATCHER PARKWAY
WESTERN KENTUCKY PARKWAY
Rough River Lake
Rough
Leitchfield
Green
Pond
Madisonville
Marion
Tradewater
Nolin River Lake
MAMMOTH CAVE NATIONAL PARK
Ohio
Paducah
Calvert City
Princeton
Birthplace of Jefferson Davis
Fairview
Hopkinsville
Bowling Green
Most extensive cave system in the U.S.; 191 miles of mapped passageways
Glas
Mayfield Creek
Mayfield
PURCHASE PARKWAY
LAND BETWEEN THE LAKES NATIONAL RECREATION AREA
Kentucky Lake
Lake Barkley
Little
Murray
Fulton
Franklin
REELFOOT N.W.R.
Mississippi
Tennessee
Cumberland
64
57
55
24
65

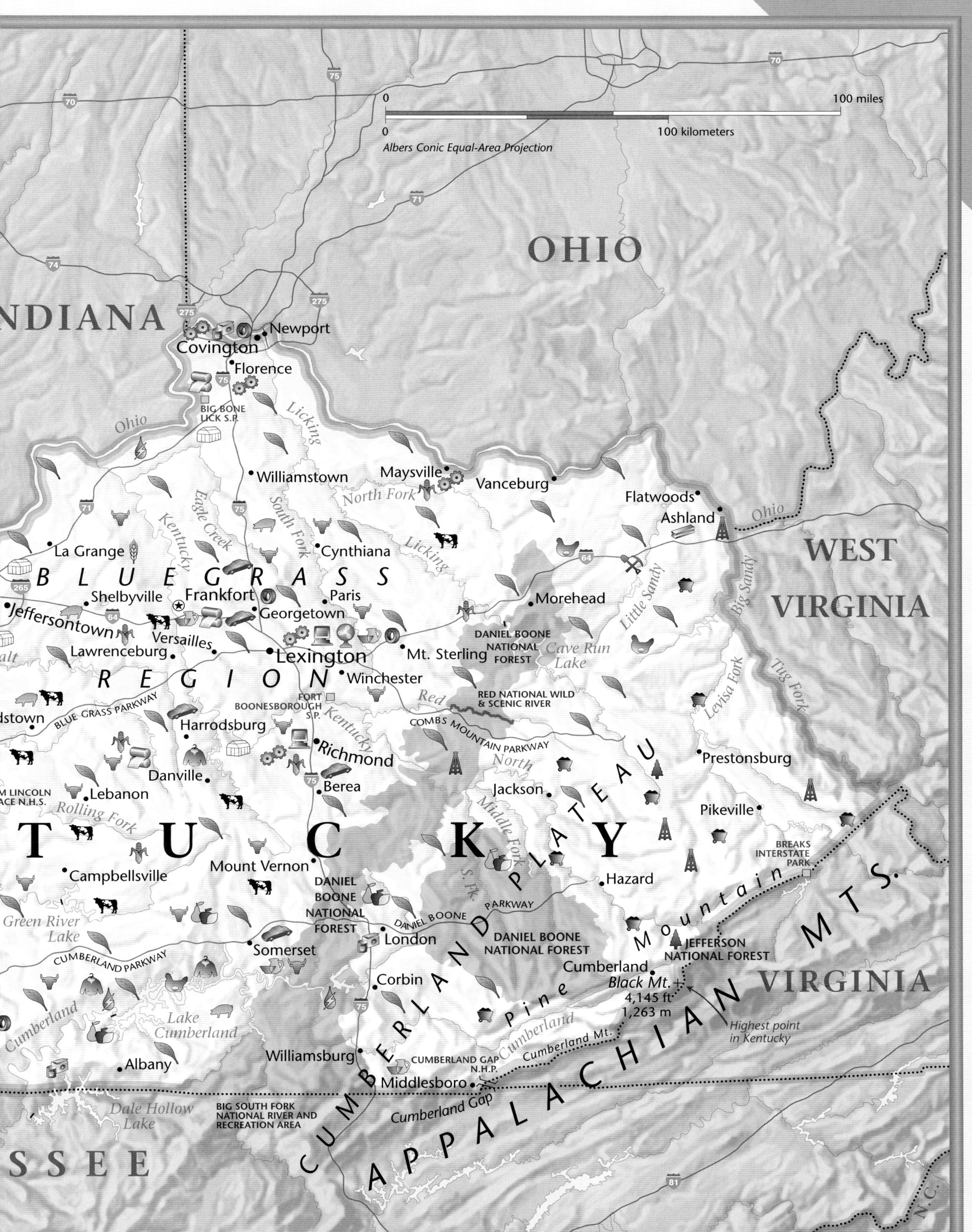
0
100 miles
0
100 kilometers
Albers Conic Equal-Area Projection
OHIO
NDIANA
WEST VIRGINIA
VIRGINIA
SSEE
N.C.
Newport
Covington
Florence
BIG BONE LICK S.P.
Ohio
Licking
Williamstown
Maysville
Vanceburg
Flatwoods
Ashland
North Fork
Eagle Creek
South Fork
Kentucky
La Grange
Cynthiana
BLUEGRASS REGION
Shelbyville
Frankfort
Paris
Georgetown
Jeffersontown
Versailles
Lawrenceburg
Lexington
Mt. Sterling
Winchester
Morehead
DANIEL BOONE NATIONAL FOREST
Cave Run Lake
Little Sandy
Big Sandy
Levisa Fork
Tug Fork
Red
RED NATIONAL WILD & SCENIC RIVER
FORT BOONESBOROUGH S.P.
BLUE GRASS PARKWAY
COMBS MOUNTAIN PARKWAY
Harrodsburg
Richmond
Danville
Berea
Prestonsburg
Jackson
Pikeville
Lebanon
Rolling Fork
North
Middle Fork
S. Fk.
CUMBERLAND PLATEAU
KENTUCKY
BREAKS INTERSTATE PARK
Campbellsville
Mount Vernon
Hazard
DANIEL BOONE NATIONAL FOREST
DANIEL BOONE PARKWAY
Green River Lake
Somerset
London
CUMBERLAND PARKWAY
Pine Mountain
JEFFERSON NATIONAL FOREST
Cumberland
Black Mt.
4,145 ft
1,263 m
Highest point in Kentucky
APPALACHIAN MTS.
Corbin
Lake Cumberland
Cumberland
Williamsburg
CUMBERLAND GAP N.H.P.
Cumberland Mt.
Middlesboro
Albany
Cumberland Gap
Dale Hollow Lake
BIG SOUTH FORK NATIONAL RIVER AND RECREATION AREA
70
75
71
74
275
64
265
81

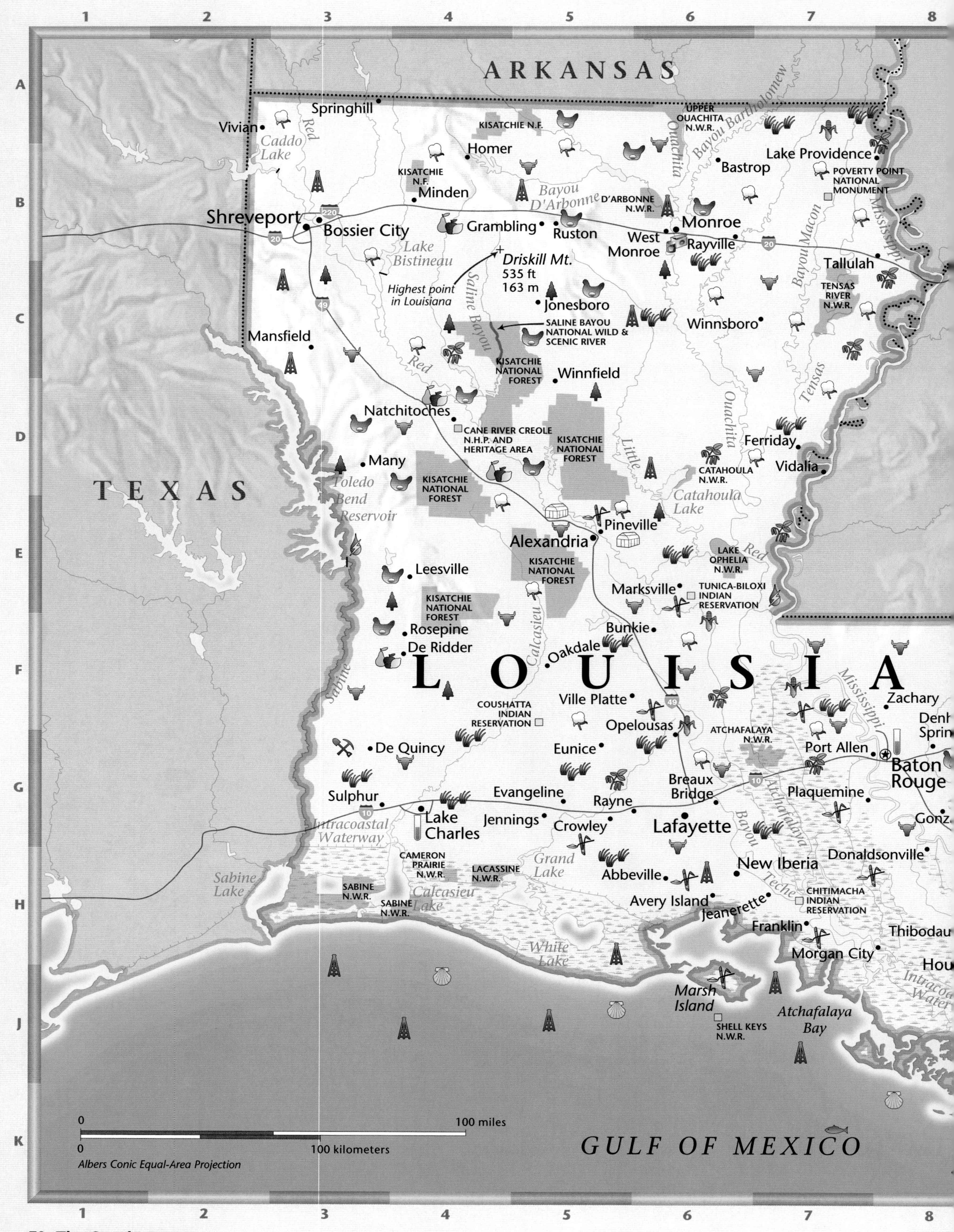
ARKANSAS
TEXAS
LOUISIANA
GULF OF MEXICO
Springhill
Vivian
Caddo Lake
KISATCHIE N.F.
Homer
Minden
Shreveport
Bossier City
Grambling
Ruston
Lake Bistineau
Driskill Mt.
535 ft
163 m
Highest point in Louisiana
Jonesboro
Mansfield
SALINE BAYOU NATIONAL WILD & SCENIC RIVER
KISATCHIE NATIONAL FOREST
Winnfield
Natchitoches
CANE RIVER CREOLE N.H.P. AND HERITAGE AREA
Many
Toledo Bend Reservoir
Alexandria
Pineville
Leesville
Rosepine
De Ridder
Oakdale
Bunkie
Marksville
TUNICA-BILOXI INDIAN RESERVATION
LAKE OPHELIA N.W.R.
Catahoula Lake
CATAHOULA N.W.R.
Ferriday
Vidalia
Winnsboro
Tallulah
TENSAS RIVER N.W.R.
Lake Providence
POVERTY POINT NATIONAL MONUMENT
Bastrop
UPPER OUACHITA N.W.R.
Bayou Bartholomew
Ouachita
Bayou D'Arbonne
D'ARBONNE N.W.R.
Monroe
West Monroe
Rayville
Bayou Macon
Mississippi
Tensas
Little
Red
Saline Bayou
Calcasieu
Sabine
COUSHATTA INDIAN RESERVATION
Ville Platte
Opelousas
Eunice
ATCHAFALAYA N.W.R.
Zachary
Port Allen
Baton Rouge
Plaquemine
De Quincy
Sulphur
Lake Charles
Evangeline
Jennings
Crowley
Rayne
Breaux Bridge
Lafayette
Intracoastal Waterway
CAMERON PRAIRIE N.W.R.
LACASSINE N.W.R.
Grand Lake
Abbeville
New Iberia
Donaldsonville
Avery Island
Jeanerette
CHITIMACHA INDIAN RESERVATION
Franklin
Morgan City
Thibodau
Hou
Gonz
Sabine Lake
SABINE N.W.R.
Calcasieu Lake
White Lake
Marsh Island
SHELL KEYS N.W.R.
Atchafalaya Bay
Bayou Teche
Atchafalaya
0
100 miles
0
100 kilometers
Albers Conic Equal-Area Projection

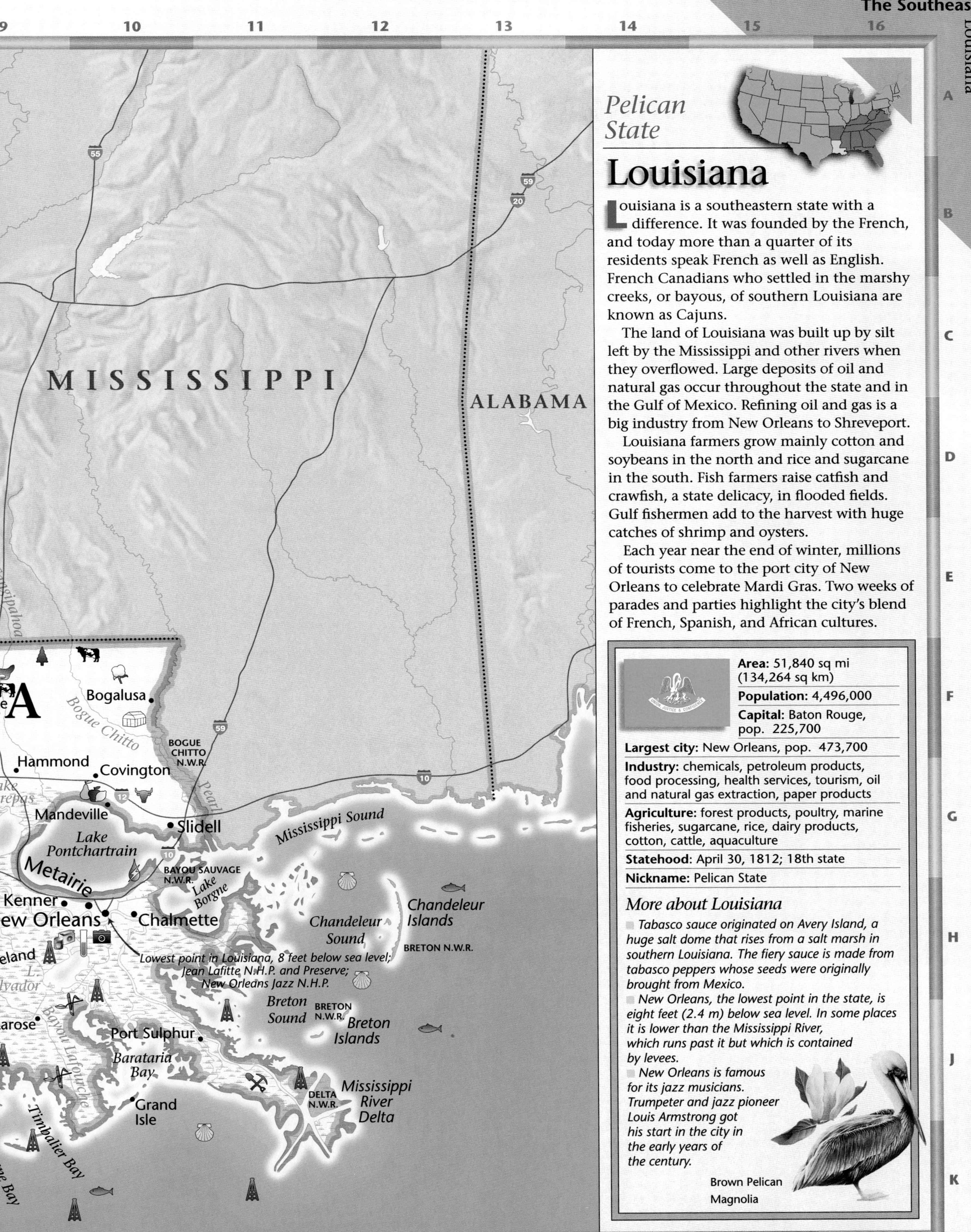

Pelican State

Louisiana

Louisiana is a southeastern state with a difference. It was founded by the French, and today more than a quarter of its residents speak French as well as English. French Canadians who settled in the marshy creeks, or bayous, of southern Louisiana are known as Cajuns.

The land of Louisiana was built up by silt left by the Mississippi and other rivers when they overflowed. Large deposits of oil and natural gas occur throughout the state and in the Gulf of Mexico. Refining oil and gas is a big industry from New Orleans to Shreveport.

Louisiana farmers grow mainly cotton and soybeans in the north and rice and sugarcane in the south. Fish farmers raise catfish and crawfish, a state delicacy, in flooded fields. Gulf fishermen add to the harvest with huge catches of shrimp and oysters.

Each year near the end of winter, millions of tourists come to the port city of New Orleans to celebrate Mardi Gras. Two weeks of parades and parties highlight the city's blend of French, Spanish, and African cultures.

Area: 51,840 sq mi (134,264 sq km)

Population: 4,496,000

Capital: Baton Rouge, pop. 225,700

Largest city: New Orleans, pop. 473,700

Industry: chemicals, petroleum products, food processing, health services, tourism, oil and natural gas extraction, paper products

Agriculture: forest products, poultry, marine fisheries, sugarcane, rice, dairy products, cotton, cattle, aquaculture

Statehood: April 30, 1812; 18th state

Nickname: Pelican State

More about Louisiana

- *Tabasco sauce originated on Avery Island, a huge salt dome that rises from a salt marsh in southern Louisiana. The fiery sauce is made from tabasco peppers whose seeds were originally brought from Mexico.*
- *New Orleans, the lowest point in the state, is eight feet (2.4 m) below sea level. In some places it is lower than the Mississippi River, which runs past it but which is contained by levees.*
- *New Orleans is famous for its jazz musicians. Trumpeter and jazz pioneer Louis Armstrong got his start in the city in the early years of the century.*

Brown Pelican
Magnolia

TENNESSEE
ARKANSAS
ALABAMA
MISSISSIPPI
Pickwick Lake
Tennessee
Highest point in Mississippi
Woodall Mt. 806 ft + 246 m
Iuka
Corinth
Southaven
Horn Lake
Arkabutla Lake
Holly Springs
HOLLY SPRINGS NATIONAL FOREST
Ripley
Booneville
Coldwater
Senatobia
Sardis Lake
Little Tallahatchie
New Albany
Baldwyn
BRICES CROSS ROADS N.B.S.
Tennessee-Tombigbee Waterway
Mississippi
Oxford
Batesville
Enid Lake
Yocona
Pontotoc
Tupelo
TUPELO N.B.
Fulton
Clarksdale
Water Valley
TALLAHATCHIE N.W.R.
Tallahatchie
Big Sunflower
HOLLY SPRINGS NATIONAL FOREST
TOMBIGBEE NATIONAL FOREST
Okolona
Amory
Shelby
Houston
Tombigbee
Grenada Lake
TALLAHATCHIE N.W.R.
Aberdeen
Cleveland
Yalobusha
Grenada
DAHOMEY N.W.R.
Ruleville
West Point
Greenwood
Winona
Columbus
Starkville
Leland
Indianola
Greenville
MATHEWS BRAKE N.W.R.
NATCHEZ TRACE PARKWAY
MORGAN BRAKE N.W.R.
Yazoo
NOXUBEE N.W.R.
TOMBIGBEE NATIONAL FOREST
Hollandale
Noxubee
Louisville
Kosciusko
YAZOO N.W.R.
HILLSIDE N.W.R.
Deer Creek
PANTHER SWAMP N.W.R.
Yazoo City
DELTA NATIONAL FOREST
Vaughan
MISSISSIPPI CHOCTAW I.R.
Philadelphia
Carthage
Canton
Pearl
Big Black
Mississippi Petrified Forest
Okatibbee Lake
Ross Barnett Reservoir
VICKSBURG N.M.P.
Ridgeland
Forest
Meridian
Vicksburg
Clinton
Pearl
Newton
Jackson
Brandon
BIENVILLE NATIONAL FOREST
NATCHEZ TRACE PARKWAY
Strong
Quitman
Tombigbee
20
55
59
40
30
A
B
C
D
E
F
G
H
J
K
1
2
3
4
5
6
7
8

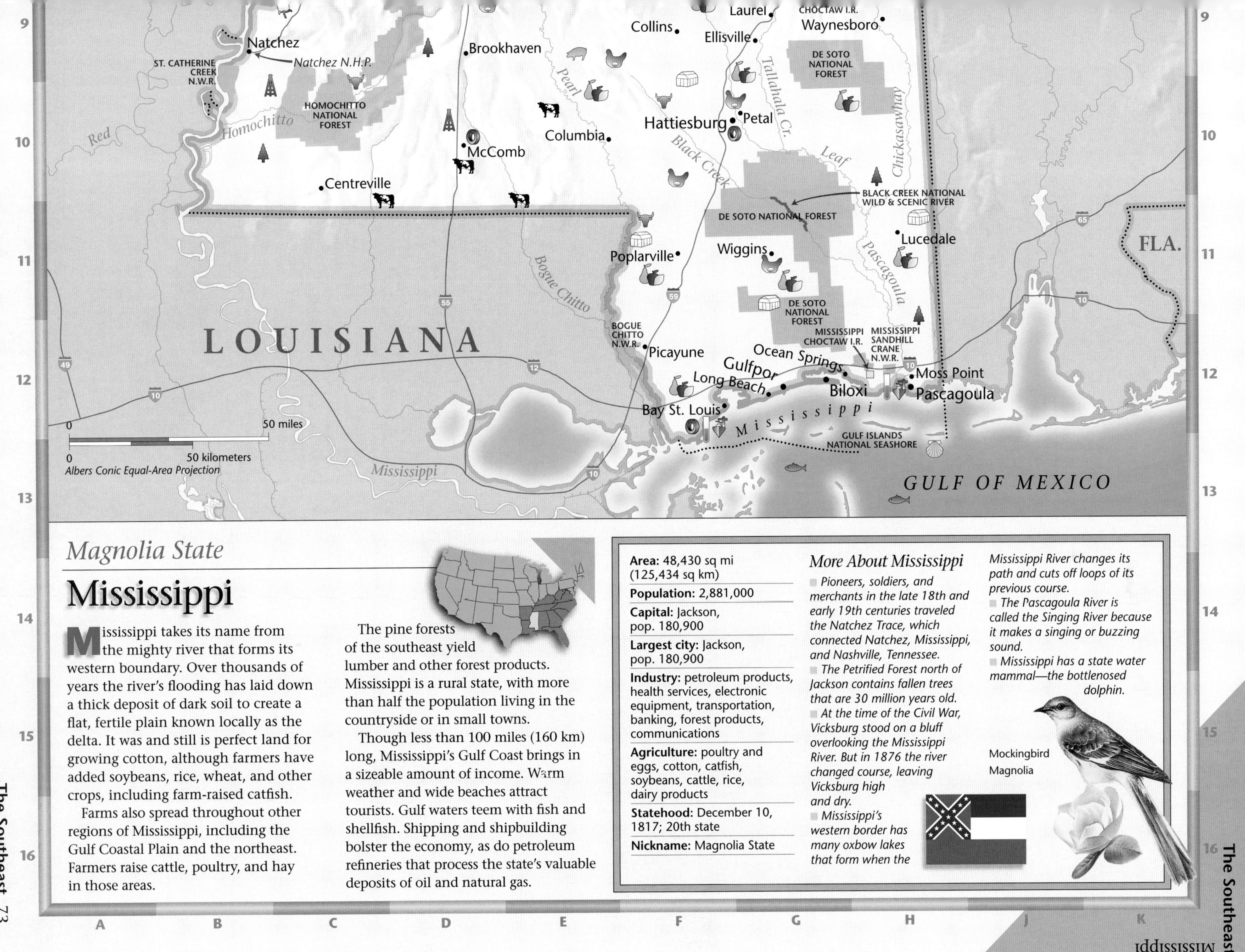

Magnolia State

Mississippi

Mississippi takes its name from the mighty river that forms its western boundary. Over thousands of years the river's flooding has laid down a thick deposit of dark soil to create a flat, fertile plain known locally as the delta. It was and still is perfect land for growing cotton, although farmers have added soybeans, rice, wheat, and other crops, including farm-raised catfish.

Farms also spread throughout other regions of Mississippi, including the Gulf Coastal Plain and the northeast. Farmers raise cattle, poultry, and hay in those areas.

The pine forests of the southeast yield lumber and other forest products. Mississippi is a rural state, with more than half the population living in the countryside or in small towns.

Though less than 100 miles (160 km) long, Mississippi's Gulf Coast brings in a sizeable amount of income. Warm weather and wide beaches attract tourists. Gulf waters teem with fish and shellfish. Shipping and shipbuilding bolster the economy, as do petroleum refineries that process the state's valuable deposits of oil and natural gas.

Area: 48,430 sq mi (125,434 sq km)

Population: 2,881,000

Capital: Jackson, pop. 180,900

Largest city: Jackson, pop. 180,900

Industry: petroleum products, health services, electronic equipment, transportation, banking, forest products, communications

Agriculture: poultry and eggs, cotton, catfish, soybeans, cattle, rice, dairy products

Statehood: December 10, 1817; 20th state

Nickname: Magnolia State

More About Mississippi

- *Pioneers, soldiers, and merchants in the late 18th and early 19th centuries traveled the Natchez Trace, which connected Natchez, Mississippi, and Nashville, Tennessee.*
- *The Petrified Forest north of Jackson contains fallen trees that are 30 million years old.*
- *At the time of the Civil War, Vicksburg stood on a bluff overlooking the Mississippi River. But in 1876 the river changed course, leaving Vicksburg high and dry.*
- *Mississippi's western border has many oxbow lakes that form when the Mississippi River changes its path and cuts off loops of its previous course.*
- *The Pascagoula River is called the Singing River because it makes a singing or buzzing sound.*
- *Mississippi has a state water mammal—the bottlenosed dolphin.*

Mockingbird
Magnolia

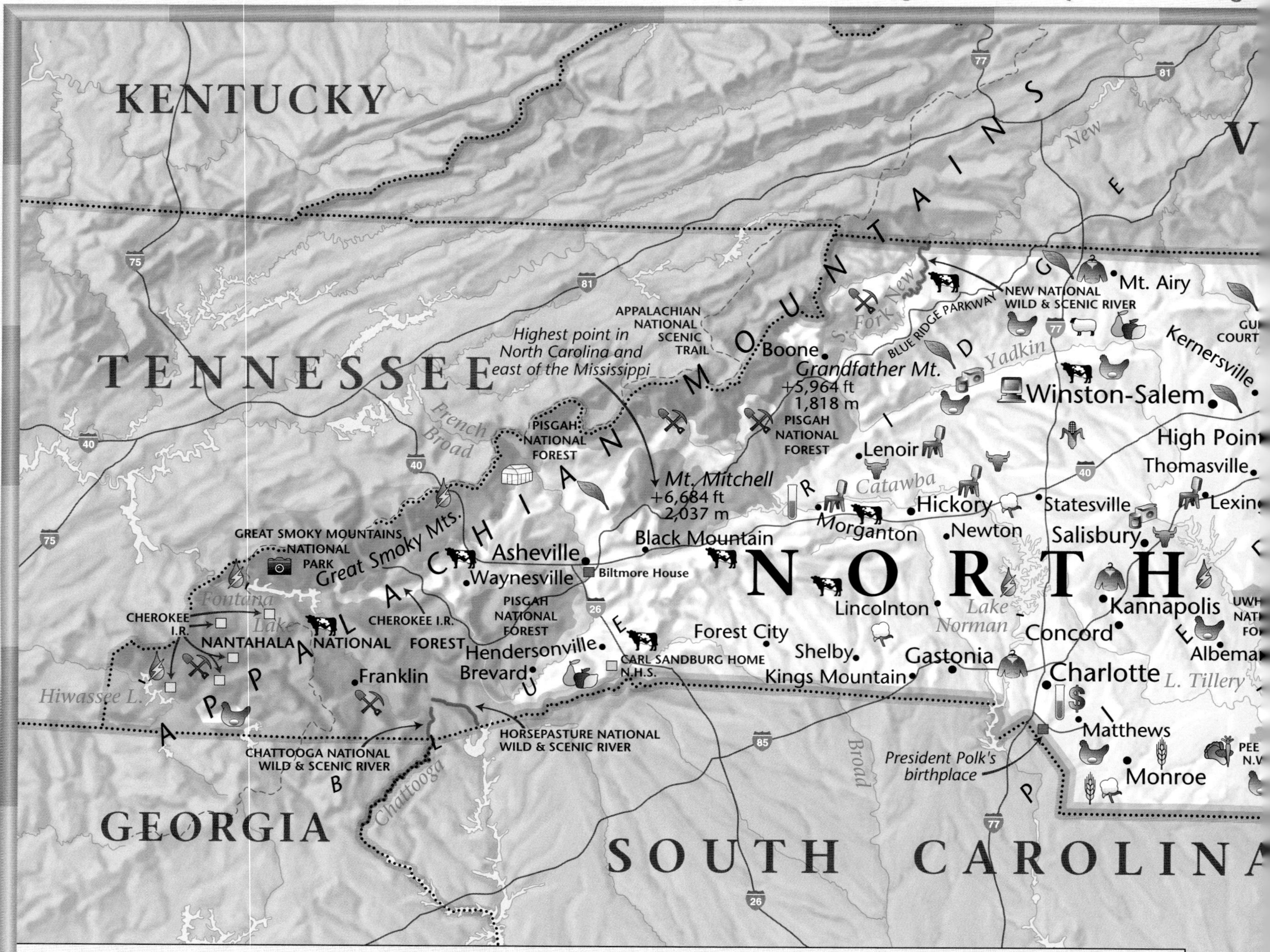

Tar Heel State

North Carolina

If you're sitting in a chair and wearing socks while you read this, there's a good chance that both the chair and the socks were made in North Carolina. North Carolina leads the country in making furniture and textiles.

Mountains belonging to the Appalachian chain rim the far western edge of the state. Most North Carolinians live in the Piedmont—the middle region where streams and reservoirs produce the electricity to run factories and mills. Three cities in the north-central part of the state—Raleigh, Durham, and Chapel Hill—form North Carolina's well-known Research Triangle. This area, which includes several strong universities, attracts researchers and businesses that specialize in electronics and high-tech medical research.

Eastern North Carolina lies on the Coastal Plain. Farmers here grow tobacco and corn and raise hogs. The shore is outlined by a string of narrow barrier islands, called the Outer Banks, that protect the mainland from gales and hurricanes that often hit the coast.

Area: 53,819 sq mi (139,389 sq km)

Population: 8,407,000

Capital: Raleigh, pop. 306,900

Largest city: Charlotte, pop. 580,600

Industry: real estate, health services, chemicals, tobacco products, finance, textiles

Agriculture: poultry, hogs, tobacco, nursery stock, turkeys, cotton, soybeans

Statehood: November 21, 1789; 12th state

Nickname: Tar Heel State

More about North Carolina

The Wright brothers made the first successful airplane flight (12 seconds) at Kitty Hawk in 1903.

Asheville is the site of Biltmore House, a 250-room mansion erected by railroad tycoon George W. Vanderbilt in the 1880s.

In the 1700s the pirate Blackbeard hid out on Okracoke Island, one of the islands in North Carolina's Outer Banks.

Grandfather Mountain, which looks like the profile of an old man, is the site of a yearly Highland festival, featuring Scottish music and games.

Old Salem, in Winston-Salem, is a restored village that shows the way of life of the Moravian people who settled the town in 1766.

Cardinal

Flowering Dogwood

VIRGINIA
NORTH CAROLINA
Reidsville
Roxboro
John H. Kerr Reservoir
Lake Gaston
Roanoke Rapids
Oxford
Henderson
President Andrew Johnson's birthplace
Burlington
Greensboro
Durham
Falls L.
Chapel Hill
B. Everett Jordan Lake
Cary
Raleigh
Garner
Rocky Mount
Tarboro
Williamston
Wilson
Greenville
Sanford
Smithfield
Goldsboro
Dunn
Southern Pines
Spring Lake
Kinston
Neuse
Fayetteville
Hope Mills
Clinton
Rockingham
Laurinburg
Lumberton
LUMBER NATIONAL WILD & SCENIC RIVER
Lumber
South
Cape Fear
Jacksonville
Whiteville
Lake Waccamaw
MOORES CREEK NATIONAL BATTLEFIELD
Wilmington
Wrightsville Beach
Green Swamp
Southport
Cape Fear
Waterway
Intracoastal
Long Bay
Little Pee Dee
Great Pee Dee
Onslow Bay
New Bern
Havelock
CROATAN NATIONAL FOREST
Morehead City
Cape Lookout
CAPE LOOKOUT NATIONAL SEASHORE
Core Sound
Raleigh Bay
CEDAR ISLAND N.W.R.
Neuse R.
Ocracoke Island
Cape Hatteras
Pamlico Sound
Outer Banks
Pamlico R.
Washington
SWANQUARTER N.W.R.
MATTAMUSKEET N.W.R.
POCOSIN LAKES N.W.R.
ROANOKE RIVER N.W.R.
Tar
Roanoke
Chowan
Ahoskie
Edenton
Albemarle Sound
Alligator R.
ALLIGATOR RIVER N.W.R.
Elizabeth City
GREAT DISMAL SWAMP N.W.R.
Great Dismal Swamp
MACKAY ISLAND N.W.R.
CURRITUCK N.W.R.
Currituck Sound
Kitty Hawk
WRIGHT BROTHERS NAT. MEM.
FORT RALEIGH N.H.S.
Roanoke Island
PEA ISLAND N.W.R.
Hatteras Island
CAPE HATTERAS NATIONAL SEASHORE
ATLANTIC OCEAN
0
100 miles
0
100 kilometers
Albers Conic Equal-Area Projection
9 10 11 12 13 14 15 16
A B C D E F G H J K
85
95
40

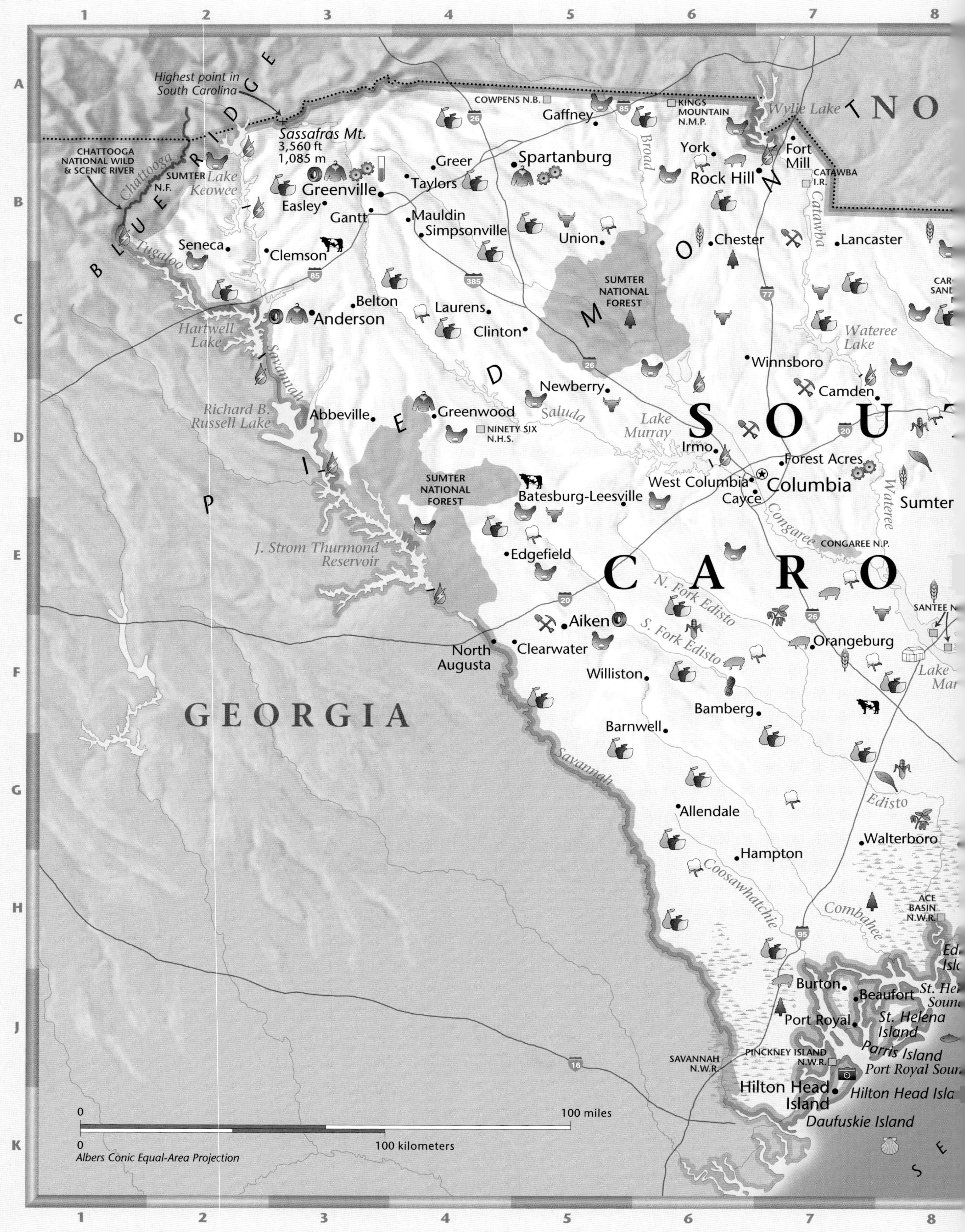

Highest point in South Carolina
Sassafras Mt.
3,560 ft
1,085 m
BLUE RIDGE
PIEDMONT
CHATTOOGA NATIONAL WILD & SCENIC RIVER
SUMTER N.F.
Lake Keowee
Greenville
Greer
Taylors
Spartanburg
Gaffney
COWPENS N.B.
KINGS MOUNTAIN N.M.P.
Wylie Lake
York
Rock Hill
Fort Mill
CATAWBA I.R.
Easley
Gantt
Mauldin
Simpsonville
Union
Chester
Lancaster
Seneca
Clemson
Belton
Anderson
Laurens
Clinton
SUMTER NATIONAL FOREST
Hartwell Lake
Wateree Lake
Winnsboro
Camden
Newberry
Abbeville
Greenwood
NINETY SIX N.H.S.
Richard B. Russell Lake
Saluda
Lake Murray
Irmo
SOUTH CAROLINA
Forest Acres
West Columbia
Columbia
Cayce
Sumter
Batesburg-Leesville
J. Strom Thurmond Reservoir
Edgefield
Congaree
CONGAREE N.P.
N. Fork Edisto
S. Fork Edisto
Aiken
Clearwater
North Augusta
Orangeburg
Williston
Bamberg
Barnwell
GEORGIA
Savannah
Allendale
Edisto
Walterboro
Hampton
Coosawhatchie
Combahee
ACE BASIN N.W.R.
Burton
Beaufort
Port Royal
St. Helena Island
Parris Island
Port Royal Sound
PINCKNEY ISLAND N.W.R.
SAVANNAH N.W.R.
Hilton Head Island
Daufuskie Island
Tugaloo
Chattooga
Broad
Catawba
Wateree
0
100 miles
0
100 kilometers
Albers Conic Equal-Area Projection

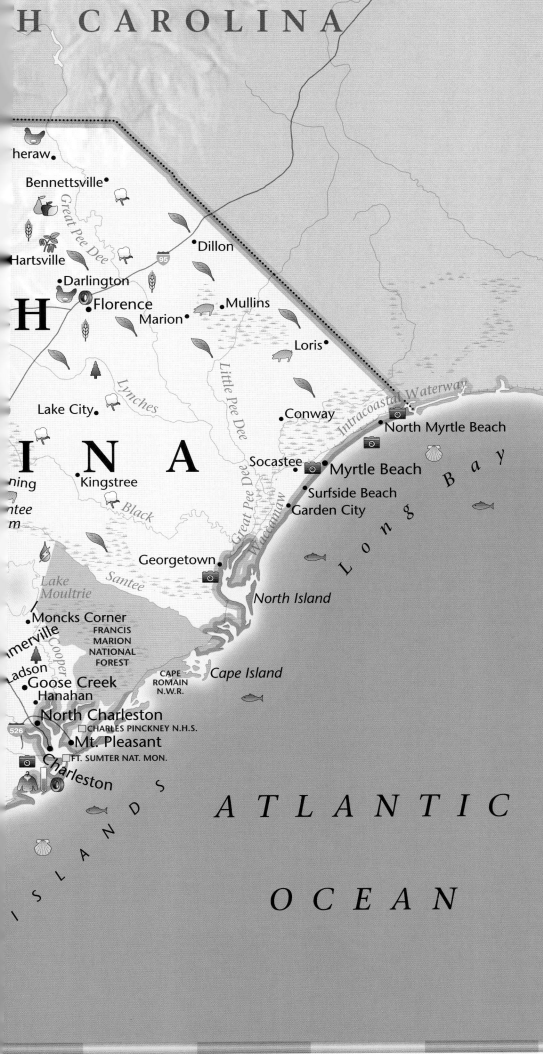

Palmetto State

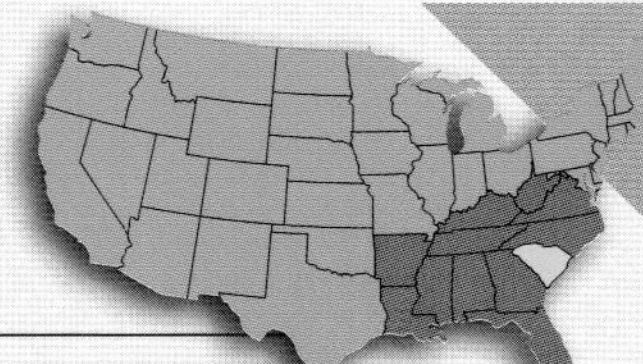

South Carolina

For one of the smallest states in the Southeast, South Carolina has had a big historical impact. In 1860 it was the first state to secede, or withdraw, from the Union. Charleston harbor was the site of the first shots of the Civil War when the Confederates fired on Fort Sumter in 1861.

Textiles and chemical manufacturing, including the making of dyes for cloth, are South Carolina's chief industries. The port city of Charleston, with its fine old houses and beautiful gardens, is a textile center.

The two-thirds of the state in the Atlantic Coastal Plain is called the Low Country. Farmers there grow cotton, tobacco, and soybeans. The rest of the state is known as Up Country and includes the Piedmont and the Blue Ridge Mountains. Swift Up Country rivers provide power for textile mills.

More than 200 years ago, pirates hid out in the many bays and inlets of South Carolina's winding coastline. Today, it is tourists who flock to warm, year-round seaside resorts such as Hilton Head and Myrtle Beach.

Area: 32,020 sq mi (82,932 sq km)

Population: 4,147,000

Capital: Columbia, pop. 117,400

Largest city: Columbia, pop. 117,400

Industry: service industries, tourism, chemicals, textiles, machinery, forest products

Agriculture: chickens, tobacco, nursery stock, dairy products, cotton

Statehood: May 23, 1788; 8th state

Nickname: Palmetto State

More about South Carolina

- *South Carolina's many swamps gave shelter to General Francis Marion, known as Swamp Fox. The daring soldier led raids against the British during the Revolutionary War, escaping capture by disappearing into the swamps.*
- *South Carolina had so much timber in its early days that settlers built their houses only from the hard "hearts of pine."*
- *Some residents of the state's southeastern Sea Islands speak a language known as Gullah, a mixture of English and West African languages.*
- *After South Carolina won a Revolutionary War battle from a fort made of palmetto logs (a palmetto is a kind of palm tree), the state picked up the nickname Palmetto State.*

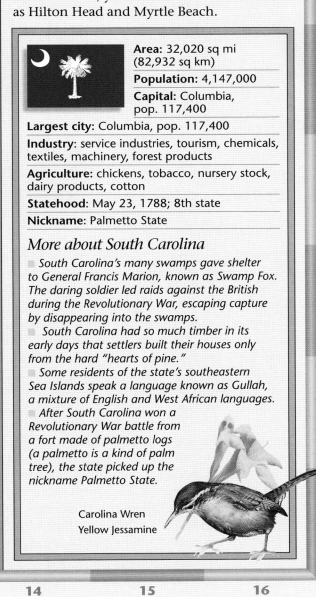

Carolina Wren
Yellow Jessamine

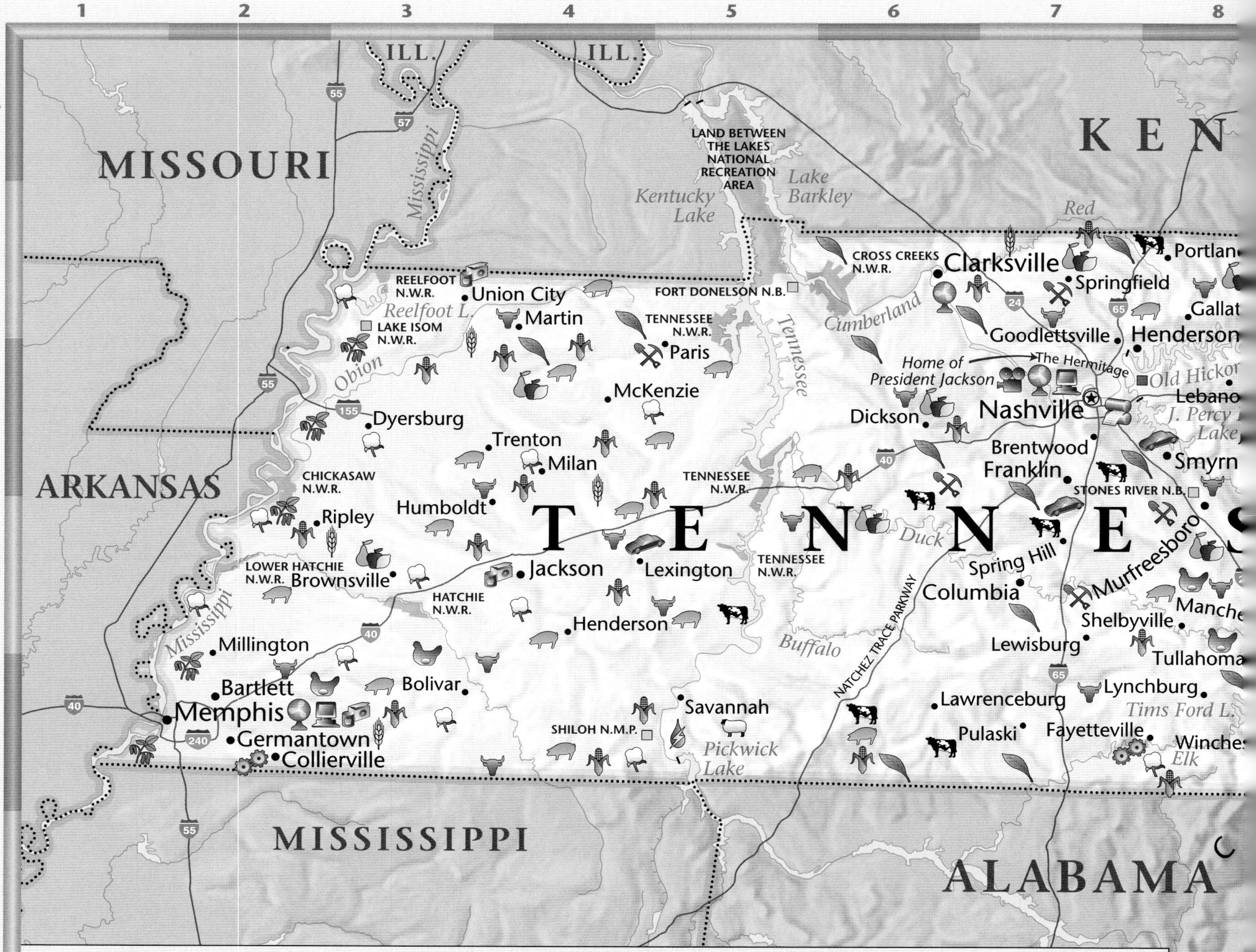

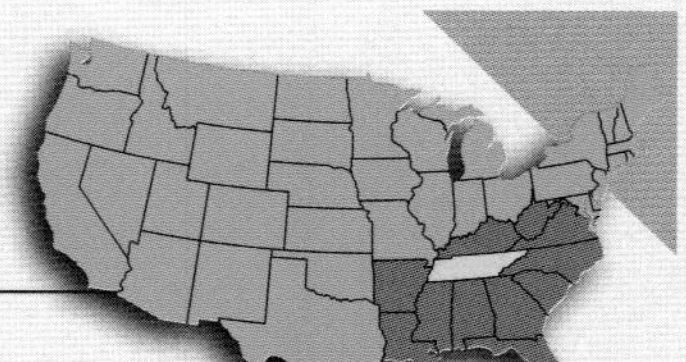

MISSOURI
ILL.
ILL.
KEN
ARKANSAS
MISSISSIPPI
ALABAMA
T E N N E S

LAND BETWEEN THE LAKES NATIONAL RECREATION AREA
Kentucky Lake
Lake Barkley
Red
Mississippi
REELFOOT N.W.R.
Reelfoot L.
LAKE ISOM N.W.R.
Union City
Martin
FORT DONELSON N.B.
TENNESSEE N.W.R.
Paris
Obion
McKenzie
Dyersburg
Trenton
Milan
CHICKASAW N.W.R.
Ripley
Humboldt
TENNESSEE N.W.R.
LOWER HATCHIE N.W.R.
Brownsville
Jackson
Lexington
TENNESSEE N.W.R.
HATCHIE N.W.R.
Henderson
Millington
Bartlett
Bolivar
Memphis
Germantown
Collierville
Savannah
SHILOH N.M.P.
Pickwick Lake
Tennessee
Buffalo
NATCHEZ TRACE PARKWAY
CROSS CREEKS N.W.R.
Clarksville
Springfield
Portland
Gallatin
Cumberland
Goodlettsville
Hendersonville
Home of President Jackson
The Hermitage
Old Hickory
Lebanon
Dickson
Nashville
J. Percy Priest Lake
Brentwood
Franklin
Smyrna
STONES RIVER N.B.
Duck
Spring Hill
Murfreesboro
Columbia
Shelbyville
Manchester
Lewisburg
Tullahoma
Lynchburg
Lawrenceburg
Tims Ford L.
Pulaski
Fayetteville
Winchester
Elk

Volunteer State

Tennessee

Tennessee stretches from the Appalachians in the east to the Mississippi River in the west. Tennessee's Appalachians include the Blue Ridge and the Great Smoky Mountains. The Smokies get their name from the mixture of mist and evaporating plant oils that creates a bluish haze over them. Hydroelectric dams built along many of Tennessee's rivers as part of the Tennessee Valley Authority (TVA) helped industry develop here.

Middle Tennessee is a large oval basin rimmed by highlands. It has prize farmland, enriched by limestone bedrock. Farmers here raise dairy and beef cows as well as chickens and tobacco. The area also is home to big automobile factories in Spring Hill and Smyrna. Nashville is the region's main city. It is both the state capital and world capital of country music. It is a center for computers and electronics as well as the recording industry.

Small farms abound in the west. The port of Memphis is a center of biomedical research and communications.

Area: 42,143 sq mi (109,151 sq km)

Population: 5,842,000

Capital: Nashville, pop. 545,900

Largest city: Memphis, pop. 648,900

Industry: service industries, chemicals, transportation equipment, processed foods, machinery

Agriculture: cattle, cotton, dairy products, hogs, poultry, nursery stock

Statehood: June 1, 1796; 16th state

Nickname: Volunteer State

Mockingbird

Iris

More about Tennessee

- *The Tennessee Aquarium, in Chattanooga, is the world's largest freshwater aquarium.*
- *During WWII scientists separated uranium isotopes for atomic bombs in secret research laboratories in Oak Ridge.*
- *In the late 18th century a section of northeastern Tennessee tried to become the separate state of Franklin, named for Benjamin Franklin.*
- *Tennessee volunteer troops fought so bravely in the war of 1812 that the state earned the nickname Volunteer State.*
- *Reelfoot Lake is the state's only large natural lake. It was formed when an earthquake caused the Mississippi River to fill a low area.*

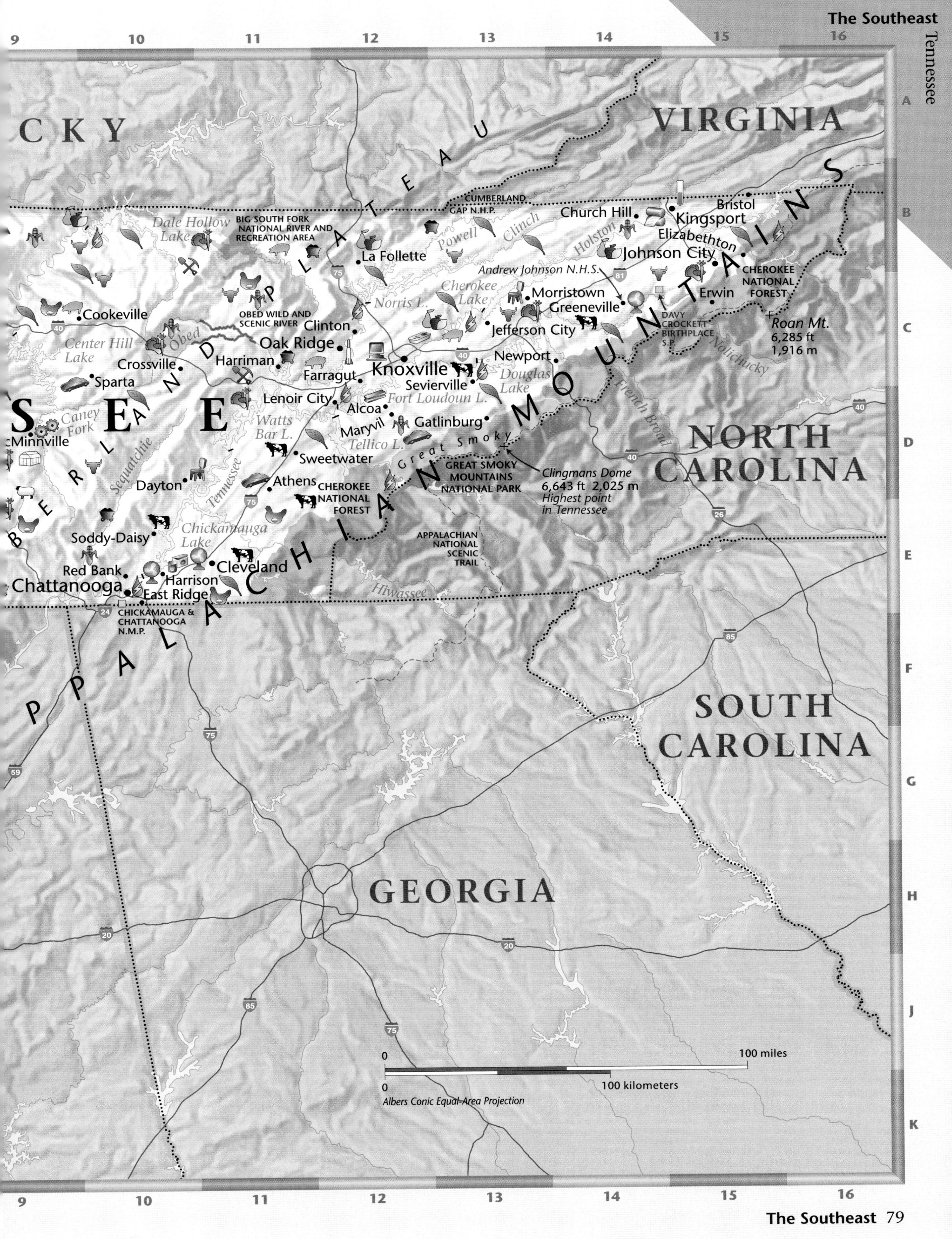
VIRGINIA
NORTH CAROLINA
SOUTH CAROLINA
GEORGIA
CUMBERLAND PLATEAU
APPALACHIAN MOUNTAINS
CUMBERLAND GAP N.H.P.
BIG SOUTH FORK NATIONAL RIVER AND RECREATION AREA
OBED WILD AND SCENIC RIVER
Dale Hollow Lake
Center Hill Lake
Cherokee Lake
Norris L.
Douglas Lake
Fort Loudoun L.
Watts Bar L.
Tellico L.
Chickamauga Lake
Cookeville
Crossville
Sparta
Clinton
Oak Ridge
Harriman
La Follette
Church Hill
Kingsport
Bristol
Elizabethton
Johnson City
Andrew Johnson N.H.S.
Morristown
Greeneville
Jefferson City
Erwin
CHEROKEE NATIONAL FOREST
DAVY CROCKETT BIRTHPLACE S.P.
Roan Mt.
6,285 ft
1,916 m
Newport
Knoxville
Farragut
Sevierville
Lenoir City
Alcoa
Maryvil
Gatlinburg
Sweetwater
Athens
Dayton
Soddy-Daisy
Red Bank
Chattanooga
Harrison
East Ridge
Cleveland
CHICKAMAUGA & CHATTANOOGA N.M.P.
GREAT SMOKY MOUNTAINS NATIONAL PARK
Great Smoky
Clingmans Dome
6,643 ft 2,025 m
Highest point in Tennessee
APPALACHIAN NATIONAL SCENIC TRAIL
Powell
Clinch
Holston
Nolichucky
French Broad
Hiwassee
Tennessee
Sequatchie
Obed
Caney Fork
Minnville
0
100 miles
0
100 kilometers
Albers Conic Equal-Area Projection

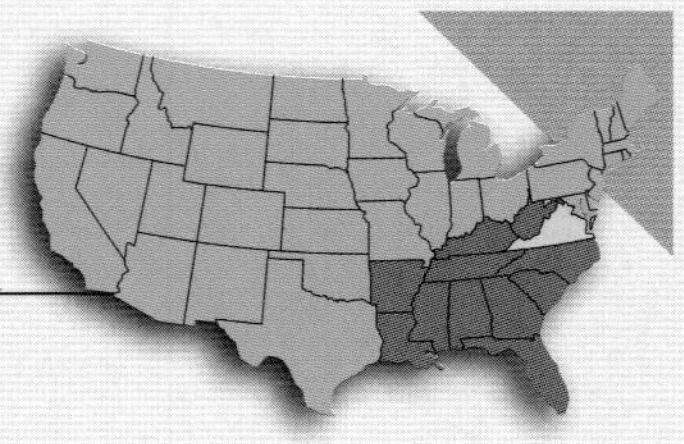

Old Dominion

Virginia

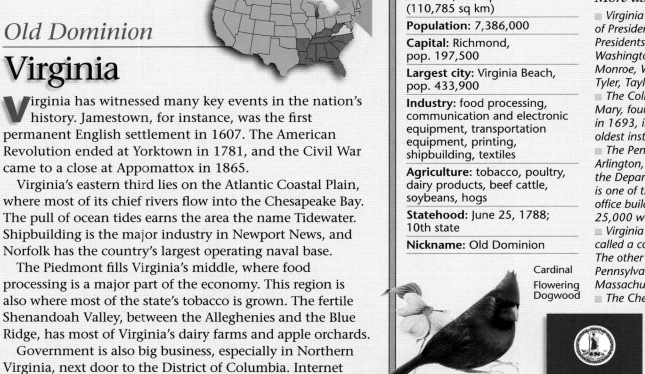

Virginia has witnessed many key events in the nation's history. Jamestown, for instance, was the first permanent English settlement in 1607. The American Revolution ended at Yorktown in 1781, and the Civil War came to a close at Appomattox in 1865.

Virginia's eastern third lies on the Atlantic Coastal Plain, where most of its chief rivers flow into the Chesapeake Bay. The pull of ocean tides earns the area the name Tidewater. Shipbuilding is the major industry in Newport News, and Norfolk has the country's largest operating naval base.

The Piedmont fills Virginia's middle, where food processing is a major part of the economy. This region is also where most of the state's tobacco is grown. The fertile Shenandoah Valley, between the Alleghenies and the Blue Ridge, has most of Virginia's dairy farms and apple orchards.

Government is also big business, especially in Northern Virginia, next door to the District of Columbia. Internet and software businesses flourish in the region as well.

Area: 42,774 sq mi (110,785 sq km)

Population: 7,386,000

Capital: Richmond, pop. 197,500

Largest city: Virginia Beach, pop. 433,900

Industry: food processing, communication and electronic equipment, transportation equipment, printing, shipbuilding, textiles

Agriculture: tobacco, poultry, dairy products, beef cattle, soybeans, hogs

Statehood: June 25, 1788; 10th state

Nickname: Old Dominion

Cardinal

Flowering Dogwood

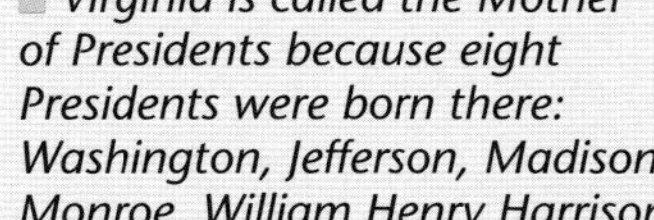

More about Virginia

- *Virginia is called the Mother of Presidents because eight Presidents were born there: Washington, Jefferson, Madison, Monroe, William Henry Harrison, Tyler, Taylor, and Wilson.*
- *The College of William and Mary, founded in Williamsburg in 1693, is the country's second oldest institute of higher learning.*
- *The Pentagon, located in Arlington, is headquarters of the Department of Defense. It is one of the world's largest office buildings, with about 25,000 workers.*
- *Virginia is one of four states called a commonwealth. The other three are Kentucky, Pennsylvania, and Massachusetts.*
- *The Chesapeake Bay Bridge-Tunnel runs 23 miles (37 km) from the tip of the Delmarva Peninsula to the shore near Norfolk.*

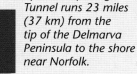

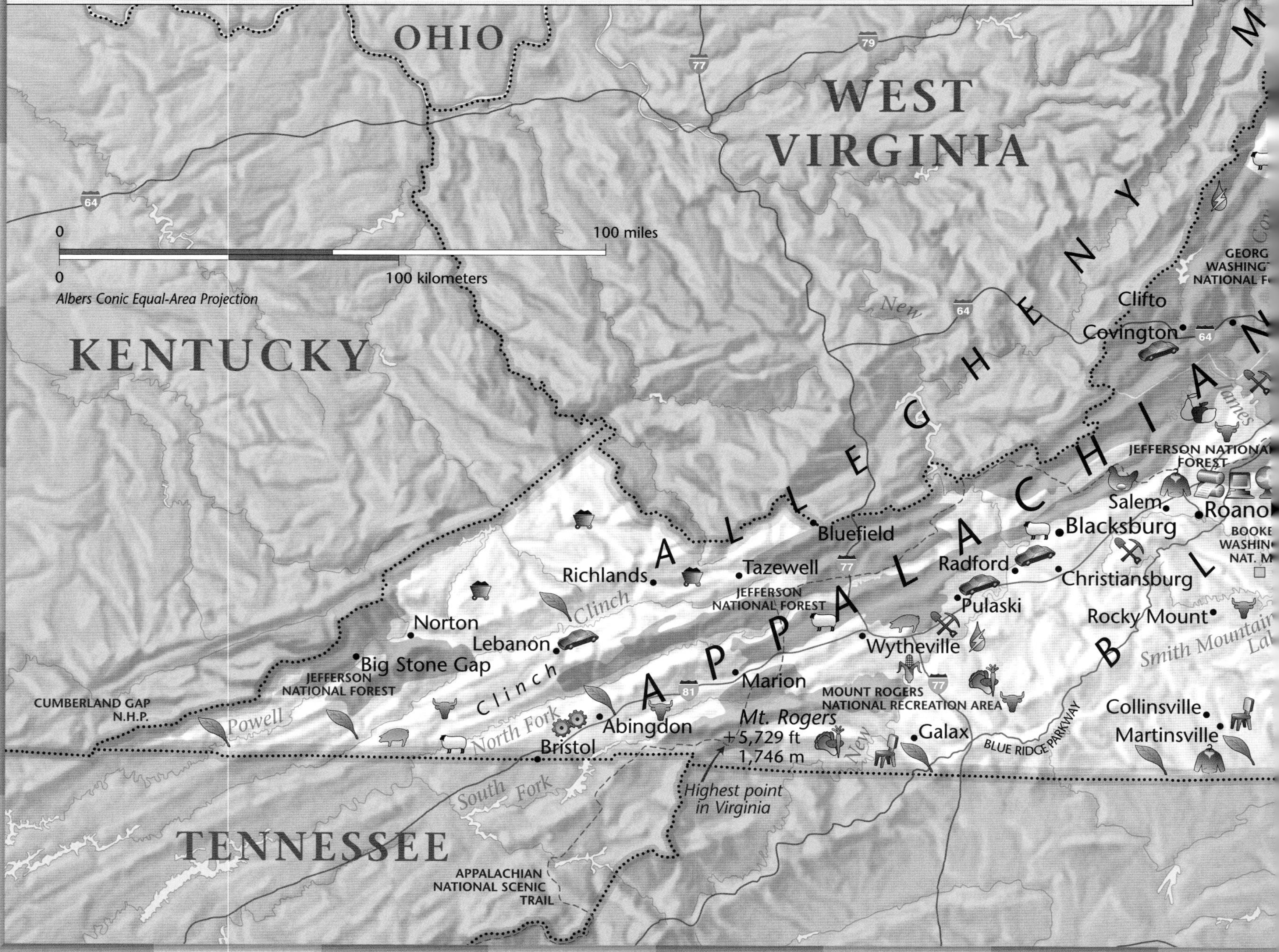

OHIO
WEST VIRGINIA
KENTUCKY
TENNESSEE
0 — 100 miles
0 — 100 kilometers
Albers Conic Equal-Area Projection
ALLEGHENY
APPALACHIAN
Clifton
Covington
JEFFERSON NATIONAL FOREST
Salem
Blacksburg
Roanoke
Bluefield
Richlands
Tazewell
Radford
Christiansburg
Pulaski
Rocky Mount
Norton
Lebanon
Big Stone Gap
Wytheville
Marion
Abingdon
Bristol
Mt. Rogers
+5,729 ft
1,746 m
Highest point in Virginia
MOUNT ROGERS NATIONAL RECREATION AREA
Galax
BLUE RIDGE PARKWAY
Collinsville
Martinsville
CUMBERLAND GAP N.H.P.
APPALACHIAN NATIONAL SCENIC TRAIL
Clinch
Powell
North Fork
South Fork
New
Smith Mountain Lake

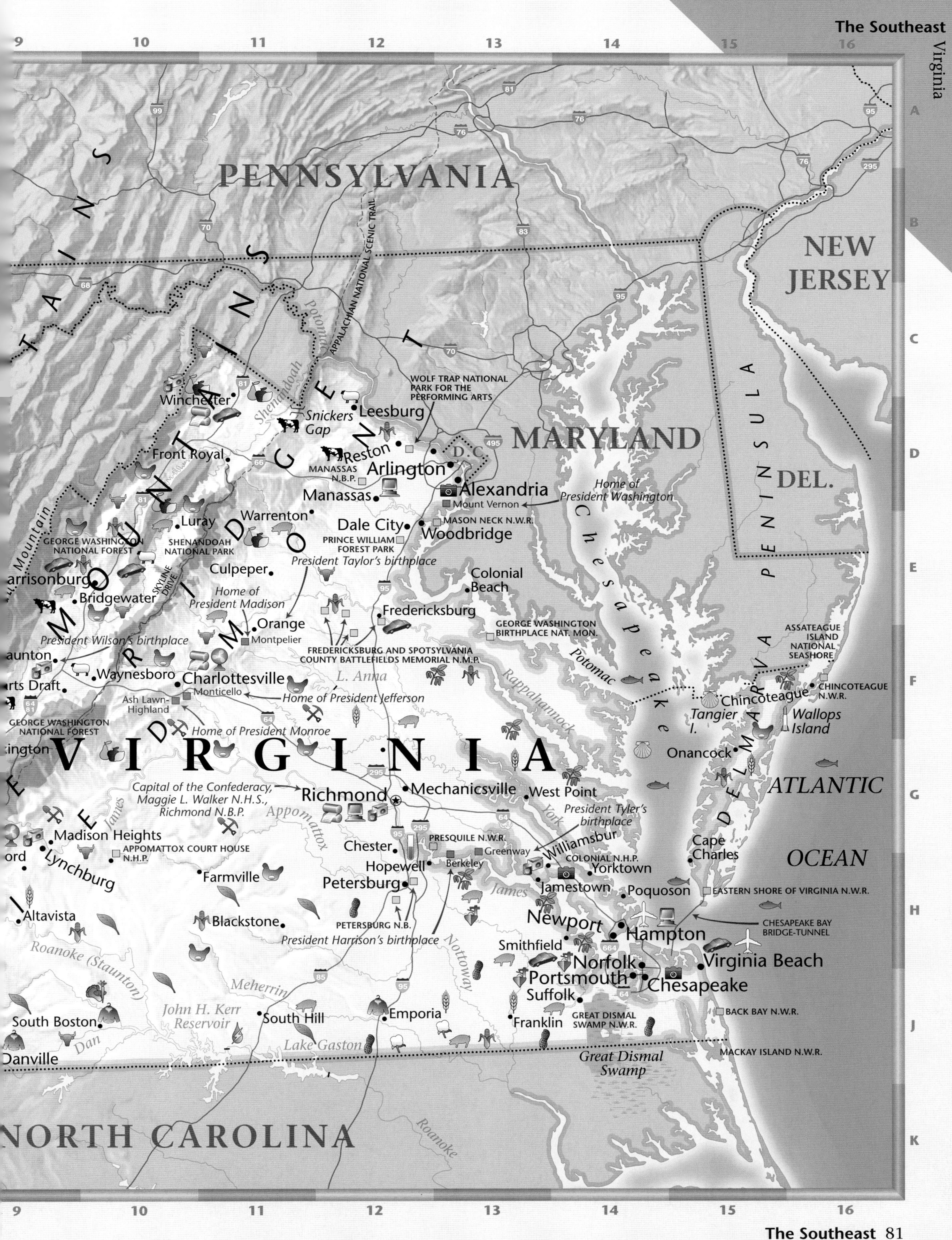
PENNSYLVANIA
NEW JERSEY
MARYLAND
DEL.
VIRGINIA
NORTH CAROLINA
ATLANTIC OCEAN
DELMARVA PENINSULA
Chesapeake
APPALACHIAN NATIONAL SCENIC TRAIL
WOLF TRAP NATIONAL PARK FOR THE PERFORMING ARTS
D.C.
Winchester
Snickers Gap
Leesburg
Front Royal
Reston
Arlington
MANASSAS N.B.P.
Manassas
Alexandria
Mount Vernon
Home of President Washington
Warrenton
Luray
Dale City
MASON NECK N.W.R.
Woodbridge
GEORGE WASHINGTON NATIONAL FOREST
SHENANDOAH NATIONAL PARK
PRINCE WILLIAM FOREST PARK
President Taylor's birthplace
Culpeper
Colonial Beach
Harrisonburg
Bridgewater
SKYLINE DRIVE
Home of President Madison
Fredericksburg
Orange
Montpelier
GEORGE WASHINGTON BIRTHPLACE NAT. MON.
President Wilson's birthplace
Staunton
FREDERICKSBURG AND SPOTSYLVANIA COUNTY BATTLEFIELDS MEMORIAL N.M.P.
ASSATEAGUE ISLAND NATIONAL SEASHORE
Waynesboro
Charlottesville
L. Anna
Potomac
Rappahannock
Monticello
Ash Lawn-Highland
Home of President Jefferson
Chincoteague
CHINCOTEAGUE N.W.R.
Tangier I.
Wallops Island
Home of President Monroe
Onancock
Capital of the Confederacy, Maggie L. Walker N.H.S., Richmond N.B.P.
Richmond
Mechanicsville
West Point
President Tyler's birthplace
Appomattox
James
York
Madison Heights
APPOMATTOX COURT HOUSE N.H.P.
Chester
PRESQUILE N.W.R.
Greenway
Williamsburg
Cape Charles
Lynchburg
Farmville
Hopewell
Berkeley
COLONIAL N.H.P.
Yorktown
Petersburg
Jamestown
Poquoson
EASTERN SHORE OF VIRGINIA N.W.R.
Altavista
Blackstone
PETERSBURG N.B.
Newport News
Hampton
CHESAPEAKE BAY BRIDGE-TUNNEL
President Harrison's birthplace
Smithfield
Roanoke (Staunton)
Nottoway
Norfolk
Virginia Beach
Portsmouth
Chesapeake
Meherrin
Suffolk
John H. Kerr Reservoir
South Boston
South Hill
Emporia
Franklin
GREAT DISMAL SWAMP N.W.R.
BACK BAY N.W.R.
Dan
Lake Gaston
MACKAY ISLAND N.W.R.
Danville
Great Dismal Swamp
Roanoke
MOUNTAINS
APPALACHIAN
BLUE RIDGE
PIEDMONT

OHIO
KENTUCKY
WEST VIRGINIA
ALLEGHENY
APPA
Chester
Weirton
Follansbee
Wellsburg
Wheeling
Moundsville
Fish Creek
New Martinsville
Paden City
Mannington
Fairmont
Morganto
Kingwood
Shinnston
Grafton
Clarksburg
Salem
Bridgeport
Tygart Lake
Philippi
Williamstown
St. Marys
OHIO RIVER ISLANDS N.W.R.
Vienna
Parkersburg
Little Kanawha
Weston
Stonewall Jackson Lake
Buckhannon
Elkins
MONONGA
Ravenswood
Point Pleasant
Ripley
Spencer
Sutton Lake
Tygart Valley
Cheat Mountain
Spruce K
Highest point West Virgini
Huntington
Kenova
Hurricane
Nitro
Dunbar
St. Albans
South Charleston
Charleston
Sissonville
Elk
MONONGAHELA NATIONAL FOREST
Summersville Lake
Summersville
Richwood
Kanawha
Gauley
GAULEY RIVER N.R.A.
Montgomery
Fayetteville
New River Gorge Bridge
Madison
Oak Hill
NEW RIVER GORGE NATIONAL RIVER
Big Sandy
Guyandotte
Big Coal
Logan
Tug Fork
Williamson
Beckley
Lewisburg
White Sulphur Springs
Greenbrier
Hinton
Mullens
BLUESTONE NATIONAL SCENIC RIVER
Bluestone Lake
JEFFERSON NATIONAL FOREST
Welch
Princeton
Bluefield
Bluestone
New
Ohio
Kanawha

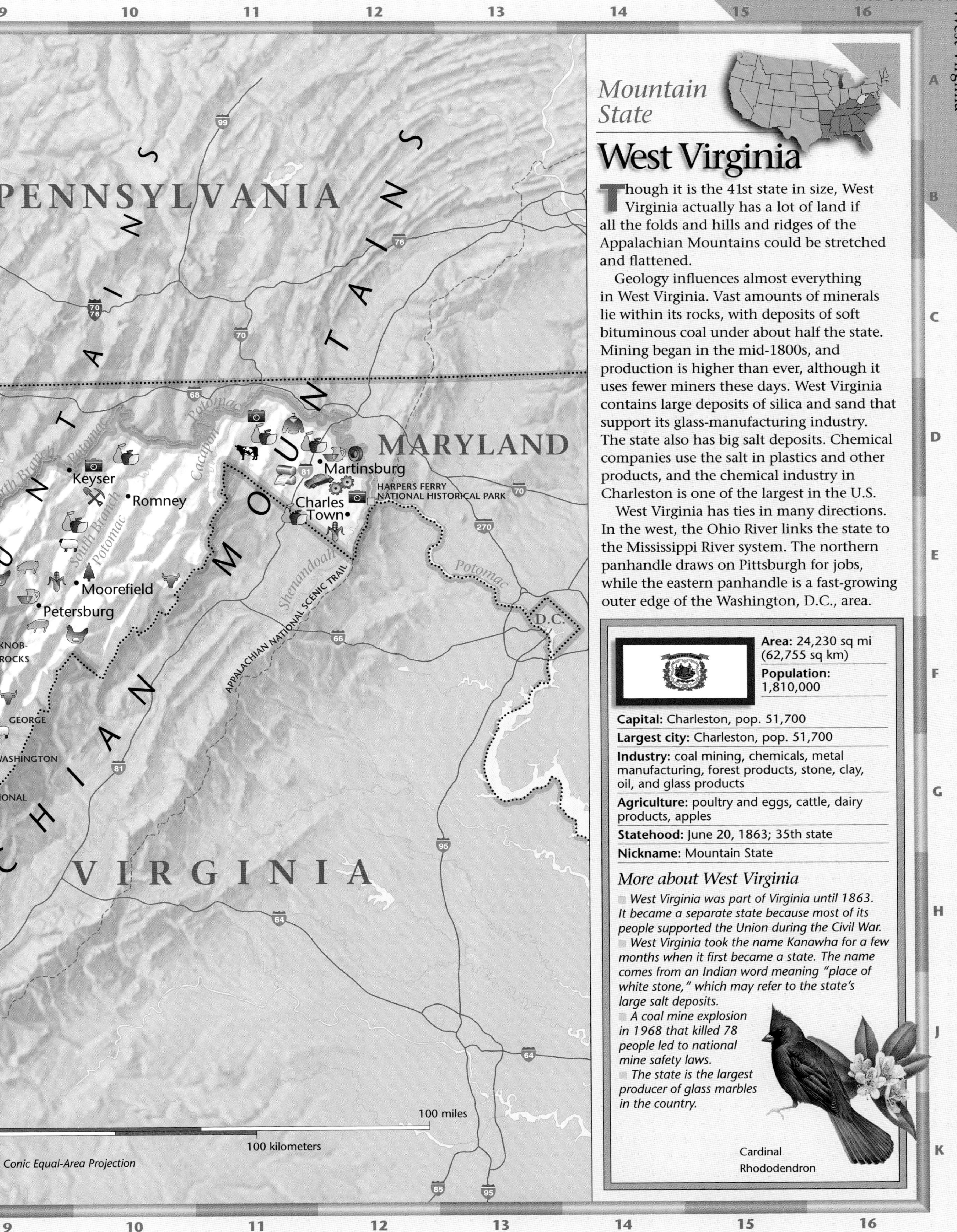

Mountain State

West Virginia

Though it is the 41st state in size, West Virginia actually has a lot of land if all the folds and hills and ridges of the Appalachian Mountains could be stretched and flattened.

Geology influences almost everything in West Virginia. Vast amounts of minerals lie within its rocks, with deposits of soft bituminous coal under about half the state. Mining began in the mid-1800s, and production is higher than ever, although it uses fewer miners these days. West Virginia contains large deposits of silica and sand that support its glass-manufacturing industry. The state also has big salt deposits. Chemical companies use the salt in plastics and other products, and the chemical industry in Charleston is one of the largest in the U.S.

West Virginia has ties in many directions. In the west, the Ohio River links the state to the Mississippi River system. The northern panhandle draws on Pittsburgh for jobs, while the eastern panhandle is a fast-growing outer edge of the Washington, D.C., area.

Area: 24,230 sq mi (62,755 sq km)

Population: 1,810,000

Capital: Charleston, pop. 51,700

Largest city: Charleston, pop. 51,700

Industry: coal mining, chemicals, metal manufacturing, forest products, stone, clay, oil, and glass products

Agriculture: poultry and eggs, cattle, dairy products, apples

Statehood: June 20, 1863; 35th state

Nickname: Mountain State

More about West Virginia

- *West Virginia was part of Virginia until 1863. It became a separate state because most of its people supported the Union during the Civil War.*
- *West Virginia took the name Kanawha for a few months when it first became a state. The name comes from an Indian word meaning "place of white stone," which may refer to the state's large salt deposits.*
- *A coal mine explosion in 1968 that killed 78 people led to national mine safety laws.*
- *The state is the largest producer of glass marbles in the country.*

The Midw

est

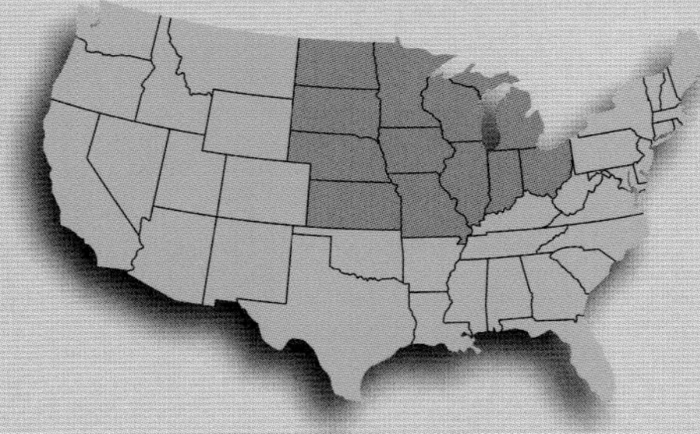

Illinois
Indiana
Iowa
Kansas
Michigan
Minnesota
Missouri
Nebraska
North Dakota
Ohio
South Dakota
Wisconsin

A farmer harvests wheat in Minnesota (left). Fertile Midwest farms grow much of the nation's food. The region's cities, on the other hand, host some major industries. Above, a factory worker in Ohio checks a sampling of molten iron.

SASKATCHEWAN
MANITOBA
CANADA
U.S.
Lake of the Woods
Rainy L.
Souris
Lake Sakakawea
Red River of the North
Upper Red Lake
Lower Red Lake
Eagle Mt.
2,301 ft
701 m
Lake Winnibigoshish
Leech Lake
NORTH DAKOTA
MONTANA
Badlands
White Butte
3,506 ft
1,069 m
Missouri
MINNESOTA
Mille Lacs Lake
Little Missouri
Lake Oahe
Mississippi
Timms
GREAT PLAINS
High Plains
SOUTH DAKOTA
Cheyenne
James
Big Sioux
Minnesota
Black Hills
Harney Peak
7,242 ft
2,207 m
L. Sharpe
White
WYOMING
Lake Francis Case
Ocheyedan Mound
1,670 ft
509 m
Cedar
Niobrara
Iowa
Sand Hills
Little Sioux
North Platte
Charles Mound
1,235 ft
376 m
IOWA
NEBRASKA
Panorama Point
5,424 ft
1,653 m
CENTRAL LOWLAND
Des Moines
South Platte
Platte
Republican
Mississippi
Illinois
COLORADO
Mt. Sunflower
4,039 ft
1,231 m
Smoky Hills
Smoky Hill
Kansas
Missouri
MISSOURI
KANSAS
Flint Hills
Neosho
Arkansas
Harry S. Truman Reservoir
Osage
Lake of the Ozarks
Taum Sauk Mt.
1,772 ft
540 m
Red Hills
Ozark Plateau
NEW MEXICO
Cimarron
Table Rock Lake
TEXAS
OKLAHOMA
ARKANSAS
1 2 3 4 5 6 7 8
A B C D E F G H J K

The Midwest

Great Lakes, Great Rivers

Reaching across the central United States, the Midwest is a land of rolling hills and grassy plains. Glaciers smoothed much of the land long ago, leaving behind rich soil in the eastern regions. Glaciers also scooped out holes that became lakes, including the huge Great Lakes. The region is drained by the Mississippi and two of its largest tributaries, the Ohio and the Missouri.

About the Region

Highest point: Harney Peak, South Dakota: 7,242 ft (2,207 m)

Lowest point: St. Francis River, Missouri: 230 ft (70 m)

Largest lakes: Superior, Michigan, Huron, Erie

Longest rivers: Mississippi, Missouri, Arkansas, Ohio

Vegetation: Grassland, broadleaf forest, needleleaf forest, mixed forest

Climate: Continental to mild, ranging from cold winters and cool summers in the north to mild winters and humid summers in the south.

The Midwest

The Heartland

A region of wide open lands and great inland waters, the Midwest spreads from the Great Lakes to the eastern foothills of the Rocky Mountains.

To pioneers moving west, the land looked like a sea of grass. Many thought the drier western part of the region was a desert. Today, farmed fields cover the land like a quilt. Rich soil, plentiful rain in the east, and vast underground reservoirs in the west make this the nation's corn and wheat belt—its breadbasket—and a major source of milk, cheese, beef, and pork. Its people include descendants of European immigrants as well as Native Americans, Hispanics, and African-Americans.

The Great Lakes form the world's largest body of fresh water. A series of locks makes it possible for ships and barges to carry goods between the Midwest and the Atlantic Ocean via the St. Lawrence River. This transportation network, linked to railroads, led to the growth of such industrial cities as Chicago, Gary, Detroit, and Cleveland.

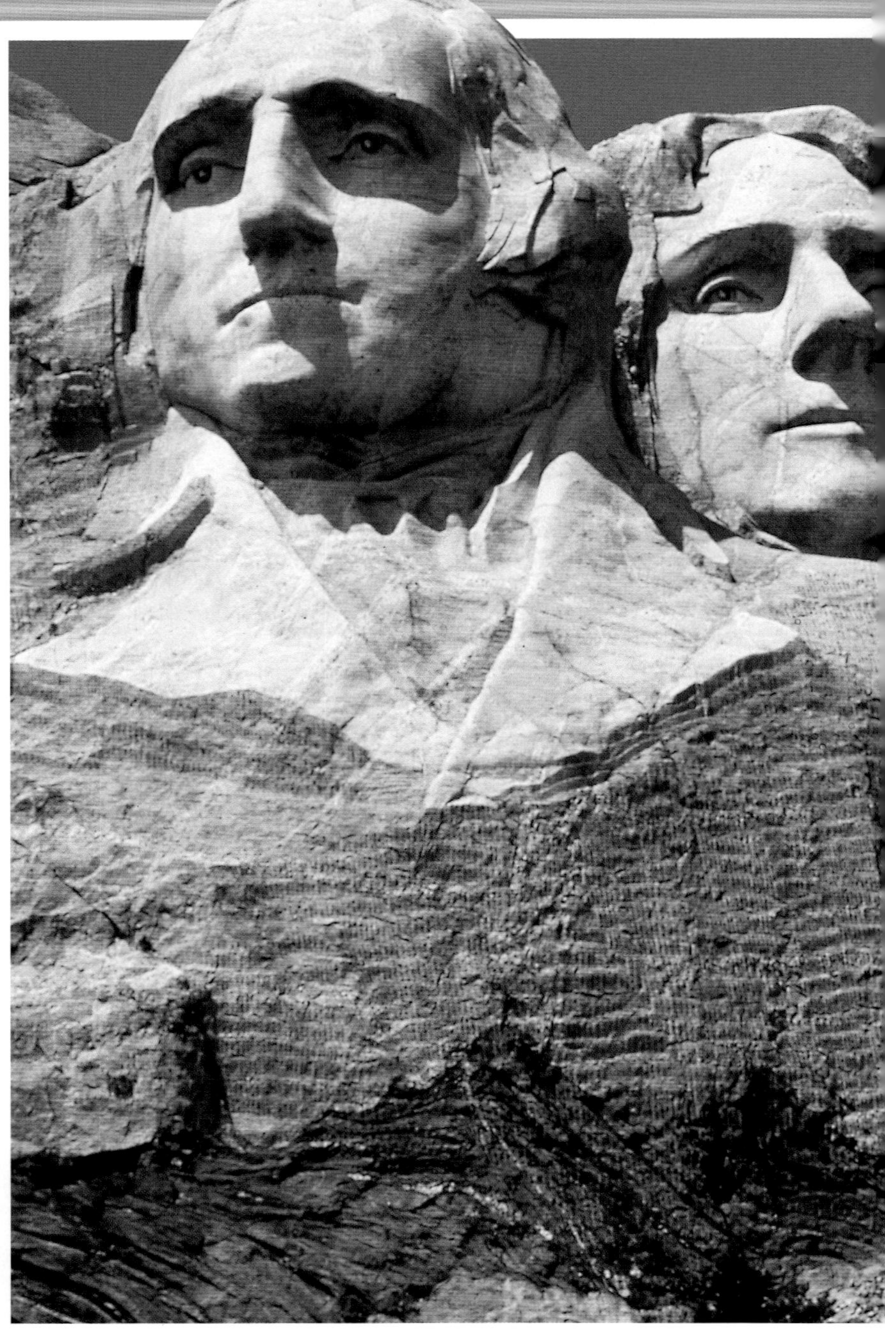

▲ **AN ORE FREIGHTER** *travels between Lakes Superior and Huron on the Soo Canals. Great Lakes ships carry iron ore, coal, and grain to the Atlantic Ocean.*

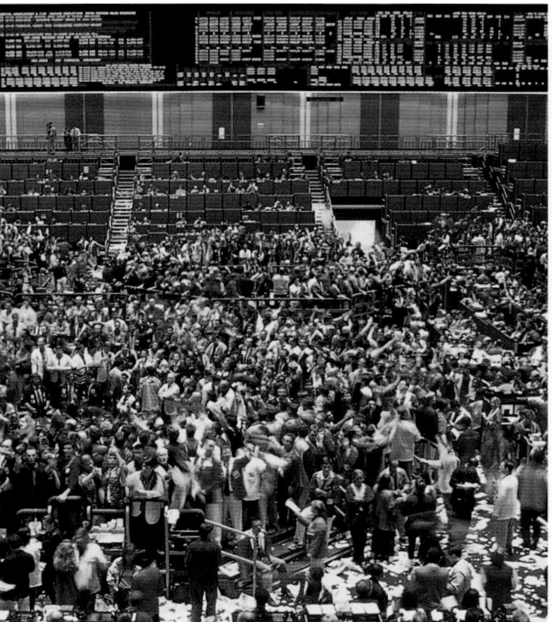

▶ **BUSY TRADERS** *crowd the floor of the Chicago Board of Trade, where they buy and sell contracts for grain, cattle, and other items. Chicago is the Midwest's finance capital.*

◀ **DAIRY COWS** *peer through a fence on a Wisconsin farm. The state is a leading producer of milk, butter, and cheese—a business worth millions of dollars. Livestock, including cattle and hogs, are an important part of the midwestern economy.*

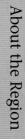

◄ **GRANITE FACES** *of Presidents George Washington, Thomas Jefferson, Theodore Roosevelt, and Abraham Lincoln rise 60 feet (18 m) high on Mount Rushmore, in South Dakota.*

▲ **A MIDWESTERN GIRL** *enjoys corn on the cob. Three-fourths of U.S. corn is grown from Ohio to Nebraska.*

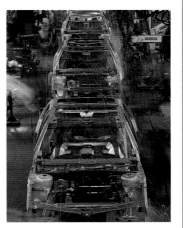

▲ **ROBOTS WELD** *new car frames in an auto plant in Illinois. Midwest assembly lines turn out thousands of vehicles a day for sale in the U.S. and abroad.*

► **A PRAIRIE DOG** *pup greets its mother by nuzzling her. These burrowing animals live in large underground "towns."*

▼ **A SOARING SPAN** *of steel, the Gateway Arch, in St. Louis, Missouri, rises 630 feet (192 m) along the waterfront.*

WISCONSIN
LAKE MICHIGAN
MICH.
INDIANA
IOWA
ILLINOIS
Highest point in Illinois
Charles Mound 1,235 ft 376 m
UPPER MISSISSIPPI RIVER NATIONAL WILDLIFE AND FISH REFUGE
MISSISSIPPI PALISADES S.P.
President Reagan's birthplace
MARK TWAIN N.W.R.
CHAUTAUQUA N.W.R.
EMIQUON N.W.R.
LINCOLN'S NEW SALEM S.H.S.
Lincoln Home N.H.S.
MEREDOSIA N.W.R.
VERMILION NATIONAL WILD & SCENIC RIVER
Galena
Freeport
Savanna
Rockford
Belvidere
Harvard
Waukegan
Arlington Heights
Evanston
Chicago
Cicero
Schaumburg
Elgin
Naperville
Aurora
Joliet
Kankakee
Sycamore
De Kalb
Dixon
Grand Detour
Sterling
Tampico
Rock Island
Moline
Geneseo
Mendota
Sandwich
Ottawa
La Salle
Peru
Morris
Streator
Pontiac
Watseka
Hoopeston
Danville
Rantoul
Urbana
Champaign
Kewanee
Galesburg
Monmouth
Macomb
Canton
Chillicothe
Peoria
Pekin
Morton
Bloomington
Normal
Clinton
Lincoln
Decatur
Tuscola
Charleston
Paris
Mattoon
Taylorville
Pana
Litchfield
Springfield
Beardstown
Jacksonville
White Hall
Carlinville
Jerseyville
Pittsfield
Quincy
Nauvoo
Carthage
Mississippi
Pecatonica
Rock
Green
Fox
Des Plaines
Kankakee
Illinois
Vermilion
Hennepin Canal
Iroquois
Middle Fork
Wabash
Mackinaw
Spoon
Salt Creek
Sangamon
Embarras
Kaskaskia
Lake Shelbyville
La Moine
McKee Creek
Macoupin Creek

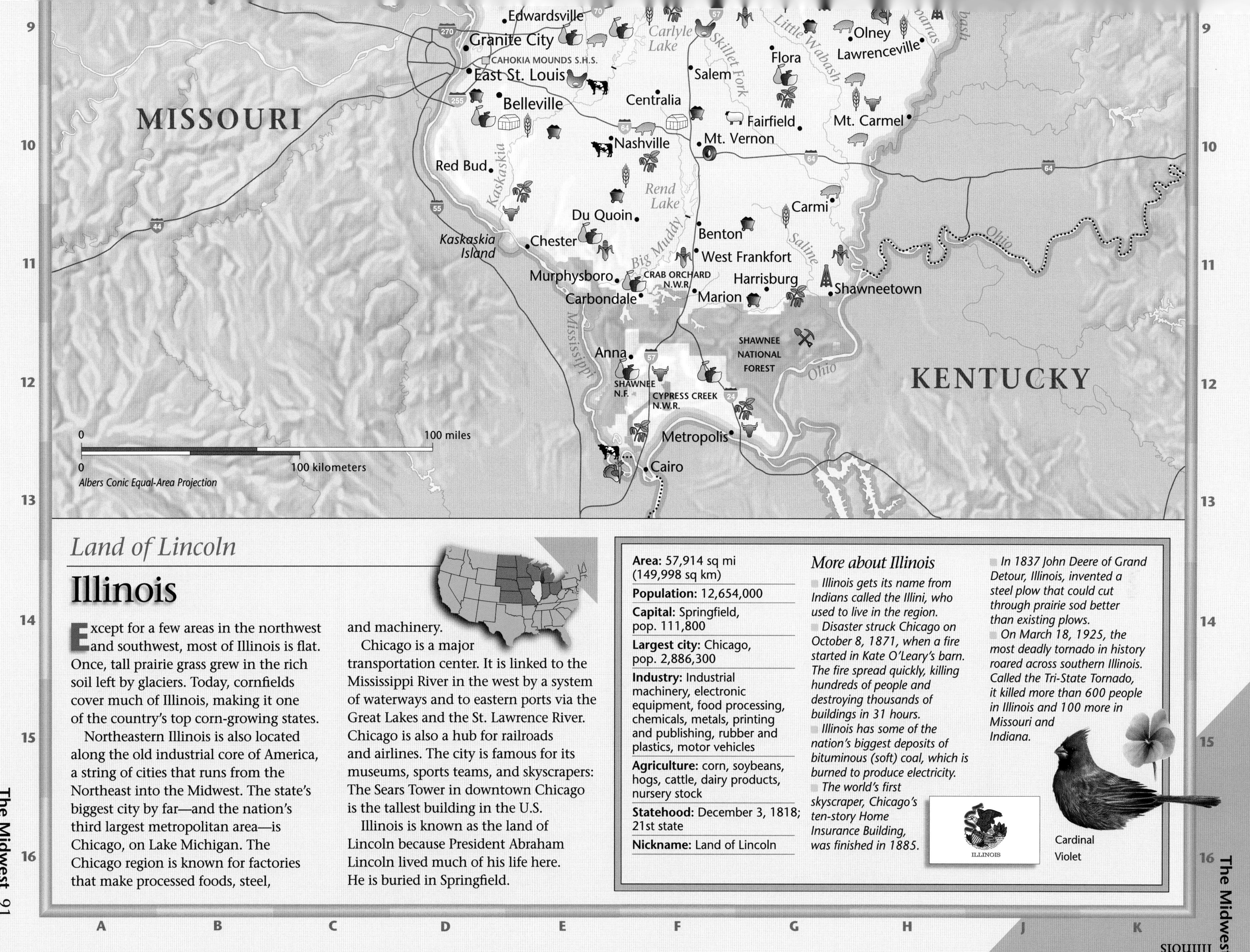

Land of Lincoln

Illinois

Except for a few areas in the northwest and southwest, most of Illinois is flat. Once, tall prairie grass grew in the rich soil left by glaciers. Today, cornfields cover much of Illinois, making it one of the country's top corn-growing states.

Northeastern Illinois is also located along the old industrial core of America, a string of cities that runs from the Northeast into the Midwest. The state's biggest city by far—and the nation's third largest metropolitan area—is Chicago, on Lake Michigan. The Chicago region is known for factories that make processed foods, steel, and machinery.

Chicago is a major transportation center. It is linked to the Mississippi River in the west by a system of waterways and to eastern ports via the Great Lakes and the St. Lawrence River. Chicago is also a hub for railroads and airlines. The city is famous for its museums, sports teams, and skyscrapers: The Sears Tower in downtown Chicago is the tallest building in the U.S.

Illinois is known as the land of Lincoln because President Abraham Lincoln lived much of his life here. He is buried in Springfield.

Area: 57,914 sq mi (149,998 sq km)

Population: 12,654,000

Capital: Springfield, pop. 111,800

Largest city: Chicago, pop. 2,886,300

Industry: Industrial machinery, electronic equipment, food processing, chemicals, metals, printing and publishing, rubber and plastics, motor vehicles

Agriculture: corn, soybeans, hogs, cattle, dairy products, nursery stock

Statehood: December 3, 1818; 21st state

Nickname: Land of Lincoln

More about Illinois

- *Illinois gets its name from Indians called the Illini, who used to live in the region.*
- *Disaster struck Chicago on October 8, 1871, when a fire started in Kate O'Leary's barn. The fire spread quickly, killing hundreds of people and destroying thousands of buildings in 31 hours.*
- *Illinois has some of the nation's biggest deposits of bituminous (soft) coal, which is burned to produce electricity.*
- *The world's first skyscraper, Chicago's ten-story Home Insurance Building, was finished in 1885.*
- *In 1837 John Deere of Grand Detour, Illinois, invented a steel plow that could cut through prairie sod better than existing plows.*
- *On March 18, 1925, the most deadly tornado in history roared across southern Illinois. Called the Tri-State Tornado, it killed more than 600 people in Illinois and 100 more in Missouri and Indiana.*

LAKE MICHIGAN
MICHIGAN
INDIANA
OHIO
ILLINOIS
INDIANA DUNES NATIONAL LAKESHORE
Michigan City
East Chicago
Gary
Hammond
Portage
Merrillville
Crown Point
Lowell
Valparaiso
LaPorte
South Bend
Mishawaka
Elkhart
Goshen
Nappanee
Plymouth
Warsaw
Kendallville
Auburn
Angola
Columbia City
Fort Wayne
Rochester
North Manchester
Huntington
Decatur
Rensselaer
Monticello
Logansport
Peru
Wabash
Marion
Gas City
Kokomo
Lafayette
Hartford City
Portland
Frankfort
Elwood
Alexandria
Muncie
Winchester
Anderson
Noblesville
Carmel
Lebanon
Crawfordsville
Indianapolis
Lawrence
Greenfield
Beech Grove
Plainfield
Greenwood
Franklin
Martinsville
Greencastle
Brazil
Clinton
Terre Haute
New Castle
Richmond
Connersville
Rushville
Shelbyville
Greensburg
Highest point in Indiana
1,257 ft
383 m
Lake Wawasee
Lake Shafer
Lake Freeman
Salamonie Lake
Mississinewa Lake
Huntington L.
Brookville Lake
Cagles Mill Lake
Cecil M. Harden Lake
Lake Lemon
St. Joseph
Pigeon
Cedar Creek
Maumee
St. Marys
Kankakee
Tippecanoe
Eel
Iroquois
Wabash
Salamonie
Mississinewa
Wildcat Creek
White
Sugar Creek
Big Raccoon Creek
Big Blue
Mill Creek
Flatrock
Great Miami
Whitewa
U.S. center of

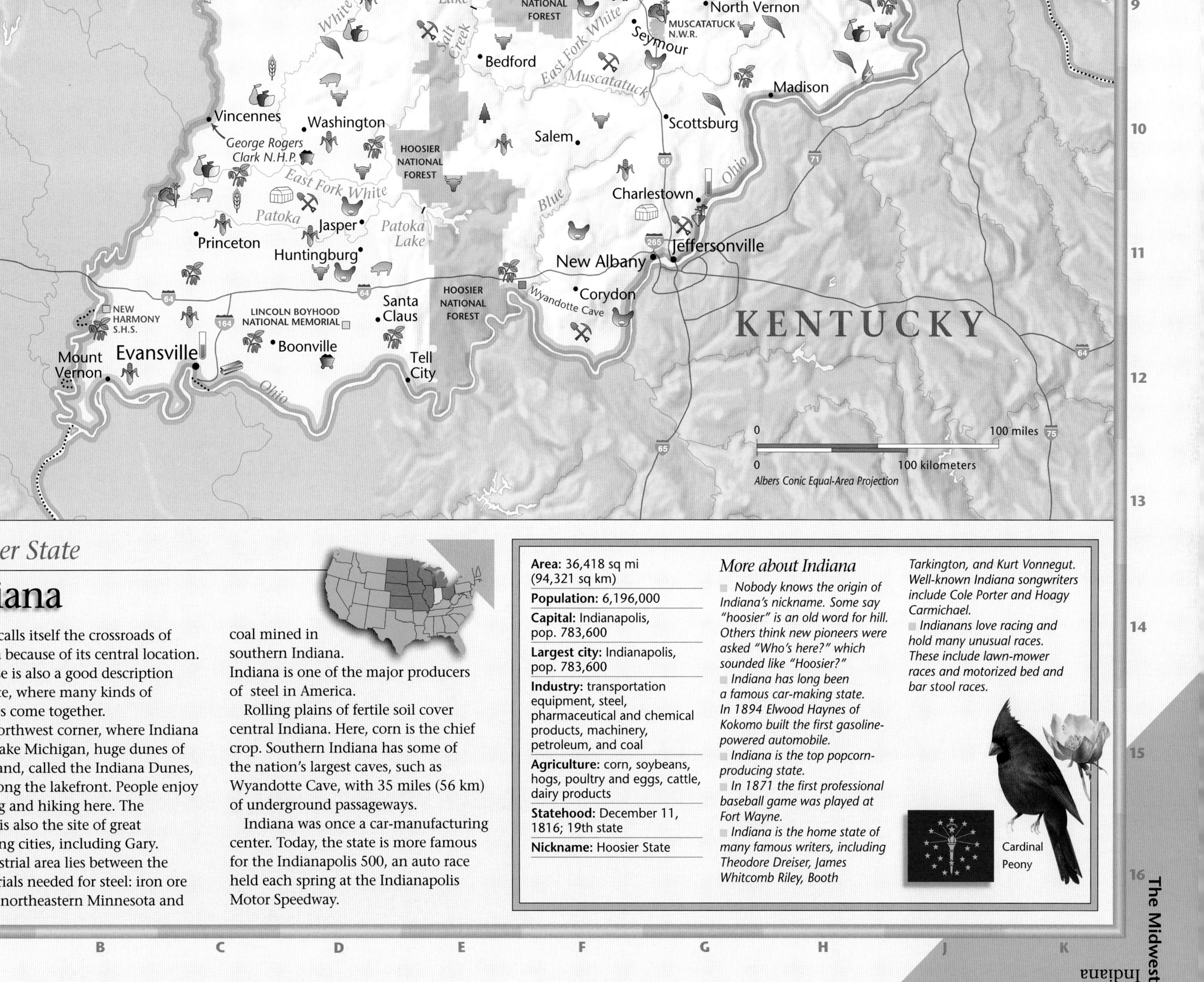

Hoosier State

Indiana

Indiana calls itself the crossroads of America because of its central location. The phrase is also a good description of the state, where many kinds of landscapes come together.

In its northwest corner, where Indiana touches Lake Michigan, huge dunes of shifting sand, called the Indiana Dunes, stretch along the lakefront. People enjoy swimming and hiking here. The lakefront is also the site of great steelmaking cities, including Gary. This industrial area lies between the raw materials needed for steel: iron ore mined in northeastern Minnesota and coal mined in southern Indiana. Indiana is one of the major producers of steel in America.

Rolling plains of fertile soil cover central Indiana. Here, corn is the chief crop. Southern Indiana has some of the nation's largest caves, such as Wyandotte Cave, with 35 miles (56 km) of underground passageways.

Indiana was once a car-manufacturing center. Today, the state is more famous for the Indianapolis 500, an auto race held each spring at the Indianapolis Motor Speedway.

Area: 36,418 sq mi (94,321 sq km)

Population: 6,196,000

Capital: Indianapolis, pop. 783,600

Largest city: Indianapolis, pop. 783,600

Industry: transportation equipment, steel, pharmaceutical and chemical products, machinery, petroleum, and coal

Agriculture: corn, soybeans, hogs, poultry and eggs, cattle, dairy products

Statehood: December 11, 1816; 19th state

Nickname: Hoosier State

More about Indiana

- *Nobody knows the origin of Indiana's nickname. Some say "hoosier" is an old word for hill. Others think new pioneers were asked "Who's here?" which sounded like "Hoosier?"*
- *Indiana has long been a famous car-making state. In 1894 Elwood Haynes of Kokomo built the first gasoline-powered automobile.*
- *Indiana is the top popcorn-producing state.*
- *In 1871 the first professional baseball game was played at Fort Wayne.*
- *Indiana is the home state of many famous writers, including Theodore Dreiser, James Whitcomb Riley, Booth Tarkington, and Kurt Vonnegut. Well-known Indiana songwriters include Cole Porter and Hoagy Carmichael.*
- *Indianans love racing and hold many unusual races. These include lawn-mower races and motorized bed and bar stool races.*

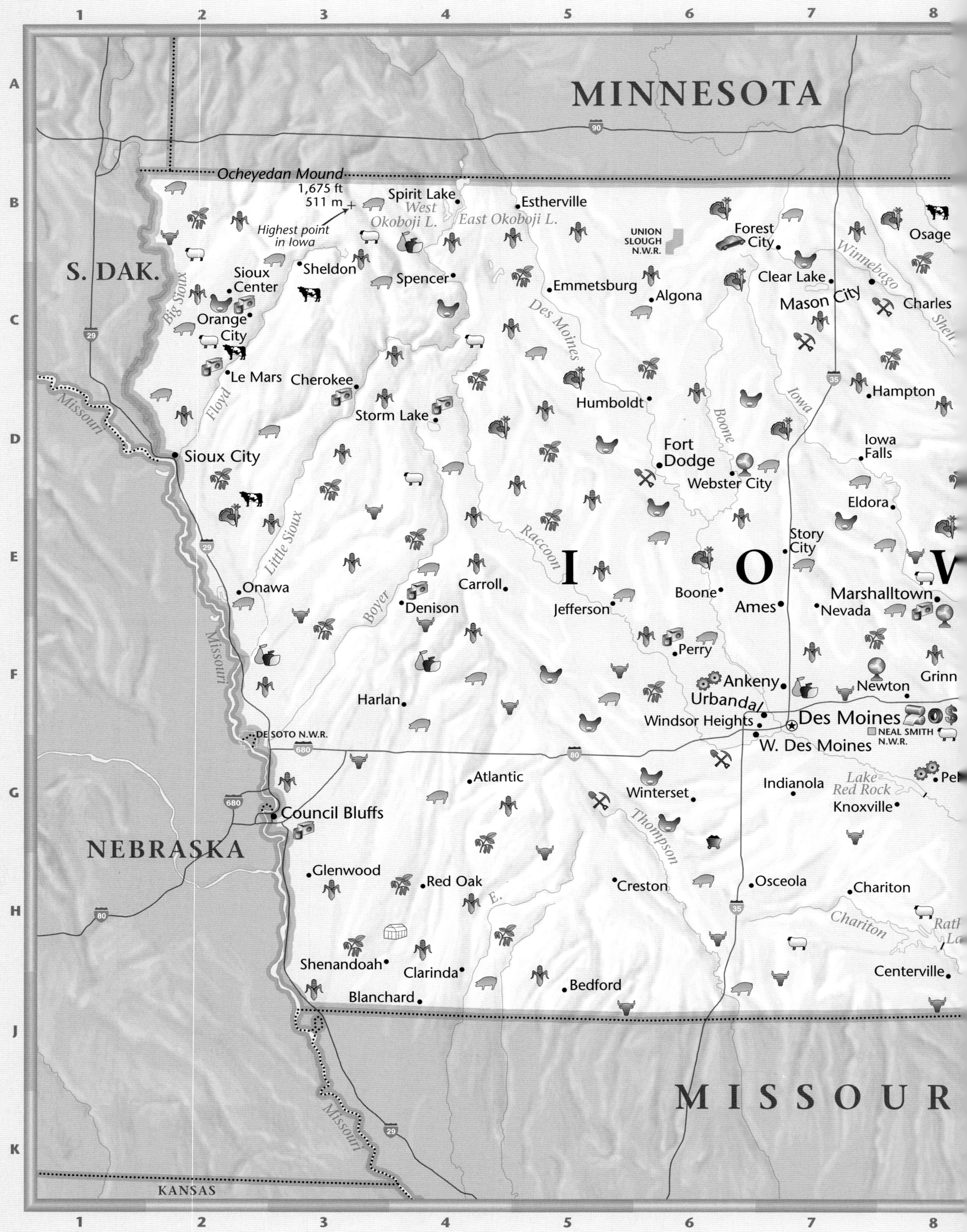
MINNESOTA
S. DAK.
NEBRASKA
MISSOUR
KANSAS
I
O
W
Ocheyedan Mound
1,675 ft
511 m
Highest point
in Iowa
Spirit Lake
West
Okoboji L.
East Okoboji L.
Estherville
UNION
SLOUGH
N.W.R.
Forest
City
Osage
Sioux
Center
Sheldon
Spencer
Emmetsburg
Algona
Clear Lake
Mason City
Charles
Orange
City
Le Mars
Cherokee
Storm Lake
Humboldt
Hampton
Sioux City
Fort
Dodge
Webster City
Iowa
Falls
Eldora
Story
City
Onawa
Carroll
Denison
Jefferson
Boone
Ames
Marshalltown
Nevada
Perry
Ankeny
Urbandale
Newton
Grinn
Harlan
Windsor Heights
Des Moines
NEAL SMITH
N.W.R.
W. Des Moines
DE SOTO N.W.R.
Atlantic
Winterset
Indianola
Lake
Red Rock
Knoxville
Council Bluffs
Glenwood
Red Oak
Creston
Osceola
Chariton
Shenandoah
Clarinda
Blanchard
Bedford
Centerville
Big Sioux
Floyd
Little Sioux
Missouri
Boyer
Raccoon
Des Moines
Boone
Iowa
Winnebago
Shell
Thompson
Chariton
E.
90
29
35
80
680
1
2
3
4
5
6
7
8
A
B
C
D
E
F
G
H
J
K

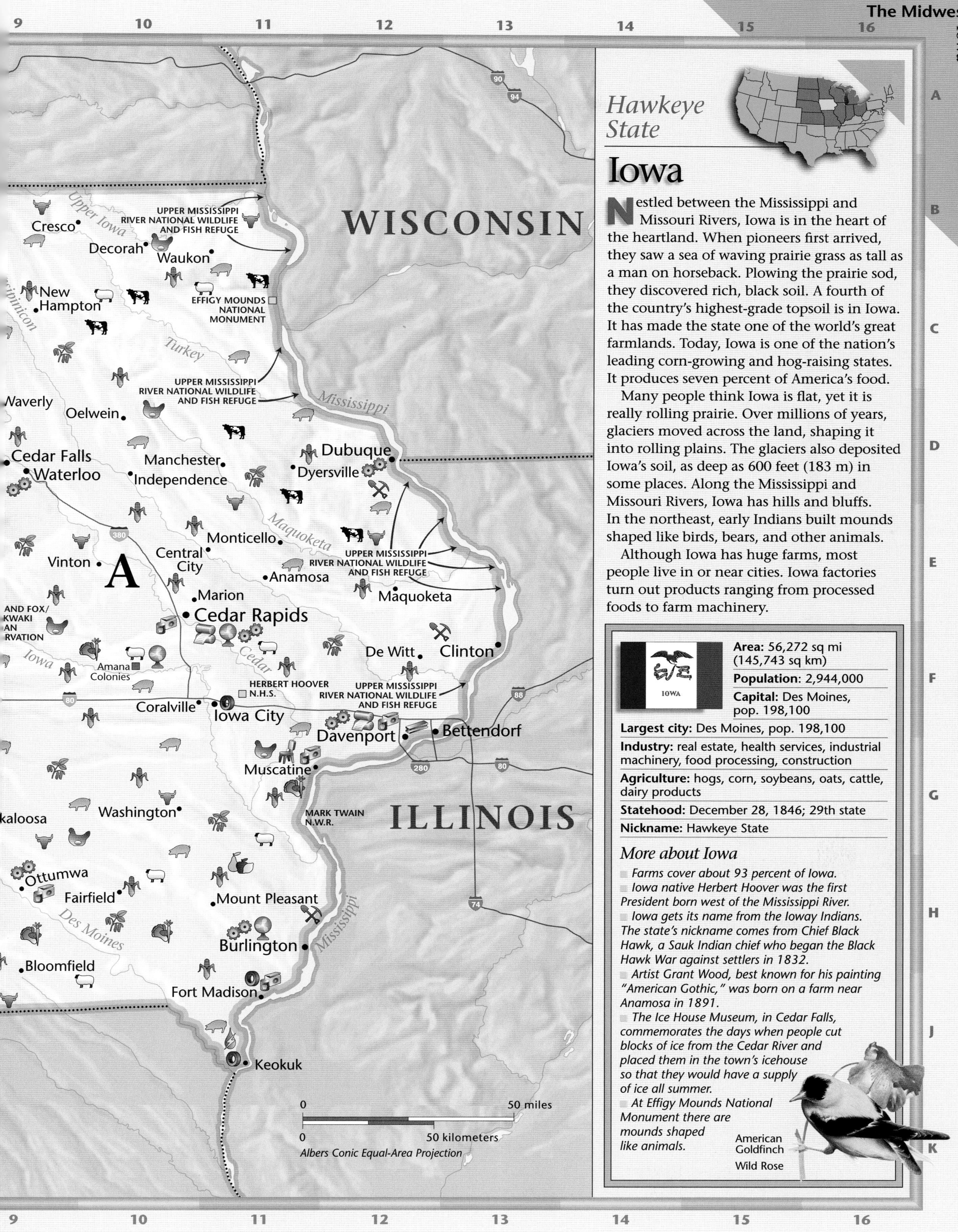

Hawkeye State

Iowa

Nestled between the Mississippi and Missouri Rivers, Iowa is in the heart of the heartland. When pioneers first arrived, they saw a sea of waving prairie grass as tall as a man on horseback. Plowing the prairie sod, they discovered rich, black soil. A fourth of the country's highest-grade topsoil is in Iowa. It has made the state one of the world's great farmlands. Today, Iowa is one of the nation's leading corn-growing and hog-raising states. It produces seven percent of America's food.

Many people think Iowa is flat, yet it is really rolling prairie. Over millions of years, glaciers moved across the land, shaping it into rolling plains. The glaciers also deposited Iowa's soil, as deep as 600 feet (183 m) in some places. Along the Mississippi and Missouri Rivers, Iowa has hills and bluffs. In the northeast, early Indians built mounds shaped like birds, bears, and other animals.

Although Iowa has huge farms, most people live in or near cities. Iowa factories turn out products ranging from processed foods to farm machinery.

IOWA

Area: 56,272 sq mi (145,743 sq km)

Population: 2,944,000

Capital: Des Moines, pop. 198,100

Largest city: Des Moines, pop. 198,100

Industry: real estate, health services, industrial machinery, food processing, construction

Agriculture: hogs, corn, soybeans, oats, cattle, dairy products

Statehood: December 28, 1846; 29th state

Nickname: Hawkeye State

More about Iowa

- *Farms cover about 93 percent of Iowa.*
- *Iowa native Herbert Hoover was the first President born west of the Mississippi River.*
- *Iowa gets its name from the Ioway Indians. The state's nickname comes from Chief Black Hawk, a Sauk Indian chief who began the Black Hawk War against settlers in 1832.*
- *Artist Grant Wood, best known for his painting "American Gothic," was born on a farm near Anamosa in 1891.*
- *The Ice House Museum, in Cedar Falls, commemorates the days when people cut blocks of ice from the Cedar River and placed them in the town's icehouse so that they would have a supply of ice all summer.*
- *At Effigy Mounds National Monument there are mounds shaped like animals.*

NEBRASKA
COLORADO
KANSAS
TEXAS
OKLA
HIGH PLAINS
Smoky Hills
Red Hills
Oberlin
Norton
Phillipsburg
Lebanon
Belleville
Geographic center of the 48 contiguous states
Concordia
Beloit
Goodland
Colby
Highest point in Kansas
Mt. Sunflower 4,039 ft 1,231 m
Oakley
WaKeeney
Plainville
Minneapolis
Hays
Russell
Salina
Ellsworth
Scott City
Ness City
Hoisington
Great Bend
McPherson
Lyons
Larned
FORT LARNED N.H.S.
QUIVIRA N.W.R.
Hutchinson
Lakin
Garden City
Kinsley
Dodge City
Ulysses
Greensburg
Pratt
Kingman
Meade
Hugoton
Liberal
Elkhart
CIMARRON NATIONAL GRASSLAND
Medicine Lodge
Anthony
KIRWIN N.W.R.
Kirwin Reservoir
NICODEMUS N.H.S.
Waconda Lake
Wilson Lake
Cedar Bluff Reservoir
Kanopolis Lake
Cheyenne Bottoms
Cheney Reservoir
South Fork Republican
Sappa Creek
Prairie Dog Creek
Beaver Creek
North Fork Solomon
South Fork Solomon
Solomon
Saline
Smoky Hill
Ladder Creek
White Woman Creek
Walnut Creek
Pawnee
Buckner Creek
Arkansas
Bear Creek
North Fork Cimarron
Crooked Creek
Medicine Lodge
Cimarron
Little Blue
0 100 miles
0 100 kilometers
Albers Conic Equal-Area Projection

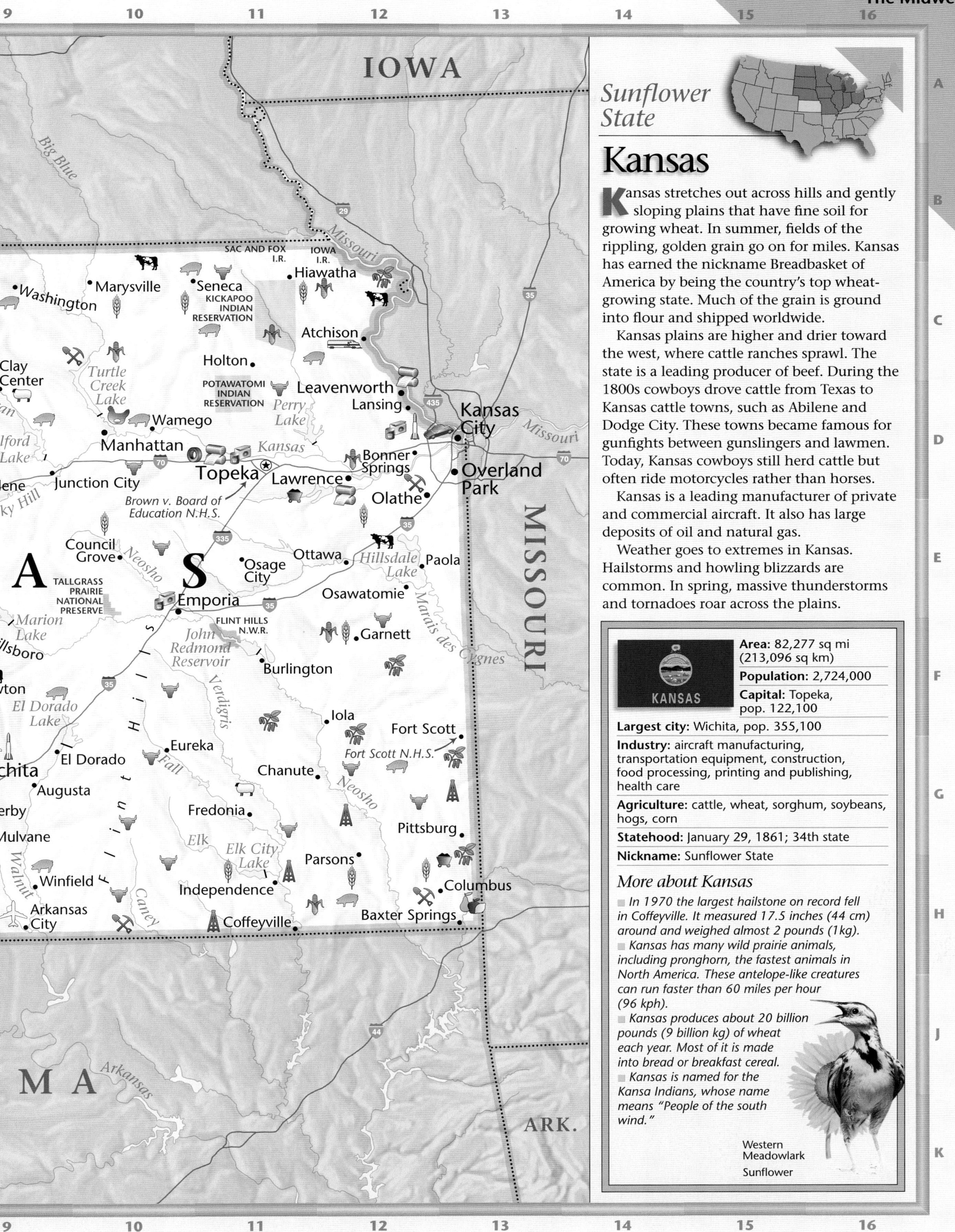

Sunflower State

Kansas

Kansas stretches out across hills and gently sloping plains that have fine soil for growing wheat. In summer, fields of the rippling, golden grain go on for miles. Kansas has earned the nickname Breadbasket of America by being the country's top wheat-growing state. Much of the grain is ground into flour and shipped worldwide.

Kansas plains are higher and drier toward the west, where cattle ranches sprawl. The state is a leading producer of beef. During the 1800s cowboys drove cattle from Texas to Kansas cattle towns, such as Abilene and Dodge City. These towns became famous for gunfights between gunslingers and lawmen. Today, Kansas cowboys still herd cattle but often ride motorcycles rather than horses.

Kansas is a leading manufacturer of private and commercial aircraft. It also has large deposits of oil and natural gas.

Weather goes to extremes in Kansas. Hailstorms and howling blizzards are common. In spring, massive thunderstorms and tornadoes roar across the plains.

KANSAS

Area: 82,277 sq mi (213,096 sq km)

Population: 2,724,000

Capital: Topeka, pop. 122,100

Largest city: Wichita, pop. 355,100

Industry: aircraft manufacturing, transportation equipment, construction, food processing, printing and publishing, health care

Agriculture: cattle, wheat, sorghum, soybeans, hogs, corn

Statehood: January 29, 1861; 34th state

Nickname: Sunflower State

More about Kansas

- *In 1970 the largest hailstone on record fell in Coffeyville. It measured 17.5 inches (44 cm) around and weighed almost 2 pounds (1kg).*
- *Kansas has many wild prairie animals, including pronghorn, the fastest animals in North America. These antelope-like creatures can run faster than 60 miles per hour (96 kph).*
- *Kansas produces about 20 billion pounds (9 billion kg) of wheat each year. Most of it is made into bread or breakfast cereal.*
- *Kansas is named for the Kansa Indians, whose name means "People of the south wind."*

Western Meadowlark

Sunflower

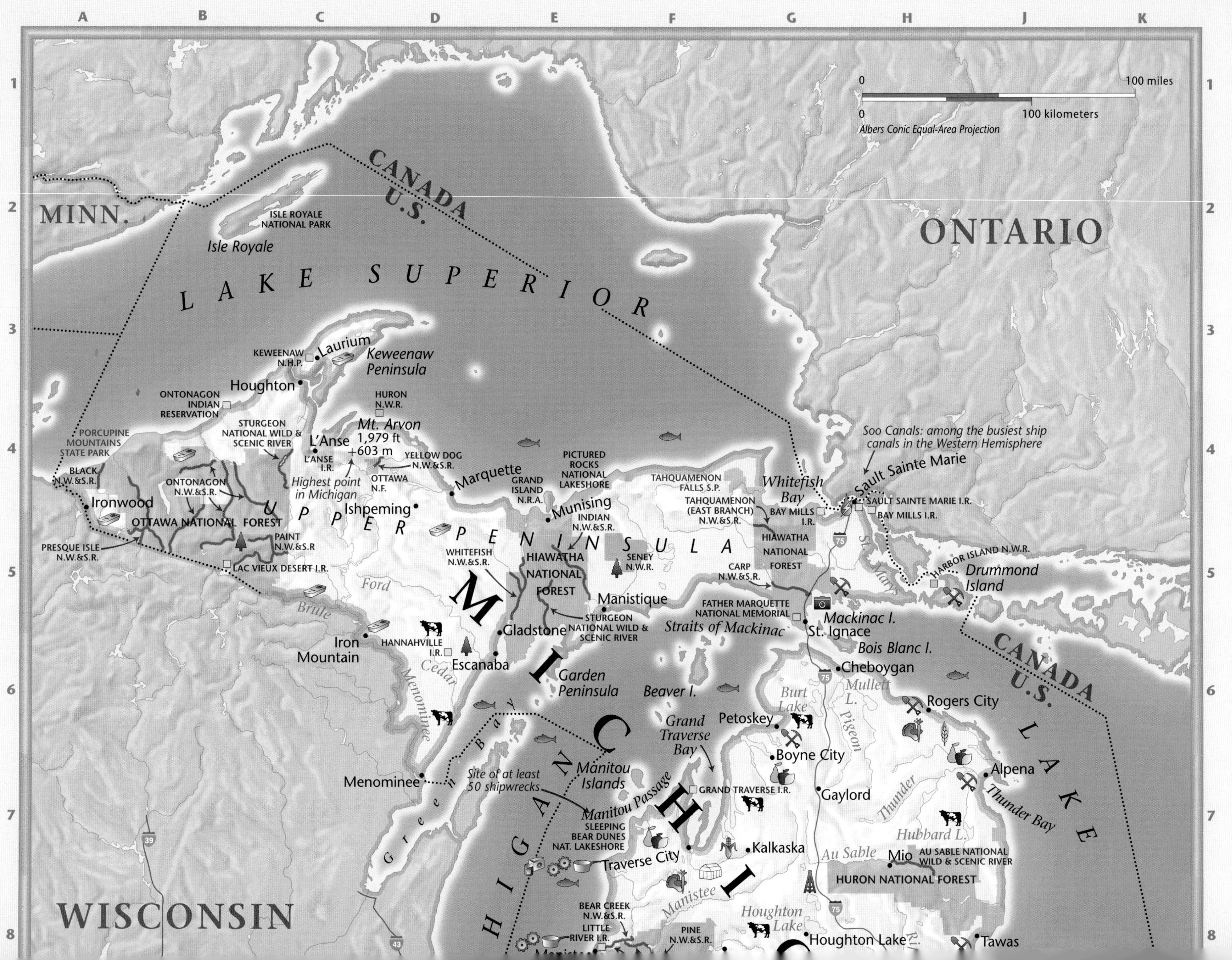
ONTARIO
MINN.
WISCONSIN
MICHIGAN
CANADA
U.S.
LAKE SUPERIOR
LAKE
UPPER PENINSULA
0 100 miles
0 100 kilometers
Albers Conic Equal-Area Projection
Isle Royale
ISLE ROYALE NATIONAL PARK
KEWEENAW N.H.P.
Laurium
Keweenaw Peninsula
Houghton
ONTONAGON INDIAN RESERVATION
HURON N.W.R.
Mt. Arvon 1,979 ft +603 m
STURGEON NATIONAL WILD & SCENIC RIVER
L'Anse
L'ANSE I.R.
Highest point in Michigan
YELLOW DOG N.W.&S.R.
OTTAWA N.F.
PORCUPINE MOUNTAINS STATE PARK
BLACK N.W.&S.R.
ONTONAGON N.W.&S.R.
Ironwood
OTTAWA NATIONAL FOREST
PRESQUE ISLE N.W.&S.R.
PAINT N.W.&S.R
LAC VIEUX DESERT I.R.
Ishpeming
Marquette
GRAND ISLAND N.R.A.
PICTURED ROCKS NATIONAL LAKESHORE
Munising
INDIAN N.W.&S.R.
WHITEFISH N.W.&S.R.
HIAWATHA NATIONAL FOREST
SENEY N.W.R.
TAHQUAMENON FALLS S.P.
TAHQUAMENON (EAST BRANCH) N.W.&S.R.
Whitefish Bay
BAY MILLS I.R.
Soo Canals: among the busiest ship canals in the Western Hemisphere
Sault Sainte Marie
SAULT SAINTE MARIE I.R.
BAY MILLS I.R.
HIAWATHA NATIONAL FOREST
CARP N.W.&S.R.
HARBOR ISLAND N.W.R.
Drummond Island
St. Marys
Ford
Brule
Iron Mountain
HANNAHVILLE I.R.
Cedar
Escanaba
Gladstone
Manistique
STURGEON NATIONAL WILD & SCENIC RIVER
FATHER MARQUETTE NATIONAL MEMORIAL
Straits of Mackinac
Mackinac I.
St. Ignace
Bois Blanc I.
Cheboygan
Garden Peninsula
Beaver I.
Burt Lake
Mullett L.
Pigeon
Rogers City
Menominee
Green Bay
Petoskey
Grand Traverse Bay
Boyne City
Site of at least 50 shipwrecks
Manitou Islands
Manitou Passage
GRAND TRAVERSE I.R.
Gaylord
Alpena
Thunder Bay
Thunder
SLEEPING BEAR DUNES NAT. LAKESHORE
Kalkaska
Hubbard L.
Au Sable
Mio
AU SABLE NATIONAL WILD & SCENIC RIVER
Traverse City
HURON NATIONAL FOREST
Manistee
Houghton Lake
BEAR CREEK N.W.&S.R.
LITTLE RIVER I.R.
PINE N.W.&S.R.
Houghton Lake
Tawas
75
39
43
A B C D E F G H J K
1 2 3 4 5 6 7 8

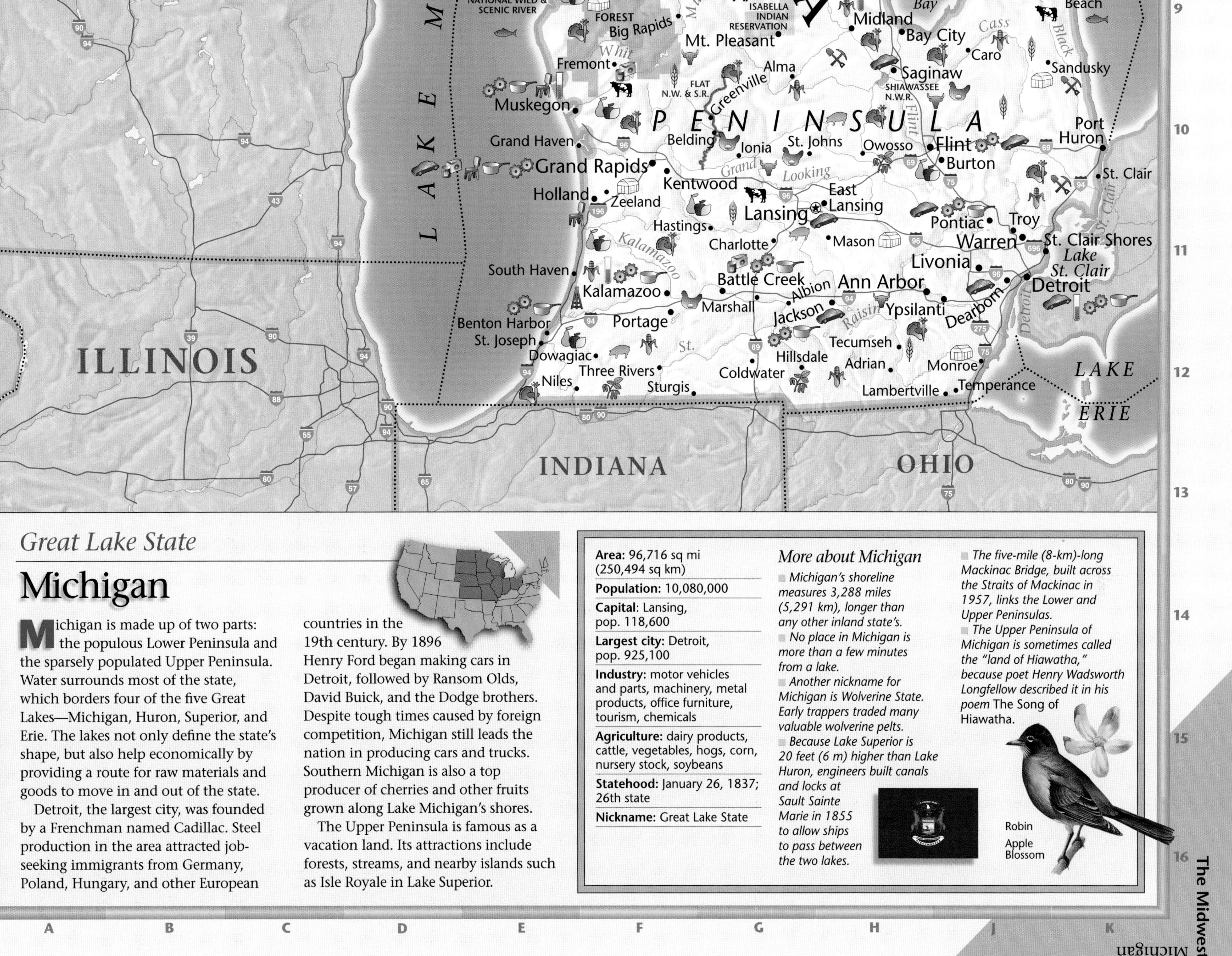

Great Lake State

Michigan

Michigan is made up of two parts: the populous Lower Peninsula and the sparsely populated Upper Peninsula. Water surrounds most of the state, which borders four of the five Great Lakes—Michigan, Huron, Superior, and Erie. The lakes not only define the state's shape, but also help economically by providing a route for raw materials and goods to move in and out of the state.

Detroit, the largest city, was founded by a Frenchman named Cadillac. Steel production in the area attracted job-seeking immigrants from Germany, Poland, Hungary, and other European countries in the 19th century. By 1896 Henry Ford began making cars in Detroit, followed by Ransom Olds, David Buick, and the Dodge brothers. Despite tough times caused by foreign competition, Michigan still leads the nation in producing cars and trucks. Southern Michigan is also a top producer of cherries and other fruits grown along Lake Michigan's shores.

The Upper Peninsula is famous as a vacation land. Its attractions include forests, streams, and nearby islands such as Isle Royale in Lake Superior.

Area: 96,716 sq mi (250,494 sq km)

Population: 10,080,000

Capital: Lansing, pop. 118,600

Largest city: Detroit, pop. 925,100

Industry: motor vehicles and parts, machinery, metal products, office furniture, tourism, chemicals

Agriculture: dairy products, cattle, vegetables, hogs, corn, nursery stock, soybeans

Statehood: January 26, 1837; 26th state

Nickname: Great Lake State

More about Michigan

- *Michigan's shoreline measures 3,288 miles (5,291 km), longer than any other inland state's.*
- *No place in Michigan is more than a few minutes from a lake.*
- *Another nickname for Michigan is Wolverine State. Early trappers traded many valuable wolverine pelts.*
- *Because Lake Superior is 20 feet (6 m) higher than Lake Huron, engineers built canals and locks at Sault Sainte Marie in 1855 to allow ships to pass between the two lakes.*
- *The five-mile (8-km)-long Mackinac Bridge, built across the Straits of Mackinac in 1957, links the Lower and Upper Peninsulas.*
- *The Upper Peninsula of Michigan is sometimes called the "land of Hiawatha," because poet Henry Wadsworth Longfellow described it in his poem* The Song of Hiawatha.

Robin

Apple Blossom

MANITOBA
ONTARIO
CANADA
U.S.
N. DAK.
MICHIGAN
MINNESOTA
LAKE SUPERIOR
The "Northwest Angle" is the northernmost point in the 48 contiguous states
RED LAKE INDIAN RESERVATION
Highest point in Minnesota
Eagle Mt.
2,301 ft 701 m
Boundary Waters Canoe Area Wilderness
SUPERIOR NATIONAL FOREST
SUPERIOR N.F.
CHIPPEWA NATIONAL FOREST
VOYAGEURS NATIONAL PARK
GRAND PORTAGE I.R.
GRAND PORTAGE NAT. MON.
BOIS FORTE I.R.
BOIS FORTE (DEER CREEK) I.R.
BOIS FORTE (VERMILION LAKE) I.R.
RED LAKE INDIAN RESERVATION
RED LAKE I.R.
LEECH LAKE I.R.
WHITE EARTH INDIAN RESERVATION
FOND DU LAC INDIAN RESERVATION
SANDY LAKE I.R.
MILLE LACS I.R.
AGASSIZ N.W.R.
TAMARAC N.W.R.
HAMDEN SLOUGH N.W.R.
RICE LAKE N.W.R.
SHERBURNE
ST. CROIX NATIONAL SCENIC RIVERWAY
Source of the Mississippi River
Mesabi Range
Lake of the Woods
Rainy Lake
Namakan Lake
Vermilion Lake
Upper Red Lake
Lower Red Lake
Lake Winnibigoshish
Leech Lake
Lake Itasca
Mille Lacs Lake
Otter Tail Lake
Mud Lake
Lake Traverse
Big Stone Lake
Rainy
Big Fork
Roseau
Red Lake
Red River of the North
Wild Rice
Mississippi
Crow Wing
Otter Tail
Chippewa
Bois de Sioux
St. Louis
St. Croix
Pigeon
Rum
N. Fork
Hallock
Roseau
Baudette
International Falls
Warren
Thief River Falls
East Grand Forks
Crookston
Red Lake
Bemidji
Walker
Grand Rapids
Hibbing
Chisholm
Virginia
Ely
Grand Marais
Two Harbors
Duluth
Proctor
Cloquet
Moorhead
Detroit Lakes
Park Rapids
Menahga
Wadena
Perham
Pelican Rapids
Fergus Falls
Aitkin
Brainerd
Little Falls
Long Prairie
Alexandria
Sauk Centre
St. Cloud
Milaca
Mora
Pine City
Sandstone
Wheaton
Morris
29
94
35
A
B
C
D
E
F
G
H
J
K
1
2
3
4
5
6
7
8

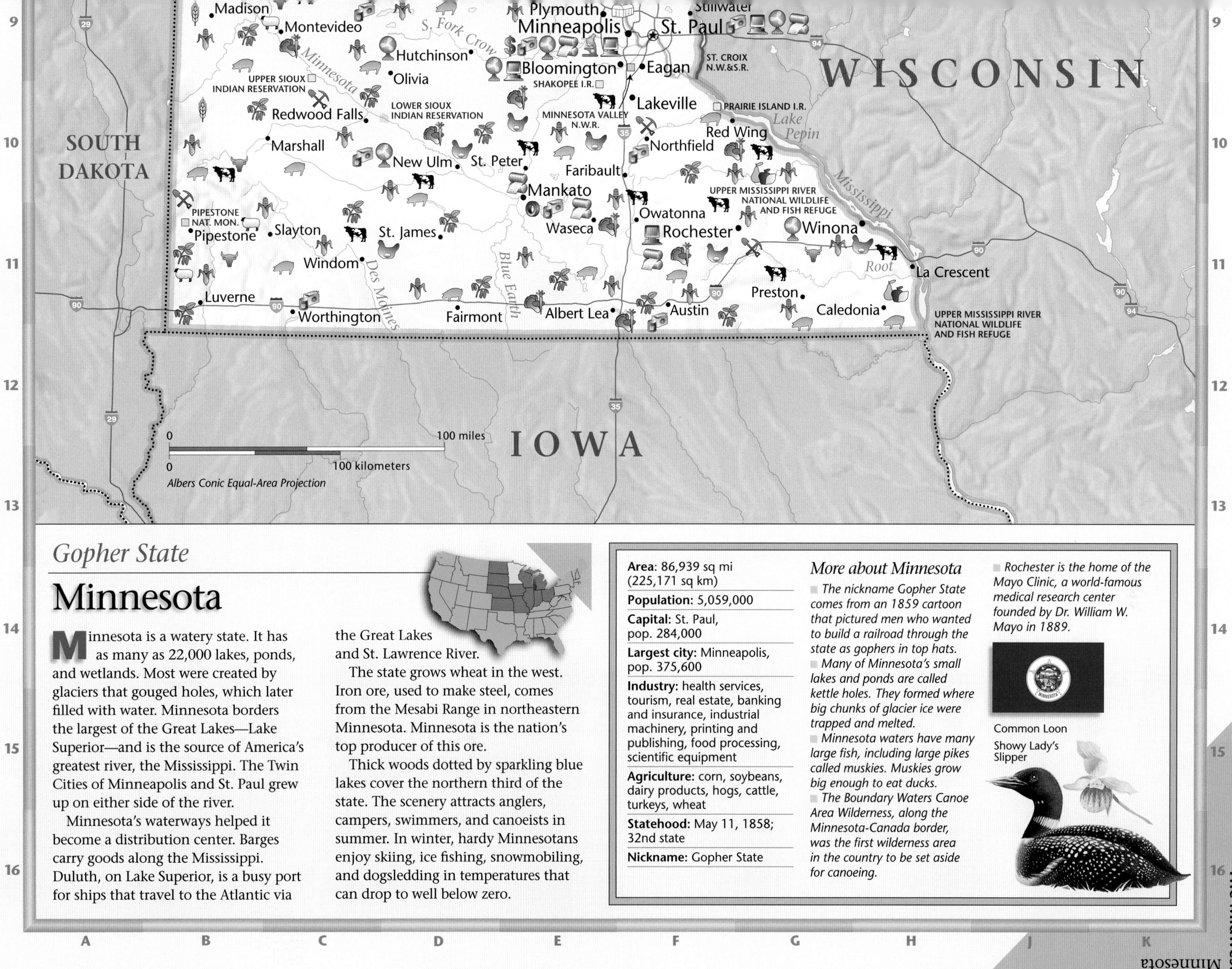

Gopher State

Minnesota

Minnesota is a watery state. It has as many as 22,000 lakes, ponds, and wetlands. Most were created by glaciers that gouged holes, which later filled with water. Minnesota borders the largest of the Great Lakes—Lake Superior—and is the source of America's greatest river, the Mississippi. The Twin Cities of Minneapolis and St. Paul grew up on either side of the river.

Minnesota's waterways helped it become a distribution center. Barges carry goods along the Mississippi. Duluth, on Lake Superior, is a busy port for ships that travel to the Atlantic via the Great Lakes and St. Lawrence River.

The state grows wheat in the west. Iron ore, used to make steel, comes from the Mesabi Range in northeastern Minnesota. Minnesota is the nation's top producer of this ore.

Thick woods dotted by sparkling blue lakes cover the northern third of the state. The scenery attracts anglers, campers, swimmers, and canoeists in summer. In winter, hardy Minnesotans enjoy skiing, ice fishing, snowmobiling, and dogsledding in temperatures that can drop to well below zero.

Area: 86,939 sq mi (225,171 sq km)

Population: 5,059,000

Capital: St. Paul, pop. 284,000

Largest city: Minneapolis, pop. 375,600

Industry: health services, tourism, real estate, banking and insurance, industrial machinery, printing and publishing, food processing, scientific equipment

Agriculture: corn, soybeans, dairy products, hogs, cattle, turkeys, wheat

Statehood: May 11, 1858; 32nd state

Nickname: Gopher State

More about Minnesota

- *The nickname Gopher State comes from an 1859 cartoon that pictured men who wanted to build a railroad through the state as gophers in top hats.*
- *Many of Minnesota's small lakes and ponds are called kettle holes. They formed where big chunks of glacier ice were trapped and melted.*
- *Minnesota waters have many large fish, including large pikes called muskies. Muskies grow big enough to eat ducks.*
- *The Boundary Waters Canoe Area Wilderness, along the Minnesota-Canada border, was the first wilderness area in the country to be set aside for canoeing.*
- *Rochester is the home of the Mayo Clinic, a world-famous medical research center founded by Dr. William W. Mayo in 1889.*

Common Loon

Showy Lady's Slipper

IOWA
NEBRASKA
KANSAS
MISSOURI
OKLAHOMA
ARKANSAS
OZARK PLATEAU
Maryville
Bethany
Trenton
Kirksville
Canton
Savannah
St. Joseph
Gallatin
Cameron
Chillicothe
Brookfield
Macon
Boyhood home of Mark Twain
SQUAW CREEK N.W.R.
SWAN LAKE N.W.R.
Jesse James Farm and Museum
Moberly
Mark Twain Lake
Liberty
Richmond
Harry S Truman N.H.S.
Kansas City
Independence
Marshall
Centralia
Mexico
Blue Springs
Lees Summit
Boonville
Columbia
BIG MUDDY N.W.R.
MARK TWAIN NATIONAL FOREST
Fulton
Belton
Warrensburg
Sedalia
California
Jefferson City
Harrisonville
Clinton
Eldon
Butler
Harry S Truman Reservoir
Lake of the Ozarks
Rolla
Nevada
Waynesville
Stockton Lake
Bolivar
Lebanon
Salem
U.S. center of population, 20
Webb City
Carthage
Springfield
Seymour
Joplin
Republic
WILSON'S CREEK N.B.
Mountain Grove
GEORGE WASHINGTON CARVER NATIONAL MONUMENT
Aurora
Monett
Neosho
Ava
West Plains
Table Rock Lake
Branson
ELEVEN POINT NATIO WILD & SCENIC R
OZARK NATION SCENIC RIVERWA
Bull Shoals Lake
Only extensive highlands in the central U.S.
One Hundred and Two
Platte
Grand
Thompson
Weldon
Locust Creek
Middle Fabius
Wyaconda
South Fabius
Missouri
Chariton
Blackwater
South Grand
Marais des Cygnes
Osage
Sac
Little Sac
Niangua
Osage Fork
Gasconade
Big Piney
Bryant Creek
White
Jacks
Eleven Point
0
100 miles
100 kilometers
Albers Conic Equal-Area Projection

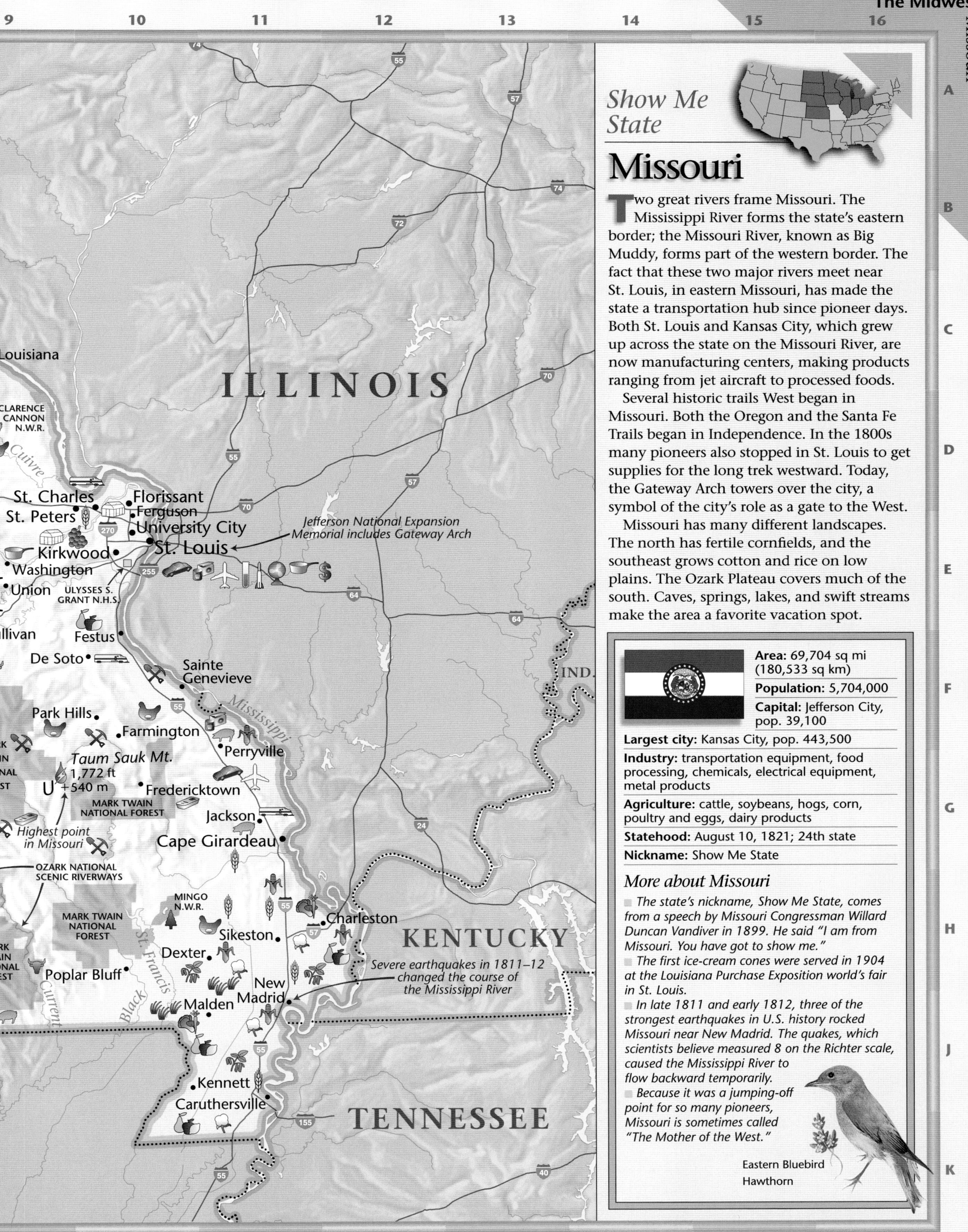

Show Me State

Missouri

Two great rivers frame Missouri. The Mississippi River forms the state's eastern border; the Missouri River, known as Big Muddy, forms part of the western border. The fact that these two major rivers meet near St. Louis, in eastern Missouri, has made the state a transportation hub since pioneer days. Both St. Louis and Kansas City, which grew up across the state on the Missouri River, are now manufacturing centers, making products ranging from jet aircraft to processed foods.

Several historic trails West began in Missouri. Both the Oregon and the Santa Fe Trails began in Independence. In the 1800s many pioneers also stopped in St. Louis to get supplies for the long trek westward. Today, the Gateway Arch towers over the city, a symbol of the city's role as a gate to the West.

Missouri has many different landscapes. The north has fertile cornfields, and the southeast grows cotton and rice on low plains. The Ozark Plateau covers much of the south. Caves, springs, lakes, and swift streams make the area a favorite vacation spot.

Area: 69,704 sq mi (180,533 sq km)

Population: 5,704,000

Capital: Jefferson City, pop. 39,100

Largest city: Kansas City, pop. 443,500

Industry: transportation equipment, food processing, chemicals, electrical equipment, metal products

Agriculture: cattle, soybeans, hogs, corn, poultry and eggs, dairy products

Statehood: August 10, 1821; 24th state

Nickname: Show Me State

More about Missouri

- *The state's nickname, Show Me State, comes from a speech by Missouri Congressman Willard Duncan Vandiver in 1899. He said "I am from Missouri. You have got to show me."*
- *The first ice-cream cones were served in 1904 at the Louisiana Purchase Exposition world's fair in St. Louis.*
- *In late 1811 and early 1812, three of the strongest earthquakes in U.S. history rocked Missouri near New Madrid. The quakes, which scientists believe measured 8 on the Richter scale, caused the Mississippi River to flow backward temporarily.*
- *Because it was a jumping-off point for so many pioneers, Missouri is sometimes called "The Mother of the West."*

Eastern Bluebird
Hawthorn

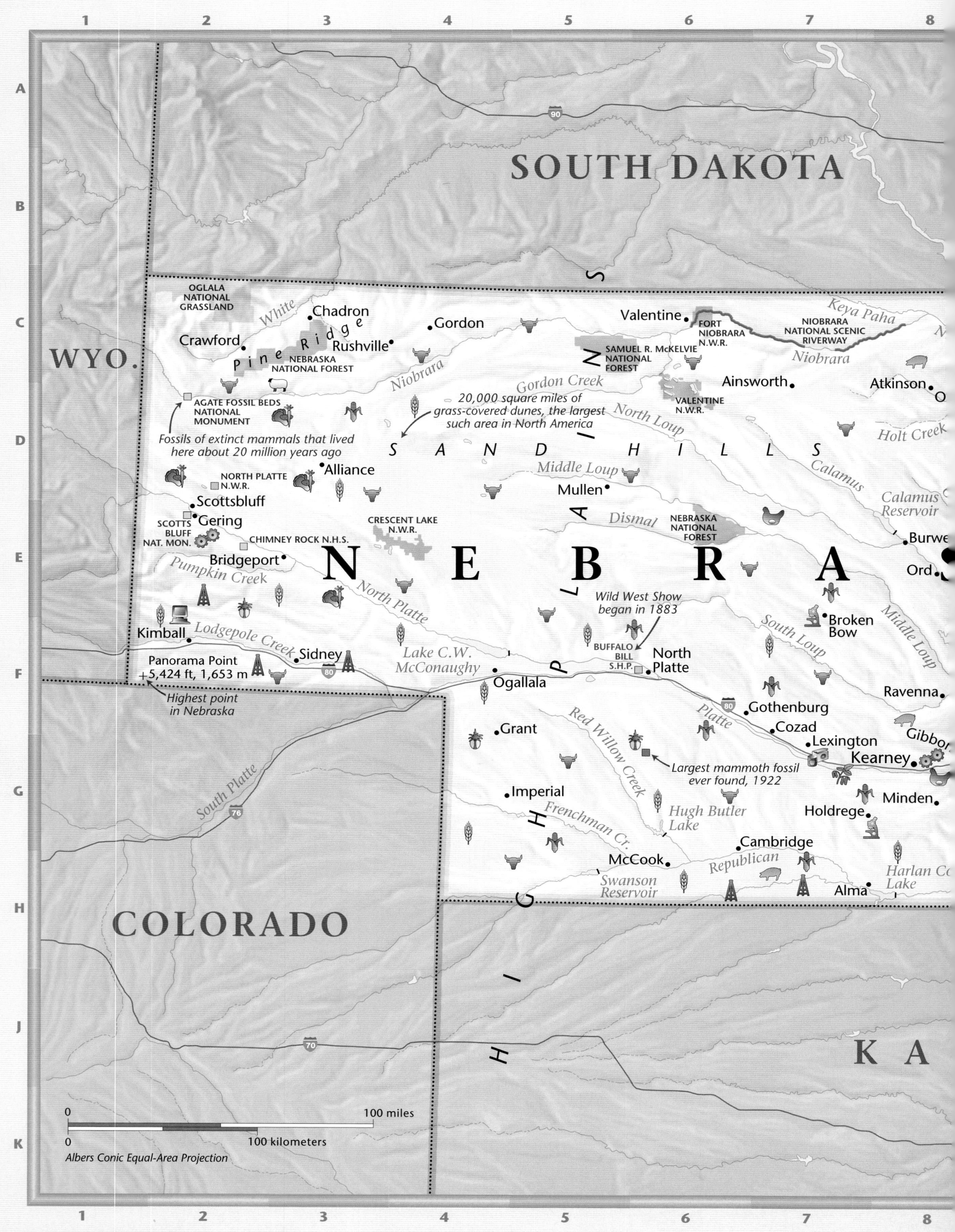

SOUTH DAKOTA
WYO.
NEBRASKA
COLORADO
KA
SANDHILLS
HIGH PLAINS
OGLALA NATIONAL GRASSLAND
Chadron
Crawford
Pine Ridge
Rushville
NEBRASKA NATIONAL FOREST
Gordon
Valentine
FORT NIOBRARA N.W.R.
NIOBRARA NATIONAL SCENIC RIVERWAY
SAMUEL R. McKELVIE NATIONAL FOREST
VALENTINE N.W.R.
Ainsworth
Atkinson
AGATE FOSSIL BEDS NATIONAL MONUMENT
Fossils of extinct mammals that lived here about 20 million years ago
20,000 square miles of grass-covered dunes, the largest such area in North America
Alliance
NORTH PLATTE N.W.R.
Scottsbluff
Gering
SCOTTS BLUFF NAT. MON.
CHIMNEY ROCK N.H.S.
Bridgeport
CRESCENT LAKE N.W.R.
Mullen
NEBRASKA NATIONAL FOREST
Calamus Reservoir
Burwe
Ord
Kimball
Sidney
Panorama Point +5,424 ft, 1,653 m
Highest point in Nebraska
Lake C.W. McConaughy
Ogallala
Wild West Show began in 1883
BUFFALO BILL S.H.P.
North Platte
Broken Bow
Ravenna
Gothenburg
Cozad
Lexington
Kearney
Gibbon
Grant
Largest mammoth fossil ever found, 1922
Imperial
Hugh Butler Lake
Minden
Holdrege
Cambridge
McCook
Swanson Reservoir
Alma
Harlan Co. Lake
White
Niobrara
Keya Paha
Gordon Creek
North Loup
Holt Creek
Calamus
Middle Loup
Dismal
Pumpkin Creek
North Platte
Lodgepole Creek
South Loup
Platte
Red Willow Creek
Frenchman Cr.
Republican
South Platte
90
80
76
70
0 100 miles
0 100 kilometers
Albers Conic Equal-Area Projection

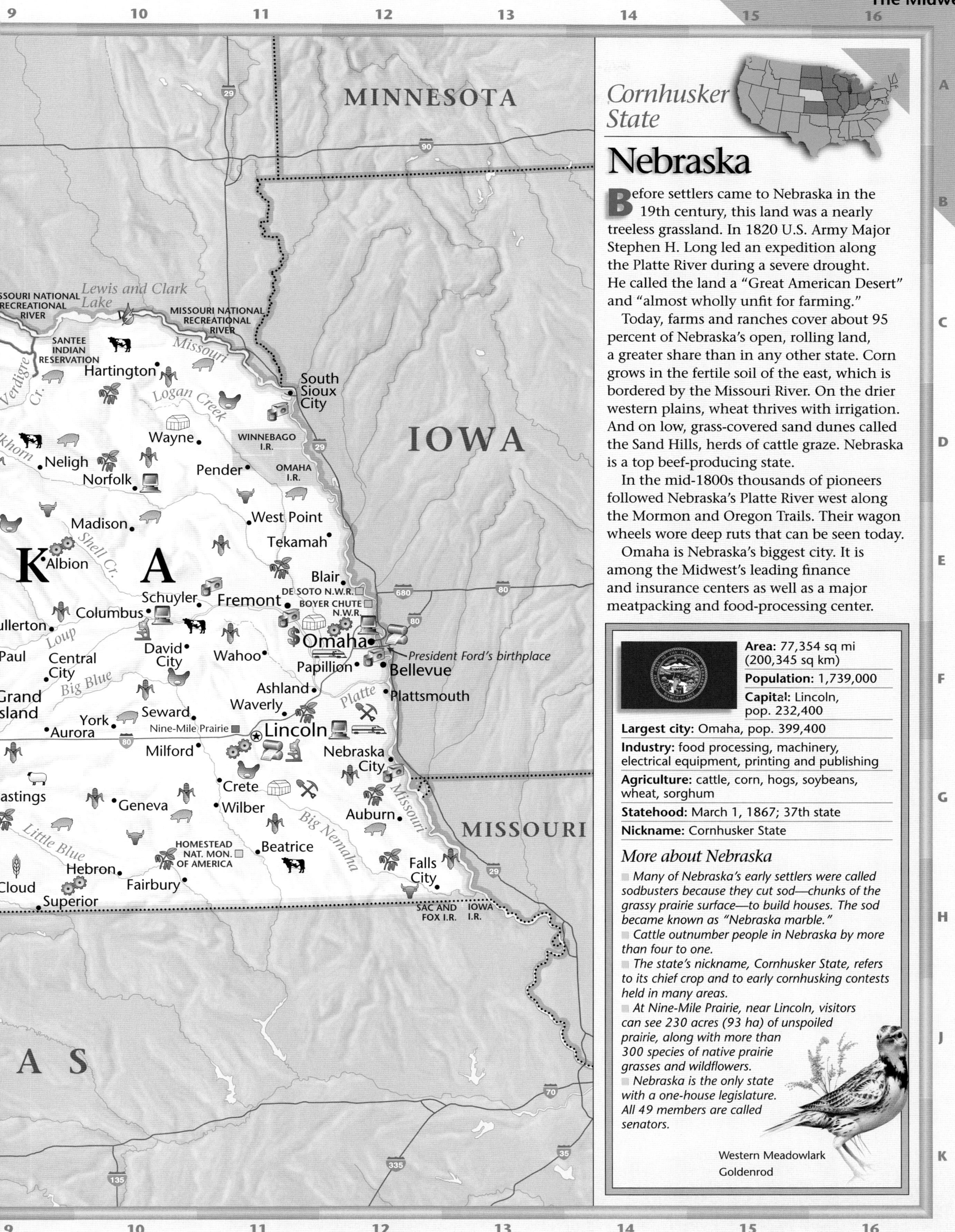

Cornhusker State

Nebraska

Before settlers came to Nebraska in the 19th century, this land was a nearly treeless grassland. In 1820 U.S. Army Major Stephen H. Long led an expedition along the Platte River during a severe drought. He called the land a "Great American Desert" and "almost wholly unfit for farming."

Today, farms and ranches cover about 95 percent of Nebraska's open, rolling land, a greater share than in any other state. Corn grows in the fertile soil of the east, which is bordered by the Missouri River. On the drier western plains, wheat thrives with irrigation. And on low, grass-covered sand dunes called the Sand Hills, herds of cattle graze. Nebraska is a top beef-producing state.

In the mid-1800s thousands of pioneers followed Nebraska's Platte River west along the Mormon and Oregon Trails. Their wagon wheels wore deep ruts that can be seen today.

Omaha is Nebraska's biggest city. It is among the Midwest's leading finance and insurance centers as well as a major meatpacking and food-processing center.

Area: 77,354 sq mi (200,345 sq km)

Population: 1,739,000

Capital: Lincoln, pop. 232,400

Largest city: Omaha, pop. 399,400

Industry: food processing, machinery, electrical equipment, printing and publishing

Agriculture: cattle, corn, hogs, soybeans, wheat, sorghum

Statehood: March 1, 1867; 37th state

Nickname: Cornhusker State

More about Nebraska

- *Many of Nebraska's early settlers were called sodbusters because they cut sod—chunks of the grassy prairie surface—to build houses. The sod became known as "Nebraska marble."*
- *Cattle outnumber people in Nebraska by more than four to one.*
- *The state's nickname, Cornhusker State, refers to its chief crop and to early cornhusking contests held in many areas.*
- *At Nine-Mile Prairie, near Lincoln, visitors can see 230 acres (93 ha) of unspoiled prairie, along with more than 300 species of native prairie grasses and wildflowers.*
- *Nebraska is the only state with a one-house legislature. All 49 members are called senators.*

Western Meadowlark
Goldenrod

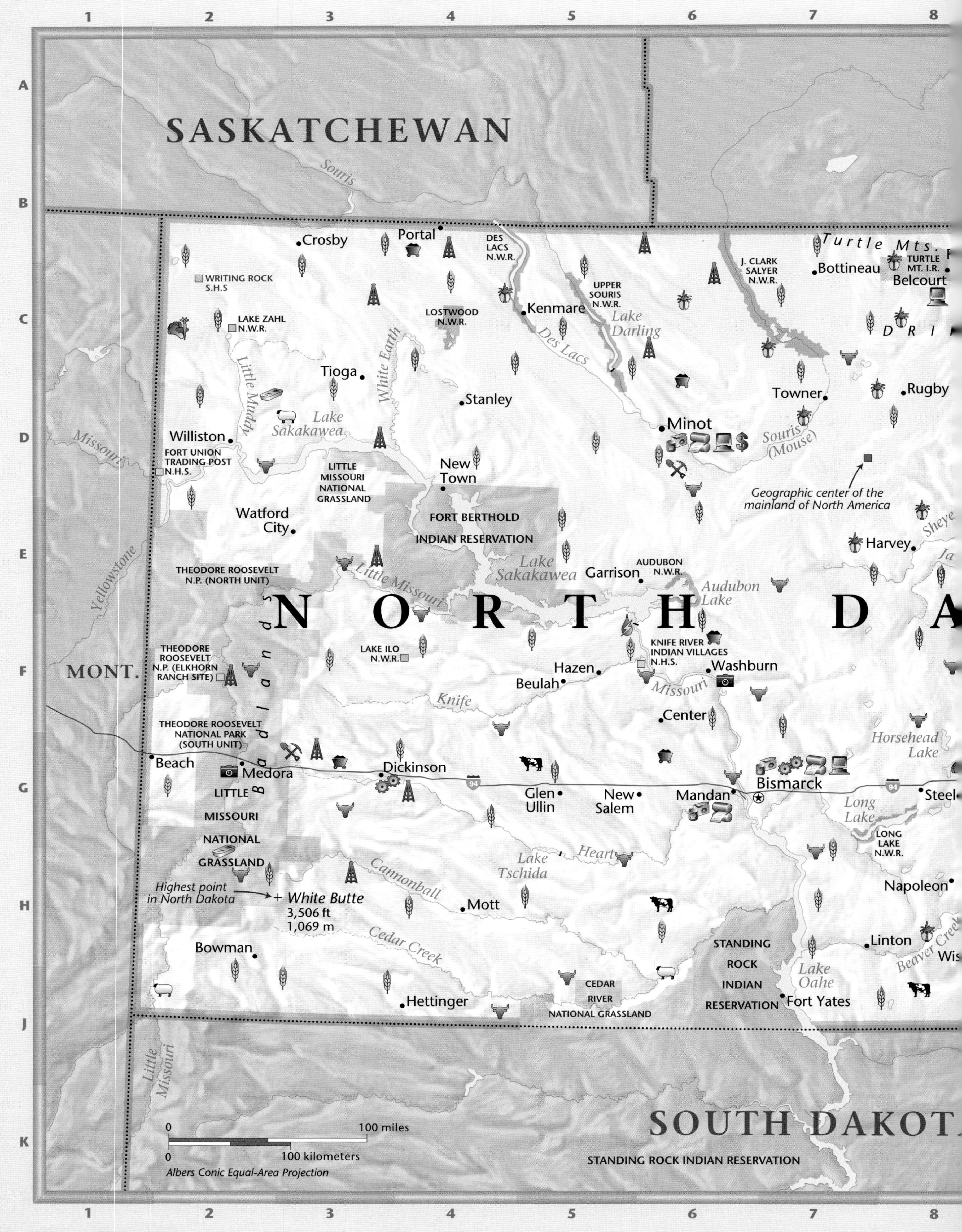
SASKATCHEWAN
MONT.
NORTH DA
SOUTH DAKOT
Crosby
Portal
Kenmare
Bottineau
Belcourt
Rugby
Towner
Minot
Tioga
Stanley
Williston
New Town
Watford City
Harvey
Garrison
Hazen
Beulah
Washburn
Center
Beach
Medora
Dickinson
Glen Ullin
New Salem
Mandan
Bismarck
Steele
Napoleon
Mott
Bowman
Hettinger
Linton
Fort Yates
White Butte
3,506 ft
1,069 m
Highest point in North Dakota
Geographic center of the mainland of North America
FORT BERTHOLD INDIAN RESERVATION
STANDING ROCK INDIAN RESERVATION
LITTLE MISSOURI NATIONAL GRASSLAND
CEDAR RIVER NATIONAL GRASSLAND
THEODORE ROOSEVELT N.P. (NORTH UNIT)
THEODORE ROOSEVELT N.P. (ELKHORN RANCH SITE)
THEODORE ROOSEVELT NATIONAL PARK (SOUTH UNIT)
FORT UNION TRADING POST N.H.S.
KNIFE RIVER INDIAN VILLAGES N.H.S.
WRITING ROCK S.H.S
LAKE ZAHL N.W.R.
LOSTWOOD N.W.R.
DES LACS N.W.R.
UPPER SOURIS N.W.R.
J. CLARK SALYER N.W.R.
TURTLE MT. I.R.
AUDUBON N.W.R.
LAKE ILO N.W.R.
LONG LAKE N.W.R.
Turtle Mts.
Lake Sakakawea
Lake Darling
Audubon Lake
Horsehead Lake
Long Lake
Lake Tschida
Lake Oahe
Souris
Souris (Mouse)
Des Lacs
Missouri
Little Muddy
White Earth
Little Missouri
Yellowstone
Knife
Heart
Cannonball
Cedar Creek
Beaver Creek
Sheyenne
Badlands
0 100 miles
0 100 kilometers
Albers Conic Equal-Area Projection

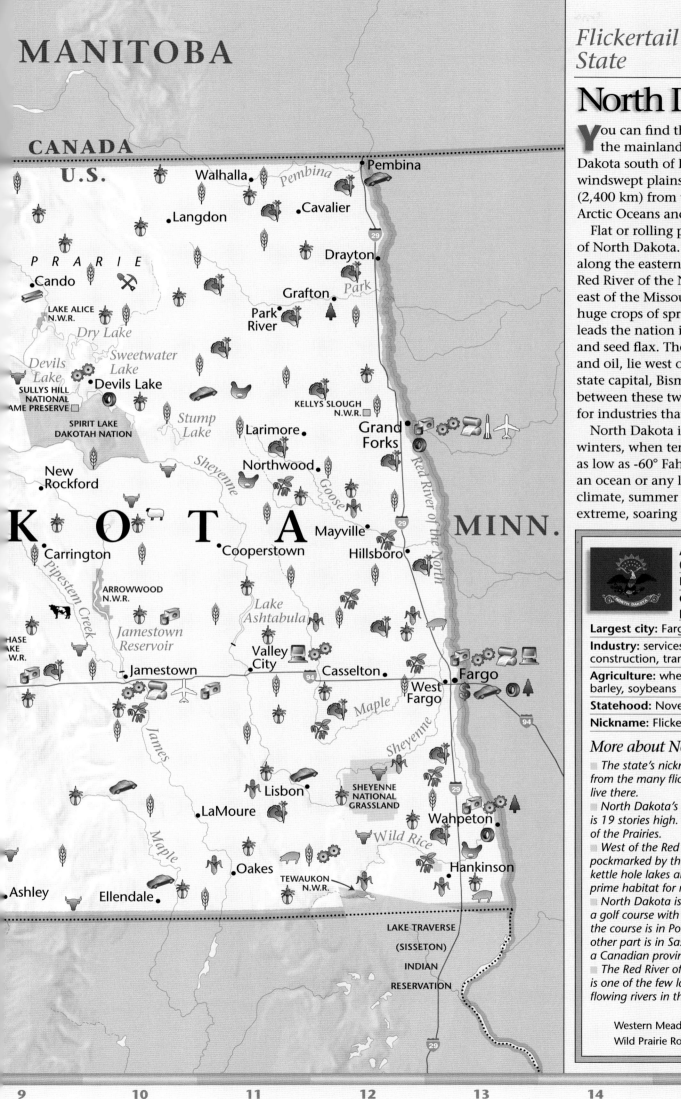

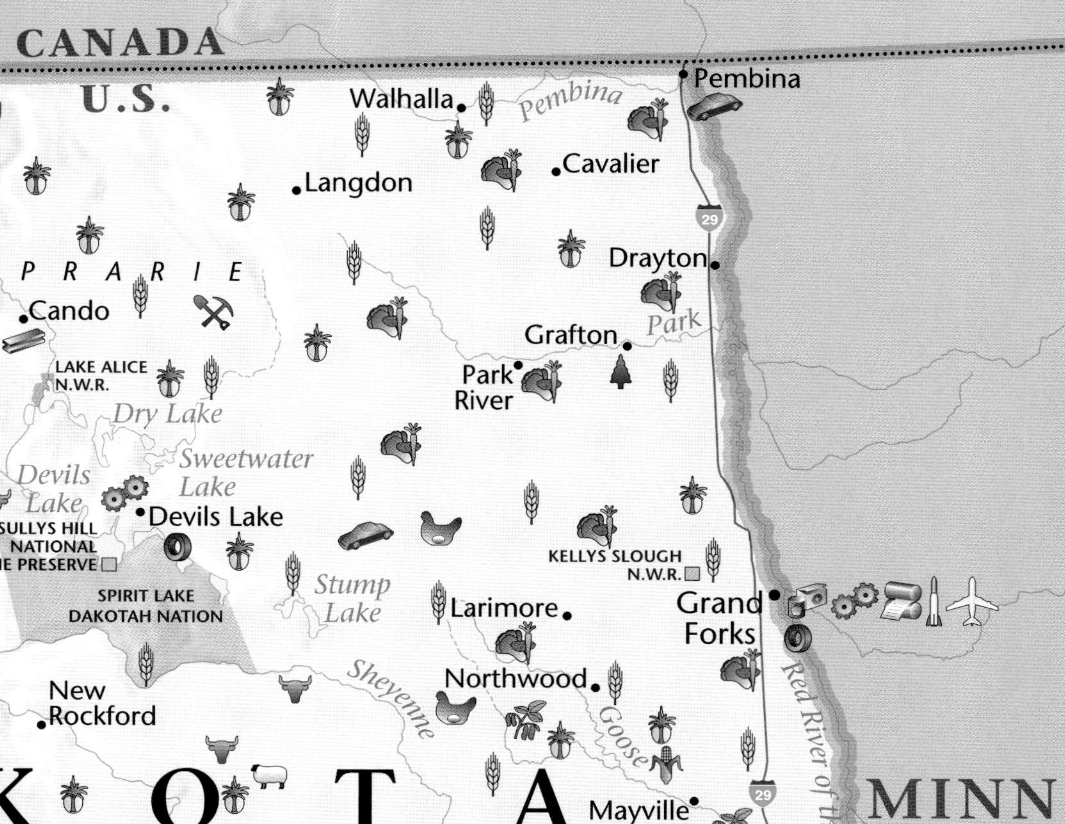

Flickertail State

North Dakota

You can find the geographic center of the mainland of North America in North Dakota south of Rugby, a small town on the windswept plains. Rugby is about 1,500 miles (2,400 km) from the Atlantic, Pacific, and Arctic Oceans and the Gulf of Mexico.

Flat or rolling plains stretch across much of North Dakota. Most North Dakotans live along the eastern border in the valley of the Red River of the North. Glaciers left rich soil east of the Missouri River. Here farmers grow huge crops of spring wheat. North Dakota leads the nation in barley, sunflower seeds, and seed flax. The Great Plains, rich in coal and oil, lie west of the Missouri River. The state capital, Bismarck, stands on the Missouri between these two regions and is the center for industries that cater to them both.

North Dakota is known for its frigid, windy winters, when temperatures may plummet as low as -60° Fahrenheit (-51°C). Without an ocean or any large lakes to moderate the climate, summer temperatures can be just as extreme, soaring to 121° Fahrenheit (49°C).

Area: 70,700 sq mi (183,112 sq km)
Population: 634,000
Capital: Bismarck, pop. 56,200
Largest city: Fargo, pop. 91,200
Industry: services, government, finance, construction, transportation, oil and gas
Agriculture: wheat, cattle, sunflowers, barley, soybeans
Statehood: November 2, 1889; 39th state
Nickname: Flickertail State

More about North Dakota

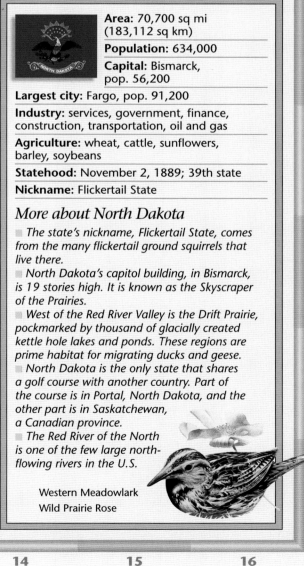

- *The state's nickname, Flickertail State, comes from the many flickertail ground squirrels that live there.*
- *North Dakota's capitol building, in Bismarck, is 19 stories high. It is known as the Skyscraper of the Prairies.*
- *West of the Red River Valley is the Drift Prairie, pockmarked by thousand of glacially created kettle hole lakes and ponds. These regions are prime habitat for migrating ducks and geese.*
- *North Dakota is the only state that shares a golf course with another country. Part of the course is in Portal, North Dakota, and the other part is in Saskatchewan, a Canadian province.*
- *The Red River of the North is one of the few large north-flowing rivers in the U.S.*

Western Meadowlark
Wild Prairie Rose

MICHIGAN
ONTARIO
LAKE ERIE
CANADA
U.S.
IND.
PA.
OHIO
Maumee Bay
Sylvania
Toledo
Oregon
OTTAWA N.W.R.
S. Bass I.
PERRY'S VICTORY AND INTERNATIONAL PEACE MEMORIAL
Kelleys Island
Port Clinton
Sandusky Bay
Sandusky
Maumee
Wauseon
Perrysburg
Bryan
St. Joseph
Napoleon
Bowling Green
Portage
Defiance
Fremont
Bellevue
Fostoria
Tiffin
Findlay
Norwalk
Willard
Lorain
North Olmsted
Elyria
Strongsville
Brunswick
Medina
Cleveland
Parma
Euclid
Mentor
Painesville
Geneva
Ashtabula
Conneaut
James A. Garfield N.H.S.
DAVID BERGER NAT. MEM.
Shaker Heights
CUYAHOGA VALLEY N.P.
Cuyahoga
Cuyahoga Falls
Kent
Akron
Barberton
Austintown
Warren
Niles
Youngstown
President McKinley's birthplace
Pymatuning Reservoir
Mosquito Creek Lake
Grand
Mahoning
Lake Milton
Berlin Lake
Alliance
Salem
North Canton
Canton
FIRST LADIES N.H.S.
Massillon
Orrville
Wooster
Tuscarawas
Ashland
Shelby
Mansfield
Loudonville
Mohican
LITTLE BEAVER CREEK NATIONAL SCENIC RIVER
East Liverpool
Atwood Lake
Leesville Lake
Toronto
Steubenville
Uhrichsville
Dover
New Philadelphia
Coshocton
Salt Fork Lake
Piedmont L.
Martins Ferry
Bellaire
Ohio
Wills Creek
Cambridge
Senecaville Lake
Zanesville
Muskin
Licking
Newark
Buckeye Lake
New
Mt. Vernon
Auglaize
Blanchard
Sandusky
Van Wert
Delphos
Lima
St. Marys
Upper Sandusky
Bucyrus
Galion
Blooming Grove
President Harding's birthplace
Olentangy
Kenton
Marion
Celina
St. Marys
Wapakoneta
Highest point in Ohio
Scioto
Grand Lake (St. Marys)
Indian Lake
Campbell Hill
1,550 ft
+ 472 m
Delaware Lake
Bellefontaine
Delaware
Birthplace of President Hayes
Sidney
Stillwater
Great Miami
Marysville
Big Darby Cr.
Piqua
Greenville
Urbana
Troy
Little Darby Cr.
Dublin
Westerville
Upper Arlington
Gahanna
Reynoldsburg
Columbus
Springfield
Huber Heights
Englewood
Trotwood
Fairborn
Dayton
BIG DARBY CREEK NATIONAL SCENIC RIVER
Dayton Aviation Heritage N.H.P.
Lancaster

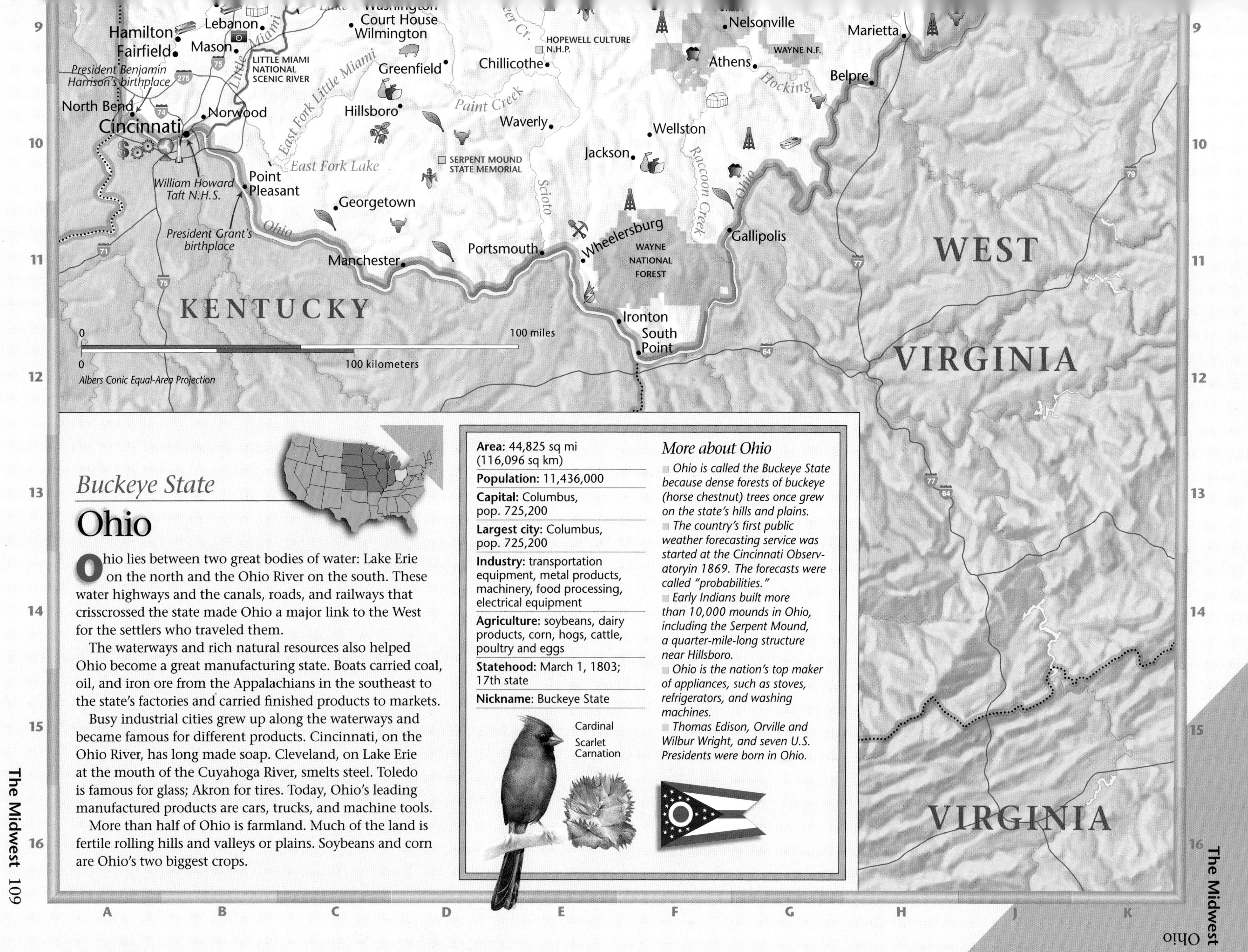

Buckeye State

Ohio

Ohio lies between two great bodies of water: Lake Erie on the north and the Ohio River on the south. These water highways and the canals, roads, and railways that crisscrossed the state made Ohio a major link to the West for the settlers who traveled them.

The waterways and rich natural resources also helped Ohio become a great manufacturing state. Boats carried coal, oil, and iron ore from the Appalachians in the southeast to the state's factories and carried finished products to markets.

Busy industrial cities grew up along the waterways and became famous for different products. Cincinnati, on the Ohio River, has long made soap. Cleveland, on Lake Erie at the mouth of the Cuyahoga River, smelts steel. Toledo is famous for glass; Akron for tires. Today, Ohio's leading manufactured products are cars, trucks, and machine tools.

More than half of Ohio is farmland. Much of the land is fertile rolling hills and valleys or plains. Soybeans and corn are Ohio's two biggest crops.

Area: 44,825 sq mi (116,096 sq km)

Population: 11,436,000

Capital: Columbus, pop. 725,200

Largest city: Columbus, pop. 725,200

Industry: transportation equipment, metal products, machinery, food processing, electrical equipment

Agriculture: soybeans, dairy products, corn, hogs, cattle, poultry and eggs

Statehood: March 1, 1803; 17th state

Nickname: Buckeye State

Cardinal
Scarlet Carnation

More about Ohio

- *Ohio is called the Buckeye State because dense forests of buckeye (horse chestnut) trees once grew on the state's hills and plains.*
- *The country's first public weather forecasting service was started at the Cincinnati Observatoryin 1869. The forecasts were called "probabilities."*
- *Early Indians built more than 10,000 mounds in Ohio, including the Serpent Mound, a quarter-mile-long structure near Hillsboro.*
- *Ohio is the nation's top maker of appliances, such as stoves, refrigerators, and washing machines.*
- *Thomas Edison, Orville and Wilbur Wright, and seven U.S. Presidents were born in Ohio.*

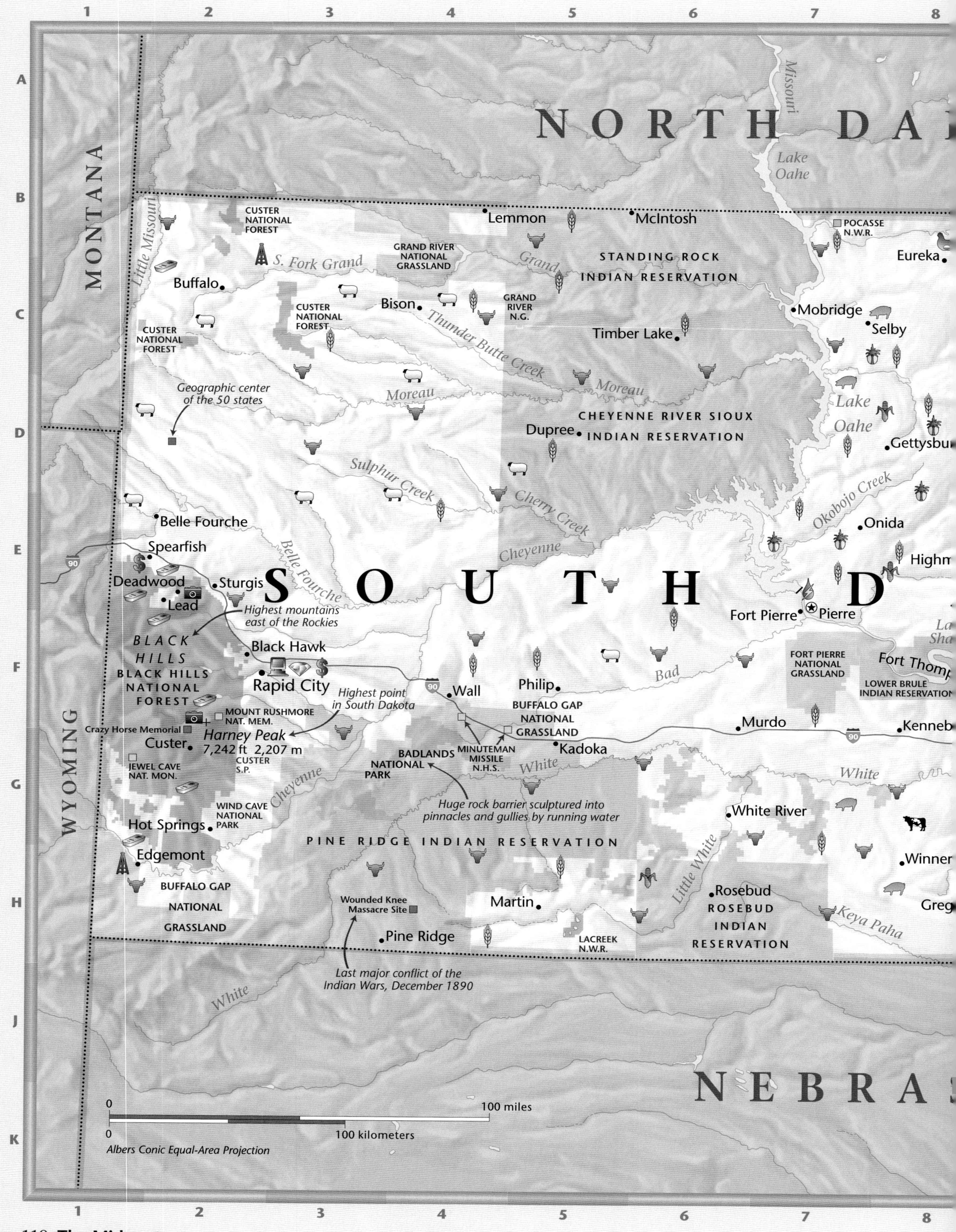

NORTH DA
MONTANA
WYOMING
SOUTH D
NEBRAS
Lake Oahe
Missouri
Little Missouri
CUSTER NATIONAL FOREST
GRAND RIVER NATIONAL GRASSLAND
STANDING ROCK INDIAN RESERVATION
POCASSE N.W.R.
Lemmon
McIntosh
Eureka
Buffalo
S. Fork Grand
Grand
Bison
GRAND RIVER N.G.
Mobridge
Selby
Timber Lake
Thunder Butte Creek
Moreau
Geographic center of the 50 states
CHEYENNE RIVER SIOUX INDIAN RESERVATION
Dupree
Gettysbu
Sulphur Creek
Cherry Creek
Okobojo Creek
Onida
Belle Fourche
Spearfish
Cheyenne
Highm
Deadwood
Sturgis
Lead
Highest mountains east of the Rockies
Fort Pierre
Pierre
BLACK HILLS
BLACK HILLS NATIONAL FOREST
Black Hawk
Rapid City
Highest point in South Dakota
Wall
Philip
Bad
FORT PIERRE NATIONAL GRASSLAND
Fort Thomp
LOWER BRULE INDIAN RESERVATION
MOUNT RUSHMORE NAT. MEM.
Crazy Horse Memorial
Harney Peak
7,242 ft 2,207 m
Custer
CUSTER S.P.
JEWEL CAVE NAT. MON.
BUFFALO GAP NATIONAL GRASSLAND
MINUTEMAN MISSILE N.H.S.
Murdo
Kennеb
Kadoka
BADLANDS NATIONAL PARK
White
Huge rock barrier sculptured into pinnacles and gullies by running water
WIND CAVE NATIONAL PARK
Hot Springs
White River
PINE RIDGE INDIAN RESERVATION
Edgemont
Winner
Little White
Rosebud
ROSEBUD INDIAN RESERVATION
Martin
Greg
Keya Paha
Wounded Knee Massacre Site
Pine Ridge
LACREEK N.W.R.
Last major conflict of the Indian Wars, December 1890
0 100 miles
0 100 kilometers
Albers Conic Equal-Area Projection

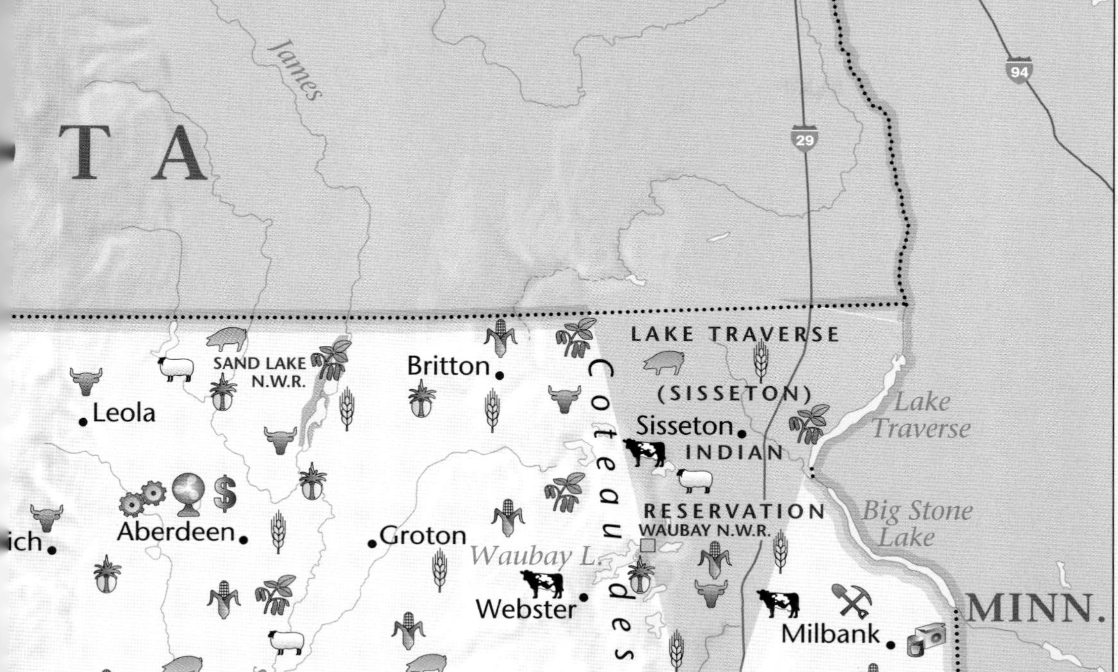

Mount Rushmore State

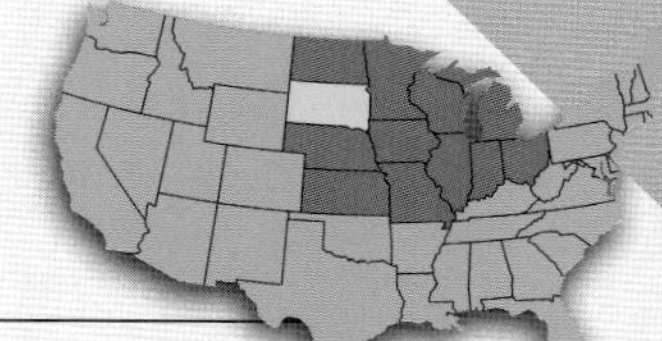

South Dakota

Named for the Dakota, or Sioux, Indians, South Dakota is sometimes called the Land of Infinite Variety, because of its many kinds of landscapes.

The Missouri River divides the state into two parts. East of the river is a land of rolling hills with fertile soil left by retreating glaciers. Here, farmers grow corn and soybeans. West of the river are the Great Plains. The land is drier here. Ranchers graze sheep and cattle on short grasses.

Close by is a barren rocky land with strangely shaped spires and canyons known as the Badlands. The Black Hills, beautiful mountains named for their dark pine and spruce trees, rise beyond them. Gold was discovered here in 1874, and South Dakota is still a leading gold-producing state.

Millions of visitors come to the Black Hills each year to visit Mount Rushmore and the nearby Crazy Horse Memorial, which is still under construction. Visitors to the memorial can also see one of the largest herds of bison in the United States.

Area: 77,117 sq mi (199,731 sq km)

Population: 764,000

Capital: Pierre, pop. 14,000

Largest city: Sioux Falls, pop. 130,500

Industry: finance, services, manufacturing, government, retail trade, transportation and utilities, wholesale trade, construction, mining

Agriculture: cattle, corn, soybeans, wheat, hogs, hay, dairy products

Statehood: November 2, 1889; 40th state

Nickname: Mount Rushmore State

More about South Dakota

- *Sculptors used dynamite to remove about a billion pounds of rock to make Mount Rushmore.*
- *In 1876 the famous bank robber Jesse James escaped from a posse by jumping his horse across Devils Gulch, a canyon 20 feet (6 m) wide and 50 feet (15 m) deep, near Sioux Falls.*
- *South Dakota has about 8,000 bison in different areas, more than any other state.*
- *The domed Corn Palace, in Mitchell, is decorated with murals made of different colors of corn and other grains.*
- *The last major conflict in the Indian Wars took place at Wounded Knee, north of Pine Ridge, in December 1890.*

Ring-necked Pheasant
Pasqueflower

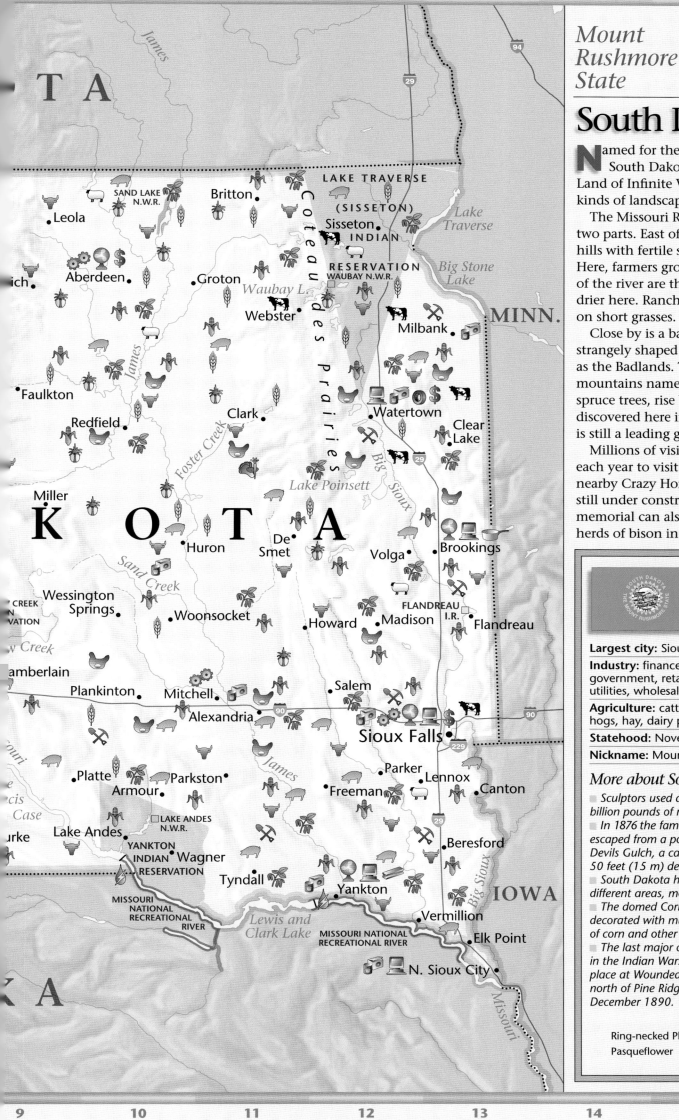

LAKE SUPERIOR
MINNESOTA
MICHIGAN
WISCONSIN
APOSTLE ISLANDS NATIONAL LAKESHORE
Apostle Islands
RED CLIFF INDIAN RESERVATION
BAD RIVER INDIAN RESERVATION
Madeline Island
Superior
Washburn
Ashland
BAD RIVER INDIAN RESERVATION
Hurley
Bois Brule
St. Croix
ST. CROIX NATIONAL SCENIC RIVERWAY
CHEQUAMEGON NATIONAL FOREST
Turtle-Flambeau Flowage
Land O'Lakes
Brule
Namekagon
Hayward
LAC DU FLAMBEAU INDIAN RESERVATION
Eagle River
Pine
Park Falls
CHEQUAMEGON NATIONAL FOREST
LAC COURTE OREILLES INDIAN RESERVATION
Lake Chippewa
Spooner
NICOLET NATIONAL FOREST
Menominee
Popple
Niagara
ST. CROIX INDIAN RESERVATION
Chippewa
Highest point in Wisconsin
Rhinelander
SOKAOGON CHIPPEWA INDIAN RESERVATION
FOREST COUNTY POTAWATOMI INDIAN RESERVATION
Rice Lake
Ladysmith
Flambeau
Tomahawk
Timms Hill
1,951ft
595 m
Wisconsin
Wolf
Washington Island
St. Croix Falls
ST. CROIX NATIONAL SCENIC RIVERWAY
Jump
NICOLET NATIONAL FOREST
Peshtigo
Apple
CHEQUAMEGON NATIONAL FOREST
Merrill
Antigo
Red Cedar
New Richmond
Yellow
Medford
Marinette
Hudson
Chippewa Falls
MENOMINEE INDIAN RESERVATION
WOLF NATIONAL WILD & SCENIC RIVER
DOOR PENINSULA
Wausau
ST. CROIX N.W.&S.R.
River Falls
Lake Wissota
Big Eau Pleine Res.
Oconto
Sturgeon Bay
Menomonie
Eau Claire
Altoona
STOCKBRIDGE INDIAN RESERVATION
Green Bay
Mississippi
Shawano
Marshfield
Lake Du Bay
Algoma
Green Bay
Ashwaubenon
Lake Pepin
Pepin
Stevens Point
Plover
ONEIDA INDIAN RESERVATION
De Pere
Fox
New London
WISCONSIN WINNEBAGO INDIAN RESERVATION
Wisconsin Rapids
Waupaca
Appleton
Black River Falls
Kaukauna
NECEDAH
UPPER MISSISSIPPI RIVER NATIONAL

Badger State

Wisconsin

Wisconsin is sometimes called the Land of Lakes. It's easy to see why. Two great lakes—Lake Superior on the north and Lake Michigan on the east—border this midwestern state. There are also about 15,000 lakes inside the state that were formed by melting glaciers. Wisconsin's lakes and its thick northern forests, called the North Woods, make it a prime vacation spot. In summer, visitors fish, swim, and sail. In winter, they ski or go ice-fishing.

In the 1800s Wisconsin farmers began raising dairy cows. Settlers from Switzerland brought traditional cheese-making skills. Today, Wisconsin is one of the nation's top producers of milk, cheese, and butter. It is known as America's dairyland.

Wisconsin has more people of German ancestry than any other state. Many live in Milwaukee, the state's largest city. Wisconsin's cities also make machinery and processed foods.

Forests cover half of Wisconsin. A century ago, lumberjacks there told tall tales about a giant logger named Paul Bunyan. Today, Wisconsin's huge forests make it a leading paper producer.

Area: 65,498 sq mi (169,639 sq km)

Population: 5,472,000

Capital: Madison, pop. 215,200

Largest city: Milwaukee, pop. 590,900

Industry: industrial machinery, paper products, food processing, metal products, electronic equipment, transportation

Agriculture: dairy products, cattle, corn, poultry and eggs, soybeans

Statehood: May 29, 1848; 30th state

Nickname: Badger State

More about Wisconsin

- *Wisconsin is nicknamed the Badger State because in the 1820s lead miners in the state lived like badgers in caves they had dug.*
- *Near Baraboo are the Wisconsin Dells, where the Wisconsin River has carved out gorges and unusual rock formations, including some called Witches Gulch and Devil's Elbow.*
- *Every February the American Birkebeiner, the largest cross-country ski race in the U.S., is held in Wisconsin.*
- *Nearly three-fourths of all the milk produced in the state goes into making cheese.*
- *Among the famous writers born in Wisconsin are novelist and playwright Thornton Wilder and Laura Ingalls Wilder, author of Little House on the Prairie. (The two writers are not related.)*

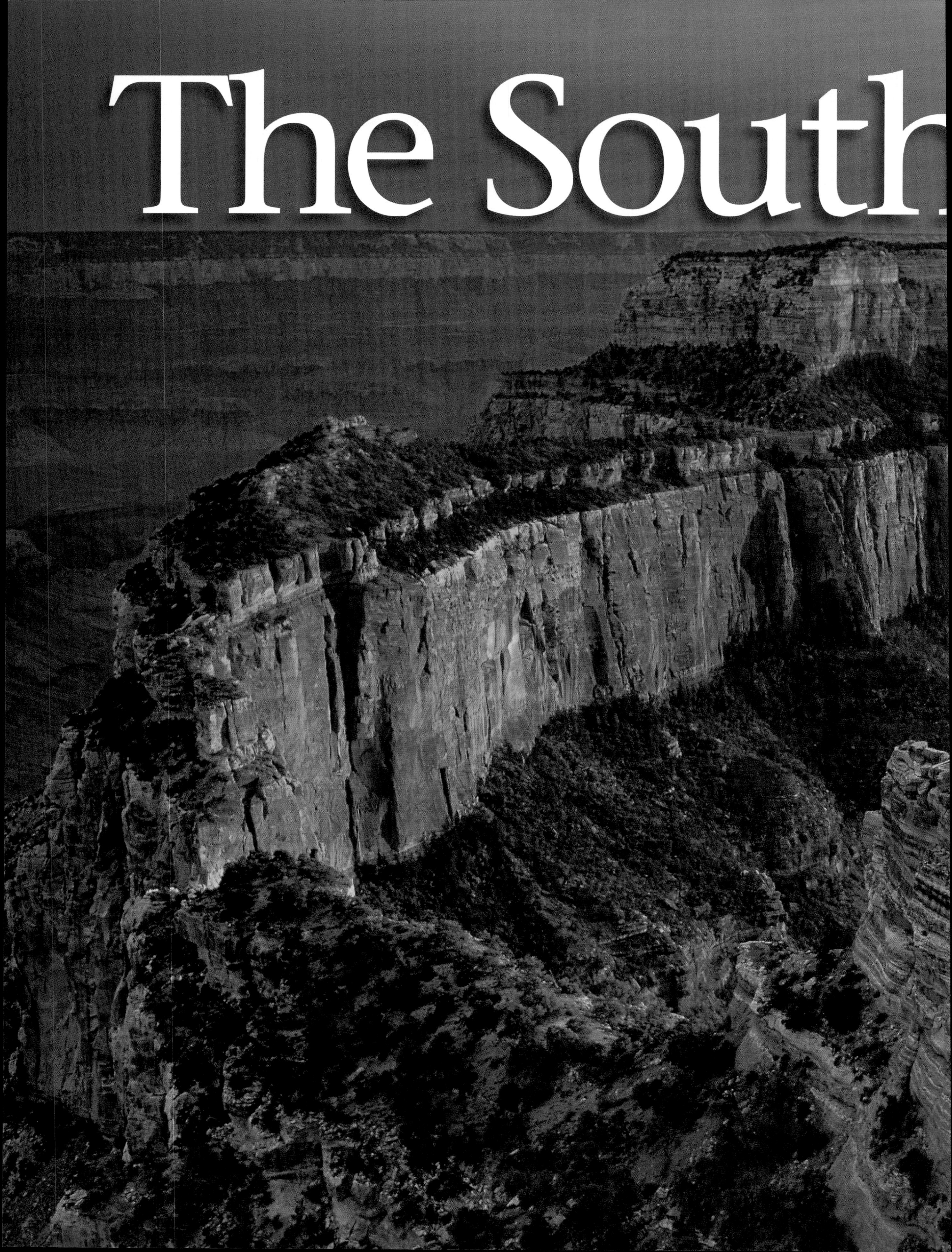

The South

west

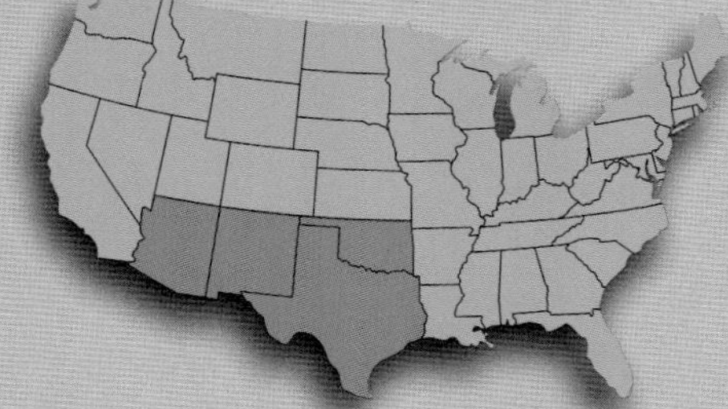

Arizona
New Mexico
Oklahoma
Texas

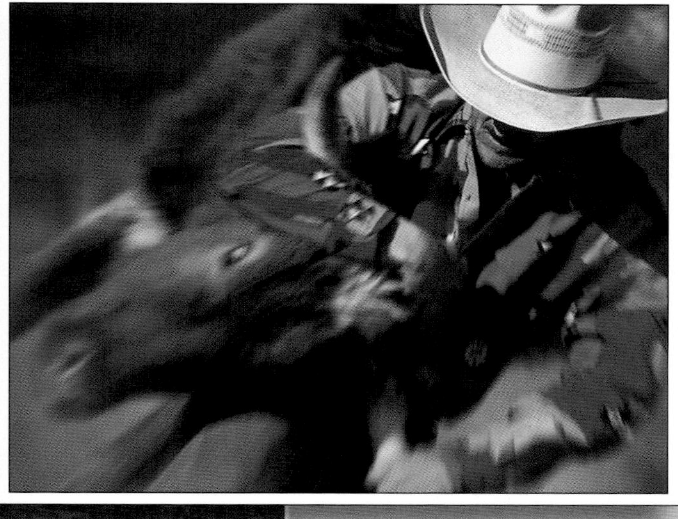

Sunset burnishes the majestic Grand Canyon (left), carved by the Colorado River over millions of years. Not far away, a cowboy takes a bull by the horns at an Arizona rodeo (above). Rodeos began as contests of cowboy skills on Southwest ranches.

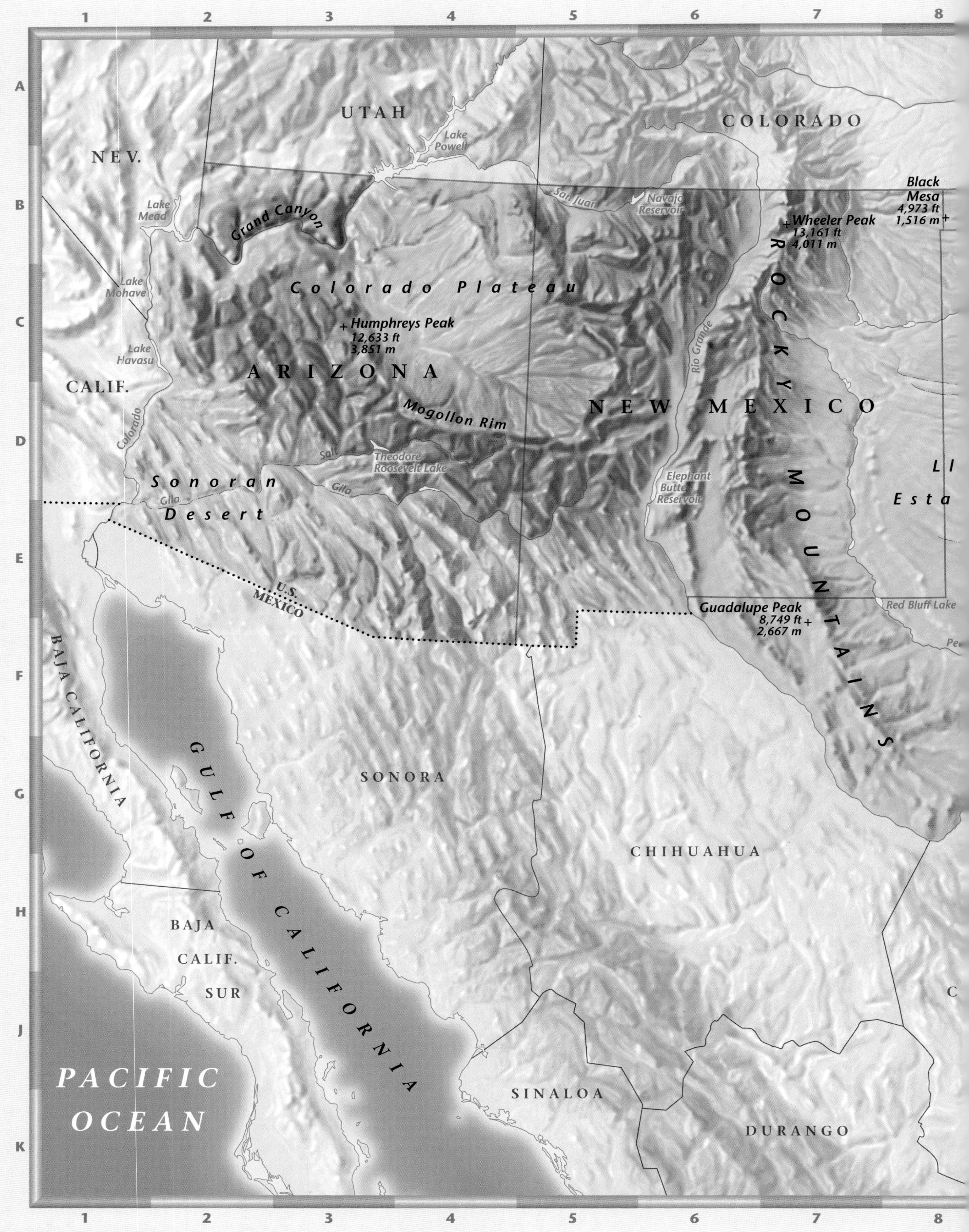
UTAH
COLORADO
NEV.
Lake Powell
Lake Mead
Grand Canyon
San Juan
Navajo Reservoir
Black Mesa
4,973 ft
1,516 m
Wheeler Peak
13,161 ft
4,011 m
Lake Mohave
Colorado Plateau
Humphreys Peak
12,633 ft
3,851 m
Lake Havasu
ARIZONA
CALIF.
Rio Grande
ROCKY MOUNTAINS
NEW MEXICO
Mogollon Rim
Colorado
Salt
Theodore Roosevelt Lake
Elephant Butte Reservoir
Sonoran Desert
Gila
U.S.
MEXICO
Guadalupe Peak
8,749 ft
2,667 m
Red Bluff Lake
BAJA CALIFORNIA
GULF OF CALIFORNIA
SONORA
CHIHUAHUA
BAJA CALIF. SUR
PACIFIC OCEAN
SINALOA
DURANGO

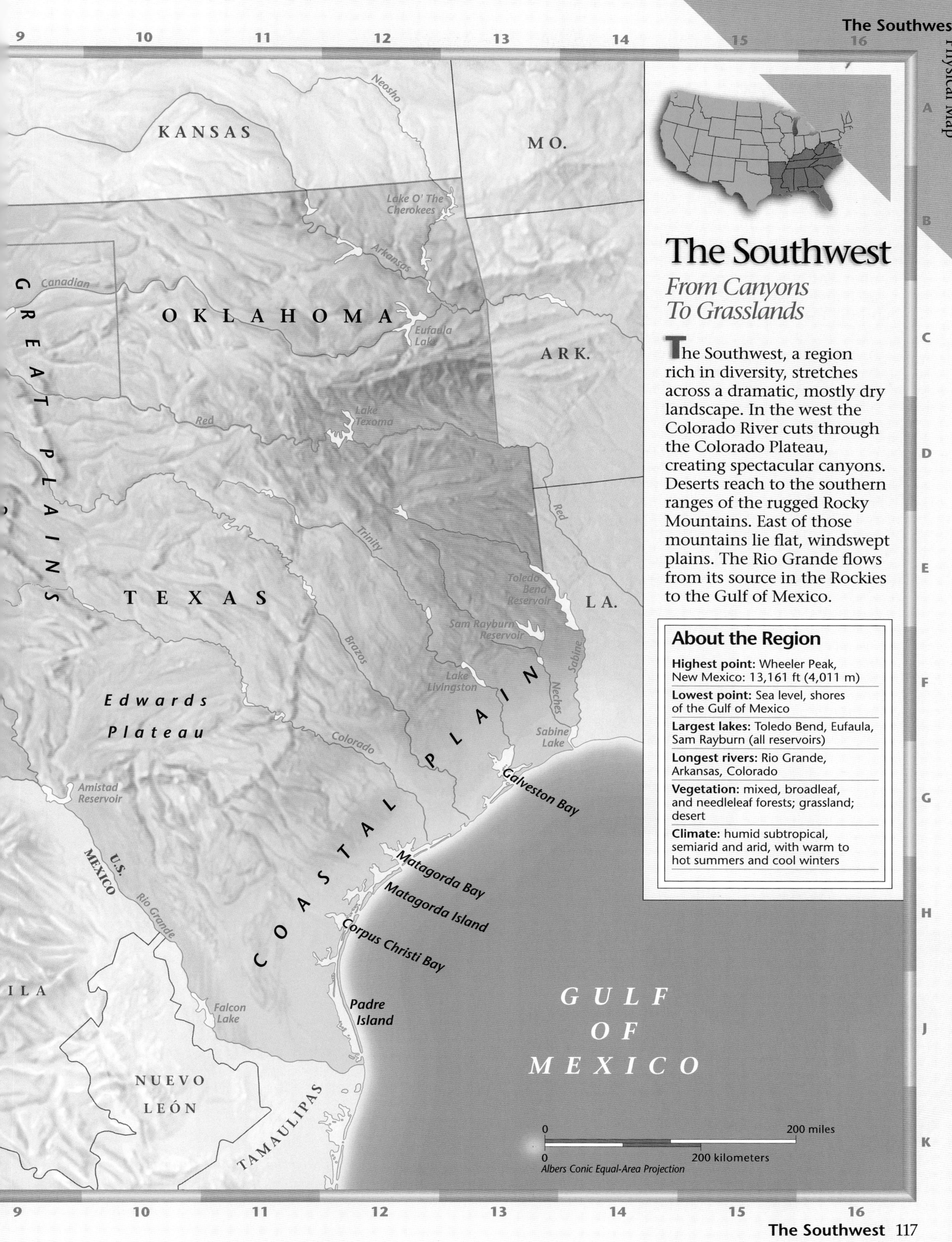

The Southwest

From Canyons To Grasslands

The Southwest, a region rich in diversity, stretches across a dramatic, mostly dry landscape. In the west the Colorado River cuts through the Colorado Plateau, creating spectacular canyons. Deserts reach to the southern ranges of the rugged Rocky Mountains. East of those mountains lie flat, windswept plains. The Rio Grande flows from its source in the Rockies to the Gulf of Mexico.

About the Region

Highest point: Wheeler Peak, New Mexico: 13,161 ft (4,011 m)

Lowest point: Sea level, shores of the Gulf of Mexico

Largest lakes: Toledo Bend, Eufaula, Sam Rayburn (all reservoirs)

Longest rivers: Rio Grande, Arkansas, Colorado

Vegetation: mixed, broadleaf, and needleleaf forests; grassland; desert

Climate: humid subtropical, semiarid and arid, with warm to hot summers and cool winters

The Southwest

Land of Natural Wonders

Vast and varied, the Southwest is a land of colorful contrasts. On the wide open plains of Texas, huge wheatfields and ranches with grazing cattle sprawl for miles. Farther west, snow-capped mountains rise above busy cities. Some, such as Phoenix, are among the fastest-growing cities in the country.

The region abounds with natural wonders: the matchless spectacle of the Grand Canyon, the strange beauty of reddish sandstone spires and sentinels in Monument Valley, and the sight of deserts blooming with cactus flowers. A history of early Indian cultures, Mexican colonization, and Wild West days gives the region a rich ethnic heritage. Today, southwestern states celebrate Mexican fiestas, Indian tribal powwows, and Frontier Days. Visitors to the area can explore ghost towns near old mining sites or boomtowns where oil first gushed. In the shadow of ancient Indian cliff-dwellings, present-day Indians make fine pottery, baskets, and silver and turquoise jewelry.

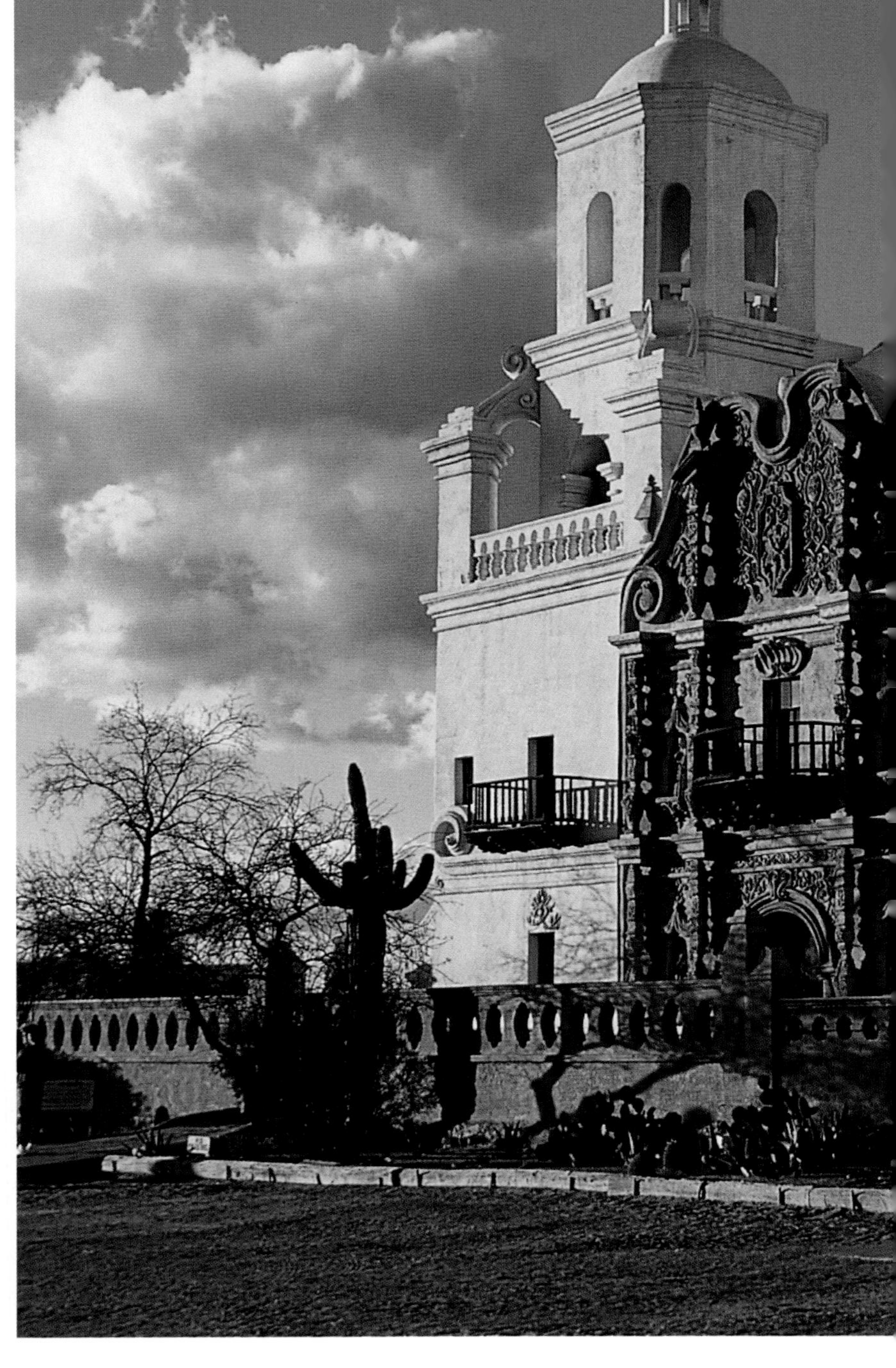

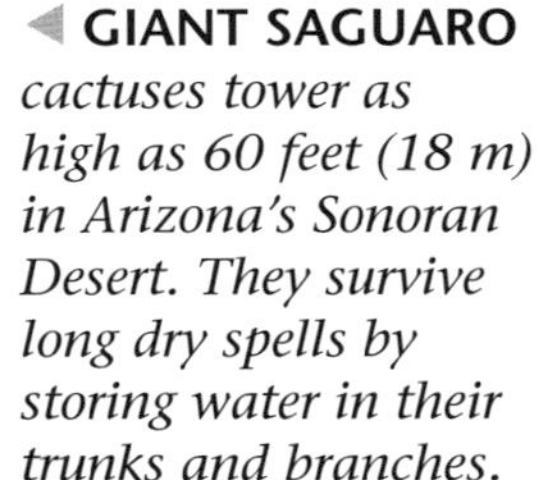

GLEN CANYON *dam, located on the Colorado River in Arizona and Utah, created Lake Powell to supply water and electricity to much of this arid region.*

GIANT SAGUARO *cactuses tower as high as 60 feet (18 m) in Arizona's Sonoran Desert. They survive long dry spells by storing water in their trunks and branches.*

NAVAJO GIRLS *play on their large reservation in Monument Valley. More than a hundred different tribes of Native Americans live in the Southwest.*

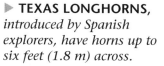

▶ **TEXAS LONGHORNS,** *introduced by Spanish explorers, have horns up to six feet (1.8 m) across.*

▼ **OIL ROUGHNECKS** *work on the drilling pipe of a Texas well. Texas produces about a fifth of U.S. petroleum.*

▲ **SAN XAVIER** *del Bac, a Spanish mission, was built about 1700 near Tucson, Arizona, by Spanish priests. It sheltered Indians learning about Christianity.*

◀ **HOT PIÑON** *chili peppers dry after harvest in New Mexico. Sold ground or whole, chili peppers add flavor to a variety of foods.*

▲ **LUSH CIRCLES OF GREEN** *are the trademark of a kind of irrigation called center pivot. Each circular field is watered by a rotating sprinkler system that draws water from a well. The system helps farmers grow crops in the dry Southwest.*

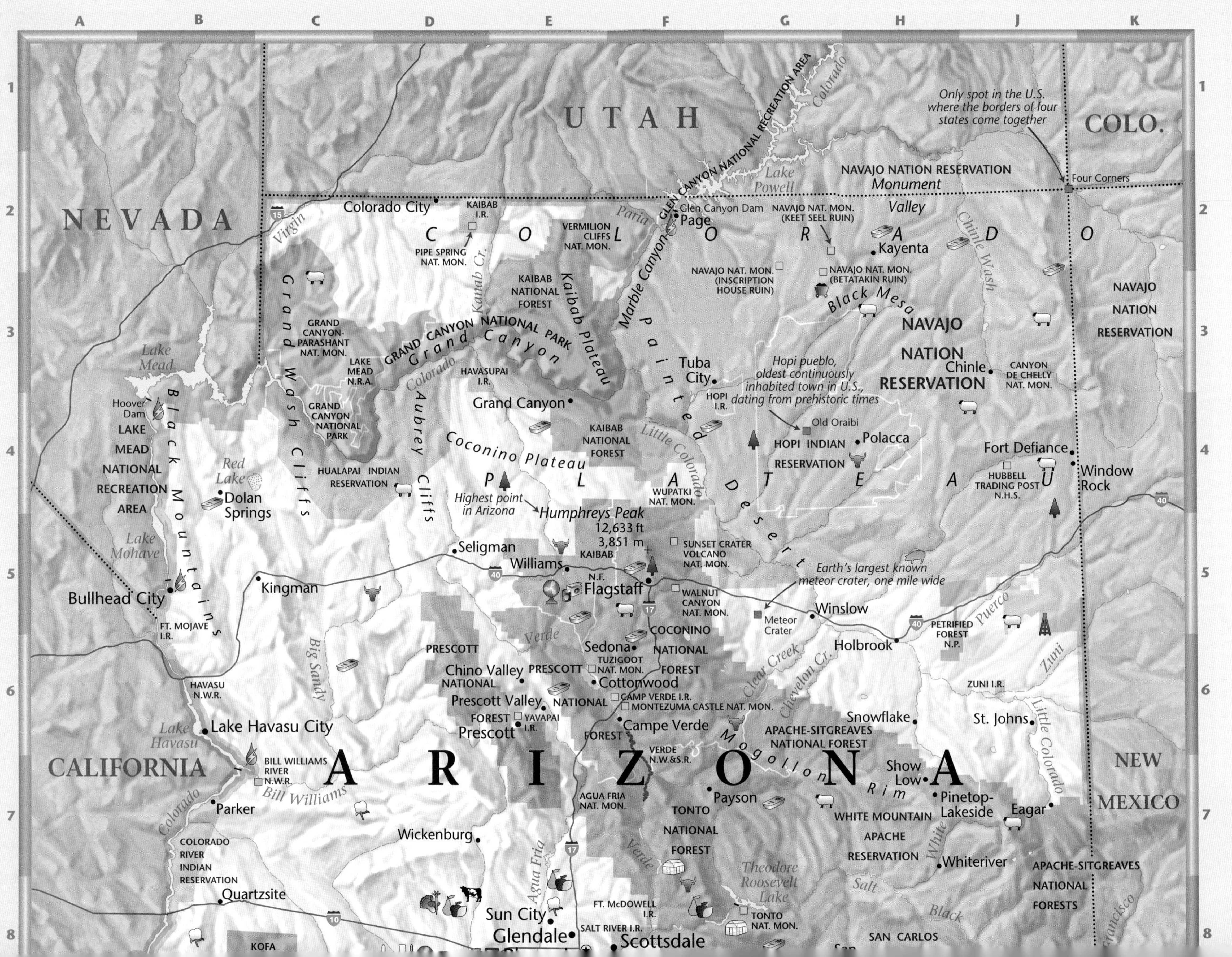

UTAH
COLO.
NEW MEXICO
NEVADA
CALIFORNIA
ARIZONA
COLORADO PLATEAU
Four Corners
Only spot in the U.S. where the borders of four states come together
NAVAJO NATION RESERVATION
Monument Valley
Kayenta
NAVAJO NAT. MON. (KEET SEEL RUIN)
NAVAJO NAT. MON. (BETATAKIN RUIN)
NAVAJO NAT. MON. (INSCRIPTION HOUSE RUIN)
Black Mesa
Chinle Wash
Chinle
CANYON DE CHELLY NAT. MON.
Fort Defiance
Window Rock
HUBBELL TRADING POST N.H.S.
GLEN CANYON NATIONAL RECREATION AREA
Lake Powell
Colorado
Glen Canyon Dam
Page
Marble Canyon
Paria
VERMILION CLIFFS NAT. MON.
Kaibab Plateau
KAIBAB NATIONAL FOREST
GRAND CANYON NATIONAL PARK
Grand Canyon
KAIBAB I.R.
PIPE SPRING NAT. MON.
Kanab Cr.
Colorado City
HAVASUPAI I.R.
Aubrey Cliffs
Coconino Plateau
Highest point in Arizona
Humphreys Peak 12,633 ft 3,851 m
Painted Desert
Tuba City
HOPI I.R.
Hopi pueblo, oldest continuously inhabited town in U.S., dating from prehistoric times
Old Oraibi
HOPI INDIAN RESERVATION
Polacca
Little Colorado
WUPATKI NAT. MON.
SUNSET CRATER VOLCANO NAT. MON.
WALNUT CANYON NAT. MON.
Earth's largest known meteor crater, one mile wide
Meteor Crater
Winslow
Holbrook
PETRIFIED FOREST N.P.
Puerco
Zuni
ZUNI I.R.
St. Johns
Eagar
APACHE-SITGREAVES NATIONAL FORESTS
Flagstaff
N.F. KAIBAB
Williams
Seligman
Sedona
COCONINO NATIONAL FOREST
TUZIGOOT NAT. MON.
Cottonwood
CAMP VERDE I.R.
MONTEZUMA CASTLE NAT. MON.
Camp Verde
Clear Creek
Chevelon Cr.
APACHE-SITGREAVES NATIONAL FOREST
Snowflake
Show Low
Pinetop-Lakeside
Mogollon Rim
WHITE MOUNTAIN APACHE RESERVATION
Whiteriver
White
Black
Salt
SAN CARLOS
Payson
TONTO NATIONAL FOREST
Theodore Roosevelt Lake
TONTO NAT. MON.
VERDE N.W.&S.R.
Verde
AGUA FRIA NAT. MON.
FT. McDOWELL I.R.
SALT RIVER I.R.
Scottsdale
Glendale
Sun City
Agua Fria
PRESCOTT NATIONAL FOREST
Chino Valley
Prescott Valley
YAVAPAI I.R.
Prescott
Wickenburg
Kingman
Big Sandy
GRAND CANYON-PARASHANT NAT. MON.
LAKE MEAD N.R.A.
GRAND CANYON NATIONAL PARK
HUALAPAI INDIAN RESERVATION
Grand Wash Cliffs
Virgin
Red Lake
Dolan Springs
Black Mountains
Lake Mead
Hoover Dam
LAKE MEAD NATIONAL RECREATION AREA
Lake Mohave
Bullhead City
FT. MOJAVE I.R.
HAVASU N.W.R.
Lake Havasu
Lake Havasu City
BILL WILLIAMS RIVER N.W.R.
Bill Williams
Parker
COLORADO RIVER INDIAN RESERVATION
Quartzsite
KOFA

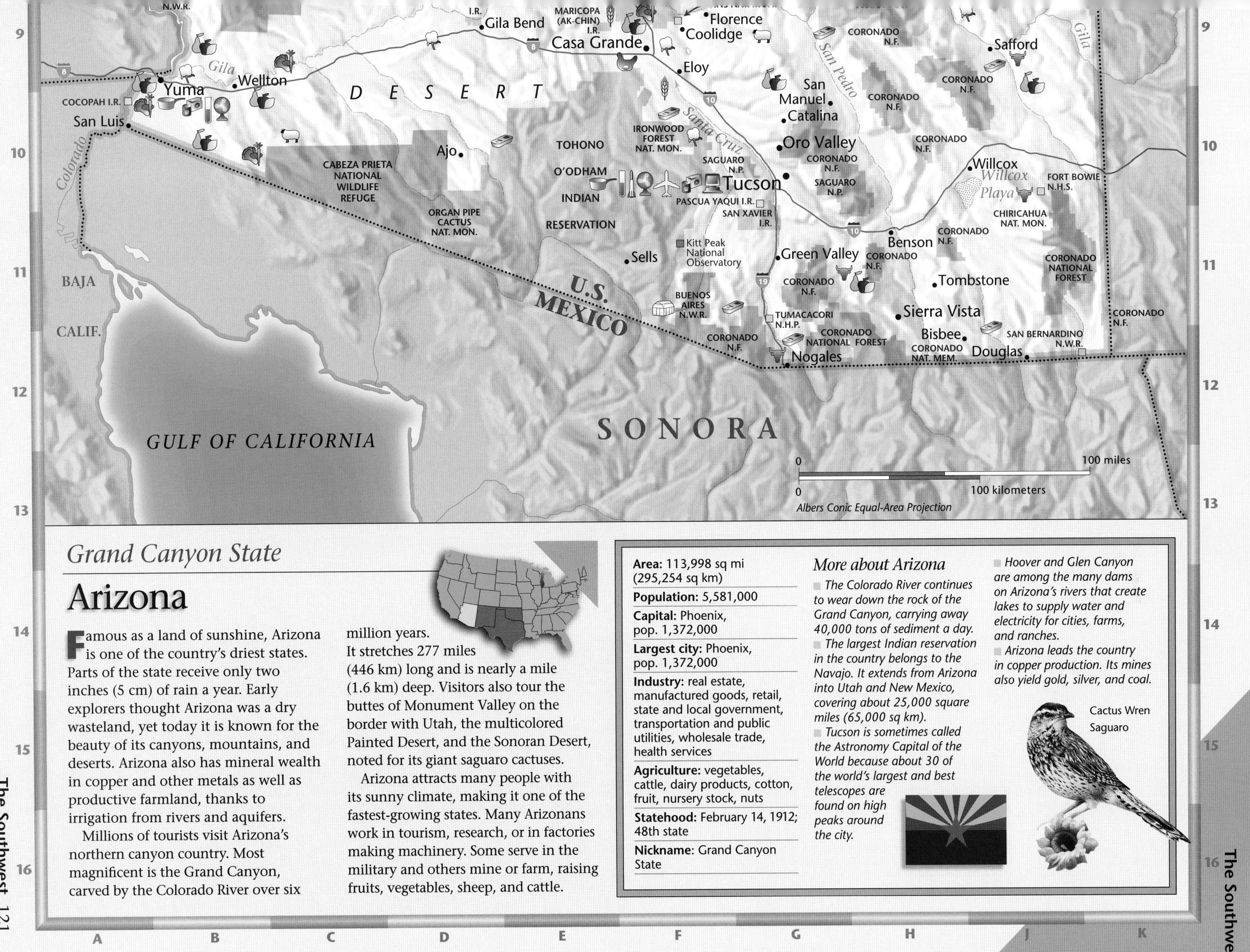

Grand Canyon State

Arizona

Famous as a land of sunshine, Arizona is one of the country's driest states. Parts of the state receive only two inches (5 cm) of rain a year. Early explorers thought Arizona was a dry wasteland, yet today it is known for the beauty of its canyons, mountains, and deserts. Arizona also has mineral wealth in copper and other metals as well as productive farmland, thanks to irrigation from rivers and aquifers.

Millions of tourists visit Arizona's northern canyon country. Most magnificent is the Grand Canyon, carved by the Colorado River over six million years.
It stretches 277 miles (446 km) long and is nearly a mile (1.6 km) deep. Visitors also tour the buttes of Monument Valley on the border with Utah, the multicolored Painted Desert, and the Sonoran Desert, noted for its giant saguaro cactuses.

Arizona attracts many people with its sunny climate, making it one of the fastest-growing states. Many Arizonans work in tourism, research, or in factories making machinery. Some serve in the military and others mine or farm, raising fruits, vegetables, sheep, and cattle.

Area: 113,998 sq mi (295,254 sq km)

Population: 5,581,000

Capital: Phoenix, pop. 1,372,000

Largest city: Phoenix, pop. 1,372,000

Industry: real estate, manufactured goods, retail, state and local government, transportation and public utilities, wholesale trade, health services

Agriculture: vegetables, cattle, dairy products, cotton, fruit, nursery stock, nuts

Statehood: February 14, 1912; 48th state

Nickname: Grand Canyon State

More about Arizona

- *The Colorado River continues to wear down the rock of the Grand Canyon, carrying away 40,000 tons of sediment a day.*
- *The largest Indian reservation in the country belongs to the Navajo. It extends from Arizona into Utah and New Mexico, covering about 25,000 square miles (65,000 sq km).*
- *Tucson is sometimes called the Astronomy Capital of the World because about 30 of the world's largest and best telescopes are found on high peaks around the city.*
- *Hoover and Glen Canyon are among the many dams on Arizona's rivers that create lakes to supply water and electricity for cities, farms, and ranches.*
- *Arizona leads the country in copper production. Its mines also yield gold, silver, and coal.*

Cactus Wren
Saguaro

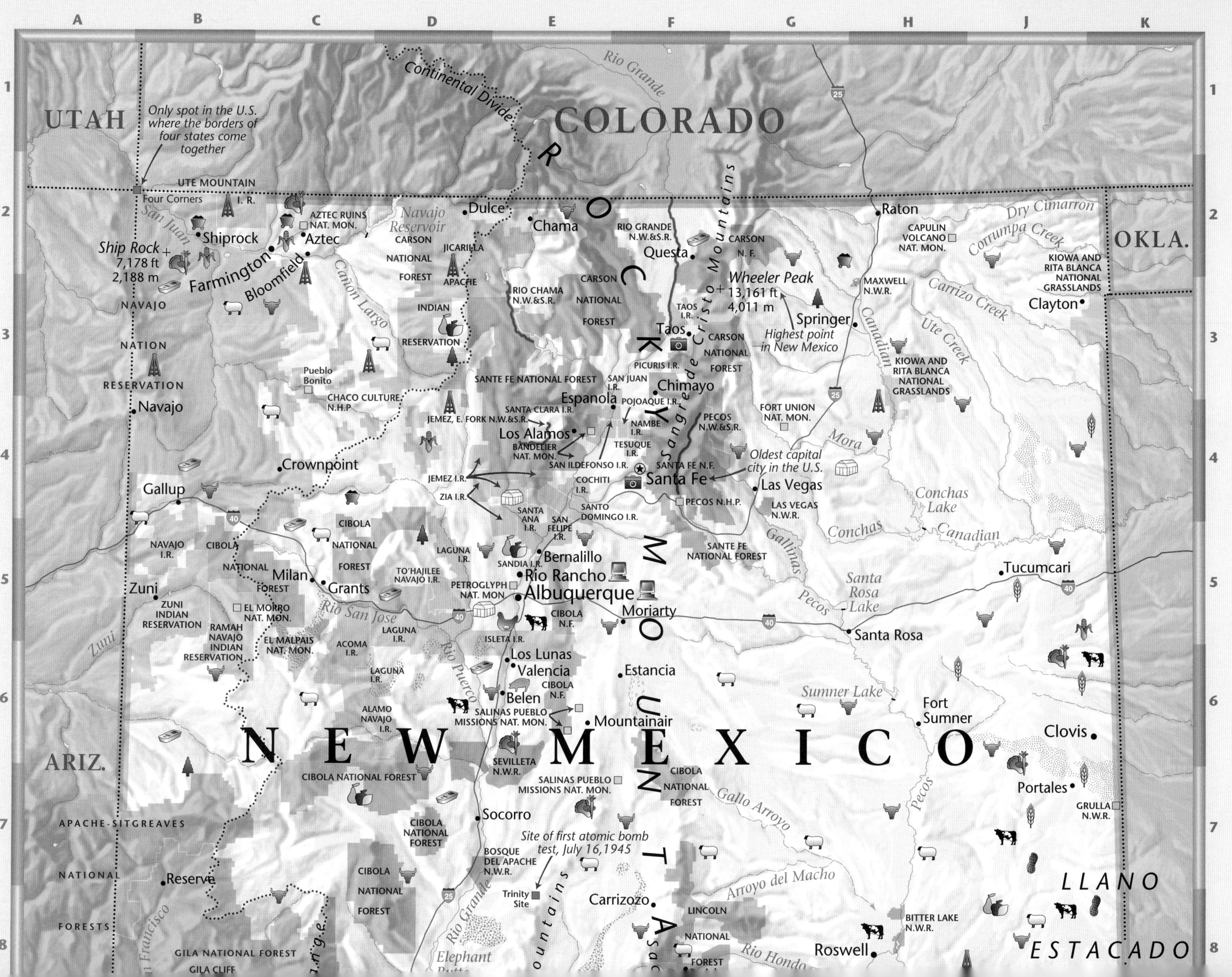

COLORADO
UTAH
OKLA.
ARIZ.
NEW MEXICO
ROCKY MOUNTAINS
LLANO ESTACADO
Sangre de Cristo Mountains
Continental Divide
Rio Grande
Only spot in the U.S. where the borders of four states come together
Four Corners
Ship Rock + 7,178 ft 2,188 m
Wheeler Peak + 13,161 ft 4,011 m
Highest point in New Mexico
Oldest capital city in the U.S.
Site of first atomic bomb test, July 16, 1945
Trinity Site
Santa Fe
Albuquerque
Rio Rancho
Bernalillo
Los Alamos
Espanola
Chimayo
Taos
Questa
Chama
Dulce
Raton
Springer
Clayton
Tucumcari
Santa Rosa
Las Vegas
Moriarty
Estancia
Mountainair
Los Lunas
Valencia
Belen
Socorro
Carrizozo
Roswell
Fort Sumner
Clovis
Portales
Gallup
Grants
Milan
Crownpoint
Zuni
Navajo
Shiprock
Farmington
Bloomfield
Aztec
Reserve
Canadian
Pecos
Conchas Lake
Santa Rosa Lake
Sumner Lake
Navajo Reservoir
Rio Puerco
Rio San Jose
Rio Hondo
Gallo Arroyo
Arroyo del Macho
Cañon Largo
San Juan
Dry Cimarron
Corrumpa Creek
Carrizo Creek
Ute Creek
Mora
Gallinas
Conchas
Zuni
Elephant Butte
KIOWA AND RITA BLANCA NATIONAL GRASSLANDS
CAPULIN VOLCANO NAT. MON.
MAXWELL N.W.R.
FORT UNION NAT. MON.
LAS VEGAS N.W.R.
PECOS N.H.P.
PECOS N.W.&S.R.
SANTE FE NATIONAL FOREST
CARSON NATIONAL FOREST
CARSON N.F.
RIO GRANDE N.W.&S.R.
RIO CHAMA N.W.&S.R.
TAOS I.R.
PICURIS I.R.
SAN JUAN I.R.
POJOAQUE I.R.
NAMBE I.R.
TESUQUE I.R.
SANTA FE N.F.
SAN ILDEFONSO I.R.
SANTA CLARA I.R.
BANDELIER NAT. MON.
JEMEZ, E. FORK N.W.&S.R.
COCHITI I.R.
SANTO DOMINGO I.R.
SAN FELIPE I.R.
SANTA ANA I.R.
ZIA I.R.
JEMEZ I.R.
SANDIA I.R.
ISLETA I.R.
LAGUNA I.R.
PETROGLYPH NAT. MON.
TO'HAJIILEE NAVAJO I.R.
ACOMA I.R.
ALAMO NAVAJO I.R.
CIBOLA NATIONAL FOREST
CIBOLA N.F.
SALINAS PUEBLO MISSIONS NAT. MON.
SEVILLETA N.W.R.
BOSQUE DEL APACHE N.W.R.
EL MALPAIS NAT. MON.
EL MORRO NAT. MON.
RAMAH NAVAJO INDIAN RESERVATION
ZUNI INDIAN RESERVATION
NAVAJO I.R.
NAVAJO NATION RESERVATION
UTE MOUNTAIN I.R.
AZTEC RUINS NAT. MON.
CHACO CULTURE N.H.P.
Pueblo Bonito
JICARILLA APACHE INDIAN RESERVATION
LINCOLN NATIONAL FOREST
BITTER LAKE N.W.R.
GRULLA N.W.R.
APACHE-SITGREAVES NATIONAL FORESTS
GILA NATIONAL FOREST
GILA CLIFF
San Francisco

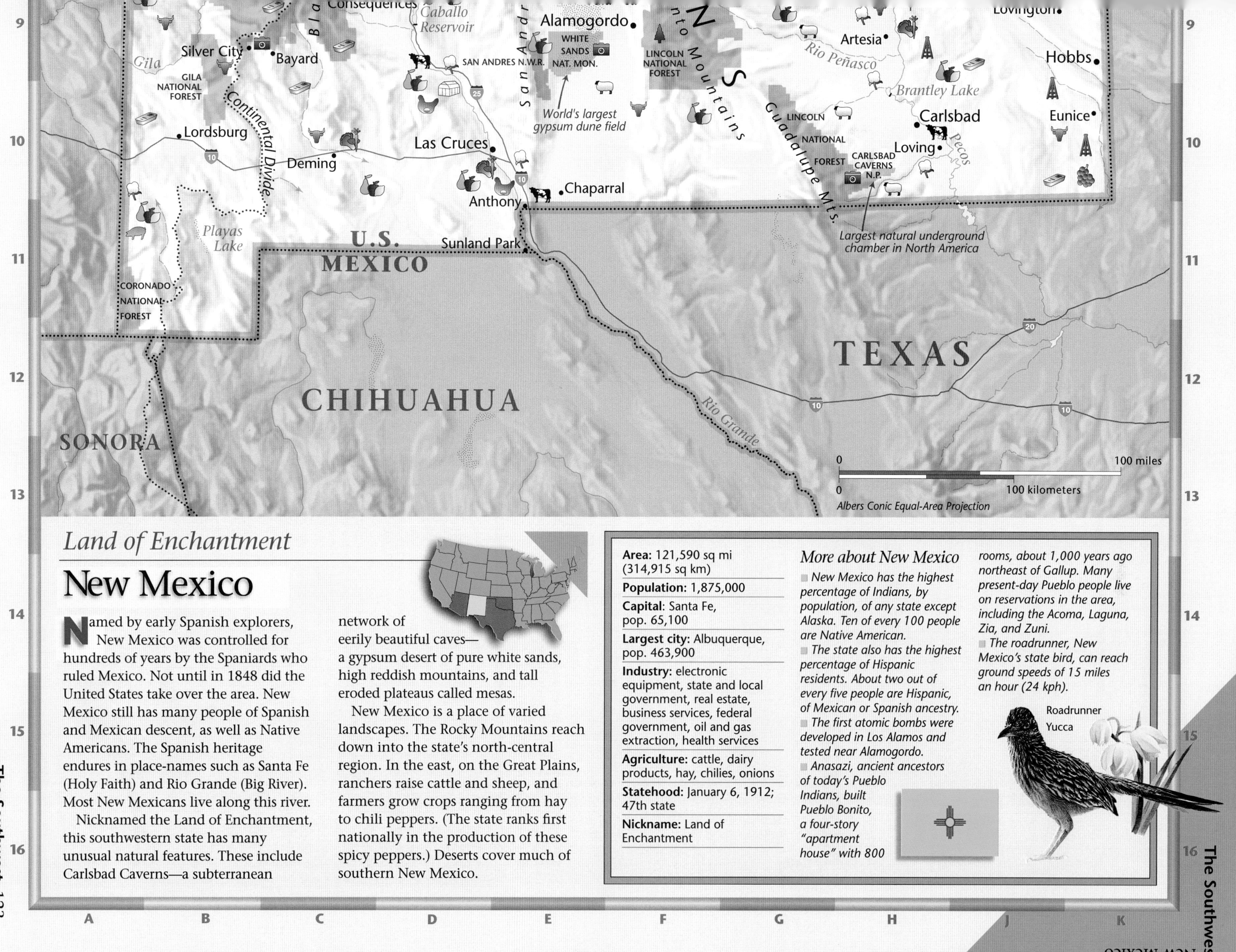

Land of Enchantment

New Mexico

Named by early Spanish explorers, New Mexico was controlled for hundreds of years by the Spaniards who ruled Mexico. Not until in 1848 did the United States take over the area. New Mexico still has many people of Spanish and Mexican descent, as well as Native Americans. The Spanish heritage endures in place-names such as Santa Fe (Holy Faith) and Rio Grande (Big River). Most New Mexicans live along this river.

Nicknamed the Land of Enchantment, this southwestern state has many unusual natural features. These include Carlsbad Caverns—a subterranean network of eerily beautiful caves—a gypsum desert of pure white sands, high reddish mountains, and tall eroded plateaus called mesas.

New Mexico is a place of varied landscapes. The Rocky Mountains reach down into the state's north-central region. In the east, on the Great Plains, ranchers raise cattle and sheep, and farmers grow crops ranging from hay to chili peppers. (The state ranks first nationally in the production of these spicy peppers.) Deserts cover much of southern New Mexico.

Area: 121,590 sq mi (314,915 sq km)

Population: 1,875,000

Capital: Santa Fe, pop. 65,100

Largest city: Albuquerque, pop. 463,900

Industry: electronic equipment, state and local government, real estate, business services, federal government, oil and gas extraction, health services

Agriculture: cattle, dairy products, hay, chilies, onions

Statehood: January 6, 1912; 47th state

Nickname: Land of Enchantment

More about New Mexico

- *New Mexico has the highest percentage of Indians, by population, of any state except Alaska. Ten of every 100 people are Native American.*
- *The state also has the highest percentage of Hispanic residents. About two out of every five people are Hispanic, of Mexican or Spanish ancestry.*
- *The first atomic bombs were developed in Los Alamos and tested near Alamogordo.*
- *Anasazi, ancient ancestors of today's Pueblo Indians, built Pueblo Bonito, a four-story "apartment house" with 800 rooms, about 1,000 years ago northeast of Gallup. Many present-day Pueblo people live on reservations in the area, including the Acoma, Laguna, Zia, and Zuni.*
- *The roadrunner, New Mexico's state bird, can reach ground speeds of 15 miles an hour (24 kph).*

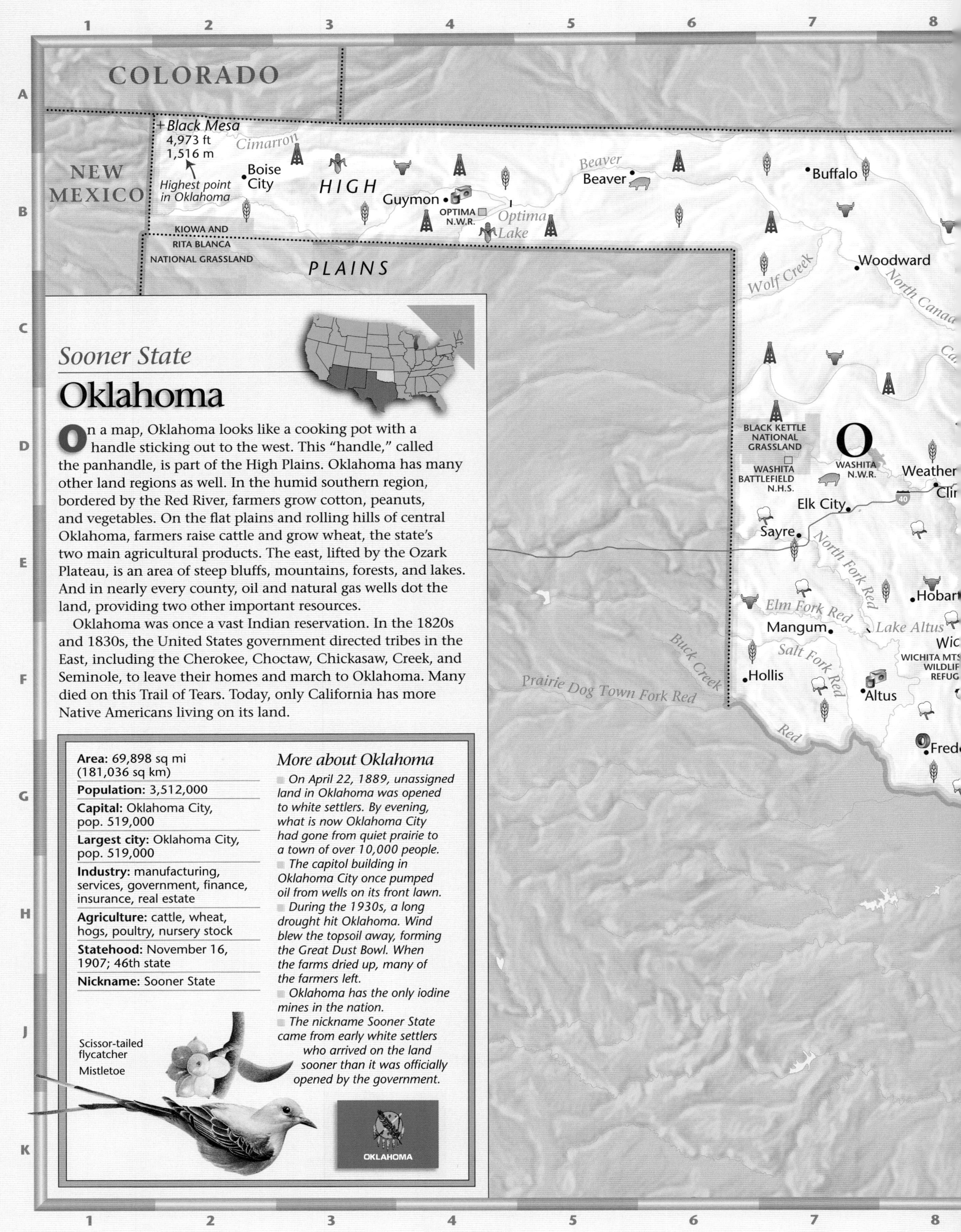

Sooner State

Oklahoma

On a map, Oklahoma looks like a cooking pot with a handle sticking out to the west. This "handle," called the panhandle, is part of the High Plains. Oklahoma has many other land regions as well. In the humid southern region, bordered by the Red River, farmers grow cotton, peanuts, and vegetables. On the flat plains and rolling hills of central Oklahoma, farmers raise cattle and grow wheat, the state's two main agricultural products. The east, lifted by the Ozark Plateau, is an area of steep bluffs, mountains, forests, and lakes. And in nearly every county, oil and natural gas wells dot the land, providing two other important resources.

Oklahoma was once a vast Indian reservation. In the 1820s and 1830s, the United States government directed tribes in the East, including the Cherokee, Choctaw, Chickasaw, Creek, and Seminole, to leave their homes and march to Oklahoma. Many died on this Trail of Tears. Today, only California has more Native Americans living on its land.

Area: 69,898 sq mi (181,036 sq km)

Population: 3,512,000

Capital: Oklahoma City, pop. 519,000

Largest city: Oklahoma City, pop. 519,000

Industry: manufacturing, services, government, finance, insurance, real estate

Agriculture: cattle, wheat, hogs, poultry, nursery stock

Statehood: November 16, 1907; 46th state

Nickname: Sooner State

More about Oklahoma

- *On April 22, 1889, unassigned land in Oklahoma was opened to white settlers. By evening, what is now Oklahoma City had gone from quiet prairie to a town of over 10,000 people.*
- *The capitol building in Oklahoma City once pumped oil from wells on its front lawn.*
- *During the 1930s, a long drought hit Oklahoma. Wind blew the topsoil away, forming the Great Dust Bowl. When the farms dried up, many of the farmers left.*
- *Oklahoma has the only iodine mines in the nation.*
- *The nickname Sooner State came from early white settlers who arrived on the land sooner than it was officially opened by the government.*

Scissor-tailed flycatcher

Mistletoe

OKLAHOMA

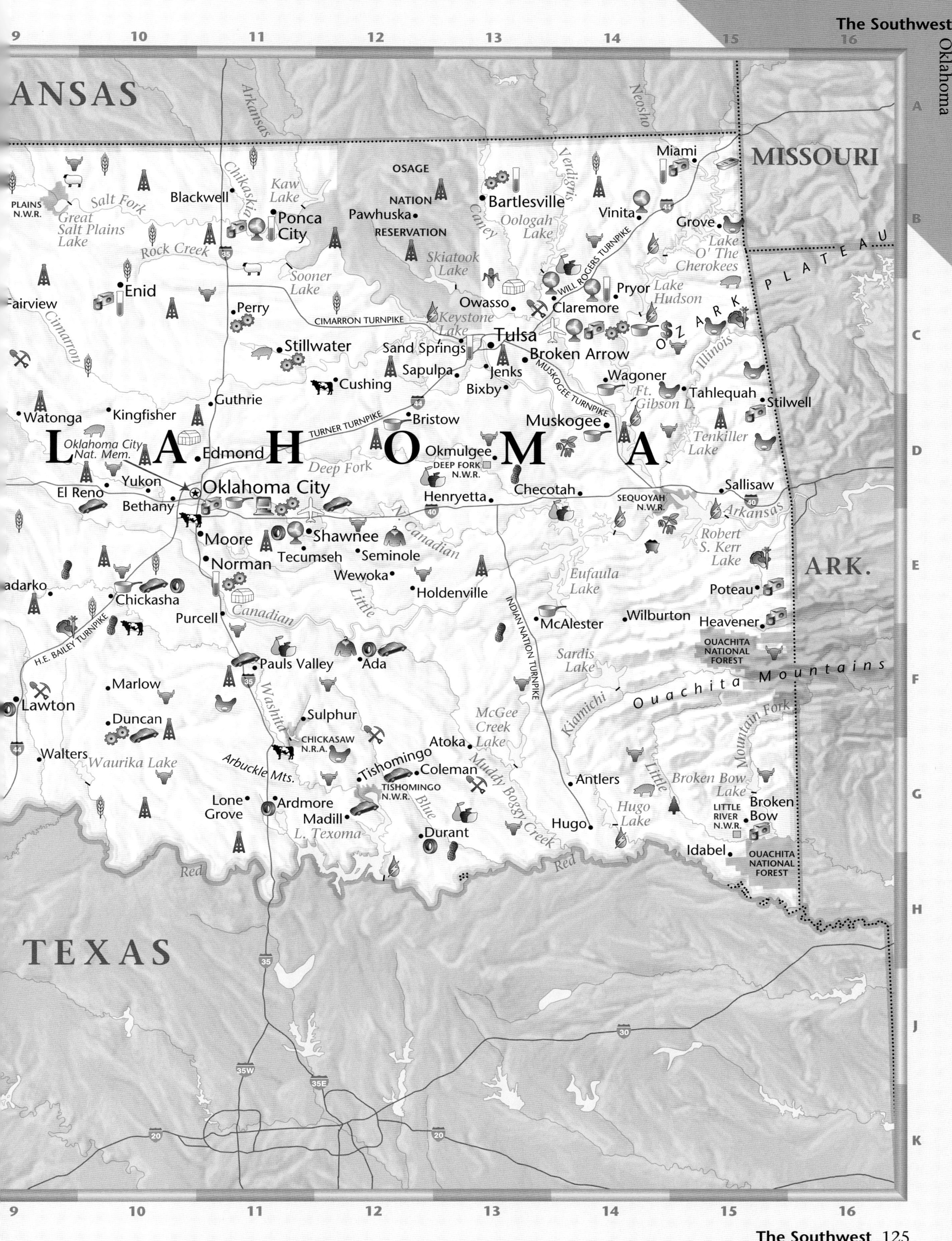
OKLAHOMA
KANSAS
MISSOURI
ARK.
TEXAS
OSAGE NATION RESERVATION
OZARK PLATEAU
Ouachita Mountains
Oklahoma City
Tulsa
Broken Arrow
Norman
Lawton
Edmond
Moore
Midwest City
Enid
Stillwater
Muskogee
Bartlesville
Shawnee
Ponca City
Ardmore
Duncan
Yukon
Bixby
Sand Springs
Sapulpa
Jenks
Owasso
Claremore
Chickasha
Durant
Ada
McAlester
Tahlequah
Bethany
El Reno
Guthrie
Miami
Altus
Elk City
Woodward
Weatherford
Clinton
Okmulgee
Seminole
Pryor
Cushing
Wagoner
Poteau
Atoka
Idabel
Hugo
Sallisaw
Stilwell
Vinita
Grove
Blackwell
Perry
Kingfisher
Watonga
Fairview
Pawhuska
Anadarko
Purcell
Pauls Valley
Sulphur
Tishomingo
Coleman
Madill
Lone Grove
Marlow
Walters
Antlers
Broken Bow
Heavener
Wilburton
Holdenville
Wewoka
Tecumseh
Henryetta
Checotah
Bristow
Oklahoma City Nat. Mem.
Great Salt Plains Lake
Salt Fork
Rock Creek
Kaw Lake
Sooner Lake
Skiatook Lake
Oologah Lake
Keystone Lake
Lake Hudson
Lake O' The Cherokees
Ft. Gibson L.
Tenkiller Lake
Robert S. Kerr Lake
Eufaula Lake
Sardis Lake
McGee Creek Lake
Broken Bow Lake
Hugo Lake
Waurika Lake
L. Texoma
Arkansas
Cimarron
Canadian
N. Canadian
Deep Fork
Chikaskia
Caney
Verdigris
Neosho
Illinois
Little
Washita
Blue
Muddy Boggy Creek
Kiamichi
Mountain Fork
Red
Arbuckle Mts.
PLAINS N.W.R.
SEQUOYAH N.W.R.
DEEP FORK N.W.R.
TISHOMINGO N.W.R.
LITTLE RIVER N.W.R.
CHICKASAW N.R.A.
OUACHITA NATIONAL FOREST
CIMARRON TURNPIKE
TURNER TURNPIKE
WILL ROGERS TURNPIKE
MUSKOGEE TURNPIKE
INDIAN NATION TURNPIKE
H.E. BAILEY TURNPIKE
9
10
11
12
13
14
15
16
A
B
C
D
E
F
G
H
J
K

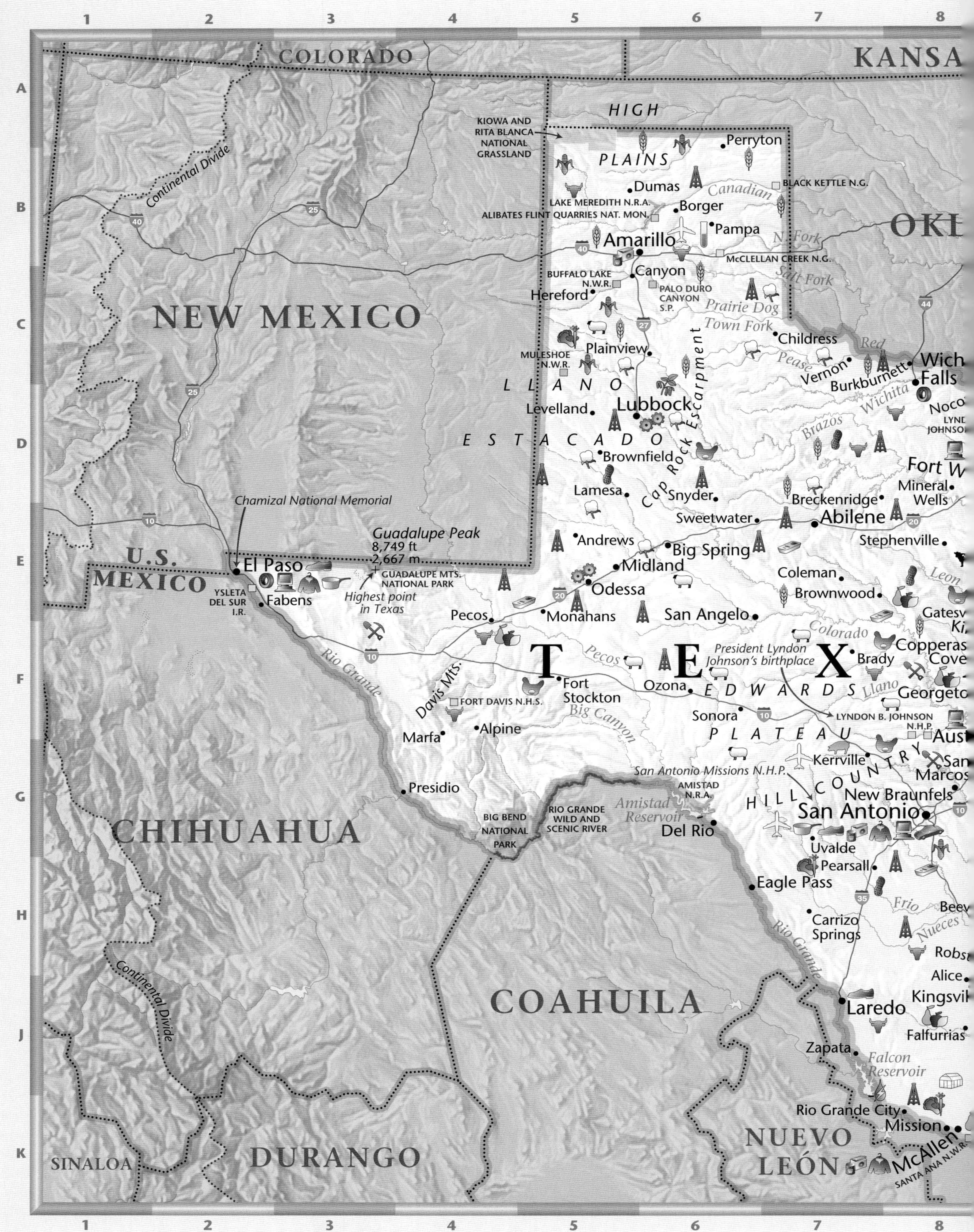

COLORADO
KANSA
HIGH
PLAINS
KIOWA AND RITA BLANCA NATIONAL GRASSLAND
Perryton
Dumas
Canadian
BLACK KETTLE N.G.
LAKE MEREDITH N.R.A.
ALIBATES FLINT QUARRIES NAT. MON.
Borger
Pampa
Amarillo
N. Fork
McCLELLAN CREEK N.G.
Canyon
BUFFALO LAKE N.W.R.
PALO DURO CANYON S.P.
Salt Fork
Hereford
Prairie Dog
Town Fork
Childress
NEW MEXICO
Continental Divide
MULESHOE N.W.R.
Plainview
Red
Pease
Vernon
Burkburnett
Wich
Falls
Wichita
L L A N O
Levelland
Lubbock
Escarpment
Brazos
E S T A C A D O
Brownfield
Cap Rock
Fort W
Lamesa
Snyder
Mineral Wells
Breckenridge
Chamizal National Memorial
Sweetwater
Abilene
Guadalupe Peak
8,749 ft
2,667 m
Andrews
Big Spring
Stephenville
U.S.
MEXICO
El Paso
GUADALUPE MTS. NATIONAL PARK
Midland
Coleman
YSLETA DEL SUR I.R.
Fabens
Highest point in Texas
Odessa
Brownwood
Pecos
Monahans
San Angelo
Colorado
President Lyndon Johnson's birthplace
Rio Grande
Pecos
T E X
Brady
Davis Mts.
Fort Stockton
Ozona
E D W A R D S
Llano
FORT DAVIS N.H.S.
Big Canyon
Sonora
LYNDON B. JOHNSON N.H.P.
Alpine
Marfa
P L A T E A U
Kerrville
San Antonio Missions N.H.P.
AMISTAD N.R.A.
H I L L C O U N T R Y
New Braunfels
Presidio
Amistad Reservoir
San Antonio
BIG BEND NATIONAL PARK
RIO GRANDE WILD AND SCENIC RIVER
Del Rio
CHIHUAHUA
Uvalde
Pearsall
Eagle Pass
Frio
Carrizo Springs
Nueces
Rio Grande
Continental Divide
COAHUILA
Laredo
Alice
Falfurrias
Zapata
Falcon Reservoir
Rio Grande City
Mission
NUEVO LEÓN
McAllen
SANTA ANA N.W.R.
DURANGO
SINALOA

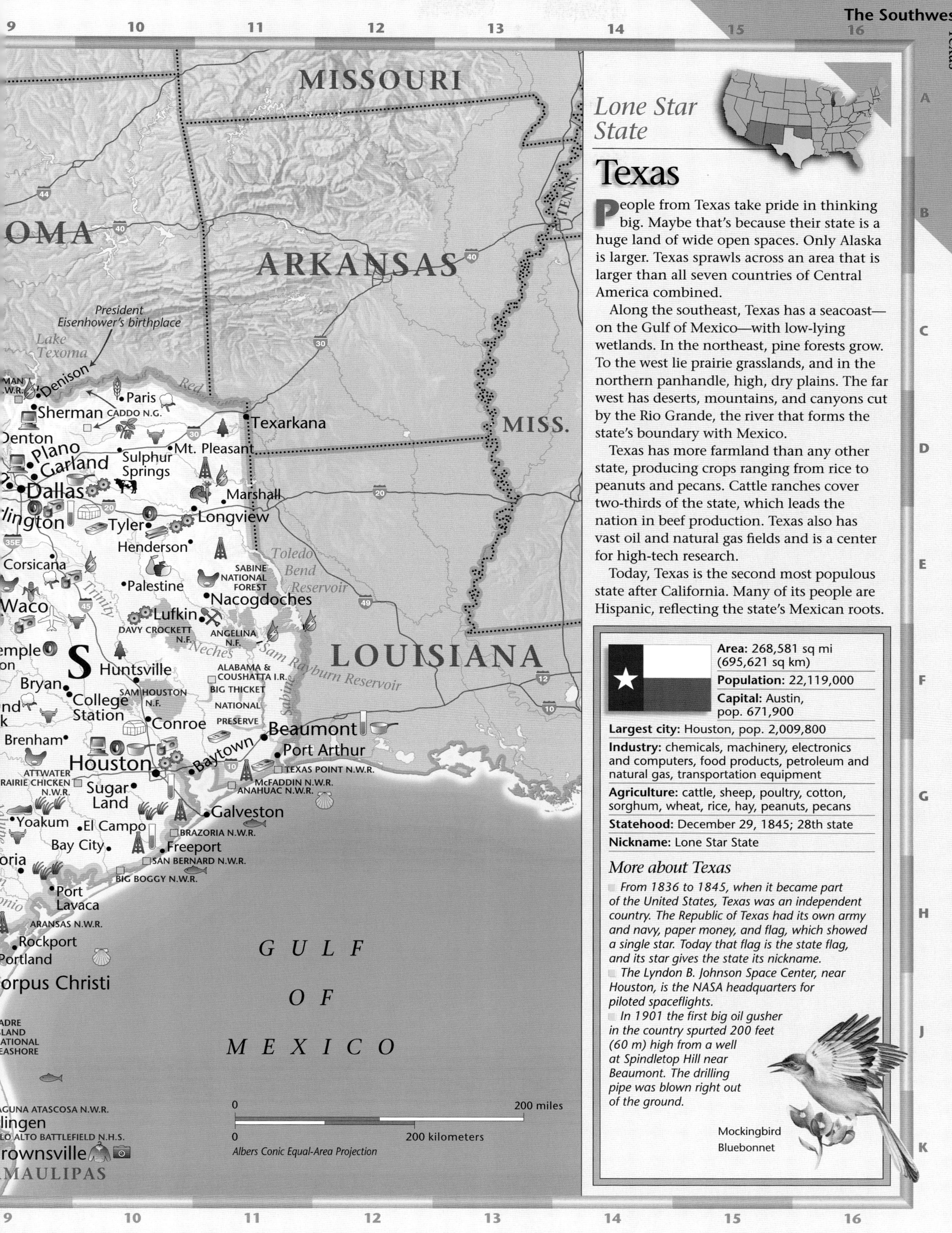

Lone Star State

Texas

People from Texas take pride in thinking big. Maybe that's because their state is a huge land of wide open spaces. Only Alaska is larger. Texas sprawls across an area that is larger than all seven countries of Central America combined.

Along the southeast, Texas has a seacoast—on the Gulf of Mexico—with low-lying wetlands. In the northeast, pine forests grow. To the west lie prairie grasslands, and in the northern panhandle, high, dry plains. The far west has deserts, mountains, and canyons cut by the Rio Grande, the river that forms the state's boundary with Mexico.

Texas has more farmland than any other state, producing crops ranging from rice to peanuts and pecans. Cattle ranches cover two-thirds of the state, which leads the nation in beef production. Texas also has vast oil and natural gas fields and is a center for high-tech research.

Today, Texas is the second most populous state after California. Many of its people are Hispanic, reflecting the state's Mexican roots.

Area: 268,581 sq mi (695,621 sq km)

Population: 22,119,000

Capital: Austin, pop. 671,900

Largest city: Houston, pop. 2,009,800

Industry: chemicals, machinery, electronics and computers, food products, petroleum and natural gas, transportation equipment

Agriculture: cattle, sheep, poultry, cotton, sorghum, wheat, rice, hay, peanuts, pecans

Statehood: December 29, 1845; 28th state

Nickname: Lone Star State

More about Texas

- *From 1836 to 1845, when it became part of the United States, Texas was an independent country. The Republic of Texas had its own army and navy, paper money, and flag, which showed a single star. Today that flag is the state flag, and its star gives the state its nickname.*
- *The Lyndon B. Johnson Space Center, near Houston, is the NASA headquarters for piloted spaceflights.*
- *In 1901 the first big oil gusher in the country spurted 200 feet (60 m) high from a well at Spindletop Hill near Beaumont. The drilling pipe was blown right out of the ground.*

Mockingbird
Bluebonnet

The West

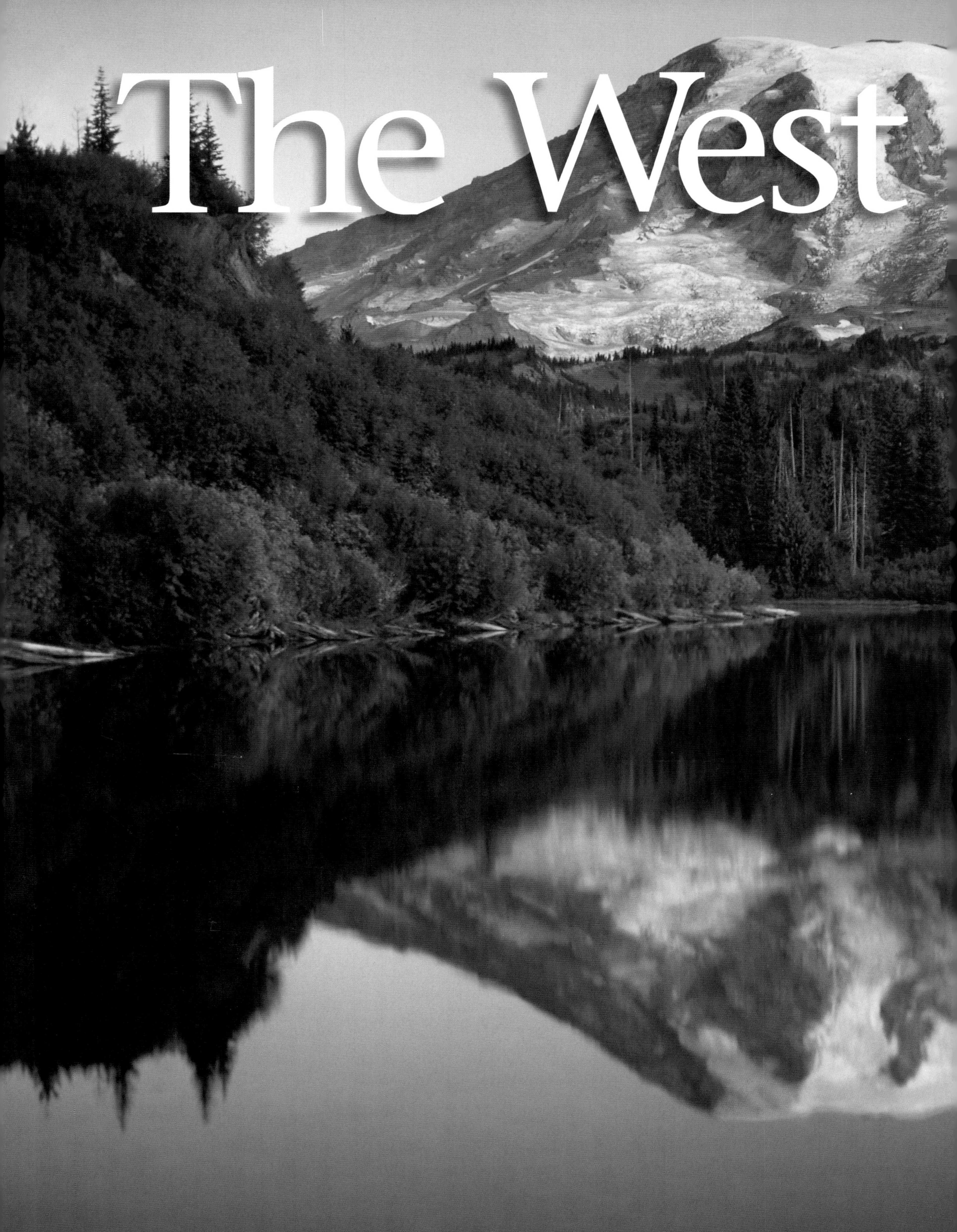

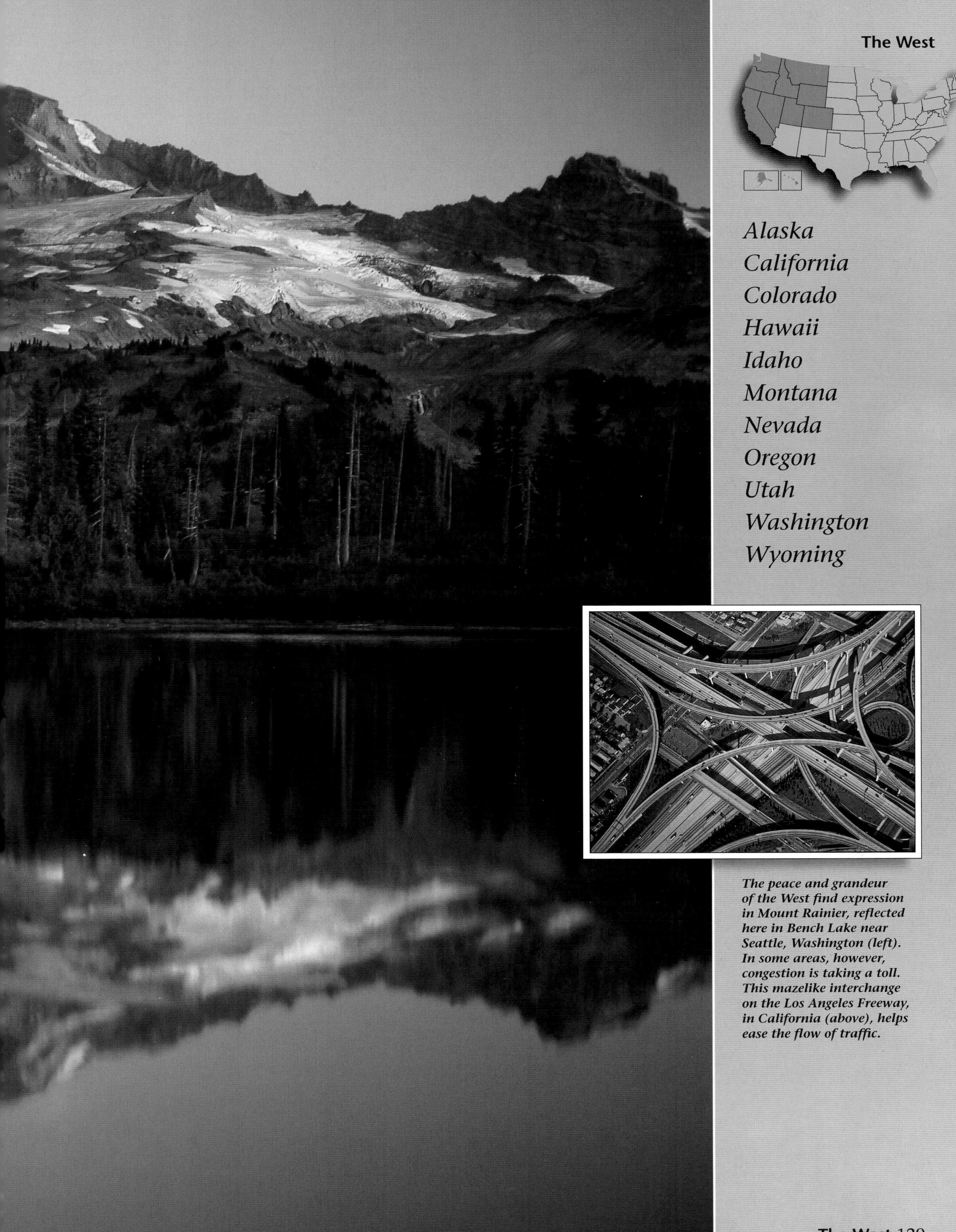

The West

Alaska
California
Colorado
Hawaii
Idaho
Montana
Nevada
Oregon
Utah
Washington
Wyoming

The peace and grandeur of the West find expression in Mount Rainier, reflected here in Bench Lake near Seattle, Washington (left). In some areas, however, congestion is taking a toll. This mazelike interchange on the Los Angeles Freeway, in California (above), helps ease the flow of traffic.

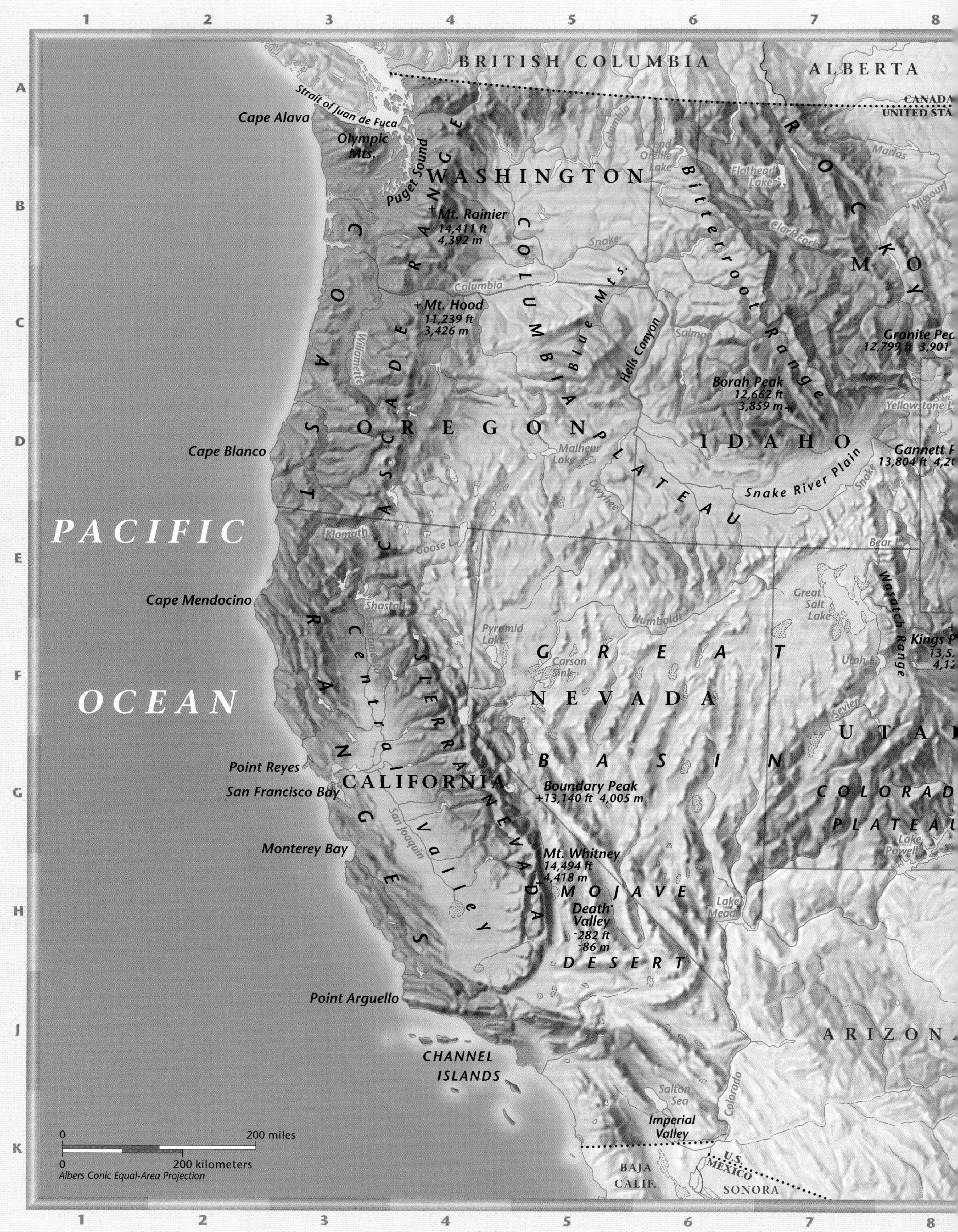
BRITISH COLUMBIA
ALBERTA
CANADA
UNITED STATES
Strait of Juan de Fuca
Cape Alava
Olympic Mts.
Puget Sound
WASHINGTON
Mt. Rainier 14,411 ft 4,392 m
COAST RANGES
CASCADE RANGE
COLUMBIA PLATEAU
Columbia
Snake
Pend Oreille Lake
Flathead Lake
Bitterroot Range
ROCKY MOUNTAINS
Marias
Missouri
Clark Fork
Mt. Hood 11,239 ft 3,426 m
Willamette
Blue Mts.
Hells Canyon
Salmon
Granite Peak 12,799 ft 3,901
Borah Peak 12,662 ft 3,859 m
Yellowstone L.
OREGON
IDAHO
Cape Blanco
Malheur Lake
Owyhee
Snake River Plain
Gannett Peak 13,804 ft
PACIFIC OCEAN
Klamath
Goose L.
Bear L.
Cape Mendocino
Shasta L.
Sacramento
Central Valley
Pyramid Lake
Humboldt
Great Salt Lake
Wasatch Range
Kings Peak
Utah L.
GREAT BASIN
NEVADA
Carson Sink
SIERRA NEVADA
Lake Tahoe
Sevier
UTAH
Point Reyes
San Francisco Bay
CALIFORNIA
Boundary Peak +13,140 ft 4,005 m
COLORADO PLATEAU
San Joaquin
Monterey Bay
Mt. Whitney 14,494 ft 4,418 m
Lake Powell
MOJAVE DESERT
Death Valley -282 ft -86 m
Lake Mead
Point Arguello
ARIZONA
CHANNEL ISLANDS
Salton Sea
Colorado
Imperial Valley
U.S.
MEXICO
BAJA CALIF.
SONORA
0 200 miles
0 200 kilometers
Albers Conic Equal-Area Projection

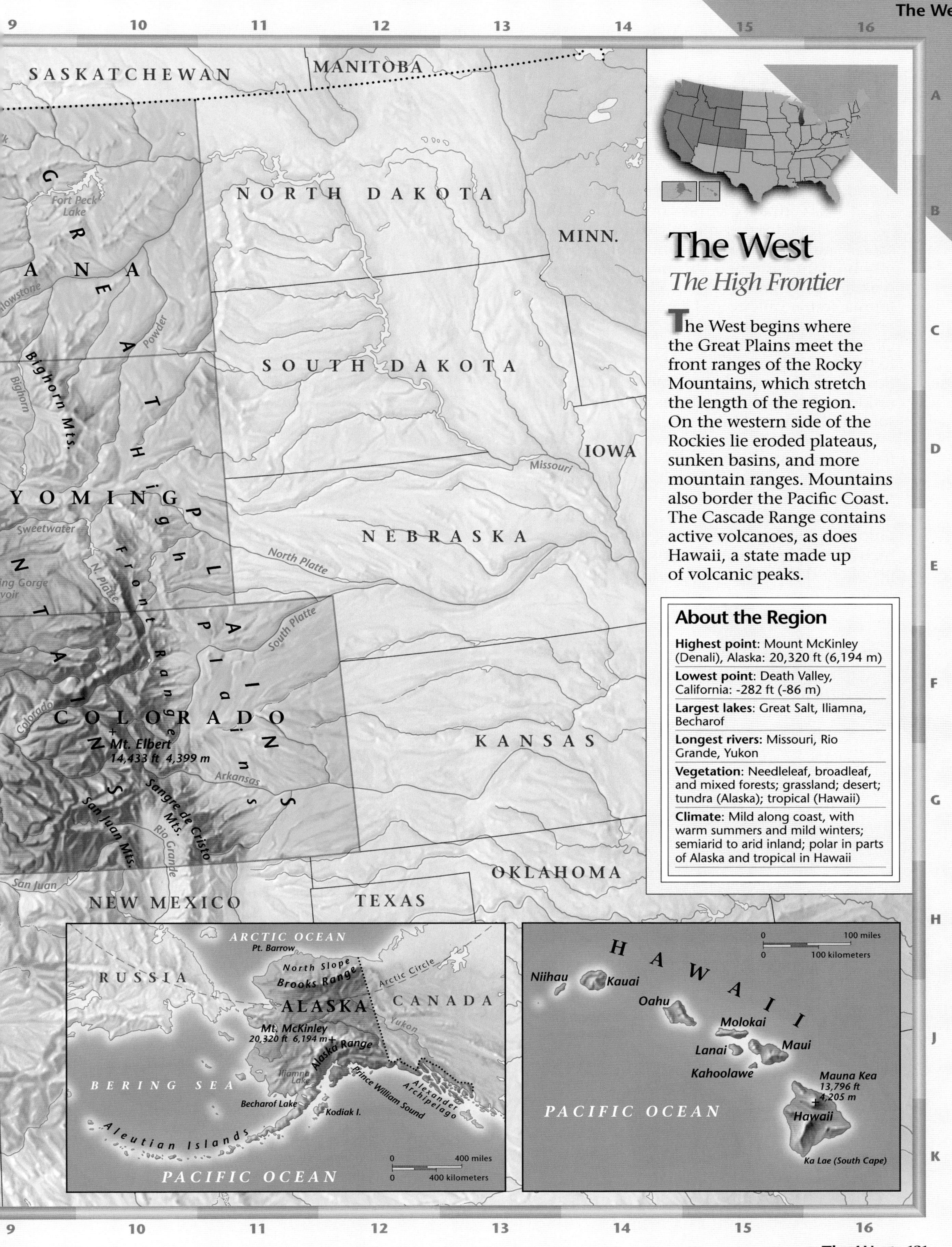

The West

The High Frontier

The West begins where the Great Plains meet the front ranges of the Rocky Mountains, which stretch the length of the region. On the western side of the Rockies lie eroded plateaus, sunken basins, and more mountain ranges. Mountains also border the Pacific Coast. The Cascade Range contains active volcanoes, as does Hawaii, a state made up of volcanic peaks.

About the Region

Highest point: Mount McKinley (Denali), Alaska: 20,320 ft (6,194 m)

Lowest point: Death Valley, California: -282 ft (-86 m)

Largest lakes: Great Salt, Iliamna, Becharof

Longest rivers: Missouri, Rio Grande, Yukon

Vegetation: Needleleaf, broadleaf, and mixed forests; grassland; desert; tundra (Alaska); tropical (Hawaii)

Climate: Mild along coast, with warm summers and mild winters; semiarid to arid inland; polar in parts of Alaska and tropical in Hawaii

The West

Land of Opportunity

Blessed with rich natural resources, the West has attracted settlers from all over the United States and the world. At different times, gold, silver—and more recently, oil—brought Easterners streaming to states such as Alaska, California, Colorado, and Nevada. Vast forests, fertile valleys, and a mild climate also lured people to California as well as to Washington and Oregon. People from Latin America and Asia came to the West Coast to find work on farms and in thriving businesses. Native Americans, the original residents, live in these states as well. In Alaska, some still hunt and fish as their ancestors did.

Except for California, most western states have few residents for their size: Giant Alaska has fewer people than tiny Rhode Island. In Wyoming and some other states, cattle nearly outnumber people. Many Westerners make their living farming, ranching, logging, and mining. But manufacturing, high-tech industries, and tourism also attract people to the West.

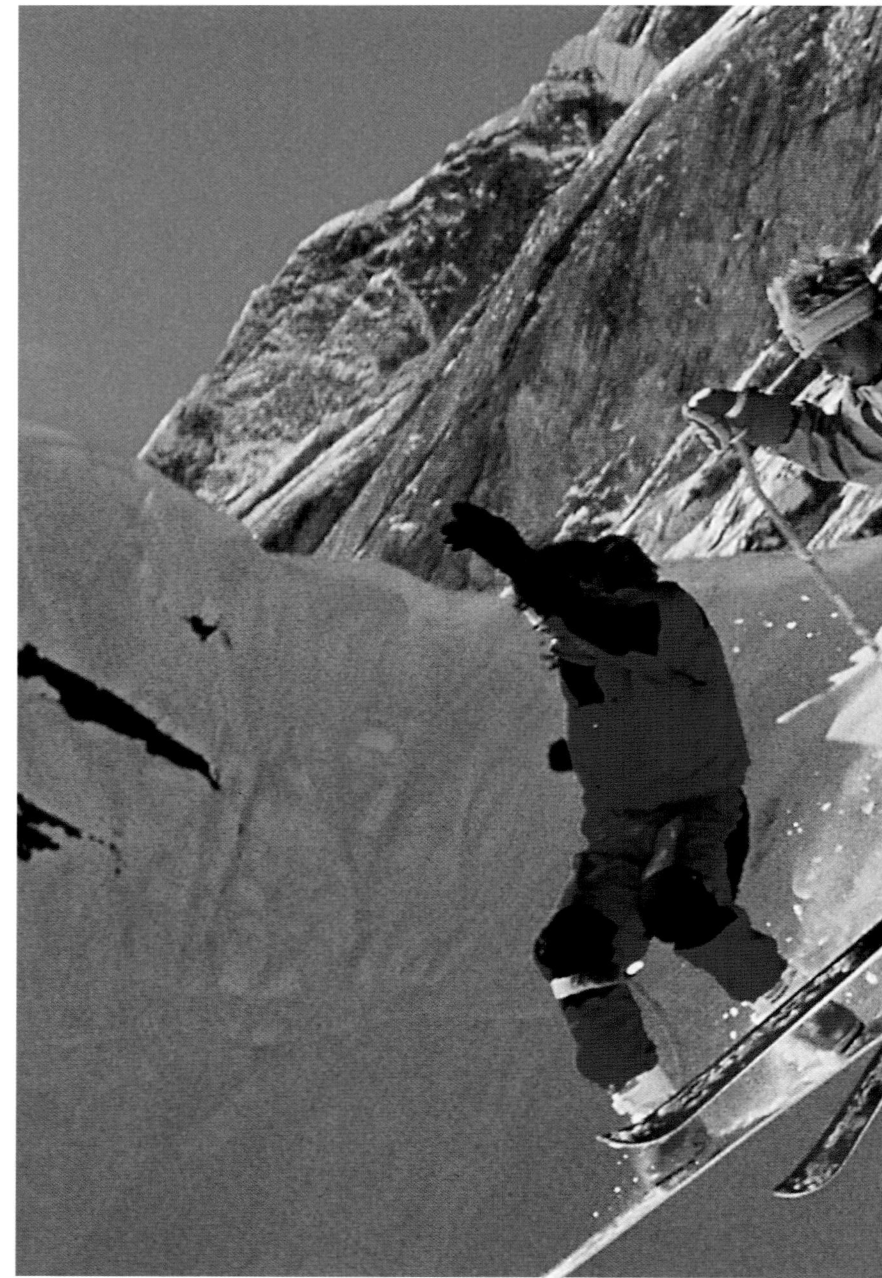

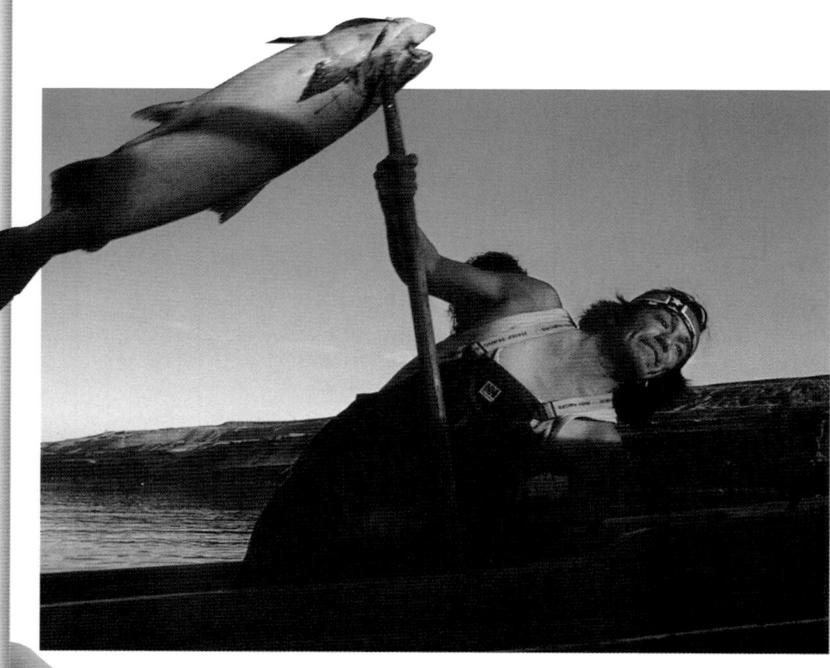

▲ **ARMED ONLY WITH MUSCLES AND A SPEAR,** *a Yakima Indian from Washington flings a king salmon into his boat. Using both traditional and modern methods, Western fishermen haul in catches worth millions each year.*

◀ **THE MIGHTY** *microchip has transformed the economy in much of the West, where computer hardware and software are big business.*

▲ **READY TO ROLL,** *freshly cut logs are loaded onto a waiting train. Generous rainfall nourishes forests in the Pacific Northwest, which supplies timber throughout the U.S. and to markets in Japan, China, and South Korea as well.*

THRILL-SEEKERS *ski off an Alaska glacier. The West boasts the country's highest mountains, offering wild—and tame—recreation.*

THE GOLDEN GATE *Bridge frames the skyline of San Francisco, California. This former gold rush town remains a banking center.*

THEME HOTELS, *such as the Luxor, attract tourists to Las Vegas. This fast-growing desert city is devoted to entertainment.*

PACIFIC WAVES *lure surfers to many Pacific beaches. In some locations, such as Hawaii's Waimea Bay, on the island of Oahu, waves can tower up to 25 feet (8 m) high.*

HMONG FARMERS *display dikon radishes in California's San Joaquin Valley. Southeast Asians, many of whom work in high-tech businesses, form a large part of the area's immigrant population.*

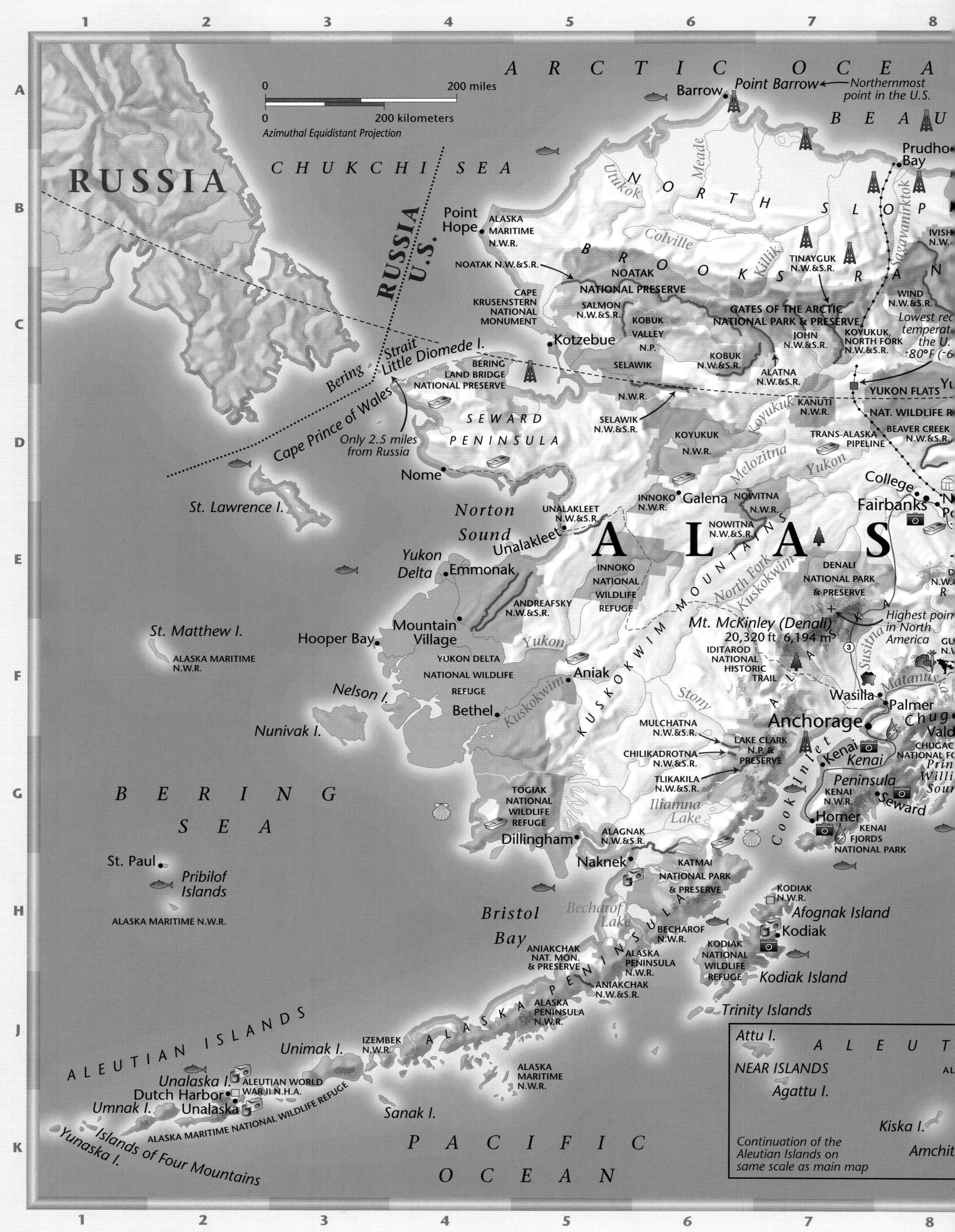

1 2 3 4 5 6 7 8
A B C D E F G H J K
ARCTIC OCEAN
0 200 miles
0 200 kilometers
Azimuthal Equidistant Projection
Barrow
Point Barrow
Northernmost point in the U.S.
BEAU
Prudhoe Bay
RUSSIA
CHUKCHI SEA
RUSSIA
U.S.
Point Hope
ALASKA MARITIME N.W.R.
Utukok
Meade
NORTH SLOPE
Colville
Sagavanirktok
BROOKS RANGE
Killik
TINAYGUK N.W.&S.R.
NOATAK N.W.&S.R.
NOATAK NATIONAL PRESERVE
CAPE KRUSENSTERN NATIONAL MONUMENT
SALMON N.W.&S.R.
KOBUK VALLEY N.P.
GATES OF THE ARCTIC NATIONAL PARK & PRESERVE
JOHN N.W.&S.R.
KOYUKUK, NORTH FORK N.W.&S.R.
WIND N.W.&S.R.
Lowest recorded temperature in the U.S. -80°F
Kotzebue
Bering Strait
Little Diomede I.
BERING LAND BRIDGE NATIONAL PRESERVE
SELAWIK
KOBUK N.W.&S.R.
ALATNA N.W.&S.R.
YUKON FLATS NAT. WILDLIFE REFUGE
N.W.R.
SELAWIK N.W.&S.R.
KANUTI N.W.R.
Koyukuk
Cape Prince of Wales
Only 2.5 miles from Russia
SEWARD PENINSULA
KOYUKUK N.W.R.
TRANS-ALASKA PIPELINE
BEAVER CREEK N.W.&S.R.
Melozitna
Yukon
Nome
College
Fairbanks
St. Lawrence I.
INNOKO N.W.R.
Galena
NOWITNA N.W.R.
NOWITNA N.W.&S.R.
Norton Sound
UNALAKLEET N.W.&S.R.
Unalakleet
ALASKA
Yukon Delta
Emmonak
INNOKO NATIONAL WILDLIFE REFUGE
North Fork Kuskokwim
DENALI NATIONAL PARK & PRESERVE
KUSKOKWIM MOUNTAINS
ANDREAFSKY N.W.&S.R.
Mt. McKinley (Denali) 20,320 ft 6,194 m
Highest point in North America
St. Matthew I.
Hooper Bay
Mountain Village
ALASKA MARITIME N.W.R.
Yukon
YUKON DELTA NATIONAL WILDLIFE REFUGE
IDITAROD NATIONAL HISTORIC TRAIL
ALASKA RANGE
Susitna
Aniak
Nelson I.
Kuskokwim
Stony
Wasilla
Palmer
Matanuska
Bethel
Anchorage
Chugach
Valdez
Nunivak I.
MULCHATNA N.W.&S.R.
LAKE CLARK N.P. & PRESERVE
CHILIKADROTNA N.W.&S.R.
TLIKAKILA N.W.&S.R.
Kenai
Kenai Peninsula
KENAI N.W.R.
Seward
Prince William Sound
Cook Inlet
BERING SEA
TOGIAK NATIONAL WILDLIFE REFUGE
Iliamna Lake
Homer
KENAI FJORDS NATIONAL PARK
Dillingham
ALAGNAK N.W.&S.R.
St. Paul
Pribilof Islands
Naknek
KATMAI NATIONAL PARK & PRESERVE
ALASKA MARITIME N.W.R.
Bristol Bay
Becharof Lake
KODIAK N.W.R.
Afognak Island
BECHAROF N.W.R.
Kodiak
ANIAKCHAK NAT. MON. & PRESERVE
ALASKA PENINSULA N.W.R.
KODIAK NATIONAL WILDLIFE REFUGE
Kodiak Island
ANIAKCHAK N.W.&S.R.
ALASKA PENINSULA
Trinity Islands
ALASKA PENINSULA N.W.R.
ALEUTIAN ISLANDS
Unimak I.
IZEMBEK N.W.R.
Unalaska I.
ALEUTIAN WORLD WAR II N.H.A.
Dutch Harbor
Umnak I.
Unalaska
ALASKA MARITIME N.W.R.
Sanak I.
ALASKA MARITIME NATIONAL WILDLIFE REFUGE
Islands of Four Mountains
Yunaska I.
PACIFIC OCEAN
Attu I.
NEAR ISLANDS
Agattu I.
Kiska I.
Amchitka
Continuation of the Aleutian Islands on same scale as main map

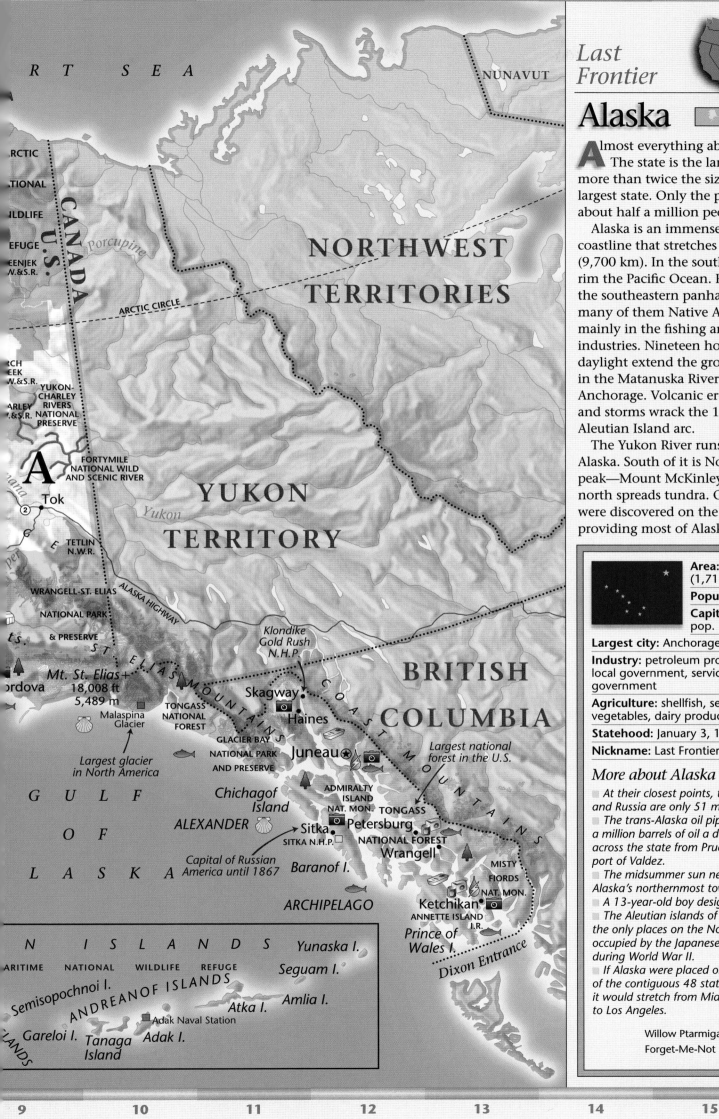

9 10 11 12 13 14 15 16

A B C D E F G H J K

R T S E A

NUNAVUT

RCTIC
TIONAL
LDLIFE
EFUGE
EENJEK
V.&S.R.

CANADA
U.S.

Porcupine

NORTHWEST TERRITORIES

ARCTIC CIRCLE

RCH
EEK
V.&S.R.
YUKON-CHARLEY RIVERS NATIONAL PRESERVE
ARLEY
.&S.R.

A

FORTYMILE NATIONAL WILD AND SCENIC RIVER

Tok

YUKON TERRITORY

Yukon

TETLIN N.W.R.

WRANGELL-ST. ELIAS NATIONAL PARK & PRESERVE

ALASKA HIGHWAY

Klondike Gold Rush N.H.P.

ST. ELIAS MOUNTAINS

Mt. St. Elias
18,008 ft
5,489 m

rdova

Malaspina Glacier

Largest glacier in North America

TONGASS NATIONAL FOREST

Skagway
Haines

BRITISH COLUMBIA

COAST MOUNTAINS

GLACIER BAY NATIONAL PARK AND PRESERVE

Juneau

Largest national forest in the U.S.

ADMIRALTY ISLAND NAT. MON.

Chichagof Island

TONGASS NATIONAL FOREST

ALEXANDER ARCHIPELAGO

Sitka
SITKA N.H.P.

Petersburg
Wrangell

Capital of Russian America until 1867

Baranof I.

MISTY FIORDS NAT. MON.

Ketchikan
ANNETTE ISLAND I.R.

Prince of Wales I.

Dixon Entrance

GULF OF ALASKA

N ISLANDS
ARITIME NATIONAL WILDLIFE REFUGE

Yunaska I.
Seguam I.
Semisopochnoi I.
ANDREANOF ISLANDS
Amlia I.
Atka I.
Adak Naval Station
Gareloi I.
Tanaga Island
Adak I.
ANDS

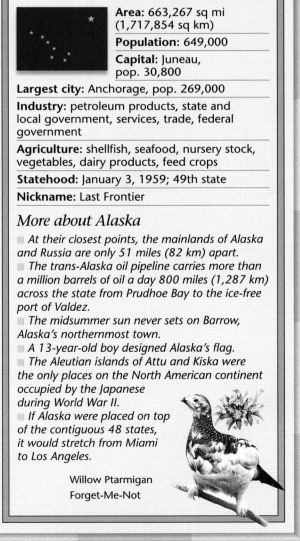

Last Frontier

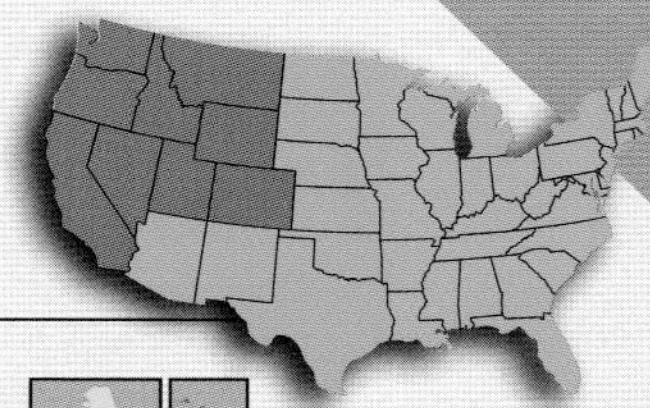

Alaska

Almost everything about Alaska is big. The state is the largest in the country—more than twice the size of Texas, the second-largest state. Only the population is small, about half a million people.

Alaska is an immense peninsula with a coastline that stretches some 6,000 miles (9,700 km). In the south mountain ranges rim the Pacific Ocean. Forested islands edge the southeastern panhandle where people, many of them Native Americans, work mainly in the fishing and lumbering industries. Nineteen hours of summer daylight extend the growing time for crops in the Matanuska River Valley north of Anchorage. Volcanic eruptions, earthquakes, and storms wrack the 1,700-mile (2,736-km) Aleutian Island arc.

The Yukon River runs east to west across Alaska. South of it is North America's highest peak—Mount McKinley, or Denali. To the north spreads tundra. Oil and natural gas were discovered on the North Slope in 1968, providing most of Alaska's current wealth.

Area: 663,267 sq mi (1,717,854 sq km)

Population: 649,000

Capital: Juneau, pop. 30,800

Largest city: Anchorage, pop. 269,000

Industry: petroleum products, state and local government, services, trade, federal government

Agriculture: shellfish, seafood, nursery stock, vegetables, dairy products, feed crops

Statehood: January 3, 1959; 49th state

Nickname: Last Frontier

More about Alaska

- *At their closest points, the mainlands of Alaska and Russia are only 51 miles (82 km) apart.*
- *The trans-Alaska oil pipeline carries more than a million barrels of oil a day 800 miles (1,287 km) across the state from Prudhoe Bay to the ice-free port of Valdez.*
- *The midsummer sun never sets on Barrow, Alaska's northernmost town.*
- *A 13-year-old boy designed Alaska's flag.*
- *The Aleutian islands of Attu and Kiska were the only places on the North American continent occupied by the Japanese during World War II.*
- *If Alaska were placed on top of the contiguous 48 states, it would stretch from Miami to Los Angeles.*

Willow Ptarmigan
Forget-Me-Not

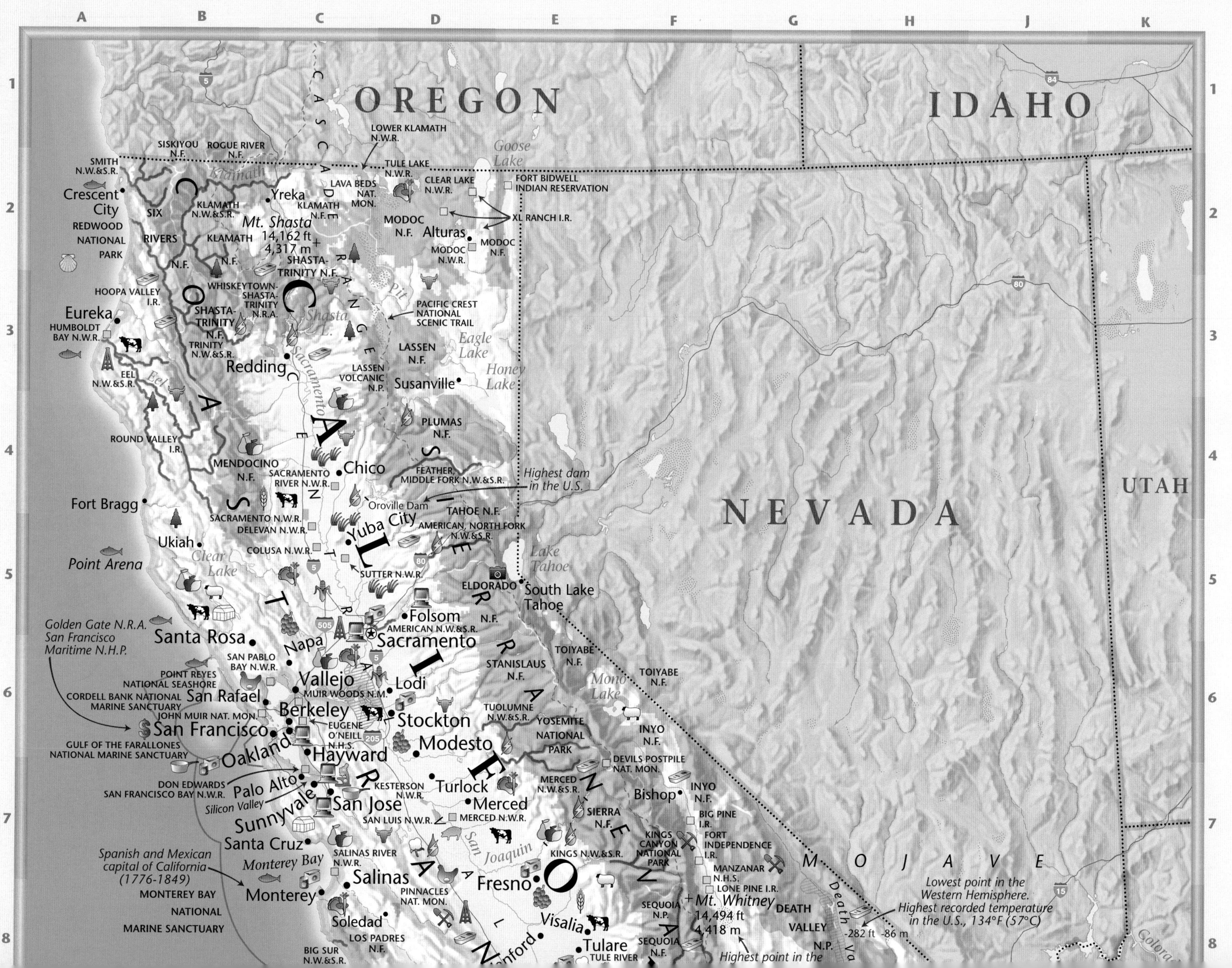

OREGON
IDAHO
NEVADA
UTAH
C A S C A D E
C O A S T
R A N G E
S I E R R A
N E V A D A
C A L I F O R N I A
M O J A V E
Goose Lake
Honey Lake
Eagle Lake
Lake Tahoe
Mono Lake
Clear Lake
Pit
Sacramento
San Joaquin
Klamath
Eel
Death Valley
SMITH N.W.&S.R.
Crescent City
REDWOOD NATIONAL PARK
SIX RIVERS N.F.
SISKIYOU N.F.
ROGUE RIVER N.F.
LOWER KLAMATH N.W.R.
TULE LAKE N.W.R.
LAVA BEDS NAT. MON.
CLEAR LAKE N.W.R.
FORT BIDWELL INDIAN RESERVATION
XL RANCH I.R.
MODOC N.F.
MODOC N.W.R.
Alturas
KLAMATH N.F.
KLAMATH N.W.&S.R.
Yreka
Mt. Shasta 14,162 ft 4,317 m
SHASTA-TRINITY N.F.
WHISKEYTOWN-SHASTA-TRINITY N.R.A.
TRINITY N.W.&S.R.
HOOPA VALLEY I.R.
Eureka
HUMBOLDT BAY N.W.R.
EEL N.W.&S.R.
Redding
LASSEN VOLCANIC N.P.
LASSEN N.F.
PACIFIC CREST NATIONAL SCENIC TRAIL
Susanville
PLUMAS N.F.
Chico
ROUND VALLEY I.R.
MENDOCINO N.F.
SACRAMENTO RIVER N.W.R.
SACRAMENTO N.W.R.
DELEVAN N.W.R.
COLUSA N.W.R.
Fort Bragg
Point Arena
Ukiah
FEATHER, MIDDLE FORK N.W.&S.R.
Oroville Dam
Highest dam in the U.S.
Yuba City
SUTTER N.W.R.
TAHOE N.F.
AMERICAN, NORTH FORK N.W.&S.R.
AMERICAN N.W.&S.R.
Folsom
Sacramento
ELDORADO N.F.
South Lake Tahoe
TOIYABE N.F.
Santa Rosa
Napa
Vallejo
Lodi
Stockton
STANISLAUS N.F.
MUIR WOODS N.M.
EUGENE O'NEILL N.H.S.
POINT REYES NATIONAL SEASHORE
SAN PABLO BAY N.W.R.
San Rafael
Berkeley
San Francisco
Oakland
Hayward
Modesto
TUOLUMNE N.W.&S.R.
YOSEMITE NATIONAL PARK
CORDELL BANK NATIONAL MARINE SANCTUARY
JOHN MUIR NAT. MON.
GULF OF THE FARALLONES NATIONAL MARINE SANCTUARY
Golden Gate N.R.A. San Francisco Maritime N.H.P.
DON EDWARDS SAN FRANCISCO BAY N.W.R.
Palo Alto
Silicon Valley
San Jose
Sunnyvale
KESTERSON N.W.R.
SAN LUIS N.W.R.
Turlock
Merced
MERCED N.W.R.
MERCED N.W.&S.R.
SIERRA N.F.
DEVILS POSTPILE NAT. MON.
INYO N.F.
Bishop
Santa Cruz
Monterey Bay
Monterey
Spanish and Mexican capital of California (1776-1849)
MONTEREY BAY NATIONAL MARINE SANCTUARY
SALINAS RIVER N.W.R.
Salinas
PINNACLES NAT. MON.
Soledad
LOS PADRES N.F.
BIG SUR N.W.&S.R.
Fresno
KINGS N.W.&S.R.
KINGS CANYON NATIONAL PARK
Visalia
Tulare
TULE RIVER
SEQUOIA N.P.
SEQUOIA N.F.
BIG PINE I.R.
FORT INDEPENDENCE I.R.
MANZANAR N.H.S.
LONE PINE I.R.
Mt. Whitney 14,494 ft 4,418 m
Highest point in the
DEATH VALLEY N.P.
-282 ft -86 m
Lowest point in the Western Hemisphere. Highest recorded temperature in the U.S., 134°F (57°C)

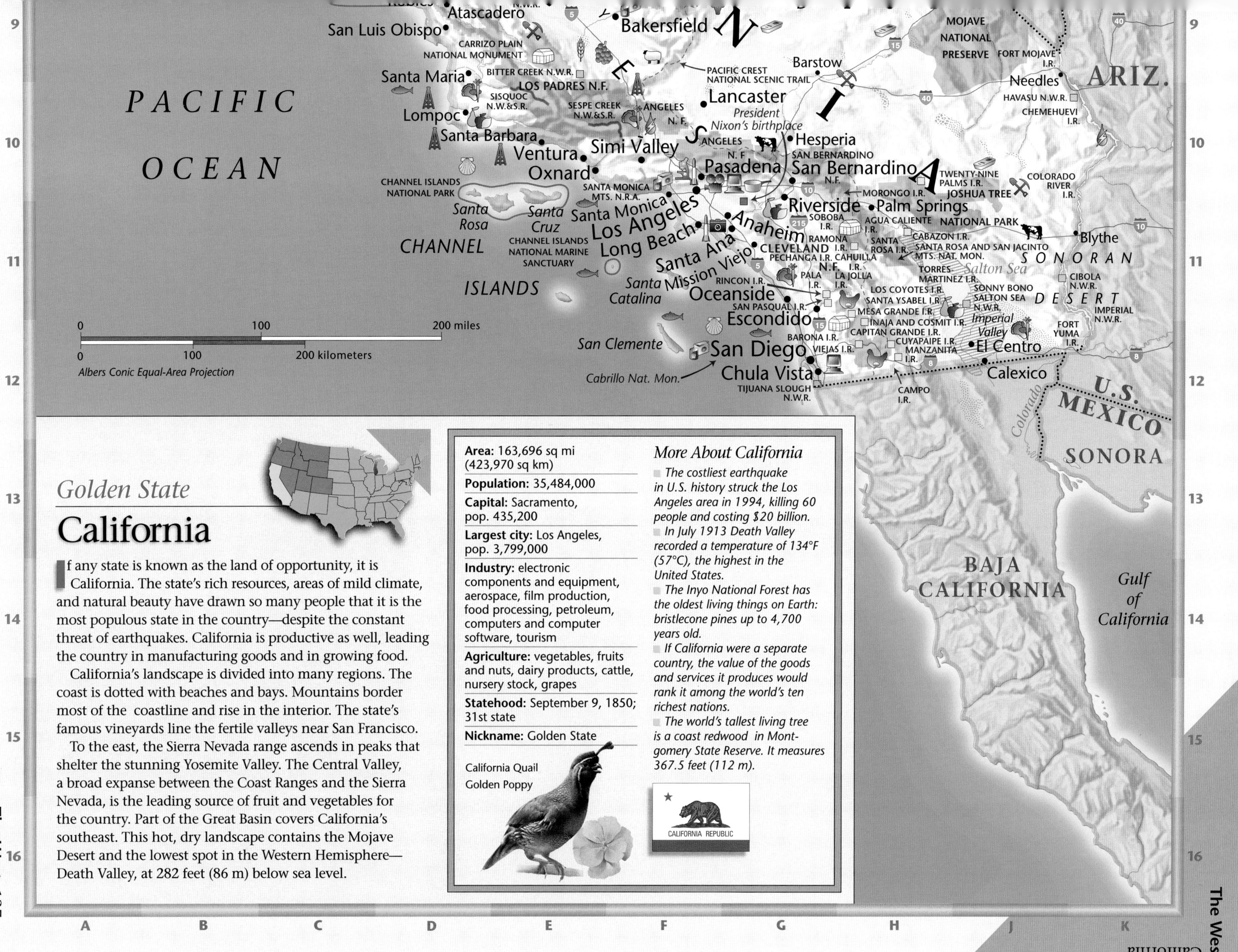

Golden State

California

If any state is known as the land of opportunity, it is California. The state's rich resources, areas of mild climate, and natural beauty have drawn so many people that it is the most populous state in the country—despite the constant threat of earthquakes. California is productive as well, leading the country in manufacturing goods and in growing food.

California's landscape is divided into many regions. The coast is dotted with beaches and bays. Mountains border most of the coastline and rise in the interior. The state's famous vineyards line the fertile valleys near San Francisco.

To the east, the Sierra Nevada range ascends in peaks that shelter the stunning Yosemite Valley. The Central Valley, a broad expanse between the Coast Ranges and the Sierra Nevada, is the leading source of fruit and vegetables for the country. Part of the Great Basin covers California's southeast. This hot, dry landscape contains the Mojave Desert and the lowest spot in the Western Hemisphere—Death Valley, at 282 feet (86 m) below sea level.

Area: 163,696 sq mi (423,970 sq km)

Population: 35,484,000

Capital: Sacramento, pop. 435,200

Largest city: Los Angeles, pop. 3,799,000

Industry: electronic components and equipment, aerospace, film production, food processing, petroleum, computers and computer software, tourism

Agriculture: vegetables, fruits and nuts, dairy products, cattle, nursery stock, grapes

Statehood: September 9, 1850; 31st state

Nickname: Golden State

California Quail
Golden Poppy

CALIFORNIA REPUBLIC

More About California

- *The costliest earthquake in U.S. history struck the Los Angeles area in 1994, killing 60 people and costing $20 billion.*
- *In July 1913 Death Valley recorded a temperature of 134°F (57°C), the highest in the United States.*
- *The Inyo National Forest has the oldest living things on Earth: bristlecone pines up to 4,700 years old.*
- *If California were a separate country, the value of the goods and services it produces would rank it among the world's ten richest nations.*
- *The world's tallest living tree is a coast redwood in Montgomery State Reserve. It measures 367.5 feet (112 m).*

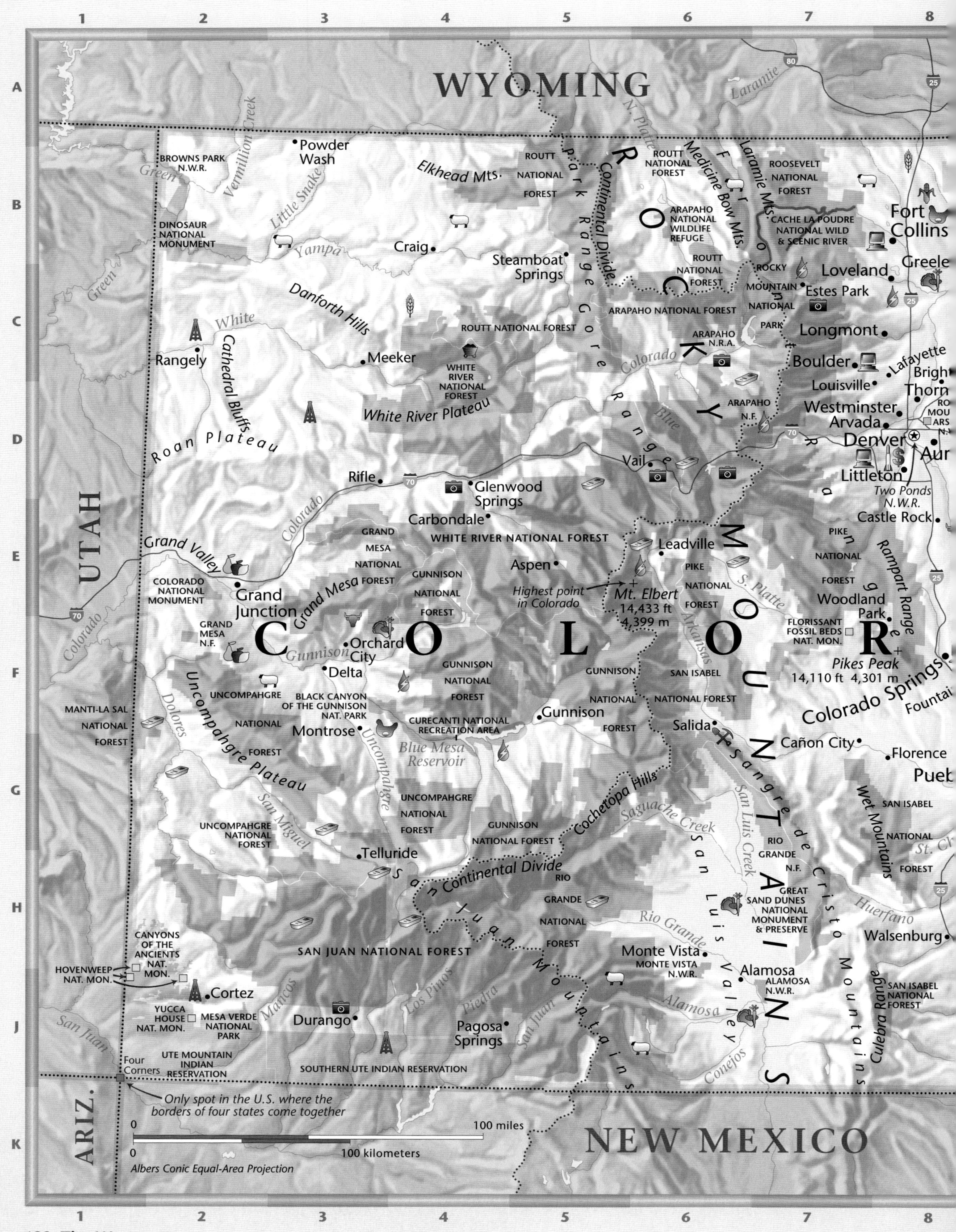

WYOMING
UTAH
ARIZ.
NEW MEXICO
COLORADO
ROCKY MOUNTAINS
Powder Wash
BROWNS PARK N.W.R.
Green
Vermillion Creek
Little Snake
Elkhead Mts.
ROUTT NATIONAL FOREST
Park Range
Continental Divide
N. Platte
Medicine Bow Mts.
Laramie Mts.
Laramie
ROOSEVELT NATIONAL FOREST
ARAPAHO NATIONAL WILDLIFE REFUGE
CACHE LA POUDRE NATIONAL WILD & SCENIC RIVER
Fort Collins
Greeley
DINOSAUR NATIONAL MONUMENT
Yampa
Craig
Steamboat Springs
Gore Range
ROCKY MOUNTAIN NATIONAL PARK
Loveland
Estes Park
Danforth Hills
ARAPAHO NATIONAL FOREST
White
ROUTT NATIONAL FOREST
ARAPAHO N.R.A.
Longmont
Rangely
Cathedral Bluffs
Meeker
WHITE RIVER NATIONAL FOREST
Colorado
Boulder
Lafayette
Louisville
Brighton
Thornton
White River Plateau
Blue
ARAPAHO N.F.
Westminster
Arvada
Roan Plateau
Front Range
Denver
Aurora
Vail
Rifle
Glenwood Springs
Littleton
Two Ponds N.W.R.
Carbondale
Castle Rock
Grand Valley
GRAND MESA NATIONAL FOREST
WHITE RIVER NATIONAL FOREST
Leadville
PIKE NATIONAL FOREST
Rampart Range
Aspen
GUNNISON NATIONAL FOREST
COLORADO NATIONAL MONUMENT
Grand Junction
Grand Mesa
Highest point in Colorado
Mt. Elbert 14,433 ft 4,399 m
S. Platte
Woodland Park
GRAND MESA N.F.
Arkansas
FLORISSANT FOSSIL BEDS NAT. MON.
Gunnison
Orchard City
Pikes Peak 14,110 ft 4,301 m
Delta
Colorado Springs
Fountain
Uncompahgre
UNCOMPAHGRE NATIONAL FOREST
BLACK CANYON OF THE GUNNISON NAT. PARK
SAN ISABEL NATIONAL FOREST
MANTI-LA SAL NATIONAL FOREST
Gunnison
Dolores
Montrose
CURECANTI NATIONAL RECREATION AREA
Salida
Cañon City
Florence
Uncompahgre Plateau
Blue Mesa Reservoir
Pueblo
Cochetopa Hills
Sangre de Cristo
San Miguel
Saguache Creek
San Luis Creek
Wet Mountains
SAN ISABEL NATIONAL FOREST
UNCOMPAHGRE NATIONAL FOREST
GUNNISON NATIONAL FOREST
RIO GRANDE N.F.
St. Charles
Telluride
San Juan Mountains
Continental Divide
RIO GRANDE NATIONAL FOREST
San Luis Valley
GREAT SAND DUNES NATIONAL MONUMENT & PRESERVE
Huerfano
Rio Grande
Walsenburg
CANYONS OF THE ANCIENTS NAT. MON.
SAN JUAN NATIONAL FOREST
Monte Vista
MONTE VISTA N.W.R.
HOVENWEEP NAT. MON.
Alamosa
ALAMOSA N.W.R.
Culebra Range
SAN ISABEL NATIONAL FOREST
Cortez
Mancos
Los Pinos
Piedra
YUCCA HOUSE NAT. MON.
MESA VERDE NATIONAL PARK
Durango
San Juan
Pagosa Springs
Alamosa
San Juan
Four Corners
UTE MOUNTAIN INDIAN RESERVATION
SOUTHERN UTE INDIAN RESERVATION
Conejos
Only spot in the U.S. where the borders of four states come together
0
100 miles
0
100 kilometers
Albers Conic Equal-Area Projection

NEBRASKA

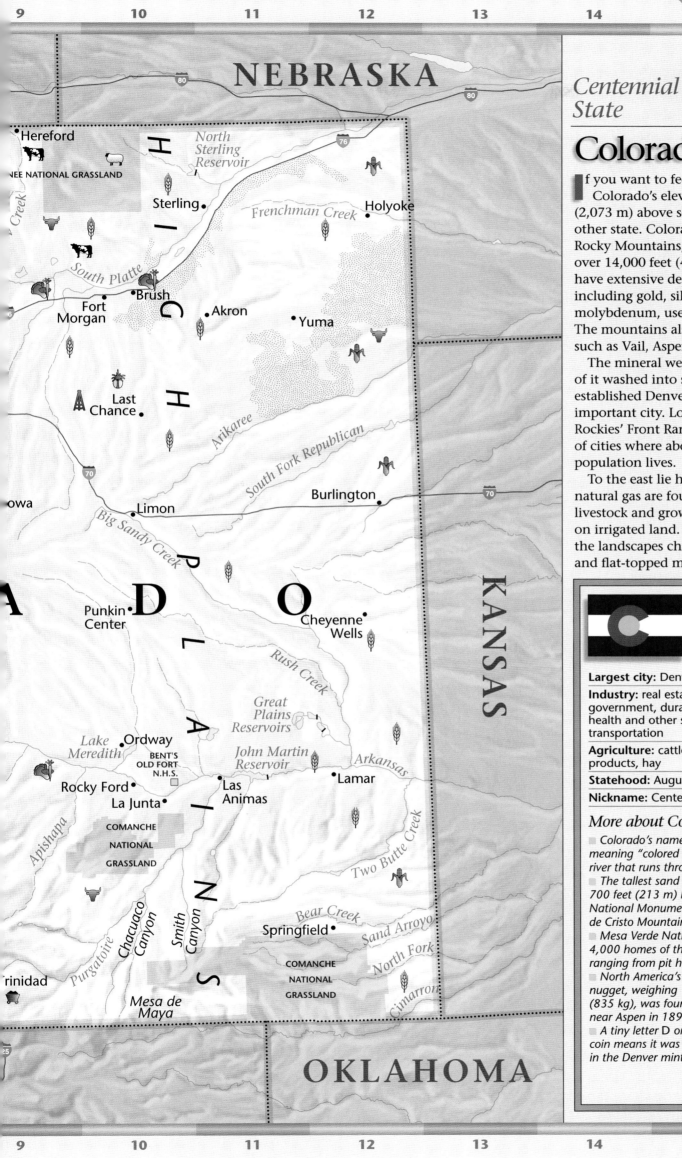

Hereford
PAWNEE NATIONAL GRASSLAND
North Sterling Reservoir
Sterling
Holyoke
Frenchman Creek
South Platte
Brush
Fort Morgan
Akron
Yuma
Last Chance
Arikaree
South Fork Republican
Burlington
Limon
Big Sandy Creek
HIGH PLAINS
COLORADO
Punkin Center
Cheyenne Wells
Rush Creek
Great Plains Reservoirs
Lake Meredith
Ordway
BENT'S OLD FORT N.H.S.
John Martin Reservoir
Arkansas
Rocky Ford
La Junta
Las Animas
Lamar
Apishapa
COMANCHE NATIONAL GRASSLAND
Two Butte Creek
Bear Creek
Springfield
Sand Arroyo
North Fork
Cimarron
Chacuaco Canyon
Smith Canyon
Purgatoire
Trinidad
Mesa de Maya
COMANCHE NATIONAL GRASSLAND
KANSAS
OKLAHOMA

Centennial State

Colorado

If you want to feel taller, head for Colorado. Colorado's elevation averages 6,800 feet (2,073 m) above sea level, higher than any other state. Colorado, in the heart of the Rocky Mountains, has more than 50 peaks over 14,000 feet (4,267 m). The mountains have extensive deposits of valuable minerals, including gold, silver, lead, iron, and molybdenum, used for strengthening steel. The mountains also bring skiers to resorts such as Vail, Aspen, and Telluride.

The mineral wealth of the Rockies, much of it washed into streams as placer deposits, established Denver as Colorado's most important city. Located at the foot of the Rockies' Front Range, Denver is one of a line of cities where about 80 percent of Colorado's population lives.

To the east lie high, dry plains. Oil and natural gas are found here, and farmers raise livestock and grow wheat, corn, and hay on irrigated land. West of the Rockies the landscapes change to plateaus, valleys, and flat-topped mesas.

Area: 104,094 sq mi (269,601 sq km)

Population: 4,551,000

Capital: Denver, pop. 560,400

Largest city: Denver, pop. 560,400

Industry: real estate, state and local government, durable goods, communications, health and other services, nondurable goods, transportation

Agriculture: cattle, corn, wheat, dairy products, hay

Statehood: August 1, 1876; 38th state

Nickname: Centennial State

More about Colorado

- *Colorado's name comes from a Spanish word meaning "colored red." It was first given to the river that runs through red stone cliffs.*
- *The tallest sand dunes in North America, some 700 feet (213 m) high, are in Great Sand Dunes National Monument at the foot of the Sangre de Cristo Mountains.*
- *Mesa Verde National Park contains more than 4,000 homes of the ancient Pueblo people, ranging from pit houses to cliff pueblos.*
- *North America's largest silver nugget, weighing 1,840 pounds (835 kg), was found near Aspen in 1894.*
- *A tiny letter D on your coin means it was made in the Denver mint.*

Lark Bunting
Columbine

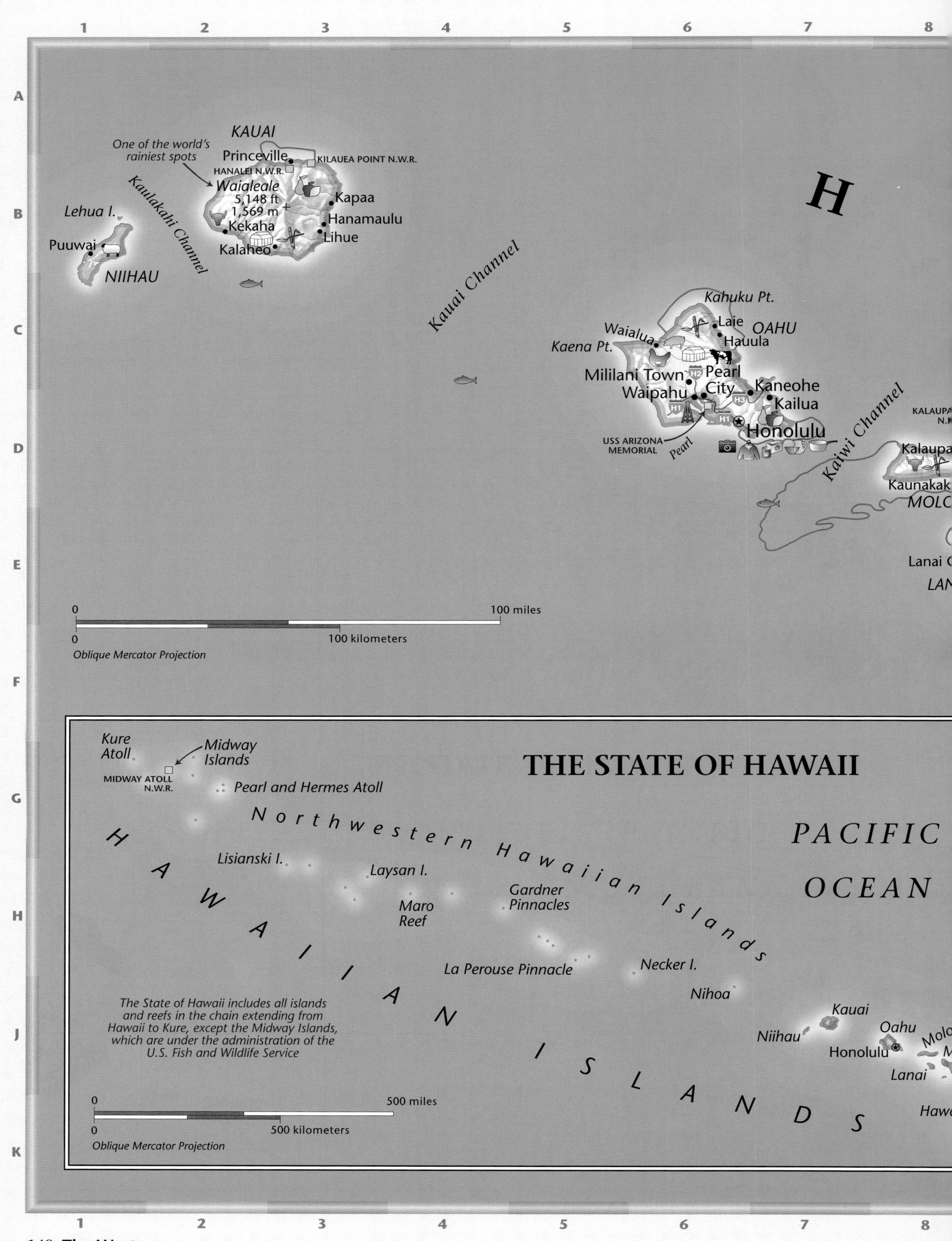
KAUAI
One of the world's rainiest spots
Princeville
HANALEI N.W.R.
KILAUEA POINT N.W.R.
Waialeale
5,148 ft
1,569 m
Kapaa
Hanamaulu
Lihue
Kekaha
Kalaheo
Lehua I.
Puuwai
NIIHAU
Kaulakahi Channel
Kauai Channel
H
Kahuku Pt.
Laie
OAHU
Hauula
Waialua
Kaena Pt.
Mililani Town
Pearl City
Waipahu
Kaneohe
Kailua
Honolulu
USS ARIZONA MEMORIAL
Pearl
Kaiwi Channel
Kalaupa
Kaunakak
MOLO
Lanai
LAN
0
100 miles
0
100 kilometers
Oblique Mercator Projection
THE STATE OF HAWAII
Kure Atoll
Midway Islands
MIDWAY ATOLL N.W.R.
Pearl and Hermes Atoll
Northwestern Hawaiian Islands
HAWAIIAN ISLANDS
PACIFIC OCEAN
Lisianski I.
Laysan I.
Maro Reef
Gardner Pinnacles
La Perouse Pinnacle
Necker I.
Nihoa
Kauai
Niihau
Oahu
Honolulu
Lanai
The State of Hawaii includes all islands and reefs in the chain extending from Hawaii to Kure, except the Midway Islands, which are under the administration of the U.S. Fish and Wildlife Service
0
500 miles
0
500 kilometers
Oblique Mercator Projection

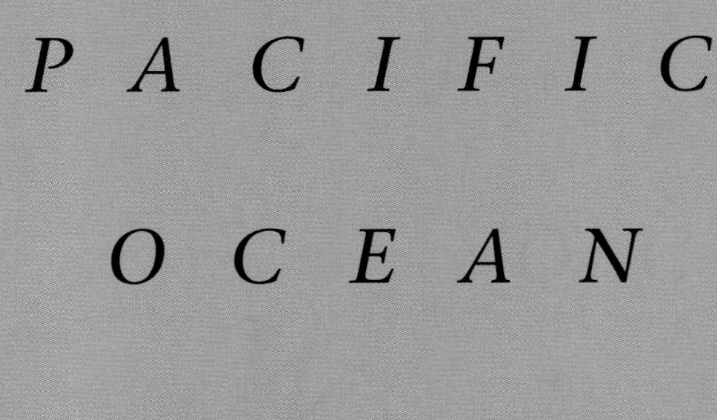

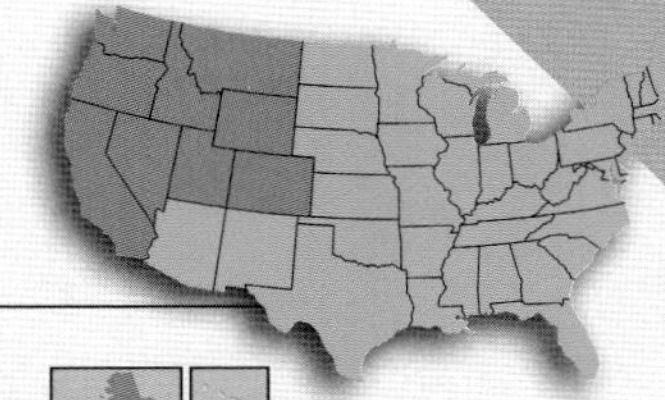

Aloha State

Hawaii

Located in the Pacific Ocean more than 2,400 miles (3,862 km) from the U.S. mainland, the southernmost state is a chain of 132 volcanic islands extending more than 1,500 miles (2,400 km). Most are small islands that total only three square miles (7.8 sq km). The eight main islands at the eastern end form most of Hawaii's territory.

People came to Hawaii as long as 2,000 years ago in twin-hulled canoes from other Polynesian islands. In the late 19th century, European and American planters established pineapple and sugarcane plantations, bringing in workers from many Asian countries. As a result, Hawaii is one of the country's most ethnically diverse states.

Most residents live on Oahu, site of Honolulu, which lures many of the state's six million annual visitors. Hawaii, the Big Island, has more than half the state's land. Lanai is known for pineapples and tourism. Among the other islands, Molokai has jagged sea cliffs, Kauai is noted for beautiful gardens, and Maui for spectacular beaches.

Area: 10,931 sq mi (28,311 sq km)

Population: 1,258,000

Capital: Honolulu, pop. 378,200

Largest city: Honolulu, pop. 378,200

Industry: tourism, trade, finance, food processing, petroleum refining, stone, clay, and glass products

Agriculture: sugarcane, pineapples, nursery stock, tropical fruit, livestock, macadamia nuts

Statehood: August 21, 1959; 50th state

Nickname: Aloha State

More about Hawaii

- *Today, less than one percent of Hawaii's population is descended from the original Polynesian settlers.*
- *There are only 12 letters in the Hawaiian alphabet—a,e,h,i,k,l,m,n,o,p,u, and w.*
- *Many of Hawaii's plant and animal species, such as the Hawaiian goose, or nene, are unique to the islands—and endangered.*
- *A new island is rising at the eastern end of the Hawaiian chain as the Pacific Plate carrying the islands slides over a hot spot. The Loihi Seamount is about 3,000 feet (914 m) below the ocean's surface and growing.*

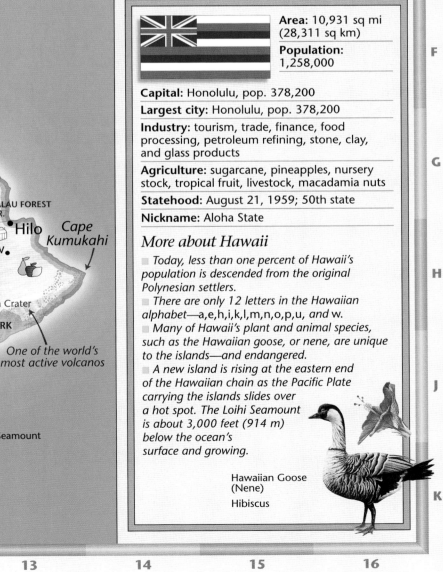

Hawaiian Goose (Nene)

Hibiscus

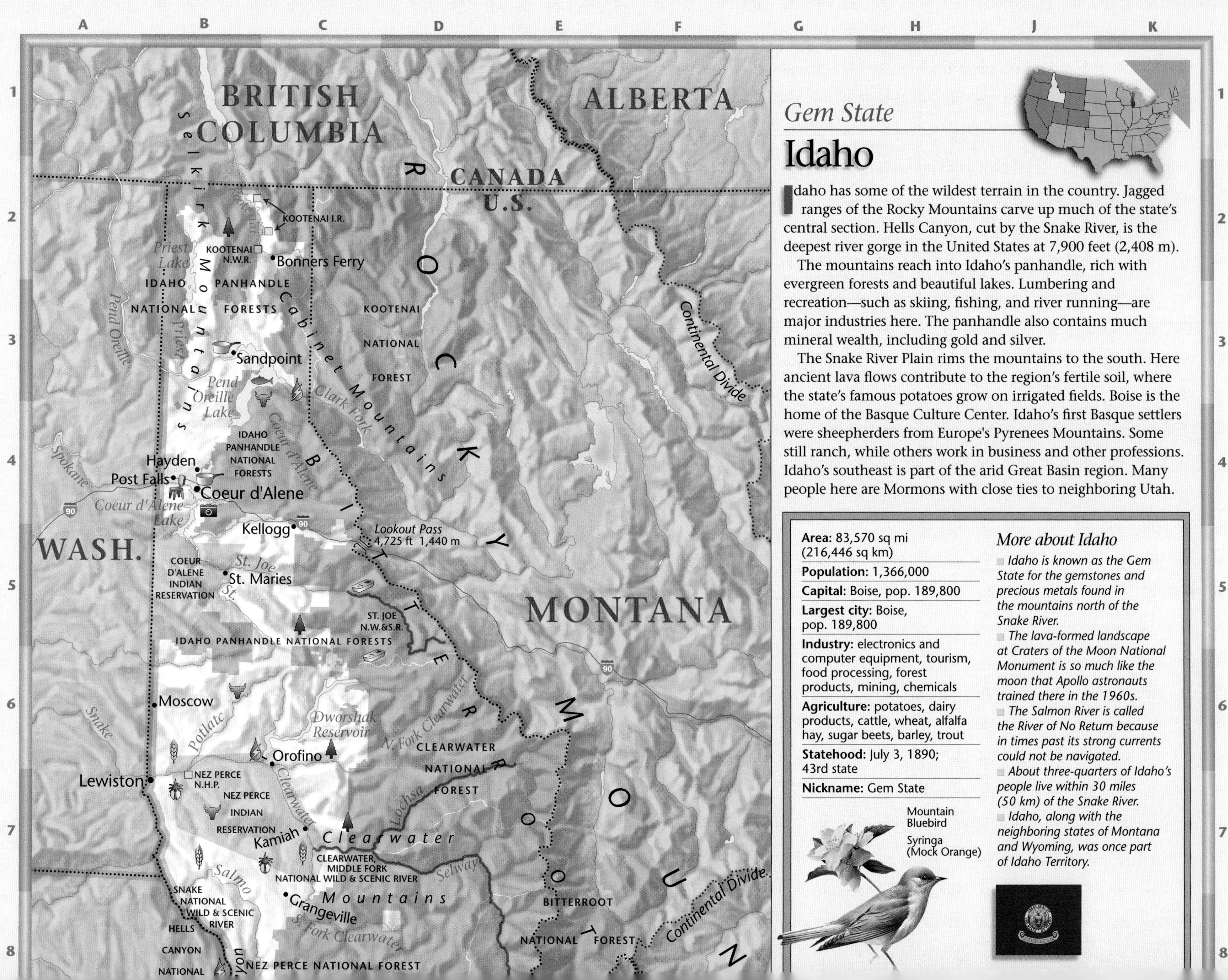

Gem State

Idaho

Idaho has some of the wildest terrain in the country. Jagged ranges of the Rocky Mountains carve up much of the state's central section. Hells Canyon, cut by the Snake River, is the deepest river gorge in the United States at 7,900 feet (2,408 m).

The mountains reach into Idaho's panhandle, rich with evergreen forests and beautiful lakes. Lumbering and recreation—such as skiing, fishing, and river running—are major industries here. The panhandle also contains much mineral wealth, including gold and silver.

The Snake River Plain rims the mountains to the south. Here ancient lava flows contribute to the region's fertile soil, where the state's famous potatoes grow on irrigated fields. Boise is the home of the Basque Culture Center. Idaho's first Basque settlers were sheepherders from Europe's Pyrenees Mountains. Some still ranch, while others work in business and other professions. Idaho's southeast is part of the arid Great Basin region. Many people here are Mormons with close ties to neighboring Utah.

Area: 83,570 sq mi (216,446 sq km)

Population: 1,366,000

Capital: Boise, pop. 189,800

Largest city: Boise, pop. 189,800

Industry: electronics and computer equipment, tourism, food processing, forest products, mining, chemicals

Agriculture: potatoes, dairy products, cattle, wheat, alfalfa hay, sugar beets, barley, trout

Statehood: July 3, 1890; 43rd state

Nickname: Gem State

Mountain Bluebird

Syringa (Mock Orange)

More about Idaho

- *Idaho is known as the Gem State for the gemstones and precious metals found in the mountains north of the Snake River.*
- *The lava-formed landscape at Craters of the Moon National Monument is so much like the moon that Apollo astronauts trained there in the 1960s.*
- *The Salmon River is called the River of No Return because in times past its strong currents could not be navigated.*
- *About three-quarters of Idaho's people live within 30 miles (50 km) of the Snake River.*
- *Idaho, along with the neighboring states of Montana and Wyoming, was once part of Idaho Territory.*

IDAHO
OREGON
NEVADA
UTAH
WYO.
Boise
Nampa
Caldwell
Emmett
Payette
Weiser
Cascade
McCall
Mountain Home
Glenns Ferry
Gooding
Twin Falls
Buhl
Jerome
Shoshone
Hailey
Ketchum
Rupert
Burley
American Falls
Chubbuck
Pocatello
Blackfoot
Shelley
Idaho Falls
Rigby
Rexburg
St. Anthony
Soda Springs
Montpelier
Preston
Malad City
Arco
Challis
Salmon
Salmon River
Mountains
Sawtooth
Smoky Mts.
Lost River Range
Lemhi Range
Centennial Mts.
Caribou Range
Portneuf Range
Bannock Range
Bear River Range
Blackfoot Mts.
Owyhee Mts.
Snake River
Borah Peak 12,662 ft 3,859 m
Highest point in Idaho
Deepest river gorge in North America
CRATERS OF THE MOON NATIONAL MONUMENT & PRESERVE
YELLOWSTONE NATIONAL PARK
HAGERMAN FOSSIL BEDS NATIONAL MONUMENT
MINIDOKA INTERNMENT CAMP NAT. MON.
CITY OF ROCKS NATIONAL RESERVE
DUCK VALLEY INDIAN RESERVATION
FORT HALL INDIAN RESERVATION
SAWTOOTH NATIONAL RECREATION AREA
CURLEW NATIONAL GRASSLAND
Great Salt Lake
Bear Lake
American Falls Reservoir
Palisades Reservoir
Island Park Reservoir
Lake Cascade
Deadwood Reservoir
Anderson Ranch Reservoir
C.J. Strike Reservoir
Magic Reservoir
Mormon Reservoir
Salmon Falls Creek Reservoir
Brownlee Reservoir
Henrys Lake
Mud Lake
Lake Walcott
100 miles
100 kilometers
Albers Conic Equal-Area Projection

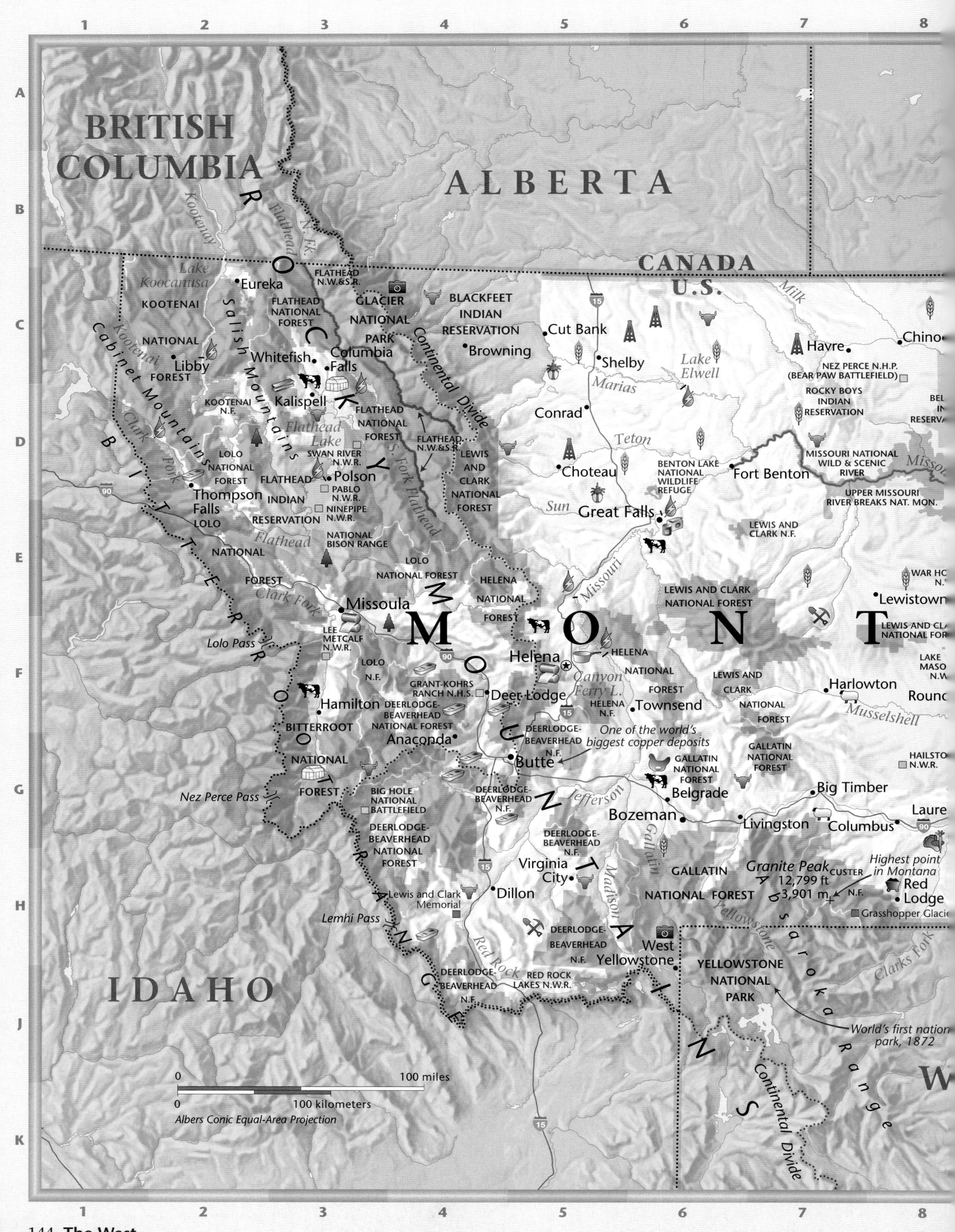

BRITISH COLUMBIA
ALBERTA
CANADA
U.S.
ROCKY MOUNTAINS
MONT
IDAHO
BITTERROOT RANGE
Absaroka Range
Salish Mountains
Cabinet Mountains
Continental Divide
Eureka
Libby
Whitefish
Columbia Falls
Kalispell
Polson
Thompson Falls
Missoula
Hamilton
Anaconda
Deer Lodge
Butte
Helena
Townsend
Dillon
Virginia City
Bozeman
Belgrade
Livingston
Big Timber
Columbus
Red Lodge
West Yellowstone
Browning
Cut Bank
Shelby
Conrad
Choteau
Great Falls
Fort Benton
Havre
Chinook
Lewistown
Harlowton
Roundup
Laurel
Lake Koocanusa
Flathead Lake
Lake Elwell
Canyon Ferry L.
Kootenay
Kootenai
Flathead
N. Fk.
S. Fork Flathead
Clark Fork
Marias
Teton
Sun
Missouri
Milk
Jefferson
Gallatin
Madison
Red Rock
Yellowstone
Clarks Fork
Musselshell
KOOTENAI NATIONAL FOREST
KOOTENAI N.F.
FLATHEAD N.W.&S.R.
FLATHEAD NATIONAL FOREST
GLACIER NATIONAL PARK
BLACKFEET INDIAN RESERVATION
LOLO NATIONAL FOREST
LOLO N.F.
SWAN RIVER N.W.R.
FLATHEAD INDIAN RESERVATION
PABLO N.W.R.
NINEPIPE N.W.R.
NATIONAL BISON RANGE
LEWIS AND CLARK NATIONAL FOREST
LEWIS AND CLARK N.F.
HELENA NATIONAL FOREST
HELENA N.F.
LEE METCALF N.W.R.
GRANT-KOHRS RANCH N.H.S.
DEERLODGE-BEAVERHEAD NATIONAL FOREST
DEERLODGE-BEAVERHEAD N.F.
BITTERROOT NATIONAL FOREST
BIG HOLE NATIONAL BATTLEFIELD
Lewis and Clark Memorial
RED ROCK LAKES N.W.R.
GALLATIN NATIONAL FOREST
CUSTER N.F.
YELLOWSTONE NATIONAL PARK
BENTON LAKE NATIONAL WILDLIFE REFUGE
MISSOURI NATIONAL WILD & SCENIC RIVER
UPPER MISSOURI RIVER BREAKS NAT. MON.
NEZ PERCE N.H.P. (BEAR PAW BATTLEFIELD)
ROCKY BOYS INDIAN RESERVATION
HAILSTONE N.W.R.
Grasshopper Glacier
Lolo Pass
Nez Perce Pass
Lemhi Pass
One of the world's biggest copper deposits
Granite Peak 12,799 ft 3,901 m
Highest point in Montana
World's first national park, 1872
0 100 miles
0 100 kilometers
Albers Conic Equal-Area Projection

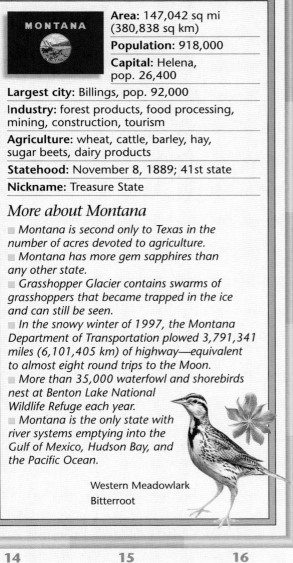

Treasure State

Montana

Montana gets its name from the Spanish word for mountains. More than 50 ranges of the Rocky Mountains rise in the western half of the state. Some peaks are so rugged that they have never been climbed. Vast stands of evergreens—fir, pine, cedar, and spruce—cover lower mountain slopes. Loggers cut them to provide timber for Montana's valuable forest products industry.

Montana's mountains are laced with gold, silver, and other minerals. Erosion often deposits these minerals in streams and rivers, forming placer deposits. Placers sparked the rush that brought gold-seekers to Montana in the mid-1800s, and mining is still an important part of the economy.

The eastern three-fifths of the state is shortgrass prairie, part of the country's Great Plains. Mighty rivers, such as the Missouri and Yellowstone, wind across the plains. This region supports most of Montana's agriculture, with wheat being the most important crop. People there raise livestock, especially beef cattle, on enormous ranches.

MONTANA

Area: 147,042 sq mi (380,838 sq km)

Population: 918,000

Capital: Helena, pop. 26,400

Largest city: Billings, pop. 92,000

Industry: forest products, food processing, mining, construction, tourism

Agriculture: wheat, cattle, barley, hay, sugar beets, dairy products

Statehood: November 8, 1889; 41st state

Nickname: Treasure State

More about Montana

- *Montana is second only to Texas in the number of acres devoted to agriculture.*
- *Montana has more gem sapphires than any other state.*
- *Grasshopper Glacier contains swarms of grasshoppers that became trapped in the ice and can still be seen.*
- *In the snowy winter of 1997, the Montana Department of Transportation plowed 3,791,341 miles (6,101,405 km) of highway—equivalent to almost eight round trips to the Moon.*
- *More than 35,000 waterfowl and shorebirds nest at Benton Lake National Wildlife Refuge each year.*
- *Montana is the only state with river systems emptying into the Gulf of Mexico, Hudson Bay, and the Pacific Ocean.*

Western Meadowlark
Bitterroot

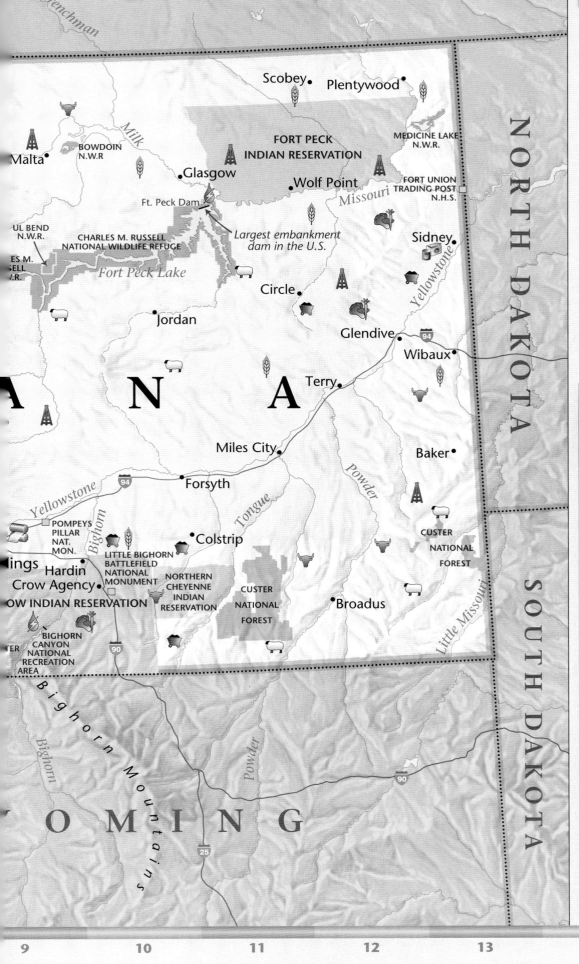

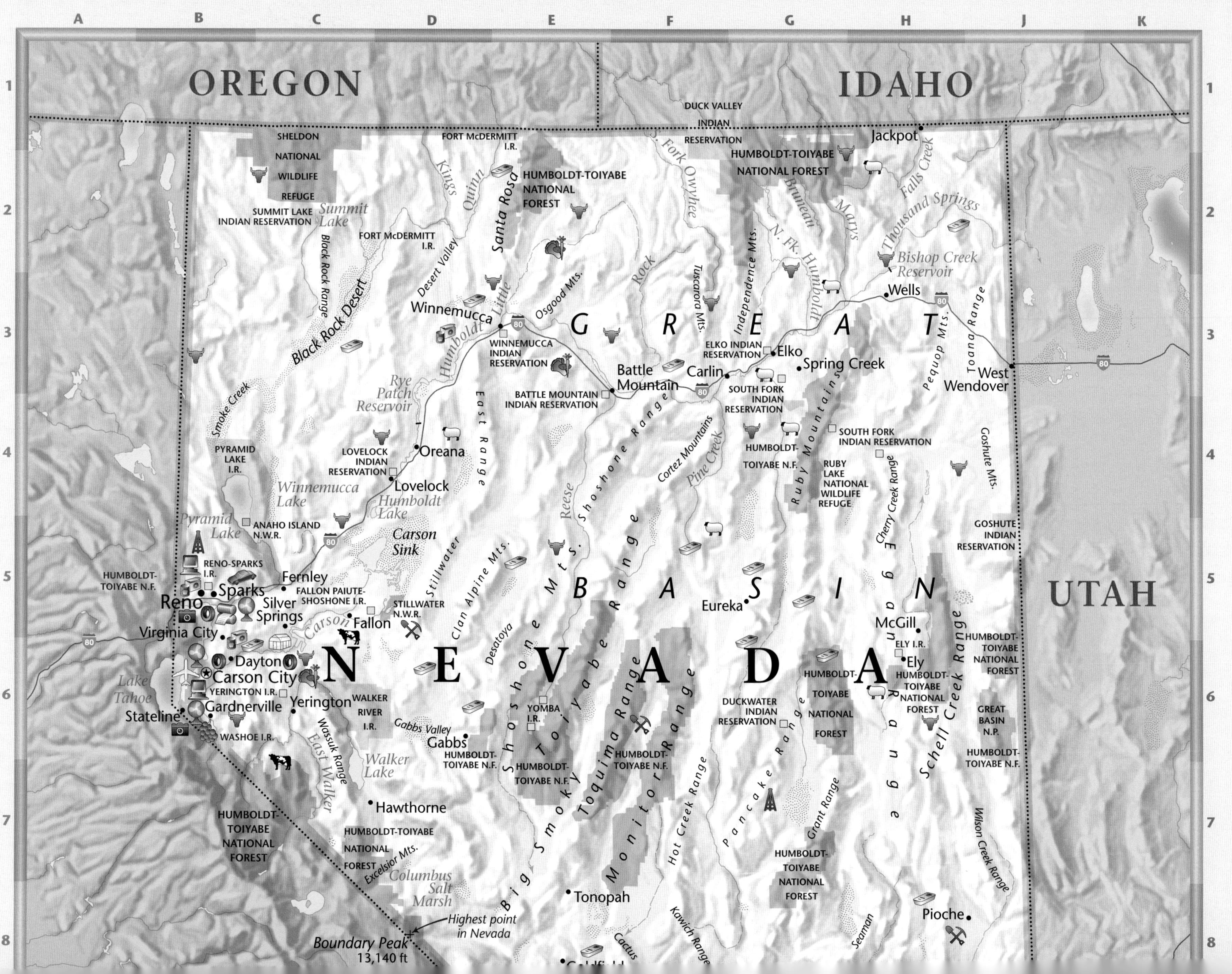

OREGON
IDAHO
UTAH
NEVADA
GREAT BASIN
Jackpot
Wells
West Wendover
Elko
Spring Creek
Carlin
Battle Mountain
Winnemucca
Oreana
Lovelock
Fernley
Sparks
Reno
Silver Springs
Fallon
Virginia City
Dayton
Carson City
Yerington
Gardnerville
Stateline
Eureka
McGill
Ely
Pioche
Tonopah
Hawthorne
Gabbs
Lake Tahoe
Pyramid Lake
Winnemucca Lake
Humboldt Lake
Carson Sink
Walker Lake
Summit Lake
Rye Patch Reservoir
Bishop Creek Reservoir
Black Rock Desert
Black Rock Range
Santa Rosa
Desert Valley
Osgood Mts.
Tuscarora Mts.
Independence Mts.
East Range
Shoshone Range
Cortez Mountains
Ruby Mountains
Cherry Creek Range
Pequop Mts.
Toana Range
Goshute Mts.
Egan Range
Schell Creek Range
Stillwater
Clan Alpine Mts.
Desatoya
Shoshone Mts.
Toiyabe Range
Toquima Range
Monitor Range
Big Smoky
Hot Creek Range
Pancake Range
Grant Range
Wilson Creek Range
Kawich Range
Seaman
Cactus
Wassuk Range
Excelsior Mts.
Gabbs Valley
Columbus Salt Marsh
Boundary Peak 13,140 ft
Highest point in Nevada
SHELDON NATIONAL WILDLIFE REFUGE
SUMMIT LAKE INDIAN RESERVATION
FORT McDERMITT I.R.
DUCK VALLEY INDIAN RESERVATION
HUMBOLDT-TOIYABE NATIONAL FOREST
HUMBOLDT-TOIYABE N.F.
WINNEMUCCA INDIAN RESERVATION
BATTLE MOUNTAIN INDIAN RESERVATION
ELKO INDIAN RESERVATION
SOUTH FORK INDIAN RESERVATION
RUBY LAKE NATIONAL WILDLIFE REFUGE
GOSHUTE INDIAN RESERVATION
LOVELOCK INDIAN RESERVATION
PYRAMID LAKE I.R.
ANAHO ISLAND N.W.R.
RENO-SPARKS I.R.
FALLON PAIUTE-SHOSHONE I.R.
STILLWATER N.W.R.
YERINGTON I.R.
WALKER RIVER I.R.
WASHOE I.R.
YOMBA I.R.
DUCKWATER INDIAN RESERVATION
ELY I.R.
GREAT BASIN N.P.
Kings
Quinn
Little Humboldt
Humboldt
N. Fk. Humboldt
S. Fork Owyhee
Bruneau
Marys
Falls Creek
Thousand Springs
Rock
Reese
Pine Creek
Smoke Creek
Carson
East Walker
80

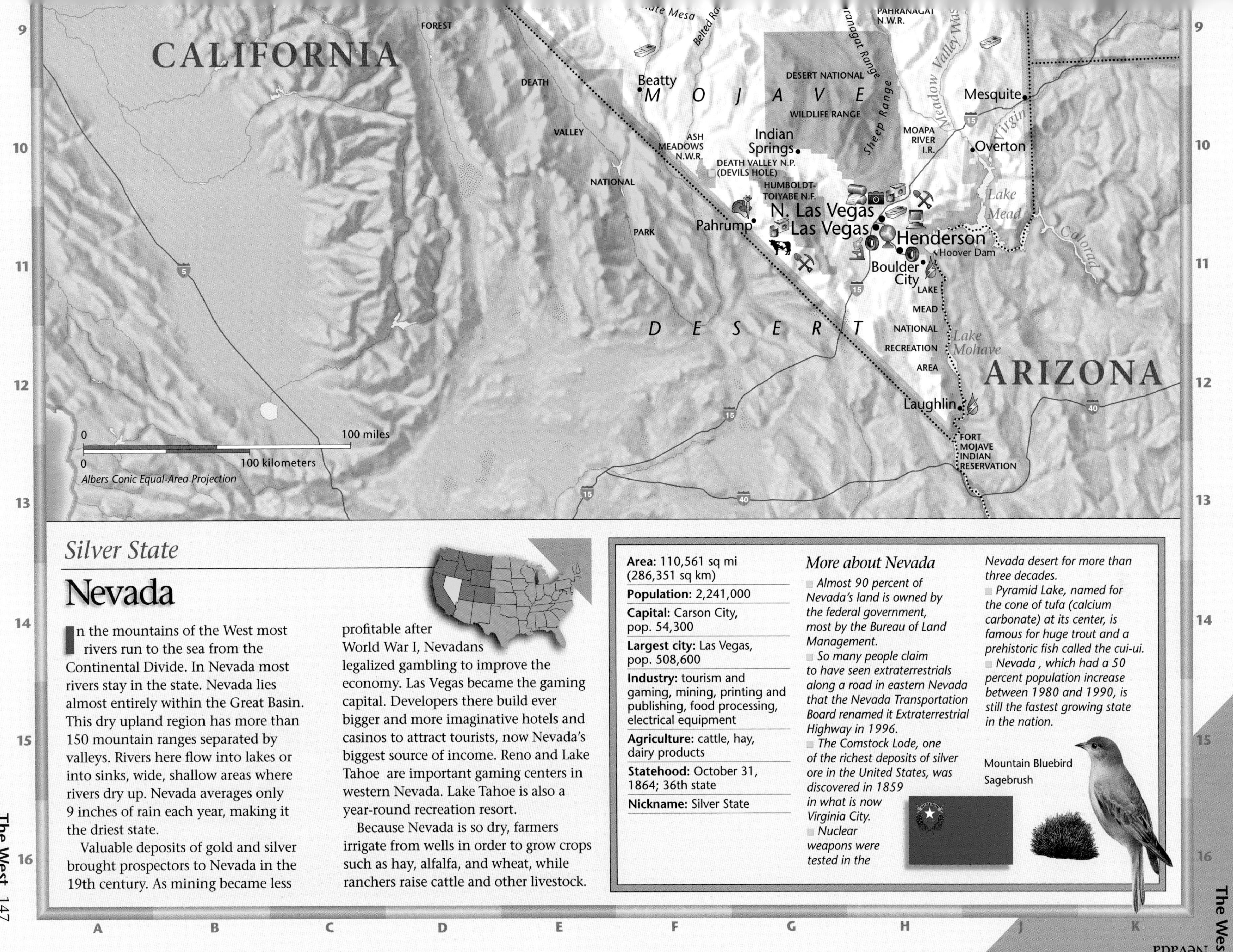

Silver State

Nevada

In the mountains of the West most rivers run to the sea from the Continental Divide. In Nevada most rivers stay in the state. Nevada lies almost entirely within the Great Basin. This dry upland region has more than 150 mountain ranges separated by valleys. Rivers here flow into lakes or into sinks, wide, shallow areas where rivers dry up. Nevada averages only 9 inches of rain each year, making it the driest state.

Valuable deposits of gold and silver brought prospectors to Nevada in the 19th century. As mining became less profitable after World War I, Nevadans legalized gambling to improve the economy. Las Vegas became the gaming capital. Developers there build ever bigger and more imaginative hotels and casinos to attract tourists, now Nevada's biggest source of income. Reno and Lake Tahoe are important gaming centers in western Nevada. Lake Tahoe is also a year-round recreation resort.

Because Nevada is so dry, farmers irrigate from wells in order to grow crops such as hay, alfalfa, and wheat, while ranchers raise cattle and other livestock.

Area: 110,561 sq mi (286,351 sq km)

Population: 2,241,000

Capital: Carson City, pop. 54,300

Largest city: Las Vegas, pop. 508,600

Industry: tourism and gaming, mining, printing and publishing, food processing, electrical equipment

Agriculture: cattle, hay, dairy products

Statehood: October 31, 1864; 36th state

Nickname: Silver State

More about Nevada

- *Almost 90 percent of Nevada's land is owned by the federal government, most by the Bureau of Land Management.*
- *So many people claim to have seen extraterrestrials along a road in eastern Nevada that the Nevada Transportation Board renamed it Extraterrestrial Highway in 1996.*
- *The Comstock Lode, one of the richest deposits of silver ore in the United States, was discovered in 1859 in what is now Virginia City.*
- *Nuclear weapons were tested in the Nevada desert for more than three decades.*
- *Pyramid Lake, named for the cone of tufa (calcium carbonate) at its center, is famous for huge trout and a prehistoric fish called the cui-ui.*
- *Nevada , which had a 50 percent population increase between 1980 and 1990, is still the fastest growing state in the nation.*

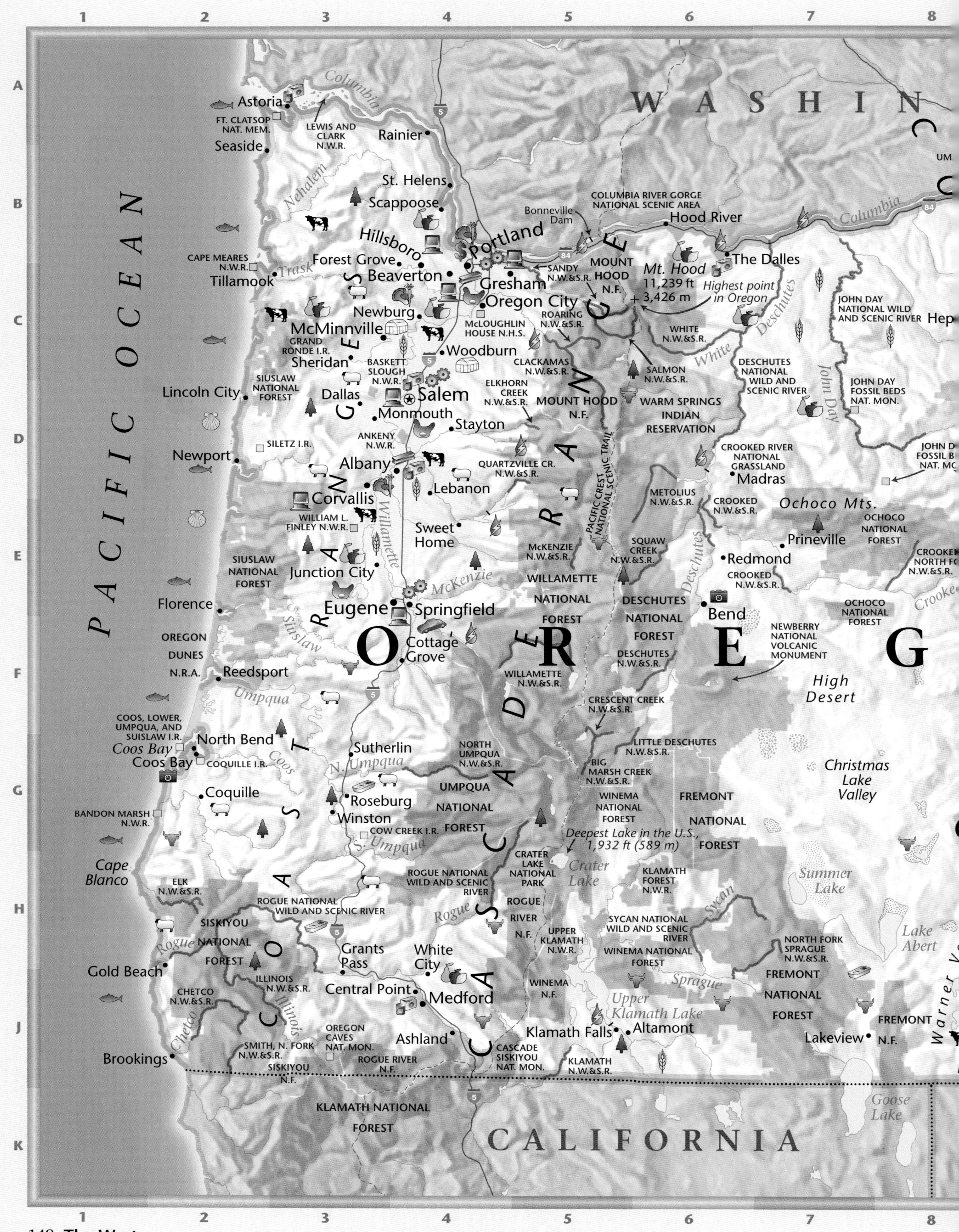

1
2
3
4
5
6
7
8
A
B
C
D
E
F
G
H
J
K
PACIFIC OCEAN
WASHINGTON
OREGON
CALIFORNIA
COAST RANGES
CASCADE RANGE
Columbia
Astoria
FT. CLATSOP NAT. MEM.
LEWIS AND CLARK N.W.R.
Seaside
Rainier
Nehalem
St. Helens
Scappoose
Hillsboro
Portland
Bonneville Dam
COLUMBIA RIVER GORGE NATIONAL SCENIC AREA
Hood River
CAPE MEARES N.W.R.
Tillamook
Trask
Forest Grove
Beaverton
Gresham
SANDY N.W.&S.R.
MOUNT HOOD N.F.
Mt. Hood
11,239 ft
3,426 m
Highest point in Oregon
The Dalles
Oregon City
McLOUGHLIN HOUSE N.H.S.
ROARING N.W.&S.R.
Newburg
McMinnville
GRAND RONDE I.R.
Sheridan
Woodburn
WHITE N.W.&S.R.
White
Deschutes
JOHN DAY NATIONAL WILD AND SCENIC RIVER
BASKETT SLOUGH N.W.R.
CLACKAMAS N.W.&S.R.
SALMON N.W.&S.R.
DESCHUTES NATIONAL WILD AND SCENIC RIVER
John Day
JOHN DAY FOSSIL BEDS NAT. MON.
SIUSLAW NATIONAL FOREST
Lincoln City
Dallas
Salem
ELKHORN CREEK N.W.&S.R.
MOUNT HOOD N.F.
WARM SPRINGS INDIAN RESERVATION
Monmouth
Stayton
ANKENY N.W.R.
SILETZ I.R.
Newport
Albany
QUARTZVILLE CR. N.W.&S.R.
CROOKED RIVER NATIONAL GRASSLAND
Madras
Lebanon
Corvallis
PACIFIC CREST NATIONAL SCENIC TRAIL
METOLIUS N.W.&S.R.
CROOKED N.W.&S.R.
Ochoco Mts.
OCHOCO NATIONAL FOREST
WILLIAM L. FINLEY N.W.R.
Willamette
Sweet Home
SQUAW CREEK N.W.&S.R.
Prineville
McKENZIE N.W.&S.R.
Redmond
SIUSLAW NATIONAL FOREST
Junction City
WILLAMETTE NATIONAL FOREST
CROOKED N.W.&S.R.
McKenzie
Florence
Eugene
Springfield
DESCHUTES NATIONAL FOREST
Bend
OCHOCO NATIONAL FOREST
Crooked
Siuslaw
OREGON DUNES N.R.A.
Cottage Grove
DESCHUTES N.W.&S.R.
NEWBERRY NATIONAL VOLCANIC MONUMENT
Reedsport
WILLAMETTE N.W.&S.R.
High Desert
Umpqua
COOS, LOWER, UMPQUA, AND SUISLAW I.R.
North Bend
Coos Bay
Coos Bay
COQUILLE I.R.
CRESCENT CREEK N.W.&S.R.
Sutherlin
NORTH UMPQUA N.W.&S.R.
LITTLE DESCHUTES N.W.&S.R.
BIG MARSH CREEK N.W.&S.R.
Christmas Lake Valley
Coos
N. Umpqua
Coquille
Roseburg
UMPQUA NATIONAL FOREST
WINEMA NATIONAL FOREST
FREMONT NATIONAL FOREST
BANDON MARSH N.W.R.
Winston
COW CREEK I.R.
Deepest Lake in the U.S., 1,932 ft (589 m)
S. Umpqua
Cape Blanco
CRATER LAKE NATIONAL PARK
Crater Lake
KLAMATH FOREST N.W.R.
Summer Lake
ELK N.W.&S.R.
ROGUE NATIONAL WILD AND SCENIC RIVER
ROGUE NATIONAL WILD AND SCENIC RIVER
SISKIYOU NATIONAL FOREST
Rogue
ROGUE RIVER N.F.
UPPER KLAMATH N.W.R.
SYCAN NATIONAL WILD AND SCENIC RIVER
Sycan
Lake Abert
NORTH FORK SPRAGUE N.W.&S.R.
Gold Beach
Grants Pass
White City
WINEMA NATIONAL FOREST
Sprague
FREMONT NATIONAL FOREST
CHETCO N.W.&S.R.
ILLINOIS N.W.&S.R.
Central Point
Medford
WINEMA N.F.
Upper Klamath Lake
Illinois
Chetco
OREGON CAVES NAT. MON.
Ashland
Klamath Falls
Altamont
Lakeview
FREMONT N.F.
Warner
SMITH, N. FORK N.W.&S.R.
ROGUE RIVER N.F.
CASCADE SISKIYOU NAT. MON.
KLAMATH N.W.&S.R.
Brookings
SISKIYOU N.F.
KLAMATH NATIONAL FOREST
Goose Lake
5
84

Beaver State

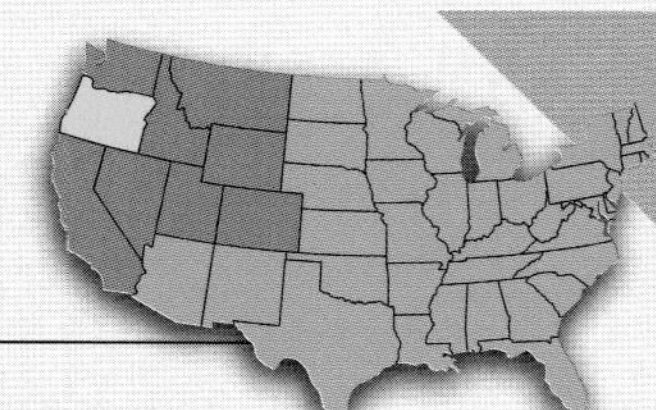

Oregon

Oregon was the end of the line for pioneers who traveled the Oregon Trail in the mid-1800s. The destination for most of them was the Willamette Valley, along the Willamette River in the western part of the state. There they found land so fertile that, as the saying went, you could poke a broomstick in the ground and it would grow.

Today, more than half of Oregon's people live in the valley. Many still farm, growing pears and other fruits and vegetables. Portland arose where the Willamette meets the Columbia River. An industrial center, Portland processes wood from the state's forests, produces computers and other electronics, and distributes Japanese cars.

Oregon's coast is rocky and edged with low mountains. It has a wet, mild climate. East of the Willamette Valley rise the Cascades, a volcanic range. Farther east the climate is drier and colder. Irrigated wheat and ryegrass grow on the rugged Columbia Plateau, built up of layers of lava. Southward, cattle ranches sprawl in the semiarid Great Basin.

Area: 98,381 sq mi (254,805 sq km)

Population: 3,560,000

Capital: Salem, pop. 141,000

Largest city: Portland, pop. 539,400

Industry: real estate, retail and wholesale trade, electronic equipment, health services, construction, forest products, business services

Agriculture: nursery stock, hay, cattle, grass seed, wheat, dairy products, potatoes

Statehood: February 14, 1859; 33rd state

Nickname: Beaver State

More about Oregon

- *Oregon produces about one-third of the country's softwood lumber and plywood.*
- *More than 90 percent of Oregon's energy needs are met by hydroelectric power, mostly from dams on the Columbia River.*
- *Local legends say that Sasquatch, an apelike creature also known as Bigfoot, roams in Oregon's Coast Ranges.*
- *Crater Lake, in the Cascade Range, was formed when a volcano called Mount Mazama erupted and blew its top about 7,000 years ago.*
- *Hundreds of sea lions find shelter in sea caves near Florence.*
- *Explorers Lewis and Clark ended their long journey in 1805 at the mouth of the Columbia River.*

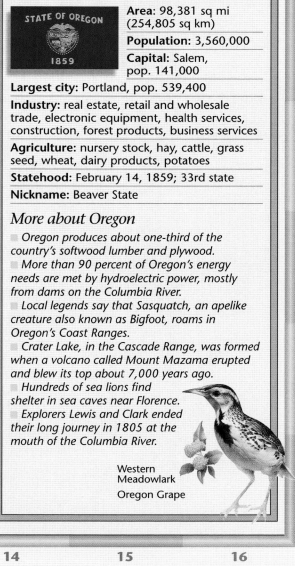

Western Meadowlark

Oregon Grape

0 — 100 miles
0 — 100 kilometers
Albers Conic Equal-Area Projection

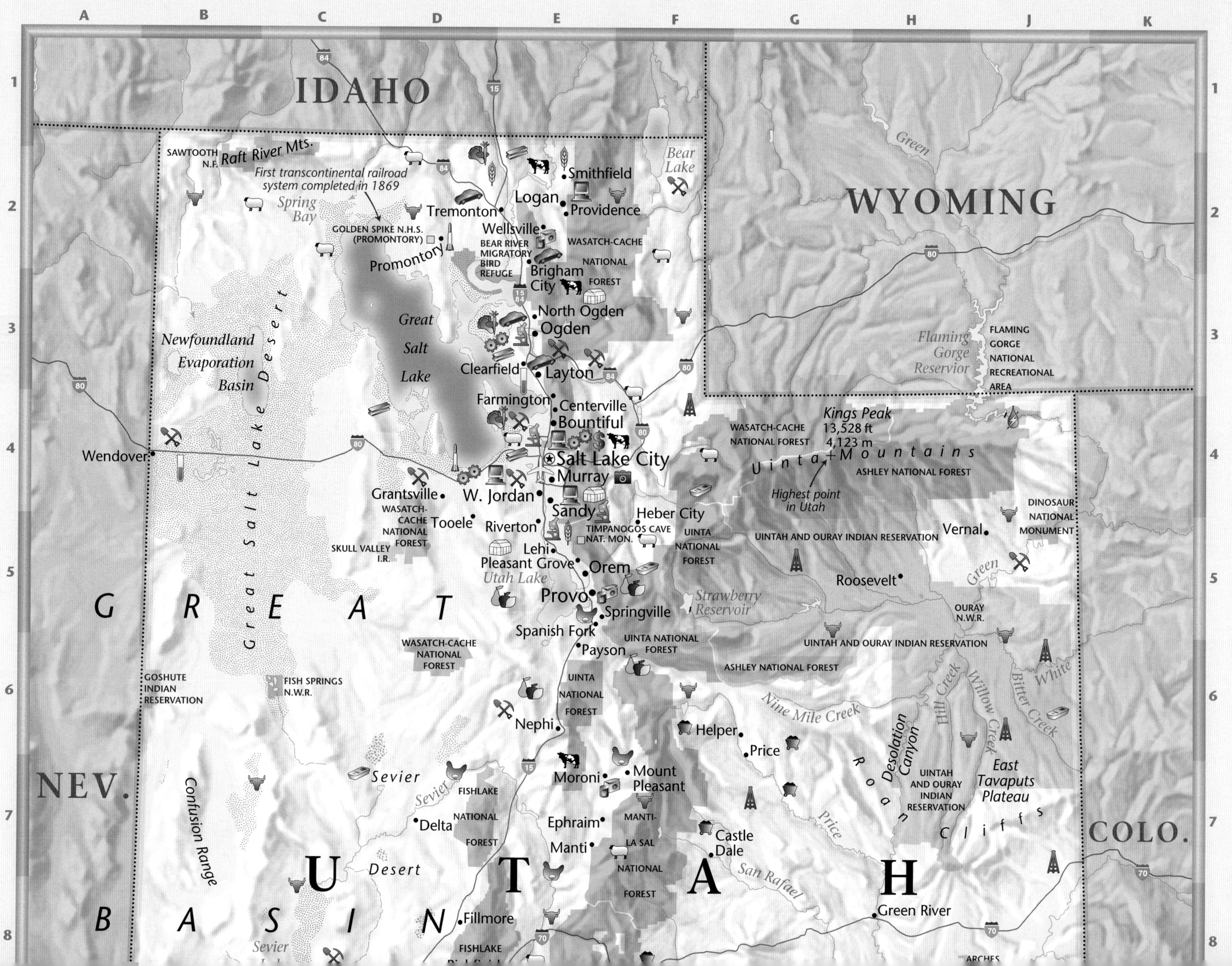

IDAHO
WYOMING
COLO.
NEV.
G R E A T
B A S I N
U T A H
Bear Lake
SAWTOOTH N.F.
Raft River Mts.
First transcontinental railroad system completed in 1869
Spring Bay
GOLDEN SPIKE N.H.S. (PROMONTORY)
Promontory
Great Salt Lake
Great Salt Lake Desert
Newfoundland Evaporation Basin
Wendover
Tremonton
Wellsville
Logan
Smithfield
Providence
BEAR RIVER MIGRATORY BIRD REFUGE
Brigham City
WASATCH-CACHE NATIONAL FOREST
North Ogden
Ogden
Clearfield
Layton
Farmington
Centerville
Bountiful
Salt Lake City
Murray
W. Jordan
Sandy
Riverton
Lehi
Pleasant Grove
Orem
Provo
Springville
Spanish Fork
Payson
Utah Lake
Heber City
TIMPANOGOS CAVE NAT. MON.
Tooele
Grantsville
WASATCH-CACHE NATIONAL FOREST
SKULL VALLEY I.R.
WASATCH-CACHE NATIONAL FOREST
GOSHUTE INDIAN RESERVATION
FISH SPRINGS N.W.R.
Confusion Range
Sevier
Sevier
Desert
Delta
Fillmore
FISHLAKE NATIONAL FOREST
FISHLAKE
Nephi
UINTA NATIONAL FOREST
Moroni
Mount Pleasant
Ephraim
Manti
MANTI-LA SAL NATIONAL FOREST
Castle Dale
San Rafael
Helper
Price
Nine Mile Creek
Price
Green River
Roan Cliffs
Desolation Canyon
UINTAH AND OURAY INDIAN RESERVATION
East Tavaputs Plateau
Willow Creek
Hill Creek
Bitter Creek
White
OURAY N.W.R.
UINTAH AND OURAY INDIAN RESERVATION
ASHLEY NATIONAL FOREST
UINTA NATIONAL FOREST
Roosevelt
Vernal
Green
DINOSAUR NATIONAL MONUMENT
FLAMING GORGE NATIONAL RECREATIONAL AREA
Flaming Gorge Reservoir
Green
WASATCH-CACHE NATIONAL FOREST
Kings Peak 13,528 ft 4,123 m
Highest point in Utah
Uinta Mountains
ASHLEY NATIONAL FOREST
UINTA NATIONAL FOREST
Strawberry Reservoir
ARCHES

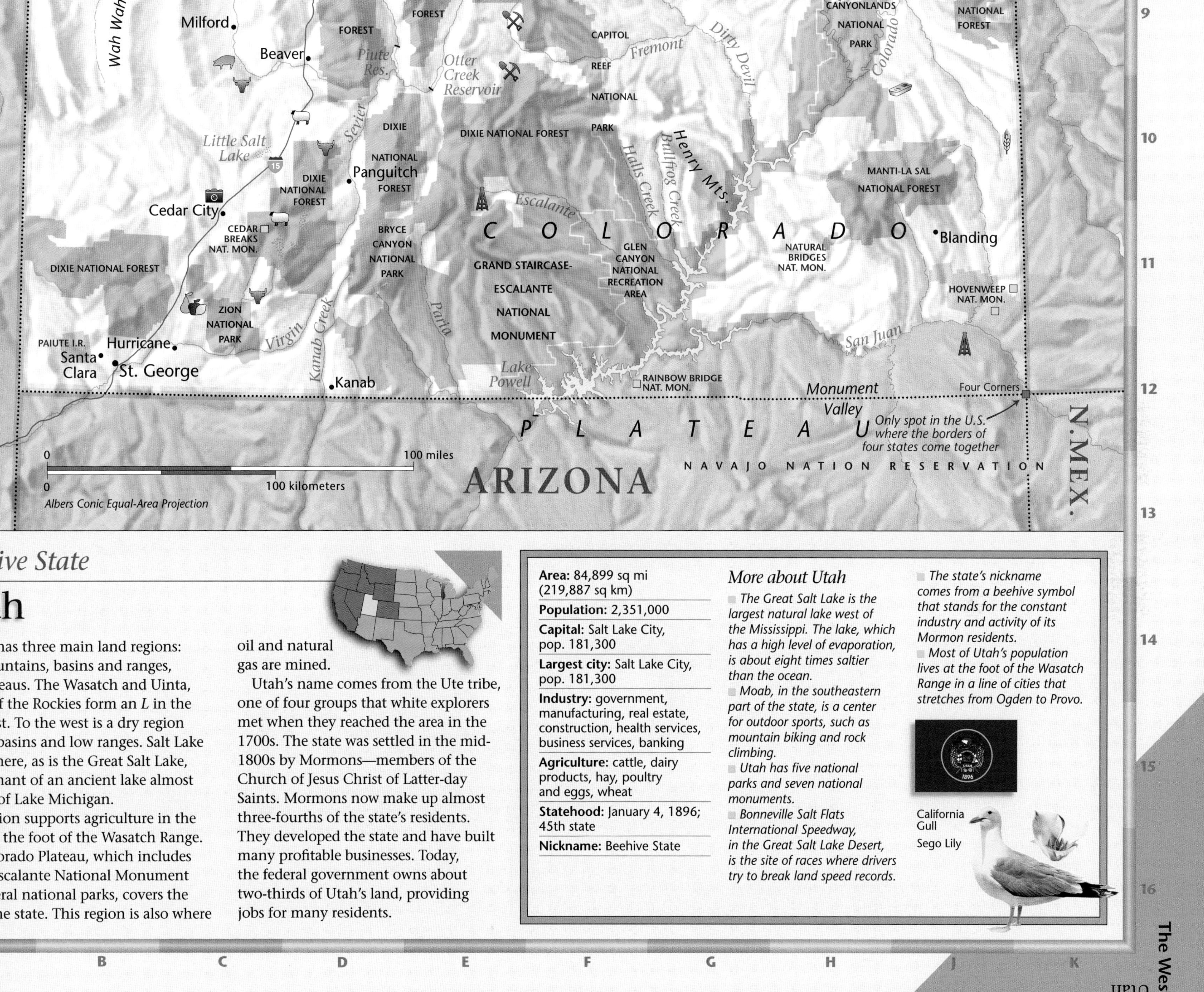

Beehive State

Utah

Utah has three main land regions: mountains, basins and ranges, and plateaus. The Wasatch and Uinta, ranges of the Rockies form an *L* in the northeast. To the west is a dry region of wide basins and low ranges. Salt Lake City is there, as is the Great Salt Lake, the remnant of an ancient lake almost the size of Lake Michigan.

Irrigation supports agriculture in the valley at the foot of the Wasatch Range. The Colorado Plateau, which includes Grand Escalante National Monument and several national parks, covers the rest of the state. This region is also where oil and natural gas are mined.

Utah's name comes from the Ute tribe, one of four groups that white explorers met when they reached the area in the 1700s. The state was settled in the mid-1800s by Mormons—members of the Church of Jesus Christ of Latter-day Saints. Mormons now make up almost three-fourths of the state's residents. They developed the state and have built many profitable businesses. Today, the federal government owns about two-thirds of Utah's land, providing jobs for many residents.

Area: 84,899 sq mi (219,887 sq km)

Population: 2,351,000

Capital: Salt Lake City, pop. 181,300

Largest city: Salt Lake City, pop. 181,300

Industry: government, manufacturing, real estate, construction, health services, business services, banking

Agriculture: cattle, dairy products, hay, poultry and eggs, wheat

Statehood: January 4, 1896; 45th state

Nickname: Beehive State

More about Utah

- *The Great Salt Lake is the largest natural lake west of the Mississippi. The lake, which has a high level of evaporation, is about eight times saltier than the ocean.*
- *Moab, in the southeastern part of the state, is a center for outdoor sports, such as mountain biking and rock climbing.*
- *Utah has five national parks and seven national monuments.*
- *Bonneville Salt Flats International Speedway, in the Great Salt Lake Desert, is the site of races where drivers try to break land speed records.*
- *The state's nickname comes from a beehive symbol that stands for the constant industry and activity of its Mormon residents.*
- *Most of Utah's population lives at the foot of the Wasatch Range in a line of cities that stretches from Ogden to Provo.*

California Gull

Sego Lily

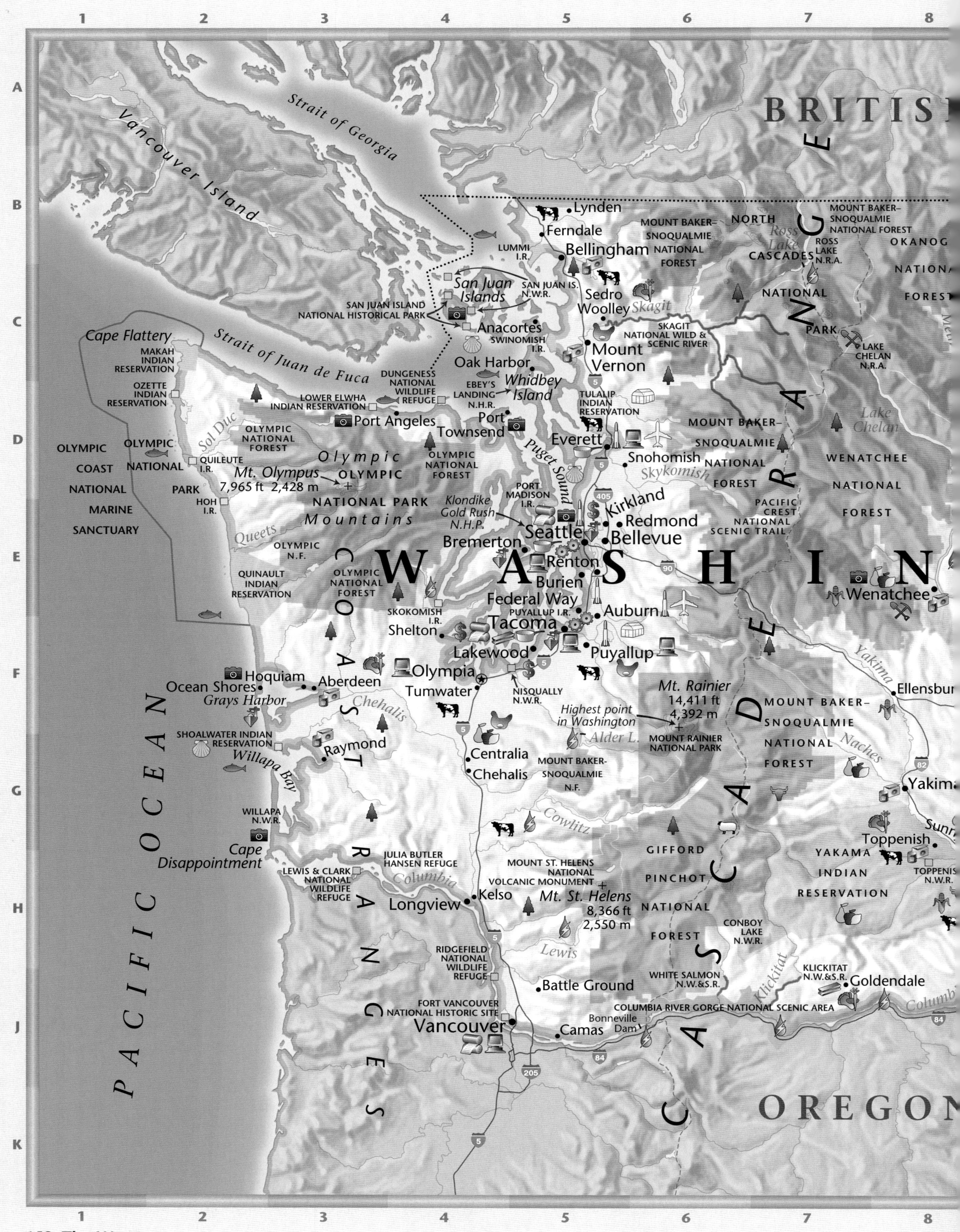

Strait of Georgia
Vancouver Island
BRITISH
Lynden
Ferndale
Bellingham
LUMMI I.R.
MOUNT BAKER–SNOQUALMIE NATIONAL FOREST
NORTH CASCADES NATIONAL PARK
Ross Lake
ROSS LAKE N.R.A.
MOUNT BAKER–SNOQUALMIE NATIONAL FOREST
OKANOGAN NATIONAL FOREST
San Juan Islands
SAN JUAN IS. N.W.R.
SAN JUAN ISLAND NATIONAL HISTORICAL PARK
Sedro Woolley
Skagit
Anacortes
SWINOMISH I.R.
SKAGIT NATIONAL WILD & SCENIC RIVER
Mount Vernon
LAKE CHELAN N.R.A.
Cape Flattery
MAKAH INDIAN RESERVATION
Strait of Juan de Fuca
OZETTE INDIAN RESERVATION
Oak Harbor
DUNGENESS NATIONAL WILDLIFE REFUGE
EBEY'S LANDING N.H.R.
Whidbey Island
LOWER ELWHA INDIAN RESERVATION
Port Angeles
Port Townsend
TULALIP INDIAN RESERVATION
Lake Chelan
Sol Duc
OLYMPIC NATIONAL FOREST
Everett
MOUNT BAKER–SNOQUALMIE NATIONAL FOREST
Puget Sound
Snohomish
Skykomish
WENATCHEE NATIONAL FOREST
OLYMPIC COAST NATIONAL MARINE SANCTUARY
OLYMPIC NATIONAL PARK
QUILEUTE I.R.
Olympic Mountains
Mt. Olympus 7,965 ft 2,428 m
OLYMPIC NATIONAL PARK
OLYMPIC NATIONAL FOREST
HOH I.R.
PORT MADISON I.R.
Klondike Gold Rush N.H.P.
Kirkland
Redmond
PACIFIC CREST NATIONAL SCENIC TRAIL
Seattle
Bellevue
Queets
Bremerton
OLYMPIC N.F.
WASHINGTON
Renton
QUINAULT INDIAN RESERVATION
OLYMPIC NATIONAL FOREST
Burien
Federal Way
Wenatchee
SKOKOMISH I.R.
PUYALLUP I.R.
Auburn
Shelton
Tacoma
Yakima
Lakewood
Puyallup
Hoquiam
Ocean Shores
Aberdeen
Olympia
Tumwater
NISQUALLY N.W.R.
Mt. Rainier 14,411 ft 4,392 m
Ellensburg
Grays Harbor
Chehalis
Highest point in Washington
MOUNT BAKER–SNOQUALMIE NATIONAL FOREST
Naches
SHOALWATER INDIAN RESERVATION
Alder L.
MOUNT RAINIER NATIONAL PARK
Raymond
Willapa Bay
Centralia
Chehalis
MOUNT BAKER-SNOQUALMIE N.F.
Yakima
PACIFIC OCEAN
WILLAPA N.W.R.
Cowlitz
Toppenish
YAKAMA INDIAN RESERVATION
TOPPENISH N.W.R.
Cape Disappointment
GIFFORD PINCHOT NATIONAL FOREST
JULIA BUTLER HANSEN REFUGE
LEWIS & CLARK NATIONAL WILDLIFE REFUGE
Columbia
MOUNT ST. HELENS NATIONAL VOLCANIC MONUMENT
Kelso
Longview
Mt. St. Helens 8,366 ft 2,550 m
CONBOY LAKE N.W.R.
COAST RANGES
CASCADE RANGE
Lewis
RIDGEFIELD NATIONAL WILDLIFE REFUGE
Battle Ground
WHITE SALMON N.W.&S.R.
Klickitat
KLICKITAT N.W.&S.R.
Goldendale
FORT VANCOUVER NATIONAL HISTORIC SITE
COLUMBIA RIVER GORGE NATIONAL SCENIC AREA
Vancouver
Camas
Bonneville Dam
OREGON

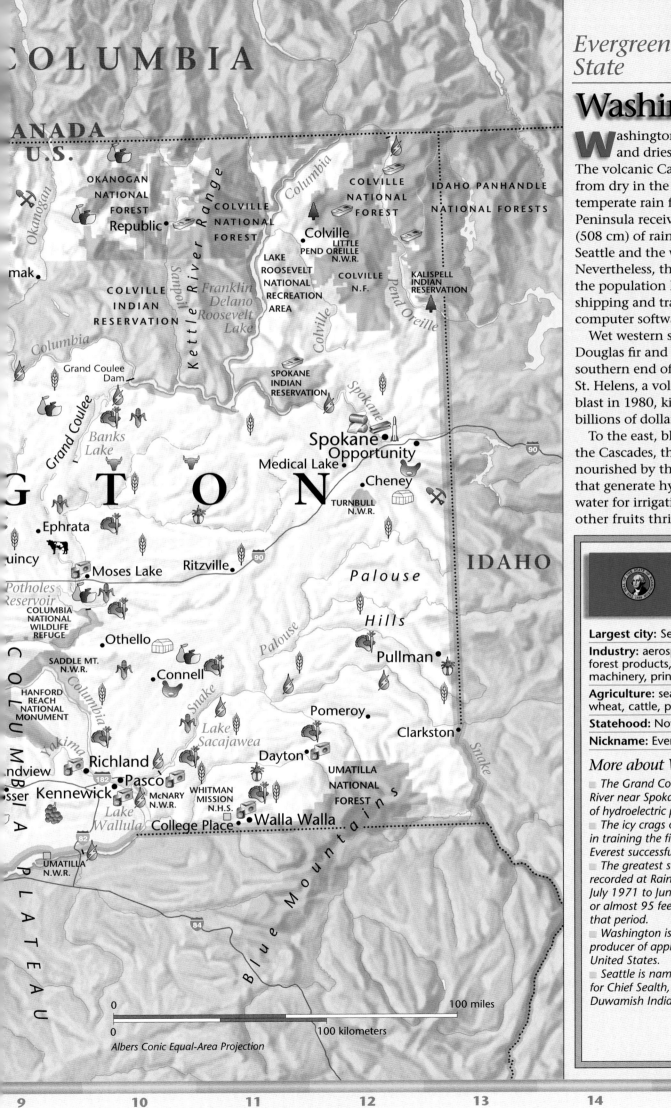

Evergreen State

Washington

Washington has some of the wettest—and driest—weather in the nation. The volcanic Cascade Range separates wet from dry in the state. Along the coast the temperate rain forests of the Olympic Peninsula receive more than 200 inches (508 cm) of rain a year. Rain also soaks Seattle and the whole Puget Sound area. Nevertheless, this is where more than half the population lives. People here work in shipping and transportation, food processing, computer software, and many other fields.

Wet western slopes support stands of Douglas fir and other timber trees. At the southern end of the Cascades rises Mount St. Helens, a volcano that erupted with a huge blast in 1980, killing 57 people and causing billions of dollars in property damage.

To the east, blocked from moist winds by the Cascades, the dry Columbia Plateau is nourished by the Columbia and other rivers that generate hydroelectric power and supply water for irrigation. Wheat, hops, apples, and other fruits thrive in eastern Washington.

Area: 71,300 sq mi (184,665 sq km)

Population: 6,131,000

Capital: Olympia, pop. 43,500

Largest city: Seattle, pop. 570,400

Industry: aerospace, tourism, food processing, forest products, paper products, industrial machinery, printing and publishing, metals

Agriculture: seafood, apples, dairy products, wheat, cattle, potatoes, hay

Statehood: November 11, 1889; 42nd state

Nickname: Evergreen State

More about Washington

- *The Grand Coulee Dam, on the Columbia River near Spokane, is the biggest producer of hydroelectric power in North America.*
- *The icy crags of Mount Rainier were used in training the first U.S. team to climb Mount Everest successfully.*
- *The greatest snowfall in North America was recorded at Rainier Paradise Ranger Station from July 1971 to June 1972. A total of 1,122 inches, or almost 95 feet (29 m), of snow fell during that period.*
- *Washington is the leading producer of apples in the United States.*
- *Seattle is named for Chief Sealth, a Duwamish Indian.*

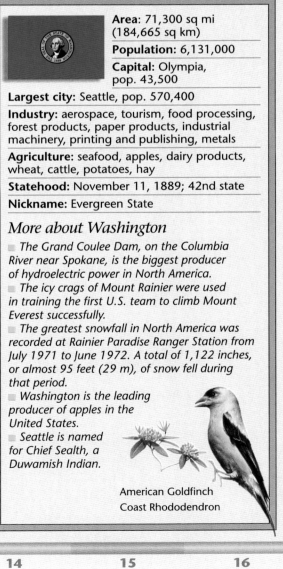

American Goldfinch
Coast Rhododendron

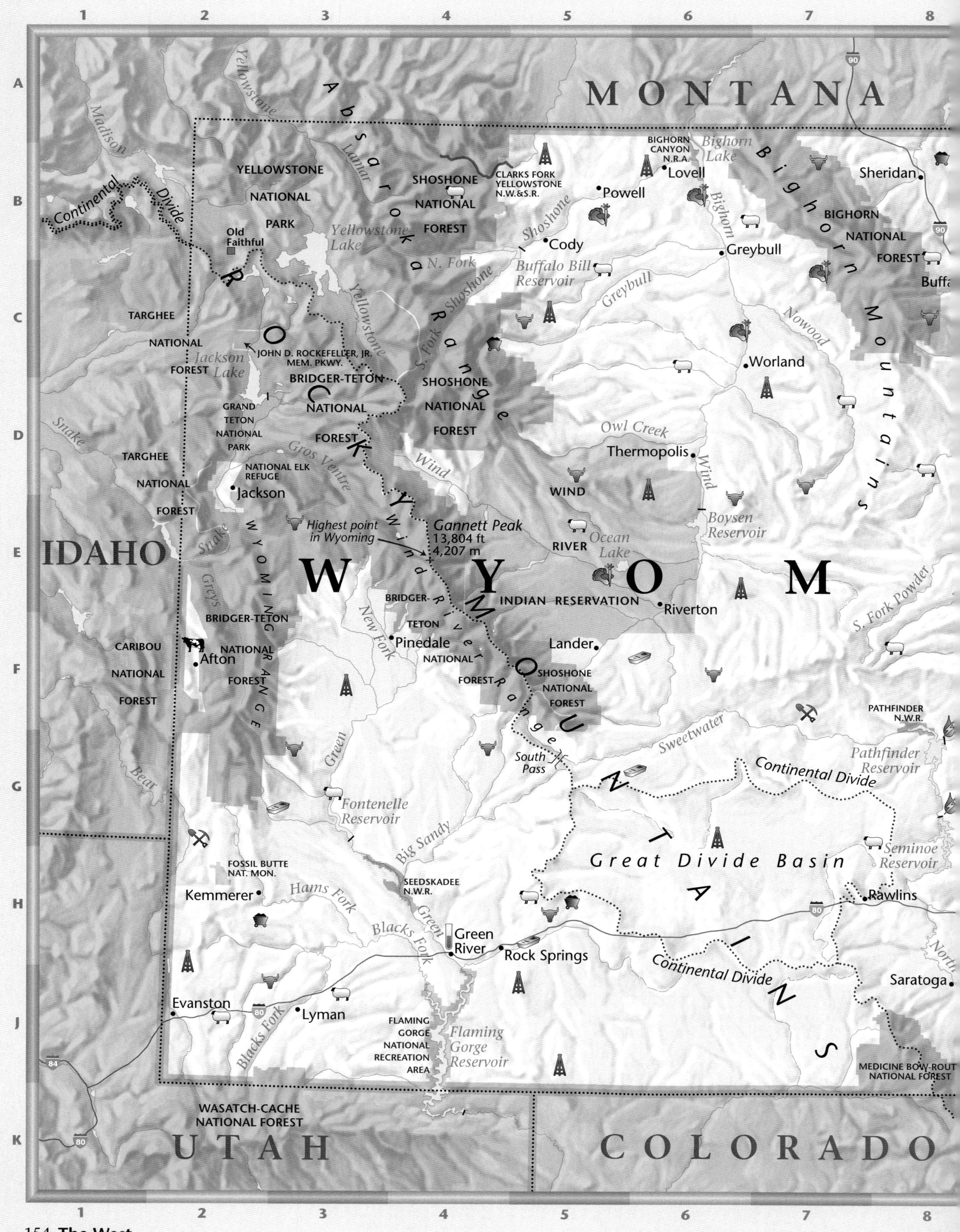
MONTANA
IDAHO
WYOMING
UTAH
COLORADO
YELLOWSTONE NATIONAL PARK
Old Faithful
SHOSHONE NATIONAL FOREST
CLARKS FORK YELLOWSTONE N.W.&S.R.
BIGHORN CANYON N.R.A.
Bighorn Lake
Lovell
Powell
Cody
Greybull
Sheridan
BIGHORN NATIONAL FOREST
Bighorn Mountains
Absaroka Range
Yellowstone Lake
Buffalo Bill Reservoir
TARGHEE NATIONAL FOREST
Jackson Lake
JOHN D. ROCKEFELLER, JR. MEM. PKWY.
BRIDGER-TETON NATIONAL FOREST
GRAND TETON NATIONAL PARK
NATIONAL ELK REFUGE
Jackson
Worland
Thermopolis
Owl Creek
WIND RIVER INDIAN RESERVATION
Boysen Reservoir
Ocean Lake
Gannett Peak
13,804 ft
4,207 m
Highest point in Wyoming
Wind River Range
WYOMING RANGE
ROCKY MOUNTAINS
Riverton
Lander
Pinedale
CARIBOU NATIONAL FOREST
Afton
PATHFINDER N.W.R.
Pathfinder Reservoir
Continental Divide
South Pass
Sweetwater
Fontenelle Reservoir
Great Divide Basin
Seminoe Reservoir
FOSSIL BUTTE NAT. MON.
SEEDSKADEE N.W.R.
Kemmerer
Rawlins
Green River
Rock Springs
Saratoga
Evanston
Lyman
FLAMING GORGE NATIONAL RECREATION AREA
Flaming Gorge Reservoir
MEDICINE BOW-ROUTT NATIONAL FOREST
WASATCH-CACHE NATIONAL FOREST

9 10 11 12 13 14 15 16

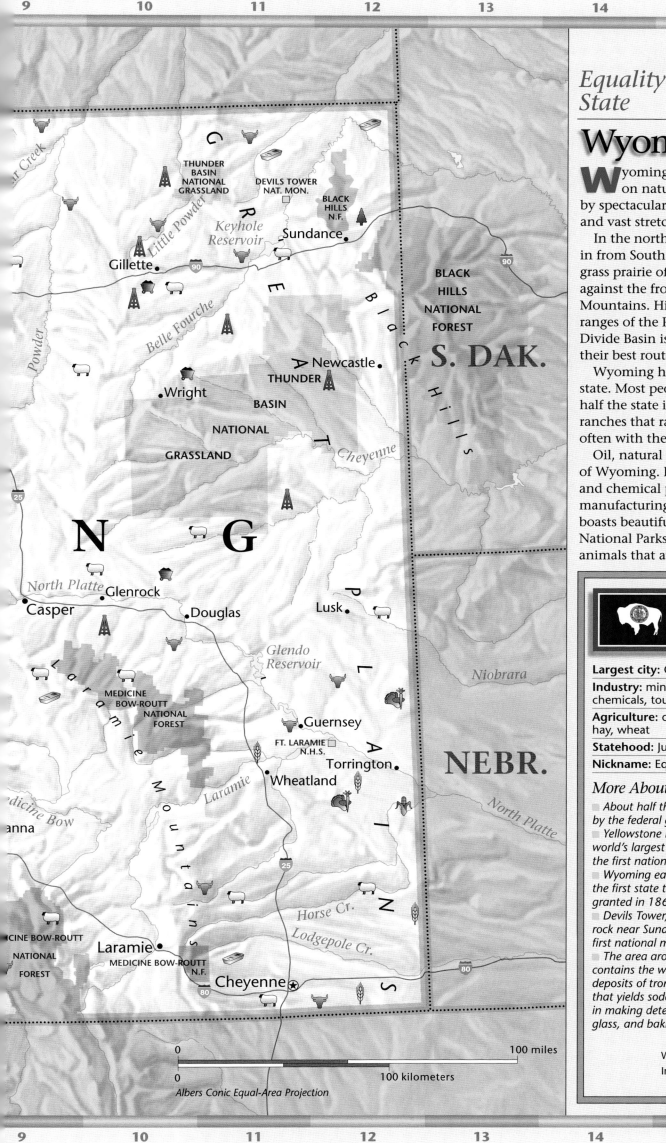

THUNDER BASIN NATIONAL GRASSLAND
DEVILS TOWER NAT. MON.
BLACK HILLS N.F.
Keyhole Reservoir
Sundance
Gillette
Little Powder
Belle Fourche
Powder
BLACK HILLS NATIONAL FOREST
Black Hills
S. DAK.
Newcastle
THUNDER BASIN NATIONAL GRASSLAND
Wright
Cheyenne
GREAT PLAINS
Glenrock
North Platte
Casper
Douglas
Lusk
Glendo Reservoir
Niobrara
MEDICINE BOW-ROUTT NATIONAL FOREST
Laramie Mountains
Guernsey
FT. LARAMIE N.H.S.
Torrington
Wheatland
NEBR.
Laramie
North Platte
Horse Cr.
Lodgepole Cr.
MEDICINE BOW-ROUTT NATIONAL FOREST
Laramie
MEDICINE BOW-ROUTT N.F.
Cheyenne

0 100 miles
0 100 kilometers
Albers Conic Equal-Area Projection

Equality State

Wyoming

Wyoming is short on people and tall on natural beauty. The state is marked by spectacular landforms, geologic wonders, and vast stretches of open space.

In the northeast, the Black Hills reach in from South Dakota. Southward, the shortgrass prairie of the Great Plains bumps up against the front ranges of the Rocky Mountains. High, windy basins lie between ranges of the Rockies. Just north of the Great Divide Basin is the pass that gave pioneers their best route through the Rockies.

Wyoming has fewer people than any other state. Most people live in small towns. About half the state is covered with large farms and ranches that raise beef cattle and sheep, often with the help of cowboys.

Oil, natural gas, and coal lie under parts of Wyoming. Except for petroleum refining and chemical production, the state has little manufacturing. Northwestern Wyoming boasts beautiful Yellowstone and Grand Teton National Parks, with waterfalls, geysers, and animals that attract millions of visitors.

Area: 97,814 sq mi (253,336 sq km)
Population: 501,000
Capital: Cheyenne, pop. 53,700
Largest city: Cheyenne, pop. 53,700
Industry: mining, generation of electricity, chemicals, tourism
Agriculture: cattle, sugar beets, sheep, hay, wheat
Statehood: July 10, 1890; 44th state
Nickname: Equality State

More About Wyoming

- *About half the land in Wyoming is owned by the federal government.*
- *Yellowstone National Park, which features the world's largest geyser area, was established as the first national park in 1872.*
- *Wyoming earned its nickname because it was the first state to give women the right to vote, granted in 1869 (when it was still a territory).*
- *Devils Tower, a huge formation of igneous rock near Sundance, was the country's first national monument.*
- *The area around Green River contains the world's largest deposits of trona, the ore that yields soda ash, used in making detergent, glass, and baking soda.*

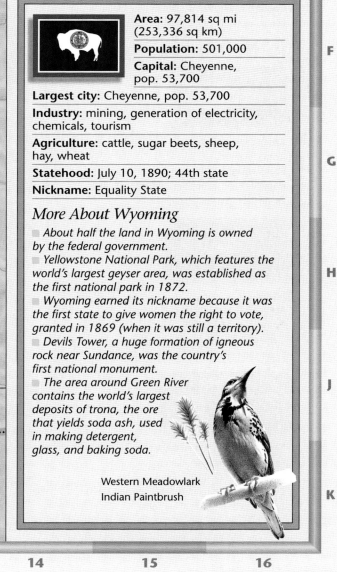

Western Meadowlark
Indian Paintbrush

The Territories

Across Two Seas

Ranging from rocks inhabited only by seabirds to a land of almost four million people, the 13 U.S. territories in the Caribbean Sea and the Pacific Ocean include thousands of islands. Listed below are the five largest in size and population, beginning with Puerto Rico.

Caribbean Territories

Puerto Rico
Area: 3,507 sq mi (9,084 sq km)
Population: 3,879,000
Capital: San Juan, pop. 433,400
Languages: Spanish, English

Virgin Islands
Area: 149 sq mi (386 sq km)
Population: 110,000
Capital: Charlotte Amalie, pop. 11,000
Languages: English, Spanish, Creole

Pacific Territories

American Samoa
Area: 90 sq mi (233 sq km)
Population: 62,000
Capital: Pago Pago, pop. 4,300
Language: Samoan, English

Guam
Area: 217 sq mi (561 sq km)
Population: 164,000
Capital: Hagåtña (Agana), 1,100
Language: English, Chamorro, Japanese

Northern Mariana Islands
Area: 179 sq mi (464 sq km)
Population: 78,000
Capital: Saipan (Capitol Hill), pop. 62,400
Languages: English, Chamorro, Carolinian

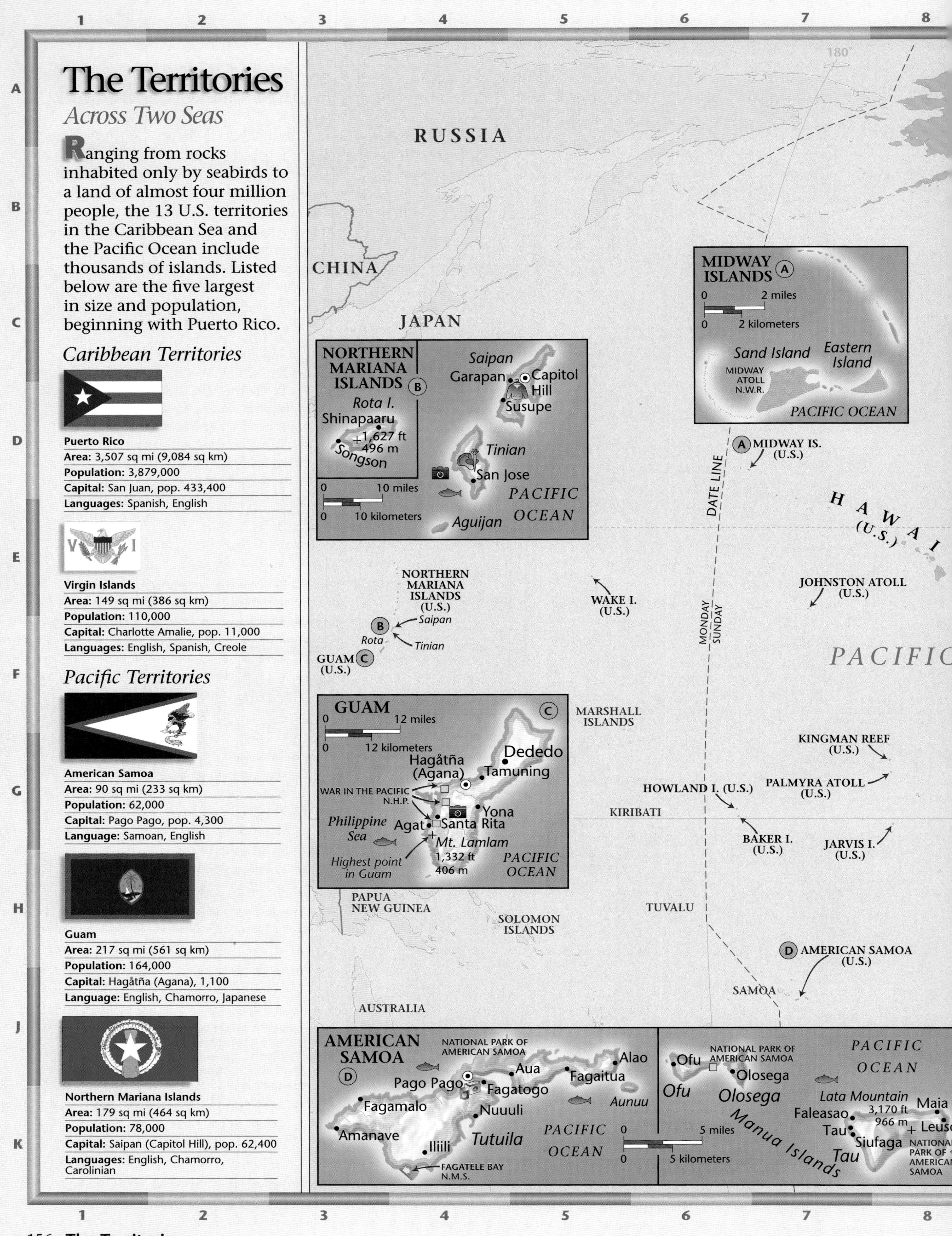

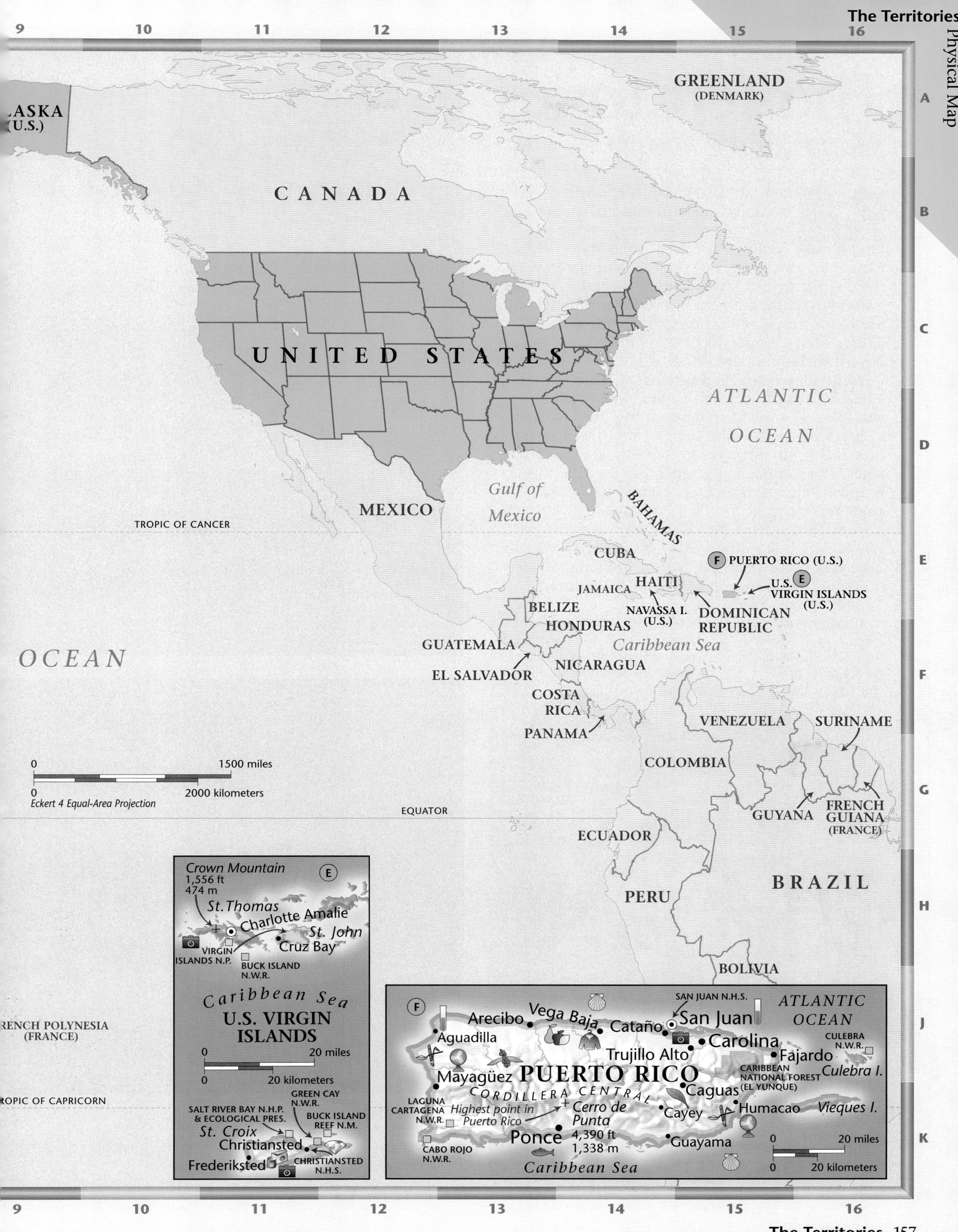
GREENLAND
(DENMARK)
ALASKA
(U.S.)
CANADA
UNITED STATES
ATLANTIC
OCEAN
Gulf of
Mexico
MEXICO
BAHAMAS
TROPIC OF CANCER
CUBA
PUERTO RICO (U.S.)
U.S.
VIRGIN ISLANDS
(U.S.)
JAMAICA
HAITI
BELIZE
NAVASSA I.
(U.S.)
DOMINICAN
REPUBLIC
HONDURAS
Caribbean Sea
GUATEMALA
OCEAN
EL SALVADOR
NICARAGUA
COSTA
RICA
PANAMA
VENEZUELA
SURINAME
COLOMBIA
0
1500 miles
0
2000 kilometers
Eckert 4 Equal-Area Projection
EQUATOR
GUYANA
FRENCH
GUIANA
(FRANCE)
ECUADOR
BRAZIL
PERU
BOLIVIA
FRENCH POLYNESIA
(FRANCE)
TROPIC OF CAPRICORN
Crown Mountain
1,556 ft
474 m
St. Thomas
Charlotte Amalie
St. John
Cruz Bay
VIRGIN
ISLANDS N.P.
BUCK ISLAND
N.W.R.
Caribbean Sea
U.S. VIRGIN
ISLANDS
0
20 miles
0
20 kilometers
GREEN CAY
N.W.R.
SALT RIVER BAY N.H.P.
& ECOLOGICAL PRES.
BUCK ISLAND
REEF N.M.
St. Croix
Christiansted
Frederiksted
CHRISTIANSTED
N.H.S.
SAN JUAN N.H.S.
ATLANTIC
OCEAN
Arecibo
Vega Baja
Cataño
San Juan
Aguadilla
Carolina
CULEBRA
N.W.R.
Trujillo Alto
Fajardo
CARIBBEAN
NATIONAL FOREST
(EL YUNQUE)
Culebra I.
Mayagüez
PUERTO RICO
Caguas
CORDILLERA CENTRAL
LAGUNA
CARTAGENA
N.W.R.
Highest point in
Puerto Rico
Cerro de
Punta
4,390 ft
1,338 m
Cayey
Humacao
Vieques I.
Ponce
Guayama
CABO ROJO
N.W.R.
0
20 miles
0
20 kilometers
Caribbean Sea

The Territories

Islands in the Family

More than 2,300 islands and islets, scattered across the Pacific Ocean and the Caribbean Sea, make up the 13 territories of the United States. These islands are not states, but they are associated with the U.S. in various ways. The five largest inhabited island territories have their own governments but receive economic and military help from the United States. Residents of these territories—except American Samoa—are U.S. citizens.

Puerto Rico is the largest territory. Three times citizens of this Caribbean island have voted on—and rejected—the idea of becoming the 51st state, in part because keeping their commonwealth status means they do not have to pay federal income taxes. The Caribbean also includes the U.S. Virgin Islands, acquired from Denmark in 1917 for strategic reasons.

Some Pacific territories were battle sites in World War II. The U.S. military still owns much of Guam. American Samoa and the Northern Marianas keep much of their traditional Polynesian culture.

▼ **A POLYNESIAN BOY** *shows off a sea turtle, flippered inhabitant of the South Pacific. Polynesians settled American Samoa.*

▶ **TURQUOISE WATERS** *ring the Midway Islands. Midway and eight other territories are administered by various departments of the U.S. government.*

▲ **LUSH BROMELIADS** *and other tropical plants thrive in the El Yunque rain forest in Puerto Rico. All U.S. territories except the Midway Islands lie in the tropical zone.*

▶ **A DIVER** *checks out life on a coral reef in the intense blue waters of the Caribbean. Excellent diving and snorkeling lure many tourists to territories in the Caribbean and Pacific.*

▲ **AN ABANDONED** *sugar mill is one of many that dot the countryside throughout the Caribbean. Cultivation and processing of sugarcane was once the area's main source of income.*

▼ **TWINKLING LIGHTS** *of a cruise ship sparkle in the harbor at Charlotte Amalie, the capital of the U.S. Virgin Islands. Tourism brings in about 70 percent of the territory's income.*

▶ **PALM-FRINGED** *beaches, such as these around Trunk Bay on St. John in the Virgin Islands, offer vacationers a year-round haven in many territories.*

▼ **SMILING FACES** *of Virgin Islands children reflect the varied African and European backgrounds of Caribbean peoples.*

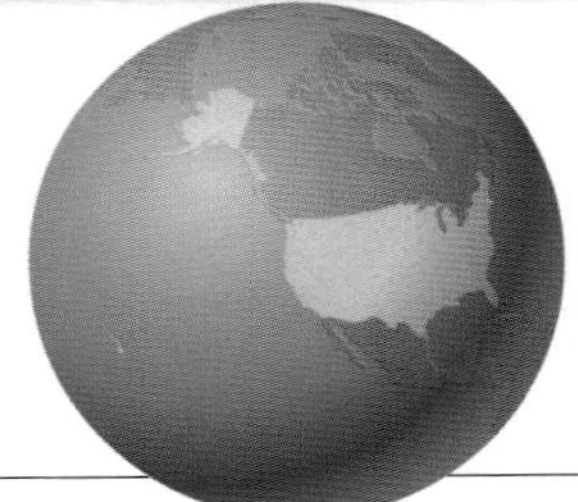

Facts & Figures

Top States

Listed below are major farm products, fish, and minerals and the states that currently lead in their production. Following each list is a ranking of the top states in each category.

Farm Products

Cattle and calves: Texas, Nebraska, Kansas, Colorado
Dairy products: California, Wisconsin, New York, Pennsylvania
Soybeans: Iowa, Illinois, Indiana, Minnesota
Corn for grain: Iowa, Illinois, Nebraska, Minnesota
Hogs and pigs: Iowa, North Carolina, Minnesota, Illinois
Broiler chickens: Georgia, Arkansas, Alabama, North Carolina
Wheat: Kansas, North Dakota, Washington, Oklahoma
Cotton: Texas, California, Mississippi, Georgia
Eggs: Georgia, Ohio, Pennsylvania, Arkansas
Hay: Texas, South Dakota, California, Kansas
Tobacco: North Carolina, Kentucky, Tennessee, South Carolina
Turkeys: North Carolina, Minnesota, Missouri, Virginia
Oranges: Florida, California, Texas, Arizona
Potatoes: Idaho, Washington, Wisconsin, Oregon
Grapes: California, Washington, New York, Oregon
Tomatoes: Florida, California, Virginia, Tennessee
Rice: Arkansas, California, Louisiana, Texas

Top Ten in Farm Products (by net farm income)

1. Texas
2. California
3. North Carolina
4. Georgia
5. Florida
6. Iowa
7. Nebraska
8. Alabama
9. Illinois
10. Arkansas

Fish

Shrimp: Louisiana, Texas, Oregon, Florida
Crabs: Alaska, Louisiana, North Carolina, Virginia, Maryland
Lobsters: Maine, Massachusetts, Florida, Rhode Island
Salmon: Alaska, Washington, California, Oregon
Pollock: Alaska, Washington

Top Five in Fisheries

1. Alaska
2. Louisiana
3. Maine
4. Florida
5. Texas

Minerals

Crude oil: Texas, Alaska, California, Louisiana, Oklahoma
Natural gas: Texas, Louisiana, Oklahoma, New Mexico
Coal: Wyoming, West Virginia, Kentucky, Pennsylvania
Crushed stone: Texas, Pennsylvania, Florida, Missouri
Copper: Arizona, Utah, New Mexico, Missouri
Cement: California, Texas, Pennsylvania, Florida
Construction sand and gravel: California, Texas, Michigan, Arizona
Gold: Nevada, Utah, Alaska, California
Iron ore: Minnesota, Michigan
Clay: Georgia, North Carolina, Wyoming, Ohio
Phosphate rock: Florida, Idaho, North Carolina, Utah
Lime: Ohio, Alabama, Pennsylvania, Texas
Salt: Louisiana, Texas, New York, Ohio
Sulfur: Texas, Louisiana

Top Ten in Minerals

1. Texas
2. Louisiana
3. Alaska
4. California
5. Oklahoma
6. Wyoming
7. New Mexico
8. West Virginia
9. Kentucky
10. Colorado

Extremes

World's Strongest Surface Wind
231 mph (372 kph), Mount Washington, New Hampshire, April 12, 1934

World's Oldest Living Tree
Methuselah bristlecone pine, California; about 4,700 years old

World's Tallest Living Tree
The "Mendocino Tree," a coast redwood at Montgomery State Reserve in California, 367.5 ft (112 m) high

World's Largest Gorge
Grand Canyon, Arizona; 290 mi (466 km) long, 600 ft to 18 mi (183 m to 29 km) wide, 1 miles (1.6 km) deep

Highest Temperature in U.S.
134°F (56.6°C), Death Valley, California, July 10, 1913

Lowest Temperature in U.S.
Minus 80°F (-62.2°C) at Prospect Creek, Alaska, January 23, 1971

Highest Point in U.S.
Mount McKinley (Denali), Alaska; 20,323 feet (6,194 m)

Lowest Point in U.S.
Death Valley, California; 282 feet (86 m) below sea level

Longest River System in U.S.
Mississippi-Missouri; 3,708 mi (5,971 km) long

Rainiest Spot in U.S.
Waialeale (mountain), Hawaii: average annual rainfall 460 in (1,168 cm)

Metropolitan Areas with More Than Five Million People
(A metropolitan area is a city and its surrounding suburban areas.)

1. New York, pop. 21,199,900
2. Los Angeles, pop. 16,373,600
3. Chicago, pop. 9,157,500
4. Washington, D.C., pop. 7,608,100
5. San Francisco, pop. 7,039,400
6. Philadelphia, pop. 6,188,500
7. Boston, pop. 5,819,100
8. Detroit, pop. 5,456,400
9. Dallas-Fort Worth, pop. 5,221,800

Glossary

bog a poorly drained area, often a kettle hole, with wet, spongy ground; usually found in cool, northern climates

bromeliad one of a family of tropical plants that grows in trees and gets nutrients from the air rather than soil

butte a high, steep-sided rock formation created by the erosion of a mesa

canal an artificial waterway that is used by ships or to carry water for irrigation

city in the U.S., usually a populated place of at least 2,500 people who work in jobs requiring various skills

continental divide an elevated area that separates rivers flowing toward opposite sides of a continent; in the U.S. this divide follows the crest of the Rocky Mountains

copra dried coconut meat from which oil is extracted to make a variety of products, including soap, candles, and cosmetics; an important export of Pacific islands

delta lowland formed by silt, sand, and gravel deposited by a river at its mouth

elevation distance above sea level, usually measured in feet or meters

fork in a river, the place where two streams come together

glacier a large, slow-moving mass of ice

gorge a deep, narrow valley with very steep sides that is usually shorter and narrower than a canyon

ice age a very long period of cold climate when glaciers often cover large areas of land; with initial capital letters, the term refers to the most recent, or Pleistocene, ice age

intermittent lake a body of water whose surface area varies with the amount of precipitation or runoff

intermittent river a stream that flows only part of the time, usually after heavy rain or snowmelt

kettle hole a glacier-created depression that contains groundwater or rainwater

lava molten rock from Earth's interior that flows out on the surface through a deep crack or during volcanic activity

mesa an eroded plateau, broader than it is high, that is found in arid or semiarid regions

metropolitan area a city and its surrounding suburbs or communities

nursery stock young plants, including fruits, vegetables, shrubs, and trees, raised in a greenhouse or nursery

plain a large area of relatively flat land that is often covered with grasses

plateau a relatively flat area, larger than a mesa, that rises above the surrounding landscape

population density the number of people living on each square mile or kilometer of a specific land area (calculated by dividing population by land area)

Richter scale a means of ranking the power of an earthquake; the higher the number, the stronger the quake

scale on a map, a means of explaining the relationship between distances on the map and actual distances on the Earth's surface

swamp wetlands where trees are the dominant vegetation

territory land that is under the jurisdiction of a country but that is not a state or a province

tropical zone the area bounded by the Tropic of Cancer and the Tropic of Capricorn where it is usually warm year-round

wetland land that is either covered with or saturated by water; includes swamps, marshes, and bogs

Abbreviations

(See also page 6)

Br.	Branch
Cr.	Creek
°C	degrees Celsius
E.	East
°F	degrees Fahrenheit
Fk.	Fork
ft	feet
Ft.	Fort
I(s).	Island(s)
km	kilometers
L.	Lake
m	meters
mi	miles
Mt(s).	Mountain(s) or Mount(s)
Nat.	National
N.	North
Pk.	Peak
Pres.	Preserve
Pt.	Point
R.	River
Sprs.	Springs
sq km	square kilometers
sq mi	square miles
St(e).	Saint(e)
Str(s).	Strait(s)
W.	West

Two-Letter State Abbreviations

Alabama	AL
Alaska	AK
Arizona	AZ
Arkansas	AR
California	CA
Colorado	CO
Connecticut	CT
Delaware	DE
Florida	FL
Georgia	GA
Hawaii	HI
Idaho	ID
Illinois	IL
Indiana	IN
Iowa	IA
Kansas	KS
Kentucky	KY
Louisiana	LA
Maine	ME
Maryland	MD
Massachusetts	MA
Michigan	MI
Minnesota	MN
Mississippi	MS
Missouri	MO
Montana	MT
Nebraska	NE
Nevada	NV
New Hampshire	NH
New Jersey	NJ
New Mexico	NM
New York	NY
North Carolina	NC
North Dakota	ND
Ohio	OH
Oklahoma	OK
Oregon	OR
Pennsylvania	PA
Rhode Island	RI
South Carolina	SC
South Dakota	SD
Tennessee	TN
Texas	TX
Utah	UT
Vermont	VT
Virginia	VA
Washington	WA
West Virginia	WV
Wisconsin	WI
Wyoming	WY

Web sites

For the 50 states:

For each of the 50 states the address is the same except for inserting the state's standard, two-letter postal abbreviation (listed above) into the Web address. For example, Alabama's address is **http://www.state.al.us**

For D.C. and the Territories:

Washington, D.C.: **http://dcpages.ari.net**
American Samoa: **www.samoanet.com**
Guam: **www.gov.gu/index.html**
Northern Marianas: **www.saipan.com/gov**
Puerto Rico: **www.prstar.net**
U.S. Virgin Islands: **www.gov.vi**

Index

Map references are in boldface (**50**) type. Letters and numbers following in lightface (D12) locate the place-names using the map grid. Illustrations appear in italic (*140*); type and text references are in lightface. The key to state abbreviations is on page 161.

A

B

F

G

M

National Geographic Society

Staff for this book

Nancy Laties Feresten
Vice President, Editor-in-Chief of Children's Books

Suzanne Patrick Fonda
Project Editor

Marianne R. Koszorus
Bea Jackson
Art Directors

Carl Mehler
Director of Maps

Dorrit Green
David M. Seager
Designers

Patricia Daniels
Editor

Marilyn Mofford Gibbons
Illustrations Editor

Thomas L. Gray
Joseph F. Ochlak
Map Editors

Thomas L. Gray
Joseph F. Ochlak
Nicholas P. Rosenbach
Mapping Specialists, Ltd.
XNR Productions
Map Research

John S. Ballay
James Huckenpahler
Michelle H. Picard
Gregory Ugiansky
Martin S. Walz
Mapping Specialists, Ltd.
XNR Productions
Map Production

Tibor G. Tóth
Map Relief

Stuart Armstrong
Map Illustration

Catherine Herbert Howell
Judith E. Rinard
Writers

Mary Collins
Kristin Edmonds
Jocelyn G. Lindsay
Ann Perry
Marcia Pires-Harwood
Jo Tunstall
Text Research

Jennifer Emmett
Asociate Editor

Janet Dustin
Illustrations Assistant

Carrie E. Young
Editorial Assistant

Connie D. Binder
Mapping Specialists, Ltd.
Indexing

Mark Caraluzzi
Heidi Vincent
Directors of Direct Response Sales and Marketing

Ellen Teguis
Marketing Director, Trade Books

Ruth Chamblee
Rachel Graham Burner
Marketing Managers

Lawrence M. Porges
Marketing Coordinator

R. Gary Colbert
Production Director

Lewis R. Bassford
Production Manager

Vincent P. Ryan
Manufacturing Manager

Consultants

Overall Consultant
Martha Sharma
National Cathedral School
Washington, D.C.

Regional Consultants

Northeast
Sari Bennett
Department of Geography
University of Maryland
Baltimore, Maryland

Southeast
Joseph T. Manzo
Department of Geography
Concord College
Athens, West Virginia

Midwest
Mark H. Bockenhauer
Department of Geography
St. Norbert College
De Pere, Wisconsin

Southwest
Sarah Witham Bednarz
Department of Geography
Texas A&M University
College Station, Texas

West
Clifford B. Craig
Department of Geography and Earth Resources
Utah State University
Logan, Utah

Illustrations Credits

Abbreviations for terms appearing below: (t)-top; (b)-bottom; (l)-left; (r)-right; (c)-center; NGS-National Geographic Staff

Photographs are from Getty Images, except where noted with an asterisk (*).

Art for state flowers and state birds by Robert E. Hynes

Locator globes pages 8 and 16 created by Theophilus Britt Griswold

Front cover (left to right) *Morton Beebe/CORBIS; *PhotoDisc; *Annie Griffiths Belt; *EyeWire; *Alan Schein Photography/CORBIS

Back Cover (top)*Jeff Vanuga; (bottom) Paul Damien/Getty Images

2 (l) Cosmo Condina; (r) Zandria Muench; 2–3 Eurimage, Space Imaging Landsat Tm30m 1991–93; 2–3 (c)Andy Sacks; 3 (l) Chad Ehlers; (r) H. Richard Johnston; 4 (l) *Howard G. Castleberry; (r) Andy Sacks; 4–5 Paul Stover; 5 (l) Paul Damien; (c) Paul Grebliunas; (r) Chris Noble; 8–9 Slim Films

The Physical United States
10 (t) Charles Doswell III; (cl) Robert Cremins; (bl) *Chris Stewart/Black Star; (br) *Ravi Miro Fry; 11 (bl) NASA/GSFC: GOES-8 Imager, 9/12/96; (c) *courtesy Melvin L. Prueitt, Los Alamos National Laboratory; (r) Robert Yager; 12 (tl) Ken Biggs; (bl) Paul Chesley; (br) Tony Tickle; 12–13 Liz Hymans; 13 (t) Stephen Frink; (br) Barbara Gibson; 14 (t) *Jeff Vanuga; (bl) *Anthony Chen; (br) *Joel Sartore; 15 (bl) *Fred Bavendam; (cl) *Joel Sartore; 15 (br) *Alan D. St. John

The Political United States
16–17 Slim Films; 18 Robert Cremins; 20 (t) Slim Films; (b) Slim Films, based on compilations provided by the Population Reference Bureau; 23 Slim Films, based on data provided by ENO Transportation Foundation; 24 (tl) Will & Deni McIntyre; (bl) George Chan; (br) Greg Pease; 24–25 Marilyn Mofford; 25 Tony Stone Images

The Northeast
26–7 Cosmo Condina; 27 Jim Pickerell; 30 (tl) Jake Rais; (tr) *James L. Stanfield NGS; (b) Dennis O'Clair; 30–31 Reuters/CORBIS; 31 (tl) Thomas Cooke; (tr) George Lepp; (c) *Howard G. Castleberry; (bl) *Pete Souza; (br) *George Grall

The Southeast
54–55 Zandria Muench; 55 Richard T. Nowitz/CORBIS; 58 (tl) Tom Raymond; (tr) Richard Howard; (bl) Owen Franken; (br) Bruce Hands; 58–59 Scott Goldsmith; 59 (t) Randy Wells; (c) Andy Sacks; (b) Bob Thomason

The Midwest
84–85 Andy Sacks; 85 Andy Sacks; 88 (t) *Phil Schermeister; (bl) Zane Williams; (br) Alan Klehr; 88–89 Paul Damien; 89 (t) Sara Gray; (cl) Gary Vestal; (cr) Mark Joseph; (b) Randy Wells

The Southwest
114–115 Chad Ehlers; 115 Tim Davis; 118 (t) David Hiser; (bl) Brian Stablyk; (br) Paul Grebliunas; 118–119 Robert Frerck; 119 (t) Gary Vestal; (c) Keith Wood; (bl) Chuck Pefley; (br) Mark Wagner

The West
128–129 H. Richard Johnston; 129 Chad Ehlers; 132 (tl) Natalie Fobes; (bl) Reg Watson; (r) Zigy Kalunzy; 132–133 Chris Noble; 133 (t) Glen Allison; (c) John Lawrence; (bl) Andy Sacks; (br) Bob Torrez

The Territories
158 (l) Grandadam; (r) Tom Bean; 158–9 *David Doubilet; 159 (tl) Randy Wells; (tr) Aldo Brando; (c) Donald Nausbaum; (bl) Cosmo Condina; (br) Cosmo Condina

The Library of Congress has cataloged the 1999 hardcover edition as follows:

National Geographic United States atlas for young explorers /
photographs by Tony Stone Images.
p. cm.
Includes index.
Summary: Maps, photographs, illustrations, and text present information about the regions and states of the United States.
ISBN 0-7922-7115-7
1. Children's atlases. [1. United States–Maps. 2. Atlases.]
I. Title. II. Title: United States atlas for young explorers
G1200 .N355 1999 <G&M>
912—dc21

99-34653
CIP
MAPS

Published by the National Geographic Society

ISBN 0-7922-6840-7 (2004 hardcover edition); 0-7922-6981-0 (2004 reinforced library binding)

Printed in Spain

Acknowledgments

We are grateful for the assistance of John Agnone, Peggy Candore, Alexander L. Cohn, Anne Marie Houppert, Sandra Leonard, and Lyle Rosbotham of the National Geographic Book Division.

180°
160°W
140°W
60°N
RUSSIA
THE WEST
128–155
160°E
40°N
PACIFIC OCEAN
0
600 miles
0
1000 kilometers
Albers Conic Equal-Area Projection
180°
20°N
THE WEST
128–155
160°W
140°W